# RAVES FOR RICHARD MATHESON

"Richard Matheson is worth our time, attention, and great affection . . . one of the most important writers of the twentieth century."

—Ray Bradbury

"His stories not only entertain but touch the mind and heart."

—Dean Koontz

"Perhaps no author living is as responsible for chilling a generation with tantalizing nightmare visions."

—*The New York Times*

"A horror story if ever there was one . . . a great adventure story—it is certainly one of that select handful that I have given to people, envying them the experience of the first reading."

—Stephen King, on *The Shrinking Man*

"Matheson, master of both horror and suspense, here gives us a picture of a man obsessed, then possessed . . . incredibly powerful."

—*Library Journal*, on *Earthbound*

"Richard Matheson is one of the great names in American terror fiction."

—*The Philadelphia Inquirer*

"Nobody can top Matheson's talent for terror."

—Robert Bloch, author of *Psycho*

# *the* TWILIGHT *and* OTHER ZONES

## THE DARK WORLDS OF **RICHARD MATHESON**

*edited by*
**Stanley Wiater, Matthew R. Bradley,
and Paul Stuve**

CITADEL PRESS
Kensington Publishing Corp.
www.kensingtonbooks.com

TADEL PRESS BOOKS are published by

Kensington Publishing Corp.

850 Third Avenue

New York, NY 10022

To Iris and Tanya, the two greatest companions and loves of my life.

And to Audrey, who remains forever in my corner,
no matter what the battle.
—S. W.

To the two Brians, one who left us far too soon, after his help and
generosity made my Matheson studies so much more complete, and
the other whose creativity and friendship placed me inside Matheson's
literary "world of his own."
—M. R. B.

To Matthew and Stanley for the great privilege of working
with them on this project.

To my pals Ben Wax, Matt Moncrief, Neil Ostercamp,
and Scottie Bahler for their serendipitous friendship.

And to The Great Richard Matheson for the words,
the words, the words . . .
—P. S.

My thanks to my family and all of the contributors in the book.
—R. M.

# Contents

# Introduction

*by Stanley Wiater and Matthew R. Bradley*

In answer to the question: *Who the hell is Richard Matheson?*

Richard Matheson may be the most influential fantasy writer in the world whose name is not recognized by most people, although when asked, they invariably know his work. They certainly don't recognize him on the street, nor do they usually recognize him (as they might with Stephen King or Dean Koontz) as a "brand name" author.

But there is hardly anyone else who has had such an impact on the genre in the media of books, television, and motion pictures. Not to mention scaring the hell out of a lot of readers and viewers along the way for more than five decades.

Matheson (born in 1926) is the *New York Times* best-selling author of such classic works as *I Am Legend, The Shrinking Man, A Stir of Echoes, Ride the Nightmare, The Beardless Warriors, Hell House, Bid Time Return* (a.k.a. *Somewhere in Time*), and *What Dreams May Come*. Incredibly, *every single one* of these novels has been made into one or more motion pictures—many of them with screenplays supplied by none other than the author himself.

He has published more than forty books, including several short story and script collections. His most recent novel of suspense, *Hunted Past Reason*, was published in 2002. The *New York Times* has said of him, "Perhaps no author living is as responsible for chilling a generation with tantalizing nightmare visions," while according to Stephen King, "The author who influenced me the most as a writer was Richard Matheson."

Matheson has also had an amazing career as a screenwriter. He is responsible for numerous popular films, including *House of Usher* and *Pit and Pendulum* (both directed by Roger Corman), and the classic made-for-television movies *The Night Stalker*, *Trilogy of Terror*, and *Duel* (directed by a then-unknown Steven Spielberg). He wrote many of the most frightening and memorable scripts for Rod Serling's *The Twilight Zone*, and contributed to other television series ranging from *The Alfred Hitchcock Hour* to *Star Trek*.

Matheson is one of the most acclaimed and influential fantasists of our time. He and his work have won the Hugo, Edgar Allan Poe, Golden Spur, and Christopher awards, plus multiple World Fantasy ("Howard"), Bram Stoker, and Writers Guild of America awards, including Lifetime Achievement awards from the World Horror and World Fantasy conventions.

Yet, quite amazingly we think, there has never been a legitimate biography of the man, or a writer's companion to his work. It is the latter that we have striven to create—the last word on the millions of words produced by Richard Matheson in a career that has already gone beyond the half-century mark, with no signs of it ending anytime soon.

Matheson fully authorized, and willingly participated in, this collection. With the exception of the tributes and appreciations, he has personally reviewed the majority of the information we have assembled. And all three editors have contributed material in which Matheson discusses his own career at length in both interviews and correspondence.

Among the essays are in-depth looks at some of his most famous tales, by Harlan Ellison, Dean Koontz, and David Morrell. Contributors who have been influenced by his work along the way include Dennis Etchison, Jack Ketchum, Joe R. Lansdale, Brian Lumley, producer Stephen Simon, and F. Paul Wilson. Gahan Wilson discusses how Matheson has affected popular culture in general, and his life in particular, while Ed Gorman casts an informed eye on some of his lesser-known but eminently worthy works.

On a more personal note, Matheson's wife, Ruth, and their children Bettina, Richard Christian, Alison, and Chris have all contributed very heartfelt observations of the man. Two of his book editors, Greg

Cox and Gary Goldstein; Gauntlet's publisher, Barry Hoffman; and artist Harry O. Morris, who has undertaken no fewer than fifteen book covers containing the words "By Richard Matheson," offer a behind-the-scenes look at working with a literary giant. And two of Matheson's fellow members of the legendary Southern California School of Writers, William F. Nolan and George Clayton Johnson, share their thoughts on his work and their longtime friendship.

The reader will find a selection of photographs of Matheson at various points in his life and career, hand-picked and supplied by the author himself. And, as a special bonus—unique to this edition—he has graciously allowed us to publish his guest of honor speech from the 1977 World Fantasy Convention, which he describes as "a public statement about the people who have been a part of my life in fantasy and about my feelings in regard to fantasy itself."

Last but not least, we bring you what may be one of the most exhaustive (certainly the most eclectic) bibliographies ever attempted on a living author. As many of those who have contributed to this volume are Matheson completists, we sincerely believe that among us we possess more Matheson material than even the man himself does.

This has admittedly been a labor of love. We did not set out to dissect Matheson's work in an academic manner, nor to critique it against or among that of any other writer or genre. We believe Matheson is a genre unto himself, and our purpose in compiling this book was simply to show our appreciation for the enduring entertainments the man has brought to us all in the past. And the pleasure he continues to bring to us today.

We hope that *The Twilight and Other Zones: The Dark Worlds of Richard Matheson* will be judged by him and by the reader to be a worthy celebration of his life and work.

# Acknowledgments

The editors wish to thank: Don Cannon, Barry Hoffman, Brian Kirby, Richard Christian Matheson, Harry O. Morris, William F. Nolan, all the contributors, and last but never least, Richard Matheson. A special mention must be made of Mark Rathbun and Graeme Flanagan, whose booklet *Richard Matheson: He Is Legend* (1984) planted the original seed for this volume. Without their efforts, none of this would have made it beyond a pleasant daydream.

# *the* TWILIGHT *and* OTHER ZONES

## THE DARK WORLDS OF **RICHARD MATHESON**

# Dark Dreamer: Richard Matheson

*Stanley Wiater*

In the time period from fall 2000 to fall 2001, I embarked on an adventure that so far has proven to be the high point of my career. Beyond my usual travails as an author, it consisted of creating a television series; making it happen with a producer, director, and film crew; and then seeing the finished episodes appear—first on cable television in Canada, then in Europe, and now available on DVD for the American market.

The television series, which I entitled *Dark Dreamers*, was inspired by two books I had previously published: *Dark Dreamers: Conversations with the Masters of Horror*, and *Dark Dreamers: Facing the Masters of Fear*. One book was a collection of original interviews, the second was a series of profiles (including marvelous photographs taken by Beth Gwinn) of the greatest practitioners of fear and suspense we have working today. The fact that both books had won the Bram Stoker Award from the Horror Writers Association also encouraged me to see if I could take the concept of interviewing horror practitioners one step further.

When I was approached to contribute to a planned documentary on horror in the popular culture, I demurred, and instead countered with the basic idea behind *Dark Dreamers*, the television series. Simply stated, I would travel around North America and visit the homes and offices of the best writers, actors, special effects teams, producers, and directors. Some of those I would visit would be Richard Laymon, Clive Barker, Larry Cohen, Peter Straub, Stan Winston, Jack Ketchum, Julie Strain, and the people at KNB Effects.

But the very first person whose doorstep I was to turn up on was

Richard Matheson. The very private Richard Matheson, who, to the best of my knowledge, had never allowed cameras in his home or sat for such an extensive one-on-one interview. (Although he would be shown only in half of a thirty-minute episode—along with the legendary Forrest J. Ackerman—the crew shot nearly two hours of footage. Usable footage, I might add, for the interest of future Matheson scholars.)

Matheson was of course incredibly gracious and witty. He later took me into his office when we were done shooting, and signed a copy of his just-published novel, *Hunger and Thirst*. On that fall day in the year 2000, it was to be an experience I would never forget.

Fortunately, the entire series is now out on DVD, so you can see Matheson himself making me look pretty damn smart.

Here's the opening to the Richard Matheson episode:

Are you a Dark Dreamer?

Richard Matheson most certainly is.

Richard Matheson is one of the most influential and respected fantasists of our time. One of his very first novels, *The Shrinking Man*, was adapted in 1957 into the classic film, *The Incredible Shrinking Man*, with Matheson himself supplying the screenplay. Incredibly, nearly all of Matheson's novels have been adapted into motion pictures, including: *Hell House, Somewhere in Time, What Dreams May Come*, and most recently, *Stir of Echoes*. His 1954 vampire novel, *I Am Legend*, has been filmed three times to date, first as *The Last Man on Earth*, starring Vincent Price, and then as *The Omega Man*, starring Charlton Heston [and as *I Am Legend* in 2007, with Will Smith]. Besides adapting his own novels and short stories, Matheson was also the screenwriter of several original Edgar Allan Poe films in the 1960s, many of which were directed by Roger Corman.

Recently, Matheson invited me to his home in the hills overlooking Los Angeles, to discuss his life and career. Beginning with something called . . . *The Twilight Zone*.

WIATER: What was your experience working on the series, and with Rod Serling?

MATHESON: I knew Rod. Occasionally I would go to his home, or we would go out to eat. But [mostly] I would go in with an idea to [his office] and walk out. Later on, I just may have given him the idea [for an episode] over the telephone; I don't remember. He would say yes or no. If he said no, I'd give him another idea. The first idea I ever gave him—I remember going in to his office and saying, "A World War One pilot gets lost and he lands, and he's on a modern SAC base." And he said, "Whoa—go home and write it!" He was a very nice man. Rod was as nice as he could be. And being a writer himself, he was very protective of the scripts of the other writers. I don't recall one word of any of my scripts ever being changed, except by actress Phyllis Kirk, who more or less said what I wrote in her own way, in the show she was in with Keenan Wynn ["A World of His Own"]. Otherwise, they all did my lines word for word. And usually very well.

WIATER: At what point did you meet Roger Corman?

MATHESON: I was just called in one day by American International [Pictures]. I didn't even know Roger was involved. I don't think I even met him until later on in the production. They thought it was going to be a one-shot—*House of Usher.* And it did so well that, producers being what they are, they did another, and then another and another. And some of them were very good! And Roger directed them quite well. Unfortunately, he used a lot of his stable of actors, some of whom were not really that good. Vincent Price of course was always wonderful! As a man and as an actor, he was probably the nicest . . . human being I ever met out here, and there's a definite lack of human beings out here.

WIATER: But your first two novels, if I'm not mistaken, were both mystery novels.

MATHESON: Yeah—that was because when I first came to California, I stayed at the home of William Campbell Gault, who was a mystery writer. He had just had his first one published. And then, through him, I met this group of writers called The Fictioneers. Most of them had come out of the pulps. Some of them were doing *Collier's*. Some of them did sports. Or they did mysteries. They did westerns. So I decided I would try a mystery myself. I had never had a great yearning to write a mystery novel, but I wrote a couple. One of which I wrote in three days. Then after that, I went back to my first love: fantasy.

If I had stuck to horror, fantasy, and science fiction, I would have done a lot better and been much more successful as a writer. But I always got bored very easily and I slipped into another genre. Mysteries. Westerns. I've done *five* westerns. A love story—*Somewhere in Time*. And a novel about the afterlife—*What Dreams May Come*. So the readers that I have must be very loyal because they faithfully trudge from one genre to another, following me.

WIATER: Another classic produced during that period was "Duel." Could you relate to us the genesis of that short story?

MATHESON: It happened on the day President Kennedy was assassinated. I was playing golf with a friend of mine. When we heard the news, we just threw our clubs in the car and started home. And as we drove through this pass, this truck started tailgating us the whole way. I was with Jerry Sohl, who's a well-known science-fiction writer. And he finally had to pull off the road in a swirl of dust. And then this crazy truck driver went roaring by. We were both infuriated, and cursing, and sweating—and then my writer's brain kicked in, and I borrowed one of the envelopes from his mail and wrote the idea down for the story.

I didn't write it, oh, for [almost] ten years. Then it was published in *Playboy*. Then Universal bought it. And then I did a script for George Eckstein, who was the producer. Then they put this young guy on as a director. Some young, hotshot director. Spillburg . . . ?

WIATER: What was that name again?

MATHESON: Spolberg? Spalberg?

WIATER: Perhaps you mean Steven Spielberg?

MATHESON: Yeah! [laughs] It was his first feature [-length project]. And you could tell right off the bat what an eye he had.

WIATER: Your 1954 novel, *I Am Legend*, has been filmed not once, but twice—

MATHESON: And now they say there'll be a third time.

WIATER: Do you have any strong feelings about it being filmed a third time?

MATHESON: I wish the whole idea would just go away. I've read the script for the new version—and it's not a bad script at all. But it's no more my book than the other two films were. And I keep thinking, "Why do they bother? Why don't they just make up something of their own?" I don't ever expect it to be done properly. There have been a number of people—Dan Curtis among them—who wanted to do my book just the way it was written. And the rights have gotten so fouled up among so many people that they couldn't get it. Michael Carerras of Hammer Films wanted to do it exactly the way I wrote it. He couldn't get the rights, either.

But that's what's special about a book. They told Raymond Chandler once about some bad film that had been made out of his novel. And they said, "It's too bad they ruined your book, Mr. Chandler." And he took it off the shelf and said, "No, no—here it is." And that's what the advantage of being a novelist is. I think that probably helped my career out here. They [the producers] kind of hold back their criticism, because they're a little awed by the fact that you're writing novels, too. You know? A scriptwriter they *know* is scum, and they can be stepped on. [laughs]

WIATER: But as a novelist you're one level above, in terms of scum.

MATHESON: That's right—I'm high-level scum. [laughs]

WIATER: If you'd put on your professor's cap for a moment, could you tell us, please, what advice you'd give to someone who is thinking of becoming a writer? Either a prose writer or a screenwriter.

MATHESON: Some schoolteacher just sent me a letter recently, saying they taught a special class to special students. And one of them wanted to be a writer, and wanted to know how you go about it. And he asked me if I would write something he could put on the bulletin board. And what I wrote was, in essence, "There are no rules." Ray Bradbury says, "Write a short story every week. Fifty-two weeks of the year." And fundamentally that's right. You've got to write. And so I said, "Create. Create! Don't think about financial success. Don't think about accolades, or being acclaimed. Don't think about anything except if you really want to write, just *write*! And keep on writing. Later on, if you're good, it will work out."

I mean, when I was just starting out, I never wrote anybody. I wrote *one* letter to Ray Bradbury, telling him how much I liked his work. He was very gracious, and he wrote back to me. But people who I graduated with from college said to me, "How long are you going to give it?"

Or someone's mother who I'd know would say, "When you going to get some work?" And I would just stare at them.

I had ambitions to do a few other things—composer, songwriter. But I chose writing. And once I had chosen that, nothing else anybody told me would mean a thing to me; I would just stare at them blankly.

And go write.

I think that's the case with most creative people. I'm sure when Stephen King was a kid, he was writing stuff. When Dean Koontz was a kid, he was writing stuff. I'm sure they didn't write other writers asking, "How do you do this?" Because I know how to do this! "Just leave me alone, and I'll do it my own way." So that's what I usually advise.

[Producer] Val Lewton had a lot of influence on me because I was drawn to that kind of film [horror]. My parents wouldn't let me go to the movies until I was seventeen! I couldn't listen to *The Lone Ranger* on the radio when I was a kid. I probably had all this bottled inside me, and when I came of age, it all came flooding out. "Scare people, scare people, scare people . . ." [laughs]

I remember seeing *Dracula* when I was a teenager. It was not the original release of it, but they were showing it again theatrically and I remember thinking as I sat there: *One vampire is scary. What if the whole world were vampires?* So that was the genesis, many years later, of *I Am Legend.*

Another movie I saw in my youth [*Let's Do It Again*] starred Ray

Milland and Aldo Ray. And Ray Milland leaves Aldo Ray's apartment, and he puts on Aldo Ray's hat, and it comes down way over his ears. I immediately thought—*what if he left his own hat on, and it came down over his ears because he was shrinking?* So that's where *The Shrinking Man* came from.

I would say the majority of my ideas have come from seeing movies. Usually, poor movies. If they're wonderful movies, you're totally involved with it. If they're poor movies that have an interesting premise, the premise intrigues you, but you pay very little attention to the movie because it's so *bad*. And that's when, for me, the ideas start coming. I grew up reading fantasy. I was never a science-fiction reader. I sort of just backed into [writing] it because there was money to be made; there were forty or fifty magazines at that time. I never intended to be a horror writer, either.

WIATER: Why not?

MATHESON: I *hate* the word horror. To me, the word horror means visceral. It's supposed to make you sick to your stomach. It can be done brilliantly, as in *Alien*, when that thing bursts out of that man's stomach. But that's horror! *That's* horror. Terror is in scaring hell out of people.

WIATER: People used to say the same of Boris Karloff, who would always explain that he made terror movies, not horror movies.

MATHESON: Yeah. He was a charming man, Karloff. He was in a couple of the [AIP] pictures that I wrote. One was *The Comedy of Terrors*; by then, he was old and could hardly move and the part was kind of strenuous. He was supposed to play the part that Basil Rathbone played. And he asked if he could switch the parts. Basil Rathbone was older than him, yet he was bouncing all over the place. They were all excited to be in it. To make a picture where you got to work with Peter Lorre. Vincent Price. Boris Karloff. Basil Rathbone. Joyce Jameson—she was so lovely! And Jacques Tourneur directed it. I personally think it's a very funny picture. And they all loved it. They were so happy to do it.

I watched a lot of the shooting. I remember spending a whole afternoon listening to Basil Rathbone tell me how they shot the duels in *Robin*

*Hood.* It took them three days to shoot the duels. They shot this whole picture in two weeks.

WIATER: Have you given any thought as to how you would like to be remembered?

MATHESON: Well, this fellow [Pat McGilligan] wrote a book about screenwriters of the sixties [*Backstory 3*]. And in one of the sections he talks about me, and the title of it is "Storyteller." I'll settle for that.


Join me here again.
On the wild side of the imagination.
Where a sense of wonder . . . and a feeling of terror can often intersect.
You'll find us waiting here.
The Dark Dreamers.

# The Matheson Years: A Profile in Friendship

*William F. Nolan*

In the spring of 1972, on the night of its first telecast, a drama centering around a vampire stalking his victims in Las Vegas drew a record viewing audience of seventy-five million. The title of this phenomenal *Movie of the Week* was *The Night Stalker*. The man who had written the teleplay, Richard Matheson, also wrote *The Incredible Shrinking Man*, *I Am Legend*, *Somewhere in Time*, *Duel*, *The Legend of Hell House*, *Dracula*, *Trilogy of Terror*, *House of Usher*—and fourteen scripts for *The Twilight Zone*.

He has earned major honors in an impressive variety of genres: three World Fantasy Awards (for a novel, a collection, and for Lifetime Achievement), two Best Teleplay Awards from the Writers Guild of America, two Bram Stoker Awards from the Horror Writers of America, the Golden Spur Award from the Western Writers of America, and the Edgar Allan Poe Award from the Mystery Writers of America. He has been named a "Grand Master" by the World Horror Convention, and his teleplay on the life of L. Frank Baum, *Dreamer of Oz*, won the coveted Christopher Award. But honors such as these mean little to him; he is much prouder of the fact that three of his four children are also professional writers, and that he has influenced them by his example.

Richard Matheson's influence in the genre of dark fantasy has been enormous. Major horror critic Douglas E. Winter credits him with having "created the modern landscape of fear, taking it from the Gothic arena of misty moors into our shopping malls and quiet suburban neighborhoods—right into the house next door." Stephen King declares that Matheson was the basic inspiration for his career: "His work hit me like a bolt of pure ozone lightning. Without Richard Matheson, I wouldn't be around today."

The man behind such well-deserved praise has used his imagination as a shield against the world. The interviews he has given reveal little of the real Matheson. He remains, essentially, a man of mystery, a deeply private individual, introspective and reserved, who has been (by his own admission) intensely paranoid for a large part of his life.

Until now, his full story has never been told. The reason that *I'm* able to tell it is simple: We've been close pals for more than fifty years. Therefore, as the subhead to this piece proclaims, this is truly "a profile in friendship."

Rich had just turned twenty-eight in February of 1954 when we met. He was already the author of two published novels, with a third due that year, and had sold enough short stories for the upcoming release of his first collection. Two years his junior, I was a raw beginner, having made my initial story sale that same month. I recall being awestruck at Matheson's vigorous professional record.

Writing was still a part-time activity for him in those days. With a wife and two young children to support, he was unable to make a living from fiction, and worked as a machine parts operator at Douglas Aircraft in Santa Monica, California.

I remember my first visit to his cramped little apartment. Rich had jammed a tiny desk and chair into an open closet, where he typed out his stories. This was Matheson's "working office" in his hours away from the aircraft plant.

Our mutual friend (who'd introduced us) was Charles Beaumont, also a young struggling author, soon to become a leading member of what *Los Angeles Times* critic Robert Kirsch would call "the Southern California School of Writers." Eventually, we would all be named as active members in this regional "school": Matheson, Beaumont, Ray Bradbury, Robert Bloch, and myself. There were others, down the years, but we five were the "creative center" of the group.

Among our favored activities in the formative days of the 1950s were all-night "gab sessions" in which we'd talk about our past lives up to then, outlining our fears, dreams, and hopes for the future. It was during these intense, extended conversations that I began to learn about the early history of Rich Matheson—about his sheltered childhood in Brooklyn, his schooling, his overseas stint in the army, and his driving determination to become a full-time professional writer.

"I was born with a proclivity toward fantasy," Rich told me. "The first important book I read, at age seven, was a wild adventure about Pinocchio in Africa, and I wrote my first story that same year, a fantasy, about a little boy who makes friends with a bird. When a neighborhood bully tries to beat him up, the bird comes to his rescue. I've explored this genre all my life. Critics and fans have dubbed me a science-fiction writer, or a horror writer, but what I've really been, all along, is a writer of fantasy."

Richard Burton Matheson was born of immigrant parents in Allendale, New Jersey, on February 20, 1926. His mother's maiden name was Svenningsen, shortened to Swanson when she came to America from Norway in her early teens.

Matheson talked about her: "An orphan before she was ten, raised by an older brother, she was insecure and frightened, thrust into this alien American environment. She met my father, also from Norway, at a dance in a Norwegian club in Brooklyn. They had a lot in common."

Matheson's father, a tile setter who had served in the Norwegian Merchant Marine, was equally uncertain and insecure, and took refuge in alcohol, which, according to Rich, "served to numb his fears and anxieties. Heavy drinking became his escape."

They married and moved to New Jersey, where Matheson's brother, Robert, and sister, Gladys, were born. "Over ten years later, I came along," Rich told me. "When I was three, we all moved back to Brooklyn, where my father left us. He just couldn't accept the responsibilities of a growing family."

His father's abandonment resulted in an emotional retreat, a "closing together of our family unit for protection against what was perceived as a hostile environment."

Matheson dates his paranoia from this period: "Existing in a shut-off, cloistered family world, I became extremely introspective at a very early age. I withdrew and lived *inside* myself. My mother joined the Christian Science Church for support, so religion provided *her* escape."

Although young Matheson also embraced these beliefs (into his college years), he found his own form of escapism within the realm of fantasy, devouring book after book of fairy tales.

"At nine, I had poems and stories printed in *The Brooklyn Eagle*," he recalled. "I vividly remember seeing my first horror movie that year, *The Werewolf of London*. Somehow, I talked my mother into taking me and when Henry Hull changed into a werewolf, I freaked! Fell out of my seat and crawled up the aisle. Thus, my introduction to terror on the screen."

Based on his superior grades in math and physics, Rich did well at Brooklyn Technical High School, once memorizing an entire textbook for a physics exam, "but it was a short-term memory, and faded away after I got an A on the test."

At Brooklyn Tech, he studied structural engineering. "This suited the practical side of my nature, which has always been a part of me. I didn't really want to become an engineer, but it seemed a safe bet for the future."

Although he continued to turn out stories, even attempting a novel at sixteen, "I never believed I could make any kind of money from writing."

At seventeen, Rich saw Val Lewton's classic fright film, *Cat People*, and wrote to Lewton about it. He had analyzed the picture in terms of its "mechanics for instilling fear in an audience." Lewton was impressed, "and that," said Matheson, "was when I thought I might work in movies someday."

He also saw *Dracula* the same year, which (more than a decade later) inspired his first horror novel, about vampires, *I Am Legend*. ("I figured that if *one* vampire is scary, then a whole world full of 'em would really shake people up.")

Music was another of Matheson's primary passions. "I began writing songs in my late teens. Wrote well over a hundred. I've always wanted to compose music, and it's been a vital part of my life since I was very young. Song writing is great fun—but I do it strictly as a hobby."

Not always. Matheson wrote the lyrics for two of Perry Como's recorded hits, and Como featured one of them as the title to an album.

World War II was in full force when Matheson graduated from Brooklyn Tech. "I knew I'd be drafted and probably tossed into the infantry, so I enlisted in Army Specialized Training, a pre-engineering program they had going at Cornell University. But they cancelled the whole program in 1944, and guess what? I ended up in the infantry!"

Young Matheson was sent to Germany with the 87th Division, and was into full combat at eighteen. A harrowing experience.

"The war was dirty, bloody, and cold. People were getting blown away around me. During battle, my blood pressure soared sky-high. Luckily, I was never wounded—but I *did* contract trench foot, ending up at a hospital in England."

While he recuperated, Matheson wrote a fantasy novelette in longhand. "I called it 'Manhattan Vampire,' and in the story, this guy kept his coffin in a subway station behind the counter of a newsstand. It was all pretty lurid."

In June of 1945, Matheson received a medical discharge from the service. He was confused about his future, torn between his love for writing and his love for music. He sought professional help. "I went to this vocational guidance counselor, who got me enrolled at the University of Missouri, in Columbia. The idea was for me to get a degree in journalism. Which seemed to make sense."

After the first two years of general education, Matheson began taking special courses toward his degree. But music still exerted a strong attraction. He joined a musical fraternity and reviewed local concerts for the school paper. ("I even wrote a full musical comedy, composing all of the songs.")

Adept at the piano, Matheson determined to compose a symphony for this instrument "in the style of Mahler. I laid the whole thing out, all the themes, and completed the first movement, then got bogged down. It became 'Matheson's Unfinished Symphony.' "

He was also active in the university drama group, and took a course in creative writing from Professor William Peden (to whom he dedicated his first published collection).

In June of 1949, at age twenty-three, Matheson graduated in the top ten percent of his class, having earned his bachelor of journalism degree. By the time he left the university, he was no longer practicing Christian Science. "In college, on weekends, I'd attend services at these various churches, just to check them out, and this ultimately soured me on all organized religion."

He attempted to find a job in the publishing world with a magazine or newspaper, but failed. An editor at *Esquire* suggested that he take "any kind of night work" so that he could devote his days to writing.

"So I did that," said Matheson. "I got a job working nights for my brother at his place in Brooklyn, typing up address plates—which allowed me to write during the daylight hours. Within a few months I'd made my first story sale, for twenty-five dollars, to editor Tony Boucher at *The Magazine of Fantasy and Science Fiction*. Opening his acceptance letter was one of the great moments in my life. I'll never forget it."

Printed in the summer 1950 issue of *F&SF*, that story was the now-classic "Born of Man and Woman," which has since often been reprinted in such volumes as *75 Masterpieces: Stories from the World's Literature*.

"It was about a mutant boy who drips green—chained in the basement by his parents," related Rich. "I considered it straight fantasy, and was shocked when Boucher informed me that it was science fiction. He told me that 'SF' was a wide-open market and that I should write more in this genre."

Matheson had never read any science fiction, but the markets were there, so he began avidly devouring every SF anthology and magazine he could lay his hands on. This intensive search paid off—and Rich was soon placing stories with *Fantastic Universe*, *Galaxy*, *Thrilling Wonder*, and *Startling Stories*.

Matheson had been considering a move to the West Coast, "out to Hollywood, where all the movie jobs were." When his feet were adversely affected by that season's severe winter cold, he decided to "take the plunge" and head for California. It was time to test himself in a new environment.

"Bill Gault, a verteran pulp writer I'd written letters to, met me at the bus depot in Santa Monica. Gault let me stay at his home until I was able to find a furnished room and a job at the local post office. And that's when I joined The Fictioneers."

This was a lively group of professional writers who met once a month for dinner, drinks, and shop talk. Most of them wrote mysteries and westerns, so Matheson turned his marketing attention to these, writing and selling in both genres. ("I had my byline in magazines like *Detective Story*, *Dime Western*, and *Fifteen Western Tales*.") Fantasy, however, remained his primary interest, and he continued to sell his science fiction.

At the beach, in 1952, he met a bright, lovely young lady, Ruth Ann Woodson, who was newly divorced with a daughter, Tina. They were married that same year, when Rich left his low-scale post office job for Douglas Aircraft.

"In those days, they paid you maybe forty or fifty dollars for a short story, and there was just no way for me to make ends meet as a full-time writer. Financial insecurity was a constant fear. Even with my weekly check at Douglas coming in, we barely paid the bills. But I had great moral support from Ruth. She believed in me, and in my talent. She never doubted for a moment that I'd eventually succeed as a writer, and that gave me the boost I needed to go on. But it was tough."

Matheson's work at the aircraft plant was what he termed "robotic," leaving his mind free to plot stories while he automatically cut out airplane parts. By October of 1953, with the birth of his first son, Richard Christian, he became a father at twenty-seven—and had sold two novels, both mysteries ("because, once again, the market was there"). But his real goal was "fantasy-terror," and this goal was fully realized with the publication, in July of 1954, of his vampire novel, *I Am Legend*, sold to Fawcett Gold Medal for an advance of $3,000. On the reverse cover of this original paperback was a very intense photo of Matheson, accompanied by the prophetic blurb: "Read this novel. Watch this young writer. You may be in at the birth of a giant."

The book indeed proved to be a major breakthrough for him. Via research in bacteriology, folklore, and psychiatry, Matheson had brought scientific validity to ancient vampire myths. *I Am Legend* generated tremendous power and freshness.

Despite this triumph, Rich was deeply conflicted regarding his future, admitting that he was "inwardly afraid to succeed completely," and that he linked such success with a betrayal of his background. "I know it sounds crazy, but that's how I felt. I later realized that I was deliberately causing myself to fail at least half the time. Bizarre!"

Such personal fears drew Matheson back to his roots, and in October of 1954, he returned with his family to the New York area, renting a small house at Sound Beach on Long Island. Instead of seeking an outside job, he decided to risk writing another novel, knowing "that I could go back to work with my brother again if the book didn't pan out."

Rich now engaged himself in a two-and-a-half-month stint of work on a new science-fiction drama dealing with a man who begins to shrink after accidentally being subjected to a toxic mist of unknown origin.

"I asked a technician at the Presbyterian Medical Center what could possibly affect the human growth system. The answer was: insecticide. I added a dose of radioactivity—and I had my toxic mist."

This resulted in the completion of another Matheson classic, *The Shrinking Man*, published by Fawcett Gold Medal in the spring of 1956.

By then, Matheson was back in Los Angeles.

"What happened was I got a call from Universal Studios," he related. "They'd seen my book in galleys and wanted to buy the film rights. I said fine—so long as they hired me to write the screenplay. If they wanted the book, I had to be part of the package. They hadn't planned on this, but agreed to my terms. They would pay me a total of fifteen thousand dollars for book *and* script. We packed and headed back to Hollywood—and that was the real start of my career."

But the sudden burst of good fortune didn't diminish Matheson's basic paranoia. Years later, in an introduction to his *Collected Stories*, he wrote openly about this troubling aspect of his life:

> My mother saw all threats to security as existing in the out-
> side world and maintained a tight nuclear family unit as pro-

tection. Her lack of knowledge concerning this outside world created mounting distrust and suspicion of it. Such was my natal environment, so it's little wonder that I fell victim to severe anxieties.

I could have turned to alcohol, as my father did, but instead of imbibing drink I imbibed stories. I escaped into fantasy, creating fictional worlds in which I could work out my paranoia. My fiction dealt with outer hostilities, isolation, loss of control, and of people—and even *things*—plotting against my besieged protagonists. Amazingly, I was being paid for such paranoid delusions.

Certainly all these elements were manifest in Matheson's novel (and screenplay). "For the movie version, the producer felt compelled to add 'incredible' to my title, expanding it to *The Incredible Shrinking Man*. Seems to me a guy who shrinks every day is incredible enough to begin with, but then I'm not into Hollywood hype."

After being exposed to the radioactive mist, Matheson's hero, Scott Carey, begins shrinking at the rate of an inch a week. Eventually, everything around him becomes a serious threat, including the family cat and a fat black spider who almost makes a meal of him. (Carey's battle with the giant spider is a high point in book and film.)

Rich told me about an amusing incident connected with the filming at Universal: "The director, Jack Arnold, got this hot query from the front office, 'What the hell is this order of yours for three dozen prophylactics?' which Jack had a big laugh over. The thing is, he'd worked out a way to show giant drops of water splashing down on Carey—by using water-filled condoms. And *that's* why he ordered three dozen of 'em!"

Released in 1957, *The Incredible Shrinking Man* is now accepted as a cinema tour de force, still as gripping today as it was five decades ago. (And, of course, it's a perfect example of paranoia.)

Also in 1957, Matheson's grim vampire saga, *I Am Legend*, was purchased by Hammer Films in England. Rich spent two months in London writing the script, but his version never reached the screen. "The

British censor killed it," he said. "Claimed it was too violent. Which was a crock. Their Dracula films had much more violence. But who can argue with a censor?"

An independent producer in the United States took over and hired another writer who drastically revised the project. Final result: a weak, watered-down film featuring Vincent Price in the title role, called *The Last Man on Earth*. (Much later, another even more inept version, starring Charlton Heston, was released as *The Omega Man*, bearing little if any resemblance to Matheson's original novel.)

Meanwhile, Rich and his family had moved to a much larger house on Venido Road in Woodland Hills. I didn't know it at the time, but this move was fated to change my life—since they proceeded to hire my future bride, Marilyn Seal, who lived in the next house up the block, as their babysitter. (Beyond Tina and Richard, Alison and Christian were soon added to the Matheson family.)

In 1958, Rich entered the financially lucrative arena of series television, writing his first teleplay in collaboration with Charles Beaumont for *The D.A.'s Man*.

"For a couple of years, Chuck and I worked as a team on scripts for such shows as *Wanted: Dead or Alive*, *Philip Marlowe*, *Buckskin*, *Markham*, and *Have Gun—Will Travel*," related Matheson. "However, in basic personality, we were total opposites. He was lively and extroverted while I was quiet and introverted. But in those beginning years, we gave each other mutual support in the strange new world of TV."

Back on the home front, Marilyn Seal had married Ruth Matheson's brother, Phil Woodson, an ex-Marine, thus becoming an official part of the Matheson family.

In television, Rich was on his own in 1959, writing episodes for *Lawman*, *Cheyenne*, and *Bourbon Street Beat*. Additionally, he had another novel published, *Ride the Nightmare*, and another feature film in release, *The Beat Generation*.

"Chuck and I had both joined the Preminger-Stuart Agency that year," Matheson stated, "and we were invited to the screening of the pilot film for a new CBS television series, *The Twilight Zone*, helmed by Rod Serling.

"Rod talked to us about his plans for the series. He was contracted to turn out most of the scripts himself, but needed backup writers. He chose the two of us. We had no idea at the time what a major cult phenomenon *Zone* would turn into. It was just another job that looked like fun. For one thing, we'd get to adapt many of our own printed stories, which was very satisfying."

Matheson won a script award from the Writers Guild in 1960 for an episode of *Lawman*, and his novel of World War II was published as *The Beardless Warriors*—a thinly fictionalized account of his own battle experiences. Four of his teleplays were telecast on the new *Twilight Zone*.

In theatrical films, he began an extremely successful relationship with AIP (American International Pictures) when studio boss James Nicholson asked Rich to script *House of Usher* based on the famous short story by Edgar Allan Poe. Roger Corman was set to direct and Vincent Price to star.

"They saw it as a low-budget quickie," declared Matheson. "Roger shot the picture in under two weeks for less than two hundred thousand dollars. AIP had no idea of what it would do at the box office."

Matheson, however, had taken his new assignment very seriously ("I was adapting Poe, after all!") and the film was a smash hit.

Personally speaking, I have Matheson and Mr. Poe and AIP to thank for what happened next—because Rich was quickly pressed into service as the writer on a second Corman/Price/Poe film, *Pit and the Pendulum*, released in 1961.

I was invited to its first showing in Hollywood, as was Marilyn Woodson (then in the process of a friendly divorce from Ruth's brother). We met for the first time that evening, dated off and on for the next several years, and have been happily married since 1970. (Having legally changed her name in court, she's now Cameron Nolan, a professional author in her own right.)

Matheson was hot in the industry. Beyond the second Poe film, his *Master of the World* (based on the work of Jules Verne) was also released in 1961, and three more of his *Twilight Zone* scripts were filmed, including the now-classic "Little Girl Lost."

With Charles Beaumont, he cowrote a screenplay based on a novel they both admired about witchcraft, by Fritz Leiber: *Conjure Wife*. (The film was produced as *Burn, Witch, Burn* by AIP in 1962.) "Chuck and I got just five grand apiece out of that one," said Matheson. "But we'd done it for our own amusement, so we didn't mind."

Then it was my turn to collaborate on three projects with Rich. The first was a wild adventure-fantasy, *Ali Baba and the Seven Marvels of the World*, for AIP, which was never produced due to the high cost of animating it in Japan.

Next, we wrote an original screenplay for comedian Tony Randall, *Double, Double*, followed by a version of the Jack Finney novel, *Assault on a Queen*, which we converted into a farce, calling it *Under the Bounding Main*. Although the Finney project was eventually filmed (with a Rod Serling screenplay), the Randall script faltered and died.

This was an incredibly active period for Matheson, and I recall a conversation we had in July of 1962 regarding his then-current workload: "In the next six weeks," he told me, "I have to write a screenplay for another Poe film, turn out a one-hour teleplay for the Hitchcock show, do an hour *Twilight Zone*, edit the final manuscript on my latest novel, and come up with a fifty-page outline for the next one. I'm so busy it's ridiculous."

But he dug in and met all these deadlines, easing down with a vacation visit to Hearst Castle, where he got the idea for the novel he would later write as *Hell House*. As Rich put it: "No matter where a writer goes, he gets ideas for new projects. You never see the world as others see it; you judge everything from a writer's perspective."

Alfred Hitchcock was planning his next picture, *The Birds*, and he called Matheson in to discuss the project. "I thought I'd be perfect to do the screenplay, but when he asked me how I'd handle the feathered menace in this story, I made the big mistake of telling him."

"What did you say?" I asked.

"I told him to go for mood and not to really show too many birds. He just stared at me. 'But that's the whole bloody idea of the picture!' he said—and that ended our interview."

By 1963, Matheson wound up his five-film AIP-Poe cycle with *The*

*Comedy of Terrors*, starring Boris Karloff, Peter Lorre, Basil Rathbone, and Vincent Price. "The AIP people *hated* my title, although they used it on the produced film. They insisted that you can't combine horror with humor, but of course they were wrong. The picture ended up with a nice profit, as did all the others in the series."

Matheson had a delightful time writing the script. "I got to create zany parts for these wonderful character actors, and they all had a grand time, proving to be excellent at comedy. I still chuckle whenever I see a rerun."

This film clearly demonstrated Matheson's flair for the absurd. As one critic observed: "Richard Matheson's work down the years reveals a delicious talent for tongue-in-cheek whimsy and biting satire."

Of Matheson's four *Twilight Zone* presentations that season, "Nightmare at 20,000 Feet" achieved the greatest impact with viewers. Star William Shatner (in his pre-Kirk days!) attempts to warn his fellow passengers during flight that a "destructive creature" was crouched outside, on the wing, beginning to tear apart the engines.

"The idea was, of course," said Matheson, "that no one on the plane believes him and he gets more and more desperate. The stunt guy on the wing almost ruined it for me. They had him dressed in this silly fur outfit and he looked about as fearsome as a panda bear—but the audience seemed to buy my concept, and thanks to a fantastic performance by Bill Shatner, the show worked."

For the closing season of this series (in 1964), Matheson had his final two *Twilight Zone* scripts produced, ending Serling's five-year run.

"I knew I'd miss Rod," said Matheson. "He was one of the nicest people I'd ever met in the film business, and a real sweetheart to work for. He saw to it that they shot my scripts just the way I wrote them, word for word, and that's rare in this industry. *Very* rare."

Tragically, during this period, Charles Beaumont became one of the youngest known victims of Alzheimer's, losing his sanity and eventually his life to this pernicious disease. For Chuck's close friends (Matheson, Bradbury, and myself) and for his family (his wife, Helen, and their four young children), Beaumont's terrible illness was truly devastating.

"I visited him in the hospital right up to the end," said Matheson. "On the night Chuck died, early in 1967, he had the face and body of a ninety-year-old man—but had just turned thirty-eight."

The Mathesons moved again, settling permanently into a spacious hilltop home in the exclusive residential area of Hidden Hills. ("Great place for a guy who's paranoid!" Rich told me with a chuckle.)

Matheson's career kept gaining momentum as he wrote an episode for *Star Trek*, had his fifth collection of short fiction published, and had teleplays produced for *Chrysler Theatre* and *The Girl from U.N.C.L.E.* He invited me to visit the set at Universal Studios where his *Beardless Warriors* was being shot.

His next major assignment was an adaptation of a Dennis Wheatley novel, *The Devil Rides Out*, for a 1968 film to be shot in England for Hammer Films. This time the censor passed his screenplay, released in the United States as *The Devil's Bride*.

As the 1960s drew to a close, Matheson became frustrated with the production of his script for AIP's *De Sade*, based on the life and works of the infamous Marquis de Sade (from whom the word "sadistic" was coined).

"They ruined it," lamented Matheson. "Only the first ten minutes represent what I wrote. The rest of it makes no sense. Just one more example of how you can get screwed in Hollywood."

In 1970, after more than two decades, Matheson lost the urge to write short stories. He'd done over a hundred, but that phase of his creative life had ended. "I don't know why, exactly. Maybe the writing of these stories satisfied a psychological need in my personality, but I also enjoyed doing them. Now that joy was gone."

He began concentrating on books, with his most horrific, *Hell House*, published in 1971. He also launched into his first extended love story, the time-travel romance *Bid Time Return*, a book that would take another four years to complete.

Universal had purchased TV rights to his *Playboy*-published suspense novelette, "Duel," and Rich was hired to write the teleplay. They wanted the story expanded to *Movie of the Week* length. Rich found this difficult, as it was a one-character piece, but he got it done. Yet he was

dubious about the actual production. "If you don't find the right director," he warned the executives at Universal, "this could turn out to be a
real turkey. A truck keeps chasing a guy in a car. Period. The guy never
sees the driver, who ultimately crashes. End of show. You'll need one hell
of a talented director to make this work."

A few days later, Rich got a call from the producer, George Eckstein.
"Some bad news," he said darkly.

"What's happened?" asked Rich. "Isn't Universal going to shoot it?"

"Oh, they're going to shoot it, all right," replied Eckstein, "but
they've foisted a young hotshot director from the lot on me—a guy
who's never directed a *Movie of the Week*. I think we're in big trouble."

Of course, the "young hotshot" was Steven Spielberg, and *Duel* became his first major credit. It is still being rerun today as an all-time TV
classic. Under Spielberg's inspired direction, Matheson's script played
out beautifully.

Rich's good luck continued when he met producer/director Dan
Curtis regarding an unpublished novel from writer Jeff Rice, featuring
a nervous reporter, Carl Kolchak, on the trail of a vampire in Las Vegas.
Matheson took on the job of scripting the story for television.

It proved to be a ratings blockbuster. *The Night Stalker*, with seventy-
five million viewers, rocked the industry. The network wanted more,
and the Curtis/Matheson team obliged them. Rich quickly followed his
initial Kolchak teleplay with a 1973 sequel, *The Night Strangler*, set in
the actual underground city below Seattle (which Matheson had visited
three years previously). Again, a huge hit.

In December of 1973, Curtis asked me to come up with a plot for
a third Kolchak *Movie of the Week*, and I supplied him with *The Night
Killers*, about robots replacing the government of Hawaii. Curtis called
in Rich for the rewrite, and the network green-lighted the project for
immediate production.

I was all set to ship off for Hawaii with Curtis and his crew, to be on
hand for any last-minute script changes, when ABC decided to opt for
a weekly *The Night Stalker* series of one-hour episodes. This killed our
project, and we were suddenly out of the Kolchak business.

By now, Matheson's 1971 horror novel had been filmed as *The Legend of Hell House*, from a script he also wrote. "When I saw it on the screen, my first reaction was very negative," declared Matheson. "In fact, I actually hated it. Having seen it a couple of times since, I've modified my opinion. I guess it's really not so bad. But one personal change emerged from this whole experience: I no longer wanted to write horror. When I got a chance to work on a totally different kind of project, I grabbed it."

This new project was a *Movie of the Week* drama for television, *The Morning After*. Its theme was alcoholism. Rich generated a very powerful script that received high critical praise—but a new Curtis/Matheson version of *Dracula* put Matheson right back on the horror shelf. And the same team was responsible for yet another classic in the fright genre, *Trilogy of Terror*, telecast early in 1975, based on three of Matheson's earlier short stories.

Again, I was called in by Curtis to write the first two short teleplays for this show. However, Rich wisely saved the plum for himself—scripting the final tale of a hideous, needle-fanged devil doll who chases Karen Black's character around her apartment, viciously slashing at her with a kitchen knife. The ending, in which the woman is consumed by the creature and literally *becomes* the killer doll, is vivid, shocking, and unforgettable.

Whether he liked it or not, Richard Matheson was firmly entrenched in the industry as a horror writer.

"I was determined to fight against this image," said Rich. "Dammit, I never wrote 'real' horror to begin with! To me, horror connotes blood and guts, while terror is a much more subtle art, a matter of stirring up primal fears. But, by the mid-seventies, I had tired of playing the fright game. Scaring the hell out of people no longer appealed to me."

As proof of his desire to break new ground, his romance novel *Bid Time Return* was published at this time, and he had embarked on his next book, a novelistic study of life after death, a metaphysical work he called *What Dreams May Come*. It boldly explored the world of reincarnation. Matheson has clearly stated his views on this subject:

> I believe that every human being is surrounded by some
> bioenergy field—what they refer to as the "aura"—that cre-

ates psychic phenomena, can affect healing, and is responsible for telepathy, telekinesis, and precognition. This field is connected to the body during our lifetime, disconnects itself at death, and is eternal. Our body is just the vehicle it uses during this particular phase of its existence. And then it comes back and attaches itself to another vehicle—which is, of course, reincarnation.

There is an overall meaning to everyone's existence, which is this constant cycle of living, dying, returning. We are headed somewhere—back to where we came from initially, when we were perfect in a very real sense.

*What Dreams May Come* was published in 1978 to a decidedly mixed reaction. Many critics and readers expressed anger at Matheson's diversion from the horror genre, while others responded with warmth and gratitude for the "mental comfort" the novel gave them.

Matheson's intense devotion to his family has given his life a rare stability, and he expressed his deep feelings for Ruth and his children in *What Dreams May Come.* The book is openly autobiographical.

"I was still doing some darker fantasy work for television," stated Matheson. "Stuff like *Dead of Night* and *The Strange Possession of Mrs. Oliver.* But my heart wasn't in it. I was totally absorbed with the filming of *Bid Time Return* [retitled as *Somewhere in Time*] and I even had a bit part in the picture."

Acting was natural to Matheson. For some years, he'd been involved with a local drama group, The Hidden Hills Players, in which he'd performed in a variety of stage roles.

"I had only one speaking line in the film," Matheson admitted. "But it was still great fun to be a part of it. No coffins or walking corpses or devil dolls—just a tender romance about a modern man who finds his way back to a woman from the past, an actress in the Victorian era. I felt renewed doing this one; it was a whole new experience."

The Mathesons took a vacation trip to Europe in 1981, visiting London, Paris, Rome, and Switzerland. "I was busy taking detailed notes on everything I saw," said Rich. "The trip proved quite valuable in terms of background because I ended up using these notes in my novel 7 *Steps to Midnight*, published in 1993."

Back in the States, Rich was signed to write the screenplay for *Twilight Zone—The Movie*, and he was also working on a massive outline for a TV series dealing with the paranormal. But not all of his assignments were to his liking.

"I got talked into writing *Jaws 3-D*, and it was a doomed venture. They threw out everything of worth that I suggested, and the final film was god-awful."

Matheson was bitter about much of his script work, and didn't hesitate to make his feelings known:

> Ultimately, I've come to the realization that the bulk of what I tried to do has not been transferred that well to the screen. Of the tremendous amount of work I've done for all these years, the amount of satisfaction is very low. Films have not served me well. I have written many good screenplays that were either ruined when they were made or that were never made at all. If I had taken that time to write novels instead, I would be a lot better off, creatively speaking. But I really had no choice with a wife and four kids to support. Unless you write a string of bestsellers, screen money is much greater than book money, and my books have always had a modest sale. Steady, but modest.

His three-year paranormal series outline had now reached the staggering total of over a thousand pages. Its final rejection by the network stunned and depressed him.

"I was trying to write something that would help people," he explained. "I've studied hundreds of books in every branch of parapsychology and metaphysics and in what I choose to call the 'supernormal'—not to be confused with the supernatural. This project meant a lot to me, and it was sad to see it die."

Helping people has always been a strong facet of Matheson's character. His charitable acts, done in conjunction with his wife, have never been publicized, nor would Rich allow them to be; they are private and numerous. (Ruth Matheson has made her own personal commitment to helping others, having become a practicing psychologist with an office in Woodland Hills.)

Matheson's next assignment, in 1986, was with Universal Studios. He was called to the studio by Steven Spielberg to act as creative consultant for the second season of the director's new anthology series, *Amazing Stories.*

"I read everything they gave me, making suggestions for changes as I saw the need. They listened politely, read all my notes and so on, but I don't think I made much of an impact. I had one of my own scripts produced on the show—but the series didn't jell and poor ratings ended it. Too bad, because I think it had real potential."

In 1989, Dream/Press issued the definitive volume of Rich's short fiction as *Richard Matheson: Collected Stories.* At a fat nine hundred pages, it also included tributes to Rich from King, Bradbury, Bloch, Finney, and several others. I was happy to contribute my own words of praise to the book, noting that it contained "some of the finest short stories of our century."

Matheson entered the 1990s with a superb *Movie of the Week*— *Dreamer of Oz*—a heartfelt drama based on the life of L. Frank Baum, author of the fabled series for children. (Who, indeed, can ever forget *The Wonderful World of Oz?*)

With his novels, Matheson was moving in a whole new direction— into the Old West. Over the next four years, he would release four books of highly-acclaimed western fiction, from *Journal of the Gun Years* to *Shadow on the Sun.* (The first of these won the Golden Spur Award as Best Western Novel of 1991.)

"I started back in the early fifties with science fiction," he said. "Then it was horror—or actually, terror-suspense—and now it's the Old West. I like to surprise people with my work, and I usually manage to surprise myself because I don't plan these phases, they just *happen.*"

Yet another facet of the Matheson talent emerged with the publication of his 1995 thriller, *Now You See It . . . ,* based on a play he'd written for Broadway.

"We had a director set, and a theater reserved, and everything was 'go' on the play when it all collapsed at the last minute. I decided to turn it into a novel since the material was just too good to waste."

The Matheson reader can never be sure of just what Rich will tackle next. But one thing's for sure: it won't be predictable or commonplace.

Richard Burton Matheson is still a major talent to be reckoned with.

I wrote this profile on Rich in the fall of 1995, over twelve years ago, and I've been asked to update it.

Certainly there have been major changes in Matheson's life and career since 1995. Now in his eighty-first year, three recent surgical operations have slowed him down—yet, as the biblio entry in this volume clearly shows, he has had no fewer than an astonishing sixty-six books and pamphlets (new and reprint) published over the last decade-plus. Many of these are novels or stories or scripts that were written much earlier.

"In the past," Matheson states, "when something of mine didn't sell right off, I'd stick it away in a drawer, so when Barry Hoffman of Gauntlet asked me for anything that hadn't been printed, I was able to resurrect all of these old manuscripts. Seeing them come to life again in print has been very satisfying."

Not to say that Rich has been inactive with new works. True enough, he no longer writes for films and television, but he has never abandoned prose. His 2002 novel *Hunted Past Reason* is stunningly good. For me, it ranks with *Bid Time Return* as his top work. It's a terror-filled deep woods drama that leaves you limp and gasping. A tour de force of suspense.

When I asked Rich if he had ever experienced such a wilderness adventure, he smiled: "No, I've never backpacked into the wilds. The novel all came from research."

He recently converted another of his plays into a novel, *Woman* (2005), and his extended paranormal TV treatment was finally published in 2006 as *The Link*.

I'm happy to report that Rich and I have also continued as a creative team into the new century. When I edited my "Southern California

School" anthology, *California Sorcery*, in 1999, I included a Matheson tale that garnered a rave in *Publishers Weekly*. Rich, in turn, wrote a warm introduction to my novel, *Helltracks*, in 2000—and we also shared creative input in Matheson's beautifully illustrated children's book, *Abu and the 7 Marvels* (2001).

In 2002, I edited *Off Beat*, a collection of early Matheson fiction—and when his Kolchak teleplays were published in 2003, the book included our never-produced collaboration, *The Night Killers*.

My move to Oregon in 2004 has not affected our close friendship, which has endured now for more than half a century.

Rich Matheson is a friend to treasure and one of the world's truly good human beings, who surely deserves all the honors and awards that have come his way.

Indeed, he is legend.

# Birth of a Writer:
# The Matheson/Peden Letters

*Paul Stuve*

A former student of mine [is] going to call you within the next few days and I think you might be interested in talking with the boy . . . The chap's name is Richard Matheson and I really believe he has possibly an extraordinary future ahead of him.

Professor William H. Peden knows of what he writes, and the above excerpt from his November 4, 1954, letter to his friend, publisher Roger W. Straus of Farrar, Straus & Young, Inc., is the recommendation of a perceptive scholar. During his lengthy career at the University of Missouri, he would shape the English Department in many important ways. He developed the University's creative writing program, established the University of Missouri Press in 1958, and in 1978 cofounded the *Missouri Review*, which awards an annual prize for short fiction in his name. Peden's impact on his students was tremendous, but his influence was felt on the national scene as well. He is the author of scholarly works on Thomas Jefferson, which are still carried in the Monticello gift shop, and on John and John Quincy Adams. He was a regular contributor of reviews and essays on English and American literature to *The Saturday Review* and *The New York Times Book Review*, which continues to this day to quote from his reviews.

Peden published several books and papers on the short story form of writing, and was part of the original editorial board of the journal

*Studies in Short Fiction* and was an editor of *Story* magazine. His short fiction has appeared in two of his own collections, and has also been published in numerous literary magazines and anthologies. Peden is credited by many with helping to establish the short story as a legitimate form of literature. When he retired in 1979, he donated his extensive personal library to the University of Missouri, a collection that contains more than 450 volumes of short story collections and anthologies with associated newspaper and magazine clippings; copies of his own books, reviews, and lectures; and boxes of correspondence with a virtual who's who of America's finest writers. One of these boxes contains a folder of nearly thirty years' worth of correspondence with one of Peden's very first students, a chap named Richard Matheson.

The correspondence offers a unique opportunity to follow Matheson's early career development, especially the first ten years. Matheson's letters convey a self-effacing wit, and yet a quiet confidence in his talent and a belief in his continued improvement as a writer. They reveal frustrations and aspirations, and include his unvarnished perspectives on the contemporary literary scene as well as the Hollywood movie-making machine. His respect and admiration for the great writers of the day is evident throughout, as is his yearning for an eventual place in their company. What follows, in more or less chronological order, is a brief tour of that correspondence, with stylistic idiosyncrasies intact.

Peden and Matheson both came to the University of Missouri in 1946, Matheson to enter the undergraduate program and Peden to join the faculty of the English Department. Although Peden would eventually spend most of his time teaching graduate students, his early work with undergraduates gave Matheson an opportunity to take two of his writing courses. From Peden he would learn the craft of writing stories—the form and structure necessary to support the story, regardless of the particular genre of writing.

Matheson chose decidedly nonmainstream themes for his stories, but he demonstrated talent for the underlying form, and Peden encouraged his work. Fellow student Maryjane Meaker would later recall in a memoir that Matheson "wrote weird fantasies I envied because they were so good, and were always read aloud in writing class by Dr. Peden" (Kerr, 1983). An early version of Matheson's short story "The Faces" made its debut in one of Peden's classes.

Matheson admired Peden greatly, and would later attribute much of his success with short stories to Peden's tutelage, but their friendship did not develop until later. In fact, Matheson's first post-graduation contact with Peden begins unassumingly with the sentence, "Trust you still recall my presence in your two advanced writing classes one and two years ago." The brief postcard, postmarked April 15, 1950, and mailed from Brooklyn, where Matheson had returned after graduating, announced an exciting event: the publication of his first story. The postcard was typed, as would be all of his letters, and was signed "Richard B. Matheson" in neat cursive handwriting that looks somewhat different from the familiar signature now embossed on the covers of his limited editions.

The story, of course, was "Born of Man and Woman." It was published in *The Magazine of Fantasy and Science Fiction*, whose editors found it to be "an extraordinarily powerful and effective piece of writing" (McComas, 1982) and erroneously assumed that Matheson was a seasoned professional writing under a pseudonym. "We do hope," they wrote, "that it will be far from the last Matheson story we'll publish" (McComas, 1982). Peden echoed their sentiments, writing Matheson on April 22, 1950, to congratulate him and to note that "I hope this will be only the first of a good many published stories."

Matheson would not disappoint. Within the year, he informed Peden (in an undated letter c. February 1951) that "I have sold twelve more stories." Several of these were to *The Magazine of Fantasy and Science Fiction*, whose pages would see nearly twice as many Matheson stories as any other publication. All of these early pieces were fantasy/science-fiction stories, and while Matheson admitted to Peden that "writing fantasy was always my best love and my best talent," he worried that "I seem to be gravitating towards specialization although I try not to." Still, he recognized that it "seems a very lucrative field. (in ideas I mean although they pay pretty well, too)," and observed, as would Rod Serling many years later, that "I can easily insert politics and personal philosophy into science-fiction and, because it is set in the future or on another planet, I can get away with it."

In spite of his love for the genre, Matheson would worry at times about its respectability and that of the "pulp" magazines that were home to so many of his stories. On March 16, 1951, he wrote Peden: "I certainly can't deny that 99% of pulp and slick writing is dull and plodding formula writing." Of his own work he reported, "Now, never in one of my stories have I tried to follow any formula . . . unless it was done unconsciously. . . . What I mean to say is that *all* stories follow a certain formula. Good characterization is certainly a 'formula' in a manner of speaking. Suspense, indirect hinting at horror, etc. All these things are, to my mind, formula. Yet when used well they add up to a good story. . . . I recently met a [man] who runs a large chain of pulps of all kinds. He told me to forget about plot or anything else and just concentrate on good characterization. This sort of knocked the props out of my old scorn for the pulp editor."

Nevertheless, scattered throughout the correspondence are indications that Matheson was always pleased to be writing other types of stories or selling to different kinds of publications. He informed Peden on March 24, 1954, that "I've also finally made the (not so big) jump into the semi-slicks out of the pulps with a sale to *Bluebook*," and on May 9, 1955, reported that "I've also sold a western novelette to a pocket-size mag. called, aptly enough, *Western*. Not much money, but I always like to sell out of my field. My next novel, I think, will be a mystery novel but of a much higher order, I hope, than my first two Lion books . . . But before that, I plan to write about ten to fifteen short stories; mostly science-fiction, but I want to try a few straight stories in there too or I'll never be able to do them."

Matheson's commitment to the craft of writing was evident from the beginning of the correspondence. When Peden published a new book with Harper's, Matheson wrote (c. February 1951), "I was very pleased to hear it and know how it must delight you, give you a needed feeling of fruition after all the time and effort you have spent on writing. I hope I shall one day reach the same point. And, when and if I do, I feel certain that attending your classes will have much to do with it." He laments young writers who give up "apparently without a fight; as the 'natural' thing to do. As if writing were something college boys did to fill in the gaps between beer busts." Matheson would persevere: "Sure it's hard . . . But the rewards are big, too. One can retain all his hopes and dreams if he writes of them. Then, of course, there seems to be an actual physical handicap which simply will not let a real writer turn to anything else without feeling sick." He states that "I am definitely started and am bound to my writing now and . . . am in no way inclined to give up and get an editorial job."

Perhaps not an editorial job, but after moving to California in May of 1951, Matheson was unable to make ends meet with his writing, and wound up taking a job with Douglas Aircraft on the swing shift, saving his days for writing. He completed his first novel during this time, and in 1952 he sent it to Peden for his comments. Of the massive manuscript, Peden, not one to mince words, replied, "you have developed considerably since you were in school. This novel, though, disappoints me." He worried about discouraging Matheson's writing efforts with his feedback, but Matheson reported that Peden's comments were consistent with the opinions of several friends and his agent, Harry Altshuler, and in that respect were "almost a relief." He abandoned plans to publish the manuscript, although he indicated that he intended to "hack up this monster and send out his legs in hopes of marketing at least his extremities." He never did so, and it would be another fifty years before *Hunger and Thirst* was finally published.

Though humble about his work, Matheson always seemed happy with the progress he was making as a writer, and appeared confident that his efforts would ultimately pay off. He generally described current novels as being his "best work" to date, and noted on March 24, 1954, that "I think I'm improving all the time and believe that, within a few years, I should make a real success of my writing." Frustrated after a brush-off from a New York publisher in December of 1954, Matheson wrote Peden: "I may not be a marvel yet, but I think my published works indicate a good deal of ability." On March 4, 1957, he reported that "I am, gradually, becoming more fussy with my work."

Matheson continued to sell short stories while working at Douglas, and in March 1954, he informed Peden of the publication of his first anthology and first hardcover book, *Born of Man and Woman*. "Chamberlain Press is a new company; as a matter of fact, this is their first book. Cross your fingers that I don't make them go broke first crack out of the bag." His comments proved to be prophetic: only about 650 copies of the print run were distributed before a flood destroyed most of the other copies. A subsequent warehouse fire destroyed remaining unbound pages, and *Born of Man and Woman* was Chamberlain Press's only publication.

The book was dedicated to Peden, who arranged to have it reviewed in the local Columbia, Missouri, newspaper and the *Missouri Alumnus* magazine. He wrote Matheson on April 21, 1954, with contacts at *The Saturday Review* and *The New York Times Book Review*, among others, and indicated that "Certainly the book is well worth reviewing, and most editors would allot it satisfactory space and a good reviewer." He would later remark in a November 4, 1954, letter to publisher Roger W. Straus that Matheson's stories display "originality, perceptiveness and great technical skill."

Matheson's first science-fiction novel, *I Am Legend*, was published in 1954, the first such novel published by Fawcett Gold Medal. Peden wrote of *I Am Legend* that he was "very much impressed"; indeed, it would remain one of his favorites of Matheson's work. But despite the success of *I Am Legend*, Matheson, now with a wife and two children, remained uncertain about the viability of a career in California. In the fall of 1954, he made the difficult decision to return to New York, where he resumed writing full time.

On May 9, 1955, Matheson wrote Peden that he was working on his second science-fantasy novel, which was bought by Fawcett Gold Medal "on the strength of the first 130 pages." The book's editor "has what he calls 'big' movie contacts," but, Matheson confided to Peden, "I don't expect anything to come of it, but it's pleasant daydreaming anyway. I'm afraid it would be much too difficult to make into a movie—unless, of course, they hoked it up as they usually do." He would have his chance to try to prevent that from happening. Just four months later, Matheson contacted Peden from California, where he had been hastily summoned from New York (and where he was temporarily staying with his friend, writer Charles Beaumont). The September 30, 1955, letter to Peden was typed on stationery from Universal-International Pictures and reported Matheson's "big news for the year—that the above studio has bought my book *Shrinking Man* and I am at the moment in the act of preparing a screen play for it . . . Sounds so simple when you write it down. Words fail sometimes. They do in this case. They fail to indicate what a tremendous thrill it was to get such news."

Still, Matheson was restless: "Oddly enough, I temper this delightful news with the report that I feel bored. Going back to an already finished work seems dull. I wish I were doing something new. Even with all this money coming in I feel tempted to go home and write stories again. . . . I want to do more movies but only once in a while. Most of the time I want for my books and stories. . . . I am going to try to do a good job on the picture so I'll have a chance to pick and choose in the future."

He did indeed do a good job on the screenplay, and by that time had permanently settled in California with his family. In mid-1956, while *The Incredible Shrinking Man* was shooting, Matheson was contacted by Universal-International about writing a story line for a sequel to the film. He wrote Peden on June 8, 1956, that they "wanted to know if I was interested in a week's work at $750. I said I was. A little better than that $33 from unemployment insurance. . . . They say if the story line is accepted, I will do the screenplay, too. Would like to refuse, but who can at those absurd prices?"

Matheson went on to profess his amazement at the Hollywood machine: "[N]othing one can say about the movie business is silly enough. Which is why a novel about Hollywood is doomed to flop, I think. If you write restrained, it's untrue. If you tell the truth, it's unbelievable. Strange circumstance of a billion dollar industry which, in its operation, is completely improbable. Like the bee that can't possibly fly with such small wings, Hollywood couldn't possibly exist and be so ridiculous. But it does and it is. What is one to do?" He visited the set of *The Incredible Shrinking Man*, reporting that, "It really awed me. . . . The producer tells me it is the longest shooting schedule of any picture the studio ever made. Costing over a million dollars. *Life* magazine to do a spread on it. All this incredible labor and output of energy just because I sat in a movie once three years ago and thought, *Gee, what if a guy started shrinking*? Biggest oak from the littlest acorn I ever heard tell of. Gives one humility. Except that humility is not saleable out here."

The planned sequel was never filmed, and Matheson returned to his books and stories. On March 4, 1957, he wrote Peden that "I may very well concentrate to a great extent on psychic phenomena in future novels—I have, at least, three planned already. It is a field which I think is important and can be popularized through fiction—intelligently popularized, that is."

Peden, at that time, had written an article for *The Saturday Review* on short stories, which Matheson indicated that he "enjoyed very much," although he remarked, "It certainly seems a commercially dying field although they are so pleasant to write." Peden would later seek a contribution from Matheson for *Story* magazine, which was resurrected in 1960 and for which he had been made co-editor. On November 25, 1959, he wrote Matheson: "I should be very pleased to have a story of yours for the first or at least for a very early issue." Matheson, however, declined three days later: "I have done very few short stories in the past few years because of the lack of market for same . . . Although I think that, toward the close of my short story production, I began to get a proper approach and feeling for them . . . The last good story I wrote appeared in *Playboy* in March 1958 and won the prize for the best story they published that year—and got mentioned in either the Foley or O'Henry collection of Best Stories, I forget which. It was called 'The Distributor.' I find it rather amusing—and somewhat irritating—that the only two mentions I got in the *Best Stories of the Year* were for two stories which had no particular plot."

He further expressed his frustration at the state of writing at that time: "I think most short story writers today—for all their skill with words—have little ability—or concern—for the craft of form: structure. All the stories we read in our texts when we were at school had a definite beginning, middle, and end. Today the stories sort of drool across the pages starting no where and getting no where. As I say, I may be conditioned to the wrong kind of short story writing by now, but I don't like it much. I feel the same about the contemporary novel—no *craft*, no *professionalism* . . . I'll take T.H. White and Joyce Carey and De Hartog and their ilk. This is CRAFT, which I admire tremendously."

Matheson reported that most of his time for the previous year and a half had been devoted to "my first so-called 'straight' novel, which is to say it isn't fantasy or science-fiction . . . It is called *The Beardless Warriors* and . . . is an immense improvement over any of my previous work. Since the field I've been working in—fantasy–science fiction is pretty well dead in prose terms, I have to expand myself. This book should do it."

While Matheson seems to have misjudged the market for fantasy and science-fiction prose, he did admit that "I *have* been doing old type work in movies and television. I have written two scripts for Rod Serling's *Twilight Zone* . . . [and] a screenplay . . . for Poe's 'Fall of the House of Usher' . . . It is the best screenplay I have done. As in the case of the Serling series, this is because I was allowed to write it precisely as I saw it and not a word has been altered."

*The Beardless Warriors* was published in 1960, and on October 20, 1960, Peden wrote Matheson: "It is a damn good book and I congratulate you on it. I found it completely convincing and thoroughly well done."

The Archive contains no additional correspondence until April 1, 1973, when Matheson contacted Peden to report, "Thanks to the Writers Guild strike currently underway (I picket five days this week at Warner Bros.—not exactly what I had anticipated as writing success) I am getting the time to finish a current novel of my own. A rather strange one for me. No shock, no gore, no suspense, just a time travel love story. I hope it does all right." Indeed it did. The first edition of *Bid Time Return* is one of Matheson's scarcest and most sought-after titles. He sent Peden a copy on August 26, 1977, writing that "I'm going to start [the] screenplay soon. . . . Dustin Hoffman likes the book and will very likely star in it." Christopher Reeve, of course, would play the role of Richard Collier in *Somewhere in Time*, which today commands a devoted cult following that is quite rare outside the realm of science-fiction and horror films.

Matheson further noted in that letter that his latest project was "a six-hour t-v movie of Ray Bradbury's *The Martian Chronicles*. I can see why he has had so much trouble getting it on the screen. Even though NBC 'agrees' that it *must* be episodic being a group of short stories, they still want 'connective tissue' and the connective tissue is getting in the way more and more. I hope not ruinously." Peden replied a week later on September 3, 1977: "It's pleasant to hear that things are going so well with you; we'll look forward to seeing your adaptation of *The Martian Chronicles*, still my favorite of all Bradbury's books . . . Incidentally—no, much more than incidentally—many thanks for *Bid Time Return*. I'm almost ¾ finished, and like it immensely, it's my favorite of yours since *I Am Legend*, which is saying a good deal."

Matheson concurred in the last piece of correspondence in the Archives. In his letter of October 10, 1977, he tells Peden: "I'm glad you like *Bid Time Return*. I like it, too. It's really the only book I've written I still re-read at all much less with any kind of pleasure." He further informs Peden that "Berkley Books is going to re-issue nine of my past books . . . the first collection will be one of them—the one I dedicated to you." Matheson would dedicate yet another book to Peden (among a list of those who had helped him in his career), his western novel, *The Memoirs of Wild Bill Hickok*.

Any further correspondence between the two men from the time of Peden's retirement in 1979 until his death in 1999 would appear to have been lost. Their thirty-year dialogue covers Matheson's formative years as a writer, and he would turn time and time again to Peden to vent his frustrations and share his successes. A number of their exchanges were in the form of brief postcards: "My first *Twilight Zone* script is to be shown on Friday, February 5," Matheson wrote on January 27, 1960. "Hope you get a chance to see it." Peden replied three days prior to the airing: "You may be sure that I will be looking out for it this Friday." It is these brief personal notes (the correspondence even contains a Christmas card from Matheson in 1961) that reveal a developing relationship from one of student and teacher to that of colleagues and friends. They even briefly discussed collaborating on a play together, but this never materialized.

Early in his career, Matheson wrote Peden on September 30, 1955, that "I'm beginning to see more and more how few genuine writers there are. I want to be one." This desire to be a "genuine writer" has been not just realized, but wildly surpassed. Peden would watch his student excel in several forms of writing, from short stories to novels to screenplays. Matheson would continue to write "outside his field," and his oeuvre defies easy categorization—he would win Life Achievement Awards from the Horror Writers Association and the World Fantasy Association, and Best Novel honors in 1991 from the Western Writers of America. Matheson is a writer's writer, revered by his colleagues who throughout the years have provided a most impressive list of accolades. Many of these can be found in this book, and all of them confirm the sentiment expressed by William Peden more than fifty years ago at the time of Matheson's birth as a writer: *I really believe he has possibly an extraordinary future ahead of him.*

Extraordinary indeed.

The correspondence cited herein is found in the following sources:

University Archives, University of Missouri-Columbia, Collection No. C:6/20/14.

Division of Special Collections and Rare Books, University of Missouri-Columbia, Collection No. Peden Ephemera FF 17.

Kerr, M.E. (1983). *Me Me Me Me Me: Not a Novel.* New York: Harper & Row.

McComas, Annette Peltz (Ed.) (1982). *The Eureka Years: Boucher and McComas's* The Magazine of Fantasy and Science Fiction *1949–1954.* New York: Bantam Books.

Special thanks to Gary Cox at the University of Missouri Archives and to Margaret "Petch" Peden for their kind assistance.

## Selected Matheson/Peden Letters

222 E. 7th Street
Brooklyn 18, N.Y.

Dear Mr. Peden:

I was at an M.U. alumni meeting yesterday.
Some friend of mine made mention of the fact
that you are having a book put out by Harpers.
Is it really so? I think that's marvelous,
Harpers being just about the best of the publishers. I was very pleased to hear it and know
how it must delight you, give you a needed feeling of fruition after all the time and effort
you have spent on writing.

I hope I shall one day reach the same
point. And, when and if I do, I feel certain that
attending your classes will have had much to
do with it.

Since I last wrote you mentioning my first
sale, I have sold twelve more stories and now
have an agent whom I like and respect. I seem
to be gravitating towards specialization although
I try not to. But most of my sales have been in
the fantasy and science-fiction field which I
like a lot and can do pretty well. As a matter
of fact, my very first published story is being
anthologized in The Best Science-Fiction Stories
of 1951. It seems a very lucrative field.( in
ideas I mean although they pay pretty well too)
For one good thing, I can easily insert politics
and personal philosophy into science-fiction and,
because it is set in the future or on another
planet, I can get away with it. And, of course,
if you recall, writing fantasy was always my best
love and my best talent.

But, at least, I am definitely started and
am bound to my writing now and, since I have made
money with it, am in no way inclined to give up
and get an editorial job.

Do you ever hear from any of the other people
who were in your Advanced Writing classes?

Undated letter (c. February 1951) from Matheson to former professor William
Peden. Courtesy of University Archives, University of Missouri-Columbia,
Collection No. C:6/20/14. Page 1.

(2)

I think it almost tragic that young people
with talent give up so soon and, shrugging their
shoulders and murmuring "let's be practical," kick
their dreams in an ashcan. Sure, it's hard. I had
a relatively easy time getting established in the
minor way I am, and, even so, I recall the long
months of seemingly wasted effort, the reams of
paper used up, the loss of social life, etc. It's
hard all right. But the rewards are big too. One
can retain all his hopes and dreams if he writes
of them. Then, of course, there seems to be an
actual physical handicap which simply will not let
a real writer turn to anything else without feeling
sick.

Well, I meant to ask if you ever heard from
any of those I worked with in your classes. Ken
Sellers, for instance. He seemed to me to have a
really fine writing talent. Do you know if he still
writes? There are several here in the city but they
have given it up, it appears. And, apparently without a fight; as the "natural" thing to do. As if
writing were something college boys did to fill in
the gaps between beer busts.

Well, this started out as a brief congratul-
ation note on your book, the person said it was a
novel. So I'll cut short the rambling and once more
say how pleased I am to hear about it. I'll be looking forward to reading it and I hope I can send you
my copy and have you autograph it for me.

Best of everything,

*Richard Matheson*
Richard Matheson

Undated letter (c. February 1951) from Matheson to former professor William
Peden. Courtesy of University Archives, University of Missouri-Columbia,
Collection No. C:6/20/14. Page 2.

P.O. Box 1082
Gardena ,Calif.
March 24, 1954

Professor William Peden
English Department
Jesse Hall
University of Missouri
Columbia, Missouri

Dear Professor Peden:

I'm sending under separate cover a collection of my short
stories. I hope you like it.

Chamberlain Press is a new company; as a matter of fact this
is their first book. Cross your fingers that I don't make them
go broke first crack out of the bag.

I've been having remarkable success lately with my writing
attempts. This month I sold my first science-fiction novel
to Gold Medal. This will be the first novel of this type
they'll do. I'm quite pleased with the book and I hope you
will be too when you read it. It's certainly the best book
I've done to date. I don't know whether I told you I've had
two mystery novels printed by Lion Books - a pocketbook house.
These aren't too good although the first got a nice review in
the New York Times.

I've also finally made the (not so big) jump into the semi-slicks
out of the pulps with a sale to Bluebook. This one, oddly enough,
is a down-beat western my agent predicted wouldn't sell because
it's told by an old man, has no hero and ends in violent death
for the main character. Bluebook bought it though first time out.

So you see I didn't let the abysmal failure of my first book (that
great monstrosity) hit me too hard. I think I'm improving all the
time and believe that, within a few years, I should make a real
success of my writing. Above all though, I'm succeeding writing
what I please. To my mind, that's the only success in writing.
Anything else is drudgery.

I hope this letter finds you well and hope too that my collection
pleases you.

                                    Best,

                                    Richard Matheson
                                    Richard Matheson

March 24, 1954, letter from Matheson to former professor William Peden.
Courtesy of University Archives, University of Missouri-Columbia, Collection
No. C:6/20/14.

June 8, 1956

Dear Bill:

Thought I'd drop you a copy of the enclosed in case you hadn't run across it in Columbia. Awful cover this time. Well, one can't complain. Those 2½ months really paid off.

Thought I was through with Hollywood until I sold them another novel but a day or so ago came a call from the Hollywood agent who told me that U-I wanted to know if I was interested in a week's work at $750. I said I was. A little better than that $33 from unemployment insurance.

Turns out - brace yourself - they are already planning a sequel to THE INCREDIBLE SHRINKING MAN to be called- what else?- THE FANTASTIC SHRINKING WOMAN. Isn't that absolute...oh well. They say if the story line is accepted I will do the screenplay too. Would like to refuse that but who can at those absurd prices?

Which all goes to prove that nothing one can say about the movie business is silly enough. Which is why a novel about Hollywood is doomed to flop, I think. If you write restrained, it's untrue. If you tell the truth, it's unbelievable. Strange circumstance of a billion dollar industry which, in its operation, is completely improbable. Like the bee that can't possibly fly with such small wings, Hollywood couldn't possibly exist and be so ridiculous. But it does and it is. What is one to do?

I was at the studio this afternoon looking over the sets for the film. (The expense of the sets is one reason they want a sequel) It really awed me. I entered this vast sound stage as big as the hugest auditorium. It is a scene of rushing din. Men hammering, sawing, filing, screaming orders. Blueprints lying around and tacked up. The air foggy with sawdust and plaster. Against the wall a giant ball of string, an orange crate as big as a house, a paint can like an oil tank. On another stage, two sets; one a normal livingroom, a little further on the same livingroom only grotesquely large giving one a feeling of strange unreality.

June 8, 1956, letter from Matheson to former professor William Peden. Courtesy of Division of Special Collections and Rare Books, University of Missouri-Columbia, Collection No. Peden Ephemera FF17. Page 1.

I stood beside Van Heflin ( ), sadly, was not aware of my estimable presence) and together we watched them photographing a tarantula on the cellar set. Sickening sight.

Picture is about half done. The producer tells me it is the longest shooting schedule of any picture the studio ever made. Costing over a million dollars. Life magazine to do a spread on it. All this incredible labor and output of energy just because I sat in a movie once three years ago and thought, Gee, what if a guy started shrinking? Biggest oak from the littlest acorn I ever heard tell of. Gives one humility. Except that humility is not saleable out here. Salable? Who knows? I've been misspelling that word since Narration.

Have a new New York agent now. Marvelous man. Name of Don Congdon with the Harold Matson Company. He also handles Ray Bradbury, Henry Kuttner, Davis Grubb, John Collier, Herman Wouk, Jack Shaak Shaeffer and a few other hacks. Friend of mine, who is also a client of Congdon's, name of Charles Beaumont, was just to Chi. where several big editors, including Spectorsky who is now an editor on Playboy said that they thought Congdon the best agent operating today in the whole world! This is going some. He has already sold another collection of my stories to Bantam Books.

I am writing my first historical novel now which I have high hopes for. It's about a religious movement that took place in the 1800's in New England; Millerism. Fascinating subject. I'm up to about page 90. Might turn out to be a long one.

Hope this letter finds you well.

                                        Best,
                                        Dick

June 8, 1956, letter from Matheson to former professor William Peden. Courtesy of Division of Special Collections and Rare Books, University of Missouri-Columbia, Collection No. Peden Ephemera FF17. Page 2.

RICHARD MATHESON

WOODLAND HILLS, CALIF. 91365

8/26/77

Dear Bill:

I received the Mizzou newspaper in the mail today and enjoyed reading
the article about you and your wife. It also reminded me that I have
not been very good about keeping in touch with you.

Enclosed is the last book I had published. The hardcover came out
in 1974. I'd send you one but I don't have any. Beside, they really
did a dreadful job on the jacket - and I did all the work getting a
gorgeous photograph taken by a friend of my son's. "They" is Viking
Press. My new novel will be published by Putnam, some time next
year. It is a realistic (I hope) story about afterlife. I read 91
books for research in addition to having read about the subject for
many years.

I'm going to start a screenplay soon on BID TIME RETURN. For Ray
Stark's company. Dustin Hoffman likes the book and will very likely
star in it. The young man who wants to produce it is trying to
get Claude Lelouche interested in the novel - which would be very
nice.

My latest project - I've been working on it since January - is a
six-hour t-v movie of Ray Bradbury's THE MARTIAN CHRONICLES. I can
see why he has had so much trouble getting it on the screen. Even
though NBC "agrees" that it <u>must</u> be epidodic being a group of short
stories, they still want "connective tissue" and the connective
tissue is getting in the way more and more. I hope not ruinously.

Have you ever thought of writing a play about Jefferson? I became
interested in him after hearing a radio program years ago starring
Claude Rains. Then I read the book by the UCLA woman professor. I
gather, from the article about you, that you are not keen on the
"psycho-history" approach to Jefferson's life - or is it just the
Sally Hennings thing? Anyway, he certainly was a fascinating man.
If he hadn't really existed, I would say he was improbable. I acted
in an educational film a few years back in which I was a kind of
bizarre moderator who brought Jefferson and Hamilton back from the
dead to debate. Maybe the University has a copy of it. I also did
about a twentysecond bit on CAPTAINS AND KINGS playing President
Garfield; my beard won me the part with a neighbor who saw me act
in our little theatre here. It was interesting if nerve-wracking.
Most of my little scene was with Henry Fonda. I can't imagine who
he thought I was. Certainly not a professional actor.

Are you in touch with Maryjane Meaker or Bill Manchester?

Hope this note finds you well,

Dick

August 26, 1977, letter from Matheson to former professor William Peden.
Courtesy of University Archives, University of Missouri-Columbia, Collection
No. C:6/20/14.

# Richard Matheson Has My Number

*Gahan Wilson*

I believe my first contact with the work of Richard Matheson was his short story "Born of Man and Woman."

There it was in the pages of *The Magazine of Fantasy and Science Fiction*, a publication I would eventually have a long and pleasurable relationship with, but which was then a monthly source of delight and instruction to me as one of its younger readers.

What I remember mostly now was not the story itself, though it was and is a pip, but the sensation I had of liking it very much in particular from its first sentence, then sinking deeper and deeper into its spell as its paragraphs progressed, and finally sitting absolutely stunned on the wicker seat of an elevated train heading from Evanston to Chicago, afloat in the joy of having had the amazing good luck to stumble upon and read such a beautifully written and marvelously profound little tale.

I don't know exactly what it is or how he does it, but Richard Matheson's stories and movies and television plays all seem to give me extraordinary pleasure. It isn't just that they're highly accomplished works of art, although they certainly are; it's that he seems to know just exactly what will widen my eyes and curl my toes and melt my heart.

No matter what medium he's working in or what style of entertainment he's exploiting, he zeros in on me every time and I find I not only heartily enjoy the first impact, I yearn for and have gone to extraordinary lengths to achieve repeated exposure to his written works or movies or television shows.

I have no idea how many times, for example, I've gloated over once again having the fun of watching Carl Kolchak eccentrically battle evil in *The Night Stalker* and *The Night Strangler* and I'm almost certain that writing this little tribute will doubtless inspire me to review Spielberg's *Duel* yet another time with equal, if not increased, pleasure.

Even the hokey delights of those Corman-driven Edgar Allan Poe takeoffs never fail to give me endless cackles and knee-slappings which I fully intend to revisit enthusiastically.

Of course it goes without saying (after what I've said) and shouldn't surprise you in the least to learn that I do, indeed, have a battered hoard of *Twilight Zone* tapes and you've probably guessed without my telling you that the most battered of them all is "Nightmare at 20,000 Feet." Who could ever get enough of that dear old fellow out there on the plane's wing? Not I.

I think the fundamental underlying charm of his works is that they are all so enormously enjoyable. They are scary, they are sensitive, they dig into forms where many find only dross and come up with pure gold, they are successfully heartbreaking and/or hilarious in exactly the right measure—they are all of these things and much, much more but they are also reliably and universally terrific fun.

Also, very importantly, his stories and the characters within them inevitably manage to inspire great affection from the reader or viewer. It's a cliché but a great and thundering truth that if you don't care about a character, don't like or feel empathy for him or her or it, you're not going to give much of a damn about what happens to him or her or it.

Take what he did with the Jack Palance *Dracula*, for instance, what he did to Dracula himself. He humanizes him. When we first see the ancient vampire making contact with a living person in the interview scene with the real estate agent Harker, Matheson sees to it that he's not wearing a dark black Dracula outfit but a bright and rather natty getup with a bow tie. Nice little touch. Matheson's grandest and most effective maneuver, however, is to show Dracula eagerly visiting the tomb of his new-made bride only to find that she has been skillfully destroyed by Van Helsing. Palance then takes full and skillful advantage of a sad and touching scene wherein the vampire goes into a lonely, raging, roaring fit of grief and tears the place apart, brutally bashing in its coffins, hurling marble urns this way and that, and raising great, choking clouds of mortal dust.

You'd have to be totally and completely made of stone not to feel a deep twinge of pity, even considerable empathy, for the poor old monster.

For all those poor old monsters.

I am deeply grateful to have had the enormous good fortune of having read and viewed and been forever haunted and warmed by the marvelous work of Richard Matheson and it's a real pleasure to be given this chance to thank him for his generosity in public.

Thank you.

# A Tribute

*Ruth Ann Matheson*

We met on the beach in Santa Monica on a sunny weekday afternoon. Both of us lived in rooming houses, neither of us had a car or money and we were both happy to meet someone in similar circumstances.

He worked at Douglas Aircraft, on the swing shift, and I worked as an X-ray tech at Santa Monica Hospital, 9 to 5. He had moved to L.A. two weeks earlier from New York, and I had left a three-year marriage at about the same time.

I was immediately drawn to his good looks, tall, blond, and soft spoken, and when he told me that he was a writer, I sensed that he was highly intelligent, creative, sensitive, and someone I wanted to know.

I had been raised in a very conventional home; my father was a captain in the navy, my mother, a homemaker, my older brother, a future graduate of Caltech, and my younger brother, still in his early teens when I left home. The arts, in my family, were not important. I was never really exposed to them, yet I equated creative people and writers in particular with people who were strong, compassionate, and sensitive. Richard was, in fact, all those things.

A year after we met, we went to Tijuana and got married. During the years that we have been together, we have raised a family of four children: Bettina, an L.C.S.W., Richard, a writer/producer, Ali, a writer/producer, and Christian, a writer/director.

As the family began to grow up, I attended college, majoring in psychology. I approached my thesis with a certain amount of awareness about creative people because of those I'd been living with. And I began to see the correlation between androgyny and creativity. Androgyny is the unconscious expression of both the male and female self—it is an ongoing experience that is felt by creative people and allows them to be integrated in their art.

In my research, I gradually began to realize that what had originally attracted me to my husband, Richard, were those things I hadn't grown up with: sensitivity and awareness; a rare and remarkable androgyny that was also his strength in loving and understanding all things.

# Horror Legend

## George Clayton Johnson

As I write this introduction to the fortieth anniversary edition of Richard Matheson's *I Am Legend*, it occurs to me that I've known Richard for thirty-seven years, although I knew *of* him long before that. In those long-ago days, I was a beginning writer still striving to become published and Richard Matheson, Charles Beaumont, Ray Bradbury, and Theodore Sturgeon were my literary heroes. To me these four contemporary writers were the chewy center. They wrote the stuff I wish I had written. They were serious storytellers whose works were artful gems of wisdom fiction. The deliciously scary stories they created were realistically mainstream in most respects but with an added touch of *strange*. The tales included not only the seen but the unseen; not only the truth but the greater truth. They provided a new slant on reality by showing both the undeniable and the unbelievable on one canvas, to convincingly create a compelling surreal image that is itself an even greater statement about the nature of existence than the particular fantasy depicted.

Fairy tales tell universal truths.

They are archetypal accounts of how the personality meets and overcomes its own dangers.

They speak in universal symbols directly to the soul.

These men showed me that a talented writer could become professional and earn a modest living over an extended length of time by remaining industrious and creative and self-searching and truthful and free—qualities that Beaumont and Sturgeon and Bradbury and Matheson displayed like flags.

I yearned to be like them.

They showed me that the bravest writer is one who dares to write about himself—his deepest fears, his darkest desires, his weaknesses, his strengths, his dreams, his visions, his rationalizations and self-deceptions, his own enemy within. The writer, though cloaking himself in the guise of a story character, must look deep within himself to lovingly understand and sympathize with that character, giving him human dimension and a certain reality by the truth revealed through his telling behavior and reactions when threatened.

When Rod Serling brought television to that state of mind inhabited by these brilliant writers, that place soon became known as TV's *The Twilight Zone*, where Matheson went on to write dozens of glittering, memorable scripts, many of them based on choice short stories of his like "Third from the Sun," "Little Girl Lost," and "Nightmare at 20,000 Feet."

So did Beaumont and Bradbury and others, each adding his own special tilt to that region "as vast as space and as timeless as infinity."

In his own extensive introduction to *Richard Matheson: Collected Stories* (Dream/Press, 1989), Richard said, "The leitmotif of all my work . . . is as follows: The individual, isolated in a threatening world, attempting to survive."

Robert Neville, the protagonist of *I Am Legend* and, for the purposes of the book, Richard's alter ego, is certainly that. He is also a very implacable individual given to sudden rages at his fate, with an analytical mind and the ability to set himself goals. He is very aware of his objective, and aware also of the means he uses to achieve his purpose. When balked in his course he immediately invents new strategies, always aware of the danger, always prepared to act ruthlessly in order to survive.

Though filled with action, *I Am Legend* is basically an interior novel of detection as Neville tries to understand the nature of his enemy—and from whence the enemy came. We are concerned with his thoughts, his fears, his feelings, his fantasies, his plans, because it is through these that we come to know him and thereby to identify with him in his terrifying world.

Richard went on to write, "[A]dd to this aspect of my paranoiac leitmotif: the inability of others to understand the male protagonist, to give him proper recognition. Their inclination (virtual insistence) on victimizing him with ignorance, stupidity, cliché thinking, and unwitting power. That I sometimes give alternative emphasis to the possibility that the male protagonist may be partially responsible for his own problems—that his real adversary is his own mind—does not alter the fact that he is, in the end, threatened by real outside forces. Or, to paraphrase an old joke, just because he's paranoid doesn't mean that someone isn't out to get him."

In rereading *I Am Legend* after almost forty years, I am made sharply aware of how much the horror scene in literature owes to the mind of Richard Matheson.

After Edgar Allan Poe himself, I consider Matheson to be the most influential writer of the genre since H.P. Lovecraft.

He has become, with the recent death of Robert Bloch, the greatest living writer of horror in America.

I knew how great he was long ago.

I made the mistake of telling him so, the first time my wife, Lola, and I met Richard and his wife, Ruth.

The place was the Alexandria Hotel in downtown Los Angeles, then a decaying pile of somber elegance, dark and imposing throughout its vaulted chambers.

The occasion was the World Science Fiction Convention, where Richard was the guest of honor, and Robert Bloch, even then a grand master of fantasy and science fiction, was master of ceremonies.

Lola and I came as guests of Charles and Helen Beaumont. Beaumont was on several panels and was scheduled to be auctioned off to the highest bidder as a dinner companion to some lucky fan. But before that took place, I urged Charles to introduce me to Richard—who had just arrived with his wife and children and remained largely untouched by the mobs of science-fiction fans, many of whom had come from as far away as the East Coast for the occasion.

At that time I was a total stranger to him, doubtless with a wild light in my eyes as I clutched his hand feverishly and tried to tell him how important I thought he was.

I did not realize at the time that a man could write so compellingly and so knowingly about paranoia while still being subject to it, as he is now quick to admit.

He immediately began to draw away from me, as though discounting my sincerity, which only drove me to new heights of frenzy. As I struggled to convince this modest young man that I was real, my intensity only made things worse, as he became fearful of me and my motives.

Fortunately we were joined by others who whisked us all away, where we found ourselves in a large suite of rooms filled with big-name science-fiction celebrities from all over the country. Soon he escaped from me, leaving me to talk to the likes of Ray Bradbury, Anthony Boucher, A.E. Van Vogt, Lester Del Rey, Clifford Simak, Jack Williamson, John W. Campbell, Poul and Karen Anderson, Walt Leibscher, Emil Petaja, Sam Mines, Leo Margulies, Rog Phillips, and Mari Wolf, to name a few of that celebrated throng, along with convention chairman Rick Sneary, who had first sounded the cry, "South Gate in '58!" All of us had come to honor Richard.

Looking back, I realize that through the years I've carefully interacted with Richard on a fairly continuous basis, with due regard for his privacy.

Despite what I took to be Richard's apprehension of me, the fact that we had mutual friends like Charles Beaumont, Theodore Sturgeon, and Ray Bradbury kept us in the same orbit and, over the years, we have become friends as have many of the science-fiction and fantasy community of writers, seeing each other more often than you might believe and not as often as I might wish: on panels at overflowing conventions and Writers Guild of America ceremonies where we are both lifetime members, at story conferences and screenings at huge studios, and at jammed signings in tiny bookstores.

We have visited in each other's homes for significant gatherings like New Year's Eve parties or to watch several of our shows on the tube.

Along with Theodore Sturgeon and Jerry Sohl, we formed a writer's company called "The Green Hand" and were well paid to develop a television project entitled *A Touch of Strange* that, unfortunately, never gained network approval.

Richard and I have worked on some of the same television shows together, including Gene Roddenberry's *Star Trek* and Rod Serling's *The Twilight Zone*. We even share a screenplay credit on *Twilight Zone—The Movie*.

We helped place Rod Serling's star on the Hollywood Walk of Fame and were both later interviewed by TV's *American Masters* for their program on Serling.

The events of all the years have only reinforced my admiration for Richard and my respect for him. I know him to be a sincere and honest man with immense integrity that manifests itself in his constancy and poise, bolstered by the great intelligence that shines from his wise eyes like a light. He has dignity and reserve and a life-giving warmth for those he has come to trust.

Both he and his fine book have become legend.

# On *I Am Legend*

———✦———

## *Jack Ketchum*

*I Am Legend* is a novel of modest length.

Weighing in at only 174 pages in my yellowing, wonderfully pulp-smelling 1979 Berkley paperback, were the book first published today and not back in 1954, some genius in marketing would probably need to call it a novella. Thus by definition unworthy of solo stance and contemplation. (We can thank our lucky stars at least that nobody uses the term *novelette* anymore. It always sounded to me like a book written by some high-stepping high school baton-twirler with a shaker on her head. Or Ike Turner's backup group.)

And most likely this self-same marketing genius wouldn't even want to publish it *at all* unless he could do so along with two or three more . . . um, *novellas* to bulk out the volume. Say we include *The Shrinking Man* and *A Stir of Echoes*. Good idea, right? Give the reader his money's worth. Call it *Echoes of a Shrinking Legend*. By Richard Matheson.

There ya go.

But like the books of James M. Cain, Dashiell Hammett, Jim Thompson, Robert Bloch, and many others, this little book has had very long legs.

To begin with, you've got the movies. It's been filmed directly twice—in 1964 as *The Last Man on Earth* with Vincent Price and again in 1971 as *The Omega Man* with Charlton Heston. Neither one's too satisfying. The first was done strictly on the cheap and the second had something to do with religious mutants. As I write this, it's being filmed again. So maybe they'll get it right this time. And we can once again thank the stars that the Arnold Schwarzenegger project died a-begging. Just imagine Arnie intoning the book's final line: *I am legend*.

Think *I'll be back*.

But direct adaptations are the absolute least of it. According to George Romero, we'd never have been blessed by *Night of the Living Dead* and its four sequels without *I Am Legend*—and since Romero is the Godfather of the modern zombie picture, by extension, we wouldn't have dozens of films—very good and utterly awful—extrapolating from his shambling example. And our imaginative lives would be much the poorer for it.

Nor would we have the modern vampire. Back in 1954, *I Am Legend* reinvented the vampire single-handedly. No longer was the suave hypnotic seducer of rich young British virgins the only kid on the block. Matheson's vampires had teeth, all right, just like Bram Stoker's. And they could seduce. But they could also throw stones through windows and haul around automatic weapons. Even Anne Rice owes a debt to him. How else Lestat, riffing on his electric guitar?

Most of us writers who essay the dark side—particularly those who write of vampires or zombies—owe him big time.

I know I do.

When I sat down in 1980 to write my first book, *Off Season*, there were two major templates that immediately came to mind. One was *Night of the Living Dead*. The other was *I Am Legend*. This was years before I'd read any of Romero's comments directly linking the two, but anybody could see that they had a number of things in common.

For one, they were both survival stories. Survival against all freaking odds and of a very specific kind. Your world's gone nuts and predatory and you're pretty much the last man standing. What do you do? How do you do it? Neville studies up on the science of the thing. Romero's characters don't have time. Finally—and no small question, this—*how far will you go in terms of sheer ferocity to go on living*? Questions about our basic humanity arise when civilization shatters and it's kill or be killed, eat or be eaten.

Book and film both hook you with siege mentality. Neville alone for years in his soundproof garlic-strewn fortress of a house supplied with industrial freezer and classical recordings. The characters of *Living Dead* scurrying from room to room with planks and hammers trying to batten down the hatches against the recently risen dead.

For a novel published in 1954, the level of closely observed violence in *I Am Legend* was stunning and remains a pulse-pounder to this day. When Neville's watch stops and night's descending and he's running like some frenzied murderous linebacker through a sea of vampires, you're in there grimly fighting for your life right along with him. And Romero's movie was far and away beyond anything that had ever been seen before in terms of pure audacious *mano-a-mano* grue. The fact that it was black-and-white grue notwithstanding.

If you've read *Off Season*, all this ought to be sounding extremely familiar.

Siege. Overwhelming catastrophic violence. And that very important question—*just how far will you go?*

The other thing I borrowed from them was the notion of a distinctly downbeat ending.

Suppose Van Helsing & Co. *don't* save The Girl. They *don't* track the vampires to their lair and exterminate them. Hell, in Neville's case they exterminate *him*. In *Night of the Living Dead*, the only survivor to have struggled his way through the night falls at dawn to deliberate, friendly fire. And my original ending to *Off Season*—cut at the editor's insistence back then as *too* downbeat, and happily now restored—had the hero shot dead in the heat of panic by the very sheriff who's ostensibly come to rescue him.

All in all, you can see why I owe Richard Matheson.

But I owe him for one thing more. A lesson.

Learned from him and many others over the years but memorably from him.

I read *I Am Legend* at a very early age. Thirteen or fourteen; I don't remember exactly, but around that age. Obviously its elements made a lasting impression. But at the time, I was and am still impressed with one key scene and one wonderful bit of writing that stuck with me.

Neville's been alone in his fortress for a whole year now. He fumes with anger and aches with loss. He's the loneliest creature on Earth.

Human life—indeed, all mammalian life—appears extinguished. His research into the vampire bacillus has stalled so completely that he trashes his microscope and stays dead drunk for two days. On the third day, he stumbles out to the porch and sees a miracle.

*A dog.*

A mangy, crippled, half-starved dog. Alive in the sunlight.

"To Neville," says Matheson, "that dog was the peak of a planet's evolution."

You can understand why.

He tries chasing him and calling him and cajoling him, but that doesn't work. The dog's terrified of him.

You can understand why.

The dog probably thought *he* was the loneliest creature on Earth, too.

And Neville can only wonder at what the dog must have gone through in order to survive for this long.

Finally he gets hold of himself, calms himself down, and tries the obvious. Food. Drink. Good raw hamburger out of his freezer, a bowl of milk, and a bowl of water. Hamburger is dear and in short supply, but there's plenty of dog food in the deserted markets so he gathers it up. Over time, the dog becomes the entire focal point of Neville's life as he tentatively and nervously takes his bait. Neville at first watches him through the peephole, then ventures outside to the porch, sitting silent and still, getting the dog used to his presence, inching closer and closer at each feeding, getting him slowly used to the human voice again. *Good dog, that's a good dog, good boy.* Delighting in him.

Then one day the dog doesn't show—and Neville's frantic. He searches everywhere. For three entire days he's gone and when he does reappear, his eyes are glazed and his legs wobbly and it's clear that not only has he been through hell out there but he's probably dying. In the dog's weakened state, Neville manages to snatch him up and bring him inside. But now the dog's trapped in some unknown place and truly scared out of his wits.

He hides in some blankets Neville arranges for him under the bed, refusing all food and drink, snapping at Neville and whining. At dinner-time, Neville hears a hideous crying and runs to the bedroom and there's the dog digging frantically at the linoleum floor. Suddenly he knows what's wrong. *It was nighttime and the terrified dog was trying to dig itself a hole to bury itself in.*

This singular night is a horror of a new and different kind. Neville can't even begin to sleep for the sounds the dog's making beneath the bed, so he switches on the bedside lamp and at that the dog panics even further, getting tangled up in the blankets and yelping and scrambling to get free. Neville reaches in and grabs him, snarling and snapping inside the blanket, and holds him firmly but gently in front of him on the floor, talking to him all the while, *good dog, we'll take care of you, you'll be better soon you'll see* for easily over an hour until at last the dog subsides and Neville exposes his poor, scarred, matted head and strokes him, scratches him, pets him, speaks to him.

*The dog looked up at him with its dulled, sick eyes and then its tongue faltered out and licked roughly and moistly across the palm of Neville's hand.*

*Something broke in Neville's throat. He sat there silently while tears ran slowly down his cheeks.*

*In a week the dog was dead.*

On that line the chapter ends.

And I remember thinking—what simple, straightforward, devastating writing. What a double sucker punch to the gut and heart.

And these finally have become the horrors that most interest me as a reader and as a writer. Not the vampires howling outside the door but the yearning and loss inside. The quiet survivals of feeling, empathy, and compassion. The courage to bind and bond which life permits us access to for only so long, but which heals us and makes life livable and allows us to go on.

When Neville emerges from the incident with the dog, he emerges a changed man. The drunk has gone. His rage has gone. He's much the better for it.

And that's the lesson.

You beat horror by reaching out beyond it. By contact.

Then you go on.

# A Tribute to Dad

## Bettina Matheson

Over the years I have noticed that whenever the subject came up that my
father and siblings are writers, inevitably I would be asked why didn't
I become a writer, too, rather than a social worker. After giving this
matter some thought, I've come to the conclusion that part of it had to
do with my own personality and interests, which led me to follow my
mother into the field of psychology. Part of it was that early on I realized
that Dad's magical way with words had not rubbed off on me. However,
I believe the deciding factor had a lot to do with birth order. Being the
oldest child, I was around during the really lean years when Dad was a
struggling writer, trying to break into the business, and we were so poor.
I think that left a profound impression on me, resulting in a deep desire
to have a steady paycheck that I could depend on when I myself became
an adult. I was never comfortable with the cycle of feast or famine that
comes with being a writer.

As I recall, we reached an all-time low financially when Mom, Dad,
my younger brother Richard, and I moved from California to New York
when I was about four. Dad was hopeful there would be more job op-
portunities out there. Although, in retrospect, it was a creatively rich
period for him, monetarily it was a disaster. We spent one winter in a
condemned building in Bay Shore. There were rats in the cupboards,
not much to eat, the pipes froze so we washed our dishes in the bathtub,
and we ran our clothesline through the kitchen. We had few belongings
and I was the proud possessor of the only bed. I've been told that during
that rather grim period, I became the inspiration for the *Twilight Zone*

episode "Little Girl Lost" about the girl who slips into another dimension. Dad said he came up with the idea late one night when he and Mom heard me crying. They came into my bedroom and, although they could hear me, they were initially unable to find me. Turns out I had fallen out of bed and somehow ended up underneath it. I find it fascinating how a pretty mundane event like that can be turned into a great story when viewed through the filter of a creative mind.

When I think back on those early years of Dad's career, I'm struck by how amazing it was that a young man with no connections but extraordinary talent, an uncanny ability to think outside the box, a strong belief in his ability, and a willingness to work harder than anyone else I've ever known, was able to become one of the top science-fiction writers of his generation. And what's really quite remarkable is that Dad pulled this off while managing to raise four relatively normal children, who were trying at times (there was a reason why Dad dedicated *Hell House* to my sister Ali and me!), and remaining married to the same woman all these years. No easy feat in Tinseltown! Dad never let on that he did anything special when we were growing up; he was never one to draw attention to himself. I kind of knew that he wasn't like my friends' fathers in that he didn't leave the house to go to work, never wore a suit and tie, and had a beard in the late 1950s and early '60s when all the other fathers were clean-cut. I also noticed that other families didn't have storyboards running through their houses or Captain Kirk coming to visit!

Looking at what Dad has accomplished, I have to say how impressed I am by the fact that while most of us spend years struggling to find ourselves and trying to figure out what it is we want to be when we grow up, Dad seemed to be born knowing that writing was his destiny. I consider him one of the fortunate ones in that writing is his passion; he truly loves what he does for a living. Lucky for him and for all those who appreciate a fantastic tale told by a true master of the art.

# Introduction to *The Shrinking Man*

## *Harlan Ellison*

There is an absolutely Cosmic Correctness in my having been granted the honor of introducing this elegant edition of Richard Matheson's classic novel. In the face of all the chaos and just general all-around random nastiness in the universe, such a demonstration of rectitude should go a long way to reassuring us that there *is* justice and order in the natural scheme of things.

Had more famous and more celebrated writers like Jack Williamson or Frederik Pohl or Michael Moorcock or Joanna Russ been tapped for this job, it would have been wrong; all wrong, I tell you.

Jack is a rangy cowboy, at least eight and a half feet tall. Pohl and Moorcock are physical giants. Joanna is but a shade under six feet. Mutants, all of them. Mutants.

I am five foot five; a lovely height to be. Optimum for doing everything noble and worthy and artful open to a member of our species. Not to mention heroic and ratiocinative.

"Are you content now?" said the Caterpillar.

"Well, I should like to be a *little* larger, Sir, if you wouldn't mind," said Alice; "three inches is such a wretched height to be."

"It is a very good height indeed!" said the Caterpillar angrily, rearing itself upright as it spoke (it was exactly three inches high).

Five foot five, incidentally, is the *average* height of the adult human race currently residing on this planet. So as a man of *average* height, you might well imagine with what jaundiced eye and torpid spirit I suffer the heightist remarks of the callow, the insensitive, the tasteless, and the tedious who, lacking any genuine personal worth, attempt to elevate themselves with bogus credentials based only on the length of their inseam. I point out to them, with oozing charm and sweet reason, that while I have no control over my height, the same cannot be said for their thuggish behavior. Thus do I demonstrate that I am very tall indeed . . . when standing on my charisma.

The very same thing may be said of this strictly terrific novel. Though it is the story of a man who grows ever smaller as the plot unfolds, it is a novel that towers over most of the genre (to which it has been unjustly consigned) by virtue of its absolutely compelling, addictive capacity to entertain. It is abundantly charismatic.

Now, dealing in such superlatives is always dangerous. To suggest that one is drawn again and again to rereadings of *The Shrinking Man* is the kind of grandiose statement that serves as scent-drag for the foxhounds of Academe. (In fact, if one looks up the vocable *Anti-Science Fiction* in, say, *Critical Terms for Science Fiction and Fantasy: A Glossary and Guide to Scholarship* [Greenwood Press, 1986], one will find the following opening sentences: "Damon Knight's description [in *In Search of Wonder*] of novels—specifically . . . *The Shrinking Man* by Richard Matheson . . . published in 1956—is characterized by 'a turning away, not merely from the standard props of science fiction [which are retained as vestiges] but from the habits of thought and belief which underlie science itself.' Such works may appeal to popular fears and concerns about science, but lack the rigor of thought that some regard as characteristic of true science fiction.")

Crotchety Damon's grumbles notwithstanding, I submit that *The Shrinking Man* is one of the most irresistibly readable books ever written. The sort of book about which blurb-writers gurgle, "A real page-turner." "Couldn't put it down!" "One helluva read."

It's a helluva read not merely because the story is so universally identifiable, has such irresistible resonances, whether the reader is male or female, young or old, in the mainstream or member of a minority; it is a helluva read because it transcends the very limitations Damon implicitly deifies when he points to *this* book and says it is found wanting, and *that* book and says it's Our Kind. It flouts Damon's rules innocently. That is to say (and I'm not suggesting Damon is merely captious), this "anti-science fiction" theory pillories *The Shrinking Man* for not being Our Kind of genre novel, when it makes no pretense ever to have been such a thing. Very much like chiding a jelly doughnut for not having the ability to bring in UHF signals.

I recognize the danger to one's critical credentials in dealing with this novel in such a fashion, lauding it so expansively not merely as a helluva read and swell entertainment (which ought to be enough of a reason for loving it, when one considers how many books embody the very antithesis of those reader friendly qualities), but as a book that may be one of the most perfect models for writing in the idiom of science-fantasy, magic realism, allegory, call it what you will. By the unarguable fact that for the last almost-thirty-five years *no one* has denied the popular appeal of Matheson's little fable, the fact that the book has continued to live, to appeal to new audiences, to capture the imagination of everyone who comes to it . . . it seems to me perfectly rational to suggest that *The Shrinking Man* may well lay claim to the appellation Contemporary Literature. (Only more time will tell us if posterity cares to drop the modifier; but if we consider how many entries in that race, trumpeted in the pages of *The Kenyon Review*, *The New York Times Book Review*, or *The New York Review of Books* as "certain to be called Literature," can now be found—if at all—on the Any 3 for a $ carts impeding foot traffic on the sidewalks outside used bookstores all across this Great Nation of Ours, I'd place my bets on Matheson over his more Establishment-acceptable competitors.)

Yet suggesting that *The Shrinking Man* may be one of a few near-perfect templates for the creation of a perfect science-fantasy novel, merely because I've reread the book a dozen times since it first appeared as a 35¢ Gold Medal Giant original paperback in 1956, merely because it has this glowing popular appeal, is to deny the craft and art Matheson brings to the work. It has all the usual requirements for Literature, in the Dickensian sense: thought, subtext, theme, pace, characterization, a message for every reader. And saying thus raises, I fear, an expectancy among those who may have been living in the Outback for the last four decades, who may never have encountered mention of the novel; an expectancy that would be hard to satisfy. Call it one of the all-time classics of imaginative literature and watch them run as if they were being stalked by *Silas Marner*.

Despite—or perhaps because of—its deceptive surface simplicity of plot, its straightforward and hard-edged drama, its uncomplicated view of the human condition as being (when you strip away all the cultural foofaraw) a birth-to-death struggle for survival with dignity, *The Shrinking Man* has survived the importunities of savants that it be more than it was intended to be: a helluva read. It remains, for all of its age and familiarity, heightened by the many imitators who have come after, a story that has captivated at least two generations of discriminating readers of the literature of the fantastic.

And when I suggest that it's one of the most nearly perfect novels of fantasy ever written, I'm elevating it to be shelved beside *Bring the Jubilee*, *Pavane*, *The Demolished Man*, *Song of Kali*, *Time and Again*, and *Kiss of the Spider Woman*.

Make no mistake, and for goodness sake stop making connections with the charming (if shallow) 1957 Universal film adaptation for which the idiotic "Incredible" was added to the title or, worse, the 1981 Lily Tomlin stinker that reduced Matheson's heartbreaking tale of human tragedy to the level of succotash. What I'm saying here is that this book is one of those rare items for which the word *mystique* was struck out of pure gold.

It is the paradigm for age, for growing old, for infirmity, for abandonment, for being excluded. It is, in short, the human drama writ at its largest for having been written at its smallest.

Which brings me back to all that tall/short business at the beginning of this essay. All that business may have seemed tangential when I started, but forms the core of my reasons for suggesting this novel is as wonderful as I say.

Since the title pretty much encapsulates the basic plot element, I won't be giving anything away to the few of you who've been living in the Outback and don't know the story, when I report that this is quite simply the logical (if you accept the basic premise) progression of exciting and emotional events that follow Scott Carey's exposure to a "warm, glittering spray" that drifts over him one afternoon when he's out sunbathing on his boss' cabin cruiser. He begins shrinking. He reports to his wife, Lou, after his first trip to the doctor: "He said my height's decreased more than half an inch in the last four days. But it's not just my height I'm losing. Every part of me seems to be shrinking. Proportionately."

Scott Carey then progressively becomes an outcast. An object of fascination, curiosity, celebrity, cruelty, insensitivity . . . all those wonderful qualities possessed by the human race which, when demonstrated, go a long way to making each of us feel like a sideshow freak. Whether we are overweight, or black, or shy, or physically impaired, or getting on in years, or bucktoothed, or sexually ambivalent, or . . . the list is endless . . . each of us has had to suffer some sort of ostracism because of a random factor over which we had no control. If we speak with a heavy Southern accent, those we work with in New York City make fun of us. If we are devoutly religious, those who are pragmatic think we are retarded, and deal with us so. If we are female and the chain of corporate command is, in reality, the Old Boy's Network, then we languish in the lower depths of unequal pay for equal work. Scott Carey is forced outside.

He becomes *excluded*. For the first time in his normal life, he is exposed to the sense of separation known to so many of us. He had always been right in there, right in the middle of living happily, socially acceptable, free of the uncertainties and fears that serve to rob the most secure and beautiful of us of our feelings of self-worth and competence. Scott Carey was the absolute societal Golden Mean, a white Anglo-Saxon male of pleasing and standard proportions. His enshrined state as unspoken paragon of the *status quo* is so wholeheartedly presented by Matheson that it need never even be explicated. At no point does the story wallow in reflections of how *normal* Carey was before the fantastic malaise struck him; it's a given. He was The American Ideal, the dominant life-form in the universe (according to our ethnocentric arrogance, supported by more than two hundred years of Manifest Destiny). Remember: Matheson wrote this novel in the mid-Fifties, after we'd "saved the civilized world from the menace of the Axis powers." The United States ruled the planet, with its opposite number, the USSR, as perfect spur and bogeyman for our justification of unchecked technological and commercial expansion. Scott Carey was Everyman . . . first as Babbitt, then as the Man in the Gray Flannel Suit, then as Cash McCall . . . finally maturing in the Eighties as Ronald Reagan, George Bush, Donald Trump, and Michael Milken: mediocrity totemized, floating ethics, form over content, public service reduced to public thespianism.

Scott Carey, at the moment disaster overtakes him, begins to lose the silent approbation of his world. He was a member of the club, without needing his ticket punched. The worst he had to fret about was selecting the correct mouthwash so he wouldn't offend. He is a character without character. But adversity pulls the rug out from under him, and he begins to live a retrograde existence, until finally he is *forced*, at peril of losing his life entirely, to become that which lurks in all of us: the hero.

I've talked to Dick Matheson about this view of the book. It all seems glowingly obvious now, more than three decades after he wrote the novel as a page-turner for Gold Medal. Neither of us believes for a moment that he had it in mind when he did the original work at his typewriter. Which is the beauty part of it!

I have this unquenchable certainty that anyone consciously setting out to write a Novel of Cultural Significance will fall on his or her duff. The three likeliest candidates for The Great American Novel—*Moby Dick, Huckleberry Finn, Gravity's Rainbow*—were created out of the honorable tradition of simply wanting to tell a good, propulsive story. But literature springs less from intent, I think, than from native talent and reverence for craft, and a well-ordered intellect. The best of us who tell stories never know when we're going to hit one of those rich veins of auctorial gold. We mine the lode as best we can, and every once in a while we hit real paydirt. *Subsequently*, when literary journals or fools like me begin to analyze the work itself, we find ourselves suddenly facing a wall of riches that seemed to be only pyrite for the thirty years preceding.

Matheson just wrote a great page-turner, a helluva read; and as the

Nineties begin we reevaluate in the light of time and place that illu-
minate what was at the moment of creation just a job, a perception of
cultural self that convinces us *The Shrinking Man* is lots and lots more
than an adventure novel.

It is a novel about the most profound alienation.

The lessons about bigotry passim this book now stand out boldly.
The human race, we must remember, has never had to look far for reasons to think one segment of itself superior to all others, for the most
elitist benefits, whether monetary or as reassurance of a proper seat in
the afterlife. Usually these high-flown statements of Manifest Destiny,
of ultimate and exclusive worthiness, these excuses for meanspiritedness
or even slavery, were eulogized as Holy Wars.

And so, to the matter of height, where I took up this cause. Matheson
eschews skin color, religious preference, sexual stereotype, or ethnicity:
he plays Aesop, and he uses *height*—one of the few absolutes every human being has in common—as emblematic cause for alienation, exclu-
sion, bigotry. He tells the story from the viewpoint of a normal, average
man of normal, "average" height, who suddenly begins to shrink into the
role of freak and outcast, alone and foredoomed.

As one who, at five foot five, has had to live in a world where the
kitchen cabinets have been hung for people over six feet tall, a world
in which bad drivers in supermarket parking lots put the word "little"
before the word "bastard" as easily as they would the words "black" or
"kike" or "crippled," a world in which one seldom finds one's clothing
size offered on the Home Shopping Network, thus reminding us end-
lessly that we ain't the model of beauty necessary for a Bloomingdale's
ad, I find the basic message of Matheson's novel a particularly affecting
plot conceit. (Not to mention ironically—if not actually Cosmically—
correct for one such as me to have been tapped to write this introduction; thus bringing to your attention your endless gaffes against those of
us of *average* height.)

Matheson, you see, understands what it is to be five foot five, or four
foot three, or three foot one.

How can this be? Richard Matheson is no Munchkin. We're talking
something like six one or two packing maybe two hundred pounds. He's

not fat, but he *is* big. The image of Gentle Ben comes to mind. (See how carelessly we describe others' physicality?)

So how can he tell Scott Carey's story so intimately? To hear Dick Matheson tell it, he just sat there in the basement of the house at Sound Beach, Long Island (just outside Port Jefferson) in 1954 and described what he saw around him.

(Except for the stairway. There wasn't a stairway. You had to go outside and open the storm cellar doors to get down into the basement.)

So how is a man who, all his adult life, has been "tall" and "large" able to write so feelingly of a situation best known to those of us built closer to the turf? Well, John Le Carré (né David John Cornwell), himself no slouch as a novelist, once said: "A good writer can watch a cat pad across the street and know what it is to be pounced upon by a Bengal tiger."

Now, that may seem mystical, not to mention self-serving; but let me digress for a moment by way of demonstration that it requires a good deal of insight to pull off what Le Carré describes. We shall digress for an emblematic anecdote.

There is a highly-acclaimed mystery-suspense writer named George C. Chesbro. He has won awards for his books, some of which feature a private eye described as follows: "Dr. Robert Frederickson, a.k.a. Mongo. He had a Ph.D. in criminology, and a black belt in karate. He teaches at a university, and is a private detective who specializes in solving cases that Sam Spade would have found too kinky to cope with. And, just incidentally, he happens to be a dwarf."

The first novel featuring Mongo appeared in 1977, and I bought it with high expectation because, 'way back in the earliest days of my career, I did a considerable amount of writing for the mystery and suspense magazines (it was not till later that I got lumbered with the misnomer "science fiction writer" grrrr), and I'd written a few stories about a midget P.I. named Big John Novak who is "just a shade over three feet." Chesbro's novel was titled *Shadow of a Broken Man*, and I plunged into it with a grin because, at long last, someone had picked up on the limitless possibilities for stories about a dwarf (or midget) detective.

Along about fifty pages into the book I suddenly cursed, ground my teeth, and threw the novel against a wall. I never went back to finish it, and I've never been able to give Chesbro a break since that time. (Though he commands the respect of a number of friends and companion writers whose taste I value, who tell me he's terrific.) His work was forever blighted for me.

What hideous sin had he committed, fifty pages into that first Mongo novel? I'll tell you, and then you'll understand why what Matheson pulls off, at six foot two, is so remarkable.

Mongo is in a phone booth at 8th Avenue and 54th Street in Manhattan. As he completes his call "Mike Foster pulled up to the curb in a late-model blue Oldsmobile . . . I slid in beside him. He checked the rearview mirror, then pulled out into traffic and drove uptown toward Harlem." A page later Mongo and the driver, Foster, who is the guy who hired Mongo to do some snooping for him, get into an argument, and Mongo makes him stop the car. He gets out and "started hoofing it back down Eighth Avenue. There was a squeal of tires as Foster's car backed past me and screeched to a halt beside a fire hydrant."

Foster doesn't want Mongo to dump the case, and argues with him to reconsider. Mongo agrees and Foster asks where he's going, if he can drop him off someplace. Mongo says he's going to the nearest car-rental agency because he has to drive over to South Jersey to talk to some cop. Now, get this; straight out of the book:

> Foster nodded toward the big Olds with the buff decoration on the windshield. "Use my car. I'll take a cab home . . ."
>
> I removed the ticket, got into the car, and pulled the seat up all the way. In the rearview mirror I saw Foster, hands jammed into his pockets, staring after me . . .
>
> I turned at the corner and Foster blinked out of sight . . .
>
> The Olds was big, powerful, smooth-riding. Slipping out of Manhattan through the stone umbilical of the Lincoln Tunnel, I made good time in the light weekend traffic. Within an hour I had passed through the depressing yellow air of northern New Jersey and was immersed in the flat, deadly monotony of the New Jersey Turnpike.

Chesbro doesn't actually ever say how tall Mongo is—as best I can tell from leafing carefully through my copy of the novel, thirteen years later—but I figure it's safe to assume he's about three feet in height, since Chesbro calls him a dwarf, and not a midget or (the term most preferred) a "little person."

You get it? You catch what pissed me off so much that I slammed that book against a wall? No?

I'm five foot five. When my assistant uses my car to run an errand, she adjusts both the rearview and the side mirrors. And she's five four, just an inch shorter than I. When it happens that she's used the car, and I don't know about it, and I get in to go somewhere, I have to *re-set* the mirrors. And that's just an inch of height difference between us. Picture the physical situation if it were, say, Dick Matheson at six two, who had borrowed my wheels. Or I, his.

Beginning to get it?

Chesbro has Mongo pulling the seat all the way up, and he thinks that'll do it for a careful reader. Yeah? Not *this* decade, sweetheart!

Have you ever seen the size of an Oldsmobile that would be "late-model" in 1977? Only slightly smaller than the *Lusitania*.

If *I*, at five five, were to get into a 1977 Olds, I would find it very difficult—even with the seat cranked as far forward as I could get it without crushing my sternum on the steering wheel—to reach the pedals, to see over the wheel, to see the road ahead over the long hood of those behemoth Olds of that period. I'd need a pillow.

But Mongo just gets in, shoves the seat up, and tools blithely out through the worst traffic-snarl streets in North America (transcended in horror only by the traffic in Rio de Janeiro or, possibly, Boston in February). He has no trouble with the Lincoln Tunnel, and no trouble with the Jersey Turnpike.

Chesbro gives us details of the size and color and model of the car, specifics of streets taken on the route, description of the terrain and air quality of northern Jersey . . . but he never lets us feel what it is to be a dwarf swallowed whole by one of the biggest Detroit trashwagons ever built. He even sees Foster on the sidewalk behind him as he pulls out, *without readjusting the rearview mirror!* Grrrrr. Toss that sucker, *bam*!

Chesbro is, I'd be willing to bet, a man of a height closer to Matheson's than mine; and a *lot* less close to mine than I am to Mongo's.

I swear I don't mean Chesbro any bad cess. But I perceive of what I've described as something more serious than sloppy writing; it is, in my view, a crippling incapacity of vision that made it impossible for me to trust, or care about, what Chesbro had in store for this "dwarf." Because, simply put, Mongo—in this sequence—is not a dwarf. He's Chesbro, at full height, pretending to write about a little person.

You never get that feeling reading *The Shrinking Man.*

Matheson, a giant of a human, writes tellingly, feelingly, cautiously, *and correctly*, about a man who is seeing the world from a starkly reduced perspective every time you start a new chapter. And the point of view changes repeatedly. Which means that Matheson had to *rethink* the totality of his fictional world, in every respect, down to the most minute detail . . . every single time he had a shift of sequence or of flashback or of time-change.

*Now* do you understand why I hold this book in such high esteem, if for no other reason (and there are plenty of other reasons) than that the craft is so dazzling?

> Upon having to suffer one too many insipid remarks about his height, Napoleon Bonaparte replied, "People are measured from the top of the head to the sky."

Richard Matheson has written a novel in *The Shrinking Man* that may be, in Damon Knight's scold, "anti-science fiction"; but I submit that's a high compliment. Most science fiction can tell a decent story; much of it can hold your interest to the end; less of it remains in memory; and the tiniest fraction of novels bearing that genre label do it all. But only the merest handful, in all the years since they were first called "scientific romances" to these dark days of "sci-fi" (yucchhh!), do all of the preceding *and* carry a universal message that can alter our world view.

And that handful, by their mere existence, ridicule the label of genre. Because they transcend the category. Whether intentionally or by glorious happenstance, they soar higher, speak more clearly, tap deeper into our consciousness, and fill us with greater wonder than all the rest. They beat the odds of The Passing Fad.

Whether a reader is attentive enough to notice it, or not, *The Shrinking Man* conveys the terror of getting smaller not just in the sense of forcing us to re-view the world around us through Scott Carey's eyes as he gets tinier, but by picking up the resonances of the powerlessness of so many of us. The powerless state of being a child in a world of adults. The powerless feelings we suffer when governments or cartels shove us around, make our lives more difficult. The powerless condition in which we flounder when death takes someone close to us, or love goes wrong and we're left in the dust, when crime touches us and we cannot defend ourselves.

Scott Carey's story is ours, each of us. It demonstrates the precariousness of our safety in an insensate universe . . . the helplessness of someone threatened by a bully . . . the world no longer taken for granted as safe and orderly.

We read about Carey, and how he fights to survive against incredible odds, and like him we feel unprotected, naked to rust and sandstorms and the inexorable truth of Berlioz's observation: "Time is a great teacher. Unfortunately, it kills all its pupils."

Suddenly an underdog, single stalk of grain before the implacable thresher, we begin to understand that when we least expect it, through fire or hail or seismic temblor or *tsunami*, the universe will always even the odds and slap little arrogant us silly.

This novel will endure, will continue to ensnare new readers and call again and again to old fans of the story. It will continue to be reprinted in Masterpiece collections such as this one, because Matheson is such an insightful, careful writer that he can take something as plebeian yet as phototonus as height, deify it as trope, and use it to tap into the universal human condition.

Matheson understands, in the writing, if not consciously when he was plotting Scott Carey's life, that parvenus and dolts, when they practice the kind of vest-pocket psychiatry that equates short people with Napoleon Complex, and Geminis with schizophrenia, and great big bearlike people with clumsiness and slow-wittedness and acting like bullies, demean the rest of the human race by categorizing it . . . without the kindness to identify with it.

He understands that as one is reduced in stature, one is reduced in received measure of dignity. In society's eyes, one is taken less seriously, is dismissed more easily, is brutalized more casually. (Short women know what I'm talking about. Tall men always want to cuddle them as if they're teddy bears. For them the words *svelte* and *coltish* and *languid* are forever verboten. They are stuck with *cute*. One calls a smurf cute, not the Dragon Lady, and certainly not Madame President.)

Matheson knows all about that kind of prejudice.

And once you've read *The Shrinking Man*, even if this Easton Press edition is your twelfth time, you will know it, too.

When they reissued this novel for the third or fourth time, in a Berkley Books paperback edition in 1979, I wrote:

> *Ambidextrous, unpredictable, always first rank . . . Matheson has been for twenty-eight years one of our most consistently original and masterful creators of imaginative literature. From the initial suspense and fantasy novels, through the vast range of uncategorizable short stories, to the visionary screenplays, there has always been one thread joining the work in one significant way: the unbroken line of absolute excellence.*

It is eleven years later,* and the sharing of pain we take away with us from reading *The Shrinking Man*, the perception of our collective humanity, is as strong now as the day the story was first written. And isn't that what Great Literature is supposed to do, that just a helluva read never does, convey a message that permits us to look out of another's eyes?

Speaking for all of us in Runt Lib, I rest my case.

*Sherman Oaks, California*
*May, 1990*

---

*Now, thirty years later. (Ellison, 2009)

# Afterword to *The Shrinking Man*

## David Morrell

An unhappy childhood can be the making of a writer, providing the compulsion to tell stories and the themes to put in them. By his own admission, that is the case with Richard Matheson. As he notes in his introduction to *Richard Matheson: Collected Stories*, his mother was an orphan before she was ten. In her early teens, she emigrated from Norway to the United States, where "insecure and frightened, thrust into an alien environment," she eventually married a fellow immigrant and fostered in her children a keen distrust of the outside world. Soon she took to religion while her husband took to drink. Three years after Matheson was born in 1926, his parents separated. Subsequently, his mother and older sister raised him.

"I found personal escape in writing," he says. "Instead of imbibing drink, I imbibed stories . . . Instead of turning to religion, I turned to fantasy . . . the creating of a new world of imagination in which I could work out any and all troubles. A therapeutic battlefield on which I could confront my enemies (my anxieties) and—in relative safety—deal with them in socially acceptable ways."

The fantasy he speaks about (most of it based on fear) led him to explore many different types of writing: science fiction (*I Am Legend, The Shrinking Man, 7 Steps to Midnight*), horror (*A Stir of Echoes, Hell House, Earthbound*),* noir suspense (*Someone Is Bleeding, Fury on Sunday,*

---

*For the record, Matheson prefers not to be associated with the term "horror," feeling that it is too suggestive of slasher pictures such as *Friday the 13th*. He believes that the explicitness of that kind of story is contrary to his usual method in which the gooseflesh detail is suggested more than described. In place of being labeled a horror writer, he favors the word "terror,"

*Ride the Nightmare, Passion Play*), combat fiction (*The Beardless Warriors*), metaphysical fantasies (*Bid Time Return, What Dreams May Come*), and westerns (*Journal of the Gun Years, The Memoirs of Wild Bill Hickok*). A mainstream novel, *Hunger and Thirst*, about a man dying from a bullet wound who recalls the various stages of his troubled life, was the first book Matheson completed, but has only recently appeared in print.

Few writers have been as skilled in so many different modes. Matheson wrote not only short stories and novels, but also scripts for episodic television (fourteen contributions to Rod Serling's *The Twilight Zone*, plus work for such diverse series as *Have Gun—Will Travel, Wanted: Dead or Alive, Richard Diamond, Star Trek, Night Gallery*, and *Lawman*, for which he received a Writers Guild of America Award), stand-alone teleplays (*Duel*, which was directed by Steven Spielberg; *The Night Stalker*; the mainstream character study of an alcoholic, *The Morning After*; plus many more), and film scripts (*The Incredible Shrinking Man*, a number of Edgar Allan Poe adaptations for Roger Corman, *The Legend of Hell House*, and *Somewhere in Time*, his moving adaptation of *Bid Time Return*). And that doesn't include his nonfiction about paranormal phenomena, *The Path* and *Mediums Rare*.

So much output. So much variety. Although diverse, however, most of Matheson's work has a common theme, which he relates to his difficult childhood and which he describes as the "individual isolated in a threatening world, attempting to survive." Often, his characters are isolated by a drastic shift in reality. In "Disappearing Act," for example, a man discovers that one by one his friends, his relatives, his employer, and his wife have disappeared as if they'd never existed. Eventually, he too vanishes, leaving only a diary on a coffee shop counter. In "The Curious Child," a man panics when his memory increasingly fails him. First he can't remember where he parked his car. Then he can't remember

---

although he admits that this may be only a matter of semantics. *Earthbound* has a complex history that merits an explanation. About a female succubus, "an earthbound spirit, probably the most insidious psychic force," the book uses sexuality as the basis for its fright. Matheson wrote it in the late sixties, cut it by about a hundred pages at the suggestion of his agent, then saw it eviscerated by two editors before it was finally published as a 1982 paperback original from Playboy Press. Matheson was so displeased by the result that he used a pseudonym, Logan Swanson. The restored text was eventually published under his own name in England in 1989 and in the U.S. in 1994.

what kind of car it is, where he lives, or even what his last name is. In a *Twilight Zone* script, "A World of Difference," a businessman enters his office one morning, picks up the phone, and is startled to hear someone yell "Cut!" The businessman is told that he's a character in a film, but he insists that he isn't an actor, that he really is the businessman. Dismayed to discover himself burdened by a shrewish wife and studio pressures, he struggles to find a way to return to the pleasant home, wife, and occupation depicted in the script.

But Matheson's most ambitious depiction of someone isolated by altered reality, struggling to survive, is his fourth novel, *The Shrinking Man* (1956), in which a veil of radioactive mist causes a man to shrink until specks of sand become boulders and a black widow spider becomes a giant. Seen strictly as a novel in which the conflict is between large and small, *The Shrinking Man* has several obvious predecessors: Odysseus's encounter with the cyclops, Beowulf against Grendel, St. George against the dragon. In Jonathan Swift's *Gulliver's Travels*, the title character journeys to Lilliput, a land in which he is a giant among tiny people (who turn out to be vicious), and to another land in which *he* is the tiny person among giants (who turn out to be gentle).

The idea of a story about shrinking also has antecedents. In 1934, for example, Harry Bates wrote "A Matter of Size" in which a scientist is taken to another planet to contribute to its gene pool. He escapes and returns to Earth, only to discover that he is now only a couple of inches high. In his struggle to stay alive, he uses burned-out matches and hairpins to construct climbing tools that get him up towering stairs. He also has a fierce battle with a giant cat. In 1936, Henry Hasse wrote "He Who Shrank" in which a scientist tests a new substance by injecting it into his assistant. The assistant shrinks to a submicroscopic level in which he descends past electrons moving planetlike around the nuclei of atoms. Occasionally, he lands on electrons which turn out to be inhabited by various types of beings: gossamer-winged sylphs, murderous robots, and stone-age hunters. In time, he lands on an electron which we learn is Earth and where he disrupts the Great Lakes before he shrinks further and enters even smaller universes.

Matheson claims that he backed into a career as a science-fiction writer because there were so many magazines of that type when he started in the fifties. Because he hadn't researched the history of the genre, it's doubtful that the stories I've just summarized had an influence on him. Even if they had, however, the influence would have been negative, for "A Matter of Size" and "He Who Shrank" are flatly written and preposterous, whereas *The Shrinking Man* brilliantly demonstrates Matheson's primary contribution to the genre: his determination to convince the reader that the events, no matter how far-fetched, are actually taking place.

This has been called (by Matheson's friend and fellow *Twilight Zone* writer, George Clayton Johnson) the "coffee and cakes" approach to scaring people. Matheson showed that a writer didn't have to imitate conventions created by Mary Shelley, Bram Stoker, or H.P. Lovecraft in order to scare readers. As Douglas E. Winter noted, Matheson along with a few other writers such as Robert Bloch and Jack Finney "created the modern landscape of fear." He took fright from Gothic "misty moors and haunted mansions to the American suburbs. He invited terror into our shopping malls and peaceful neighborhoods—into the house next door." There, coffee and cake were being served. We could smell them. We could taste them. Meanwhile, something unspeakable was about to smash through the kitchen door.

In *The Shrinking Man*, this realistic approach is achieved in part by its emphasis on sensate description: "He was still shivering. He could smell the dry, acrid odor of the cardboard close to his face, and it seemed as if he were being smothered." Every scene is depicted in that palpable detail. The hero, Scott Carey, is physically present in the extreme. The pain and deprivation he suffers—his scraped hands, his sprained joints, his cuts, his fever, his sore throat, his hunger and thirst—are so vividly communicated that we feel we are in his place.

*The Shrinking Man*'s realism is achieved also by its candid (for its time, amazingly so) treatment of sex. Scott's preoccupation about sex is so constant that references to it have a structural function. Scenes involving it become a way of measuring his torturous descent. The first reference is early in the novel. Five-sevenths of an inch tall, he has been sleeping on a crumpled pink rag, which he suddenly realizes is part of a slip that his wife threw away. Once it had "rested against her warm, fragrant flesh." Frustrated and angry, he kicks at it. But with sex on his mind, he soon comes across a gigantic magazine with an alluring photograph of a young woman leaning over a rock, "a pair of clinging black shorts cut just below the hips." He "could almost feel the curved smoothness of her legs as mentally he ran his hands along them." He fantasizes about the feel of her breasts. Abruptly he recalls a tense evening with his wife in which, at four feet tall, he wanted to have sex with her but couldn't bring himself to ask. When his wife finally realized what was bothering him, she reacted with surprise and pity. After an awkward discussion ("I guess it would be rather grotesque"), they finally did have sex, but it's as if the wife were having intercourse with a child.

Scott becomes so small that he goes to bed with a carnival midget (he tells his wife and asks her to drive him home from the midget's trailer the next morning). After that, he becomes a miniature Peeping Tom, staring "rigidly tensed" out a cellar window at his daughter's babysitter lying in the backyard in a bathing suit. When she leans forward to pick up a ball, her breasts slip out. "Oops," she says. Soon he lives in a dollhouse, where his wife supplies him with a toy female figure, "legs spread apart, arms half-raised, as though she contemplated a possible embrace." Trying to sleep with it, he "pressed close to her and slipped his arm around her body."

Not all encounters involve women. At one point, he looks so much like a boy that a pervert picks him up when he has car trouble. "Scott jumped up as he sat on the man's thick hand. The man drew it away, held it before his eyes. You have injured the member, my boy." Later a group of teenage thugs surrounds him. Realizing that he is the famous shrinking man, they call him "Freako" and want to pull his pants down to "see if *all* of him shrunk." He says, "If you want my money, take it." One answers, "Bet ya shrinkin' *butt* we'll take it." (Matheson's italics.)

If Matheson's realism was innovative for science fiction, so was his unusual structure. In this regard, it's useful to compare the novel with the well-known movie adaptation which came out in 1957, a year after the novel. Although Matheson had published three prior novels and dozens of much-praised short stories, his income still wasn't enough to pay the bills (for a time he worked as a machine operator at Douglas Aircraft). So when Universal-International wanted to purchase the film rights for *The Shrinking Man*, he refused to agree unless he was hired to write the screenplay (which later won a Hugo).* The successful result (in documentary black and white, with *Incredible* added to the title) gave him a sufficient reputation in Hollywood that more screen work followed.

For the film, he wanted to use the novel's complex back-and-forth time scheme, beginning with a dramatic scene in the middle of the story. But Universal-International objected in favor of a traditional chronological approach. It's interesting to compare the two versions. While on a boating holiday, Scott (played by Grant Williams) is engulfed by an eerie mist. In rapid succession, his clothes become too big for him as does the furniture around him. Medical specialists are mystified until they finally conclude that the mist, which was radioactive, must have altered some insecticide with which he'd accidentally been sprayed, causing a molecular mutation that shrinks him. This scientific rationale is no more convincing in the movie than it is in the book, by the way. It isn't necessary. We take for granted that the mist was toxic.

In 1954, two years before *The Shrinking Man* was published, the United States exploded the world's first hydrogen bomb on Bikini Island in the Marshall Islands. The blast was a thousand times greater than the atomic bomb dropped on Hiroshima. Radioactive ash struck an American destroyer, three inhabited islands, and a Japanese fishing boat. The ash resembled a huge mist in which some substance drizzled. As one of the fishermen said, "Some kind of white sand is falling from the heavens." The fisherman was dead in seven months. By the time the film adaptation of Matheson's novel was released three years after the blast, the Cold War had intensified. As the United States and the USSR competed to build more and deadlier nuclear weapons, as we worried

---

*I've already mentioned that Matheson received a Writers Guild Award for his television work. His other awards include the Bram Stoker (Horror Writers Association), the Edgar (Mystery Writers of America), the Golden Spur (Western Writers of America) and the Howard. The latter is named after fantasist Robert E. Howard, the creator of Conan the Barbarian, and is given each year at the prestigious World Fantasy Convention, where on one occasion Matheson was selected for the rare distinction of being called a Grand Master. The Horror Writers Association also gave him that honor.

about strontium-90 and other toxic elements floating around in the atmosphere, it made perfect sense that a radioactive mist engulfed our hero. It's what everyone feared.

Once Matheson gets the explanation out of the way (one of the few places in the movie where the sets look cheap), he proceeds to the movie's point, which is Scott's vulnerability as he gets smaller. While Scott resides in the dollhouse, the family cat attacks him. He tries to hide in the cellar, becomes trapped down there, and finds himself being stalked by a towering spider. The film's climax is his fight to the death with it. Subsequently, he becomes so small that he can step between the wires of a screen and enter the backyard, a brave new world where the infinite and the infinitesimal are linked and he looks forward to new adventures that will show him the beauty of the universe.

Character and texture aren't important here. Basically this is a special-effects movie that uses trick sets, split-screen techniques, and process shots to put the viewer in awe of Scott's ordeal in the basement. During the nineteen fifties, the visual illusions were effective but now seem primitive, yet the film still engages the viewer, a tribute to Jack Arnold's speedy direction and the strong situations in Matheson's screenplay. Some of the best of these aren't in the novel. For example, in the film the hero comes upon a mousetrap, figures out how to spring it without hurting himself, but causes the cheese to flip away and drop down a drain. Later, he is almost washed down the same drain in a flood caused by a ruptured water heater.

As positive as the movie was for Matheson's career, it was negative in this respect—many people who have seen the film think that they know the story and hence haven't bothered to read the book. A pity, because the novel is far more accomplished than the film and has more surprises. The structure is particularly noteworthy. In a stark one-page opening chapter: "First he thought it was a tidal wave. Then he saw that the sky and ocean were visible through it and it was a curtain of spray rushing at the boat." The spray hits him, making him tingle. He towels himself, and the feeling is gone. "It was the beginning."

Wham! The still-unnamed hero is suddenly racing for his life across an alien landscape, pursued by a spider whose "body was a giant, glossy egg that trembled blackly as it charged across the windless mounds." How he got to be in this alien environment we're not told, although we can guess from the title. There's a huge red snake and a great orange mass. A steel-encased flame glares behind him. Thunder shakes the air. The descriptions are maddeningly vague. Only when he eludes the spider (once again after from what we gather were dozens of times) do we learn that the flame in the steel tower is from an oil burner. The thunder is the sound of the fuel igniting. The red snake is a garden hose. The orange structure is a stack of lawn chairs. "And the tanklike cans were used paint cans, and the spider was a black widow." Then comes a hammering single-sentence paragraph: "He lived in a cellar."

Thereafter, Matheson shifts to a scene in which Scott (we learn his name casually in the middle of a paragraph) tells his incredulous wife that he just measured his height and he's not six feet tall anymore. Almost at once, the novel switches back to Scott, a half-inch tall and getting smaller, continuing to fight to survive in the basement. Sometimes his memories make him recall a scene from the past, but often the flashback has no transition. Sometimes there are flashbacks within flashbacks. In addition, the flashbacks are not in chronological order. They describe disparate events in which he's short, then tall, then really short, then not so tall. Only a few pages from the book's end do we learn how Scott came to be trapped in the basement to begin with. In this universe where big has become small and small has become big, the fractured structure is appropriate—convention no longer applies.

These days, after the fictional experiments of the 1960s, after what was called metafiction which drew attention to the techniques of storytelling, a fractured structure isn't unusual. Indeed, some writing classes experimented with creating novels in which each chapter was on a note card. If you shuffled the cards and jumbled the structure, you instantly achieved a new version of the novel, whose message was how arbitrary and disjointed life could be. Before 1956, however, few novelists had experimented in this manner. Faulkner's *The Sound and the Fury* (1929) comes to mind. So does Proust's *A la recherche du temps perdu* (1913–27). The reader no doubt has pre-fifties favorites in which chronology is shattered. But there aren't many, for this type of experimentation didn't gain great interest (and mostly among academics) until the last third of the century. From this perspective, *The Shrinking Man* wasn't only innovative within the science-fiction genre; it was ahead of most experimental fiction also.

Not that anyone would try to make a case that Matheson is equal to Faulkner. This is a genre piece. It never pretends otherwise, although it accomplishes its purpose with remarkable technical sophistication. But it is interesting to note that the novel's thematic concerns are very comparable to those of some nongenre "serious" novelists, particularly the French Existentialists Albert Camus and Jean-Paul Sartre. At its core, Existentialism links these three statements: There is no God. Everybody dies. It's difficult to find meaning in a universe that consequently seems pointless and absurd.

In his influential essay, "The Myth of Sisyphus" (1942), Camus compared our existence to that of the mythic Greek figure, Sisyphus, who was doomed to push a huge boulder up a hill, only to have it crash to the bottom and be forced to push it to the top again and again and again. "It is legitimate and necessary to wonder if life has a meaning," Camus said. "Therefore it is legitimate to meet the problem of suicide face to face." His conclusion was that suicide was not a valid course, "that even within the limits of nihilism it is possible to find the means to proceed beyond nihilism." One method that he and Sartre advocated was to find meaning in being what they called "authentic," which basically meant being what *we* wanted to be rather than what *others* wanted us to be. A corollary is that the past and the future shouldn't dictate how we behave in the present. Now is all that matters. We are free to reinvent ourselves with each second, finding meaning in the moment, regardless of the strictures of society and those around us. In contrast, the worst thing to do is to live by default, by going through the motions without any appreciation of existence.

Now consider the theme of *The Shrinking Man*. When we first see Scott in the basement, he is less than an inch tall. He calculates that he has only six days to live. Despair so overwhelms him that he debates letting the spider catch and kill him.

The thing would be out of his hands then. It would be a hideous death, but it would be quick; despair would be ended. And yet he kept fleeing from it, improvising and struggling and existing.

In subsequent scenes, his mood worsens.

Poets and philosophers could talk all they wanted about a man's being more than fleshly form, about his essential worth, about the immeasurable stature of his soul. It was rubbish.

More and more, he begins to sound like an Existentialist.

He still lived, but was his living considered, or only an instinctive survival? . . . Was he a separate, meaningful person; was he an individual? Did he matter? Was it enough just to survive? He didn't know.

It might be that "he was a pathetic fraction of a shadow, living only out of habit, impulse-driven, moved but never moving, fought but never fighting."

It's worth nothing that while the radioactive mist is the literal cause of Scott's shrinking, there are numerous metaphoric causes: the insane international politics that made a radioactive mist all too believable in the fifties, the increasing tension within Scott's marriage, and the economic hardships that would have struck Scott even if he hadn't gotten sick (his brother for whom he works has major business problems, for example). Now, a half-inch tall in the basement, his face is unusually calm for a man "who lived each day with dread and peril."

Perhaps jungle life, despite physical danger, was a relaxing one. Surely it was free of the petty grievances, the disparate values of society. It was simple, devoid of artifice and ulcer-burning pressures. . . . There were no political connivings necessary, no financial arenas to struggle in, no nerve-knotting races for superior rungs on the social ladder. There was only to be or not to be.

As things get worse, however, Scott keeps asking himself,

Why do I go on? . . . Why do I try so hard? Instinct? Will? . . . It would have been so much better if his brain had lost its toxic introspections long before. Much better if he could have concluded life as a true bug instead of being fully conscious each hideous, downward step of the way.

That thought startles him, making him realize that "so long as he had his mind, he was unique. . . . His mind could be his salvation, as it had been his damnation." Throwing himself into the search for food, he becomes a version of Sisyphus, repeatedly climbing and descending huge heights. He eventually fixates on the spider as the ultimate goal—not to let it kill him, but to manage the reverse, to kill *it*.

True satisfaction was based on struggle. . . . He was alive, he was trying. Suicide was a distant impossibility. He wondered how he could ever have considered it.

The spider takes on metaphysical dimensions. It "was immortal."

It was more than a spider. It was every unknown terror in the world fused into wriggling, poison-jawed horror. It was every anxiety, insecurity, and fear in his life given a hideous, night-black form.

I'm reminded that the early-American Calvinists thought of humanity as bugs so disgusting that they deserved to be consumed by God, whom they saw as a vengeful spider. In *The Shrinking Man*'s climax, Scott finally manages to kill the spider. In his victory, he suddenly realizes that he isn't going to shrink into nothingness, that instead he's going to enter a new level of existence. Finding a way into the backyard, he concludes,

How could he be less than nothing? . . . Last night he'd looked up at the universe without. Then there must be a universe within, too . . . He'd always thought in terms of man's own world and man's own limited dimensions. He had presumed upon nature . . . But to nature there was no zero. Existence went on in endless cycles . . . There was no point of *non-existence* in the universe.

Thus from despair, the hero passes through what amounts to the principles of Existentialism to arrive at a new (indeed, mystical) appreciation of reality:

He stood in speechless awe looking at the new world with its vivid splashes of vegetation, its scintillant hills, its towering trees, its sky of shifting hues . . . It was a wonderland.

His mind teems with "questions and ideas and—yes—hope again" as he races into his new world. The significant final word is "searching."

I have no way of knowing whether this remarkably textured novel which almost transcends its genre was influenced by Camus's essay. It's interesting that an English translation of his collection, *The Myth of Sisyphus*, appeared in 1955, a year before *The Shrinking Man* was published. But whether Matheson read that book isn't known. Sometimes ideas are in the air. American writers were very interested in Existentialism during the 1950s. It's possible that Matheson came across these ideas in conversations with friends, or maybe he worked out these ideas on his own. If the latter, I am amazed when I read the following final words of Camus's essay and realize how easily they could have been added to the final page of Matheson's novel with only a few changes (the tense, for example) to keep anyone from suspecting that Matheson hadn't written them:

Each atom of that stone, each mineral flake of that night-filled mountain, in itself forms a world. The struggle toward the heights is enough to fill a man's heart.

# A Tribute to Richard Matheson

*Dennis Etchison*

The most common question asked of writers is, "Where do you get your ideas?" God knows it's impossible to answer. If I knew the source of the Nile, I could come up with new stories on demand. The truth is that ideas are all around, like mosquitoes on a summer's day, and until one bites they tend to go unnoticed. Why do some penetrate the skin and get into the blood? I wish I could tell you. A working gazetteer for writers would be more valuable than a copy of the *Necronomicon*.

It's easier to talk about the things we love: music, paintings, books, poetry, movies that transform and inspire by example. We can't duplicate something that's unique and fully realized. But the knowledge that such things exist motivates us to search for the wellspring of creativity in ourselves.

I have my heroes. They set me on the path and kept me going during times of self-doubt. When I was fifteen, my favorite writers were guests of honor at the World Science Fiction Convention: Richard Matheson and Charles Beaumont, with Special Guest Ray Bradbury. My mother drove me there on Saturday morning so I could see these great men in the flesh. The price was three dollars a day or five dollars for the weekend. My first Matheson sighting was in the Hucksters' Room, as he strolled the aisles with his wife and small children. Beaumont appeared onstage that afternoon, in the main meeting hall, all sandy hair and good humor as he fielded questions, including the one about ideas. There were panels and readings and a costume ball and Forrest J. Ackerman and Rog Philips and other stars of the science-fiction world. Late in the day the Los Angeles Science Fantasy Society held an auction to raise funds for their clubhouse, and by the end there were so few people left in the room that I managed to make the winning bid of $2.20 for a Bradbury story manuscript. (A couple of years later, I lent it to a girl in high school English class, hoping to impress her, but neither she nor the manuscript have been seen since.)

Matheson was dignified and reserved, befitting the author of *Third From the Sun* and *The Shores of Space* and *The Shrinking Man* and *I Am Legend*, all of which I cherished in their first paperback editions. I don't remember the sound of his voice or his words, but that doesn't matter because he said everything he needed to say on the printed page. A few years later I was introduced to him by George Clayton Johnson, who befriended me when I was twenty, and for a while I had the loan of a typewriter that actually belonged to Matheson, a clean Olympia portable with book-face type. I wrote stories and even a couple of pseudonymous novels on it. Unfortunately the magic did not rub off. Play a Stradivarius when you're tone-deaf and the result is still noise.

I have learned a few things about stories, though. I don't yet have a map to the headwaters of the Nile, but I can now spot ideas when they flash by on the air. They have a certain weight to them, born of the intersection between fantasy and reality, where creative thinking resides. I do my best to put them on paper with as much clarity and honesty as possible, measuring their quality against the stories of my heroes, foremost among them Richard Matheson. He is the paradigm of an artist who always tells the truth because he cannot bring himself to settle for anything less. I have a long way to go, but at least I know the general direction, thanks to giants like Matheson who have been there so many times before.

# The Great, the One and Only, Richard Matheson

*Joe R. Lansdale*

When I was a kid, two things really struck me hard. The discovery of comic books, and a little later on, the discovery of a wonderful television show titled *The Twilight Zone*.

The minute I saw this program, I somehow knew that my life and the types of stories this television program told would be linked. I was right about this. The impact those stories had (along with, of course, comics, and books, short stories, movies, real life) gave me a direction out of a financially poor existence, as well as a pretty culturally poor one. This influence even led to my writing for *Twilight Zone Magazine* some years later. It was a major component in my career, and helped lead to better and greater things.

The stories that struck me hardest on this fine and wonderful television show turned out to be written by the same person. Richard Matheson. Oh, there were other shows I loved on this program, but Matheson's tales were the cleverest and the most amazing. Later on, this led me to reading his short story collections, which knocked me flat at the time. There were not only the stories I had seen on *The Twilight Zone* in these collections, there were other equally wonderful and very often more spectacular tales between these softcover books.

I kept encountering the name. There was a nifty television movie called *Trilogy of Terror* with three Richard Matheson stories, two scripted by William F. Nolan, and one by Richard Matheson himself, which was the best of the lot, and it was called "Prey," about a very angry little Zuni doll. This led to my finding the source story of the same title in one of his collections. I was amazed at this guy. He could do whimsy, science fantasy, and outright horror. And then I thought, wonder if he did any novels?

Yep.

I read one called *I Am Legend*. It was and is still, after *Dracula*, the best vampire book I ever read, and one of the finest novels I've read. Here Matheson outdid himself. He not only had a clever idea, he created a wonderful character in Robert Neville. The book was strange, suspenseful, and has been not only the direct source for three films, but the indirect source for many others. None of them have captured Matheson's magic.

*The Shrinking Man* was next. Also brilliant. *The Beardless Warriors*, a not-bad Norman Mailer-style novel about World War II, fell into my line of fire. And then *Bid Time Return*, which knocked me flat. I sought out all I could find by Matheson, and pretty soon I was soaked in his tales, and highly influenced by them. I found his rare crime novels and read them. I made a point of seeing everything filmed from his work that I could find.

This guy could do anything, I thought, but westerns. And then, I found in one of his collections a western short story and learned he had written for western television shows back in their heyday.

Damn the man.

Some years later, an editor named Gary Goldstein told me he had a western novel by Richard Matheson that he was thinking about publishing, and would I read it? I said, "Hell, yeah." He sent the manuscript to me. I loved it. It had some historical problems, but it was a killer. I called Gary immediately, said, "Publish. You got to. This is great."

And with a few historical changes, Matheson was a western novelist.

Yep, this guy could do anything.

Somewhere in all this, I met Richard Matheson. It was one of the two or three times I've ever felt speechless, or really impressed. Movie stars. Sports stars. None of these people have made me feel what I felt meeting Richard Matheson and shaking his hand.

I had met one of my mentors, although he didn't know it. But his stories had taught me much. His clean, straightforward style. His tight dialogue. His wonderfully clever plots.

I was proud to meet him. Proud to just be there. And I'm proud now to tell you how much he and his work have meant to me.

You're the best, Mr. Matheson. I look forward to new stories, new magic.

# The *Shock!* of Recognition

## F. Paul Wilson

My first knowing contact with Richard Matheson's fiction came in the summer of 1961. I say *knowing* because I'd had many previous contacts without connecting them to his name. (Like with any kid, credits on TV or in the movies existed to be ignored, a penance you paid before getting to the good stuff, the stuff you came for.)

While browsing the paperback rack of the local drugstore, looking for something to read, a book caught my eye. It had a cool cover very similar to my beloved Ballantine SF paperbacks (later I'd learn the artist's name was Richard Powers), but it was the title that made me snatch it from its slot.

*Shock!*

Could this be another horror anthology like *The Graveyard Reader* or *Deals with the Devil*? I couldn't get enough of those. But no, this was by just one guy named Richard Matheson. Never heard of him.

Still . . . it was titled *Shock!*

So I checked out the back cover where, instead of telling me about the contents, it asked questions like

HAVE YOU EVER WONDERED—

Who is really at the other end when you pick up a ringing phone and hear a soft, breathing silence?

Why do quiet little men suddenly go berserk?

Where do dirty jokes come from?

Why do traffic cops seem so anxious to catch you speeding?

How do national safety councils get their holiday casualty figures?

Why is Los Angeles County growing so rapidly—so purposefully?

Huh? This didn't sound like horror. Or even SF. The bottom of the back cover called it "a collection of fiction fantastique," whatever that was. Well, the rack held nothing else of interest so I plunked down thirty-five cents and took it home.

Am I ever glad I did. Of course I eventually would have discovered Richard Matheson, but I'm glad it was sooner rather than later.

*Shock!* was a revelation. To this point in my experience, what little horror fiction I could find had been peopled with eccentric professors or intrepid explorers or mad scientists. This guy Matheson's stories concerned everyday people in everyday lives in everyday towns and cities—people I might know, people who might live next door, people like—*gasp!*—my folks.

A few of the stories left me cold—like the one about the relentless growth of Los Angeles County—because I had no frame of reference for them. But the rest were creepy and disturbing. (One of them, "Dance of the Dead," recently showed up on Showtime's *Masters of Horror.*) I read them in order, and that turned out to be a good thing because the last piece in the book was "The Distributor."

I've gone on at length in *My Favorite Horror Story* about my love affair with "The Distributor," so I'll not repeat myself here. I will say that I remember being a bit disappointed at the ending because it offered no closure. Like most people, teenagers especially, I liked stories with a beginning, a middle, and an end. This one didn't really end. The guy in the story simply packed up and moved on to the next town. Who did he work for? Why was he causing all this trouble?

Dumb story.

But I found myself thinking about it when I went to sleep and again when I woke up. Who . . . ? Why . . . ? I must have missed something. So I read it again. And again.

I'd already had my I-want-to-write-horror epiphany years earlier after reading Ray Bradbury's "The October Game," so perhaps I was subconsciously on the lookout for techniques to disturb readers. Bradbury's story is filled with emotion and slowly growing menace, and then ends with a karate chop to the throat that leaves you gasping.

"The Distributor" takes a different tack. It is utterly devoid of emotion and leaves you unsettled and scratching your head.

I learned something from Richard Matheson then. I realized a story that leaves readers wondering will follow them around long after they've closed the cover. But beware: It's a delicate balance. Leave too many questions and you have angry, dissatisfied readers who feel the author has let them down. Leave just enough uncertainty and the story will cling like a bad debt.

*Shock!* proved to be a tipping point. Thereafter, everywhere I looked I saw Richard Matheson's name. I'd spot it in *Thriller* and *The Twilight Zone* credits (Oh my God, he wrote that one about the demon on the wing of the plane!), rerun movie credits (*The Incredible Shrinking Man*), and in new movies as well (*Pit and the Pendulum* and *Master of the World*).

But it was the written word I craved.

*Shock!* sent me on a Matheson hunt. *Shock II* and *Shock III* wouldn't be published for years, and hardly anything of his was in print at that time. I did find a used copy of *The Shores of Space* with the terrifying "Little Girl Lost." Then Bantam reprinted an earlier collection, *Third From the Sun*, wherein I found the horrifying and heartbreaking "Born of Man and Woman," parts of which I stole decades later for my own "Faces." (Unconscious theft, I swear. When I reread "Born of Man and Woman" sometime in the mid-1990s, I realized what I'd done. The story still moves me. So let me cop my plea: My guess is that "Born of Man and Woman" left an open, festering wound in my psyche, and perhaps the only way I could heal it was to write about the adult that poor, deformed child would become.)

So I owe you, Richard Matheson. Not just for "Faces," but for showing this would-be writer that horror need not drip ichor, need not befall eccentrics seeking Forbidden Knowledge in ancient ruins. It could happen next door, or be found simply by peeking behind the veil of everyday reality. I owe you too for demonstrating again and again that what you don't say can be as important as what you do say.

Thank you.

# For Dad...

*Alison Matheson*

One of the earliest memories I have of my father is that of his office. It was a mysterious yet magical place full of old books, paintings (the one that fascinated me the most was of the lost Atlantis), a majestic black typewriter, and a chair. It was a cozy leather special that I used to love to sit in, especially if my father's lap was available. I liked to pretend I was writing like him, scribbling on sheets of paper with his (seemingly endless) supply of Scripto pencils. Or better yet, he would read stories to me (from books I usually brought along with me).

As I grew older, the office became a place of refuge to do my homework (or better yet, to get my dad to type it up for me!), play music, or look at the books there. The latter is what fascinated me the most; my dad had a great collection that ranged from classic to contemporary. I think he realized that he had in me a fellow bibliophile, for Dad was soon buying me books for my own little library. Once a week, he would come home with treasures for me. I remember the colored fairy books, the stories about horses, princesses, great journeys through the world. A new book every week and I devoured them all gratefully . . . as I did the musical knowledge he shared with me when he realized he had a fellow classical music aficionado on his hands, too.

My brothers went to baseball games and golf with Dad, but I think I was even luckier as we went to splendid concerts together at the Dorothy Chandler Pavillion, which I loved. It was my special time to get dressed up and drive downtown with my dad, just the two of us. We would have a nice dinner (with me trying very hard to remember all my etiquette lessons and remember which fork to use) and then sit together enjoying the music. (And if I got bored, there were always binoculars available to spy on the other music fans; or a stifled giggle at the old man with his wife, who had subscription seats like us—and always fell asleep within ten minutes, snoring away.)

Forty years later, I am still an aficionado of books and classical music. They are two of my most treasured "friends" as the years go by, and something special that my father and I still happily share, via "Name that Classical Tune," a game we indulge in whenever possible—and he *still* beats me at it!

I am forever grateful for the fact that he introduced me to both—and for his love and support over the years also.

I love you forever, Mr. Pop.

# Introduction to *Hell House*

## *Dean Koontz*

When Richard Matheson launched his formidable career in 1950, with the now classic short story, "Born of Man and Woman," I missed his debut. After all, I was only five years old, and my reading was limited to picture books about adventuresome puppies, cute but mischievous kittens, and clever pigs. If I had been able to read his first published work—or to have it read to me—his vivid portrait of a slime-dripping mutant child chained in the cellar of an ordinary suburban home would no doubt have traumatized me for life.

On a wintry evening ten years later, having become a voracious reader, I was churning through story after story in a thick science-fiction anthology, when I discovered "Born of Man and Woman"—and was thunderstruck by the power of it. I reread it five times, pausing between readings to stare out of my bedroom window at the night and the falling snow. Shivering. At first the shivers were in part a reaction to the horror with which Mr. Matheson had infused the piece, but after the third reading, I was shivering solely in wonder, in *awe* of the author's ability to handle such a complicated theme and elicit such a gut-clenching reaction from the reader in considerably fewer than two thousand words. Even at the age of fifteen, I had dreams of building a career as a writer; that night, however, I didn't merely want to be a writer—I wanted to be *Richard Matheson*.

So you will know why this piece affected me so strongly, I'm going to spend more words analyzing it than were in the story itself! Writers of introductions, who put their words down for no reason but love of the subject, have to be granted every license except the license to kill, so you're just going to have to bear with me here—or do the smart thing and skip ahead to *Hell House*.

"Born of Man and Woman" is written in staccato prose, fractured grammar, and twisted syntax, because it is told from the first-person point of view of the deformed child whose parents keep him chained in the basement, too ashamed of him even to admit his existence to their neighbors, friends, and relatives. This unusual narrative voice, expressed in six diarylike entries, is effective and profoundly affecting.

Perhaps Mr. Matheson's most admirable achievement in this story is the singular grace with which he brings the reader through a 360-degree emotional and intellectual circle. In the first of the six entries, our sympathy lies strictly with the child, because we are led to believe that the only things wrong with him are hideous facial deformities and, perhaps, mild mental retardation. The parents appear hateful and ignorant, cold and abusive, utterly incapable of loving anything but a "pretty" child.

The second entry continues to lay on the pathos: the child is beaten when he dares to try to come upstairs from the cellar to see why there's so much laughter during a social gathering of his parents' friends; his father ties his legs and arms, and chains him to his bed. Hidden in this entry are three disquieting facts that should indicate all is not quite what it seems, but because the author deceives us so brilliantly, we do not fully appreciate the meaning of these clues. First, the child tells us: "In this day when it got dark I had eat my food and some bugs." We take this to mean that his parents don't even provide him with sufficient food and that in desperation he eats insects when he can find them. Second, the child reports: "I walked squish to the stairs. They creak when I walk on them. My legs slip on them because I don't walk on stairs. My feet stick to the wood." The startling truth of what he's saying doesn't register with us, because we have already learned that his uneducated yet convoluted manner of expression, arising from his limited life experience after spending all of his eight years in a cellar, makes simple events sound alien; for instance, instead of saying that it's raining, he tells us, "This day it had water falling from upstairs." The third clue is more direct. Describing the beating by his father, the boy tells us: "The anger came in his eyes. He hit me. I spilled some of the drip on the floor from one arm. It was not nice. It made ugly green on the floor." We think the "drip" is blood—but *green*? Still, we credit the confusion to the peculiarities of the narrative voice.

Entry three is the shortest of the six, and it quickly shifts our attention away from that disturbing remark about green drip by emphasizing the pathos again. We see the boy alone in his dark cellar, in pain from the beating, desperately lonely. In entry number four, he looks wistfully from a cellar window as normal children play and laugh in the backyard. When his mother beats him for showing his face at the window, the reader would like to wrench the stick out of her hand and club *her* senseless with it. The boy says, "I didn't cry. I can't do that." We interpret this to mean that his suffering has been so great for so long that he is beyond tears—or that he refuses to give his mother the twisted satisfaction of seeing him cry. As she's beating him, "the drip ran all over the bed. She saw it and twisted away and made a noise." This could, indeed, be blood again, though there's no reference to it being green; more likely, we think, it is urine, which makes the early reference to the green color slightly more understandable.

In the fifth entry, a little girl, having glimpsed the narrator's deformed face at the cellar window the previous day, is overcome by curiosity and descends into his realm with her cat. The boy hides in the coal bin, but when the cat finds him, he kills it. "I didn't want to hurt it. I got fear because it bit me harder than the rat does." Before we can be put off by his killing a cat, we learn for the first time that this little boy shares his dank cellar with a rat that has obviously bitten him more than once, and again the author uses the pathos of the situation to misdirect our attention as cleverly as any magician who appears to make a live dove vanish before our eyes. The boy tells us, "I grabbed the live thing tight. It made sounds I never heard. I pushed it all together. It was all lumpy and red on the black coal." Although we might question how an eight-year-old boy would have the strength to *crush* a cat into a bloody wad—something a grown man couldn't do—we are still thinking of that rat, appalled at the sheer loathsomeness of the parents, and we read on with total sympathy for the narrator; after all, the cat *bit* him.

In the sixth and final entry, the father beats the boy again and chains him tighter than ever to the bed. "This time I hit the stick out of his hands and made noise. He went away and his face was white. He ran out of my bed place and locked the door." We almost cheer at the boy's display of courage and defiance. But with the last paragraphs of the story, Mr. Matheson's genius becomes manifest when he slams us through a 180-degree emotional arc:

> I am not so glad. All day is cold in here. The chain comes slow out of the wall. And I have a bad anger with mother and father. I will show them. I will do what I did that once.
>
> I will screech and laugh loud. I will run on the walls. Last I will hang head down by all my legs and laugh and drip green all over until they are sorry they didn't be nice to me.

*Wait, wait, wait!* Run on the *walls*? Hang head down by *all* his legs? Suddenly the dripping green stuff sounds like noxious slime exuded by an alien *thing*. The hair goes up on the back of the reader's neck, and his mind spins through an entire reconsideration of the parents. Perhaps they were operating more out of terror than out of ignorance or bigotry or hatred. How would *you* feel if you'd given birth to something more insectoid or reptilian than human, something that could climb walls with its sticky feet and hang from the ceiling, something that ate bugs and was capable of crushing a cat into bloody pulp, something that screeched and gibbered and drooled green slime from one orifice or another? You might just lose it, go a little nuts, and be guided more by fear and repulsion than by compassion, because by keeping this creature chained in a cellar, you're probably saving the lives of your neighbors at least, and by preventing it from raping someone and thus breeding more of its kind, *maybe you're even saving the world!* Don't judge the parents until—God forbid—you have to walk a mile in their shoes.

Having been slung around a 180-degree emotional arc, you then read the last two sentences: "If they try to beat me again Ill [*sic*] hurt them. I will." For an instant, this confirms your new sympathy for the mother and father, because here's proof that the bizarre mutant in the cellar is dangerous, strong enough to crush a cat to death in its bare hands—tentacles, pincers?—and now contemplating violence against human beings. But the shiver of horror passes as you adjust to these shocking revelations, and you realize that the narrator has never hurt anything in eight years until, bitten and terrified, he crushed the cat. He has endured countless beatings, deprivation of every kind, humiliation, cold, rat bites, soul-withering loneliness—and through it all he has remained timid and fearful, with a sort of childlike wistfulness when he hears laughter up-stairs and can't be part of it, or secretly watches other "normal" children at play. That he should at last turn violent is understandable.

As your sympathy for the parents begins to waver—*wham!*—the full meaning of the title hits you, and you come around another 180 degrees: it isn't only this creature who was born of man and woman; our kind has also brought hatred and intolerance and cruelty into the world, for no other species exhibits those qualities. This physically repulsive—and now physically threatening—child is in his appearance the embodiment of the darkness in the human heart and, although for eight years he has not acted out the evil he symbolizes, his parents have treated him in such a fashion as to ensure that he will ultimately fulfill that part of his fate as well. In the end, the reader has come 360 degrees and again has more sympathy for the monstrous offspring than for the mother and father—although it is no longer possible to entirely despise or unconditionally pity either the child or the parents. Thus the story attains a bleakness that leaves us more chilled by the human condition than by the image of the narrator hanging from the ceiling by all his legs, screeching and dripping green slime. Indeed, it's especially impressive that Mr. Matheson can achieve all these effects and leave us this deeply affected while using such a pulp-magazine monster at the center of his tale, which in less talented hands would have resulted in unintended humor.

On that wintry night, when I was fifteen, after reading "Born of Man and Woman" five times in an hour, I scrambled to find other stories by Richard Matheson, and many more of them knocked me out as completely as did that first tale. I moved on to the novels, beginning with *I Am Legend* and then *The Shrinking Man*. I was blown away by these books when I was fifteen, and recently when I reread them, I was blown away yet again. These books not only introduced high-concept ideas that inspired numerous works by other writers during the past five decades; they brought to science fiction and horror a degree of psychological realism that had seldom been seen previously, setting new standards toward which other writers thereafter had to aspire.

A writer who was well known in the science-fiction community in another era, and who fancied himself a singularly perceptive critic, once wrote an essay in which he took Richard Matheson to task for perceived scientific blunders and inconsistencies, most especially in *The Shrinking Man*. I wouldn't attempt to defend the science in either novel, but it's patently clear to me that neither story was intended to work on a purely scientific level in the same way that Hal Clement or Isaac Asimov's novels do. Instead, Mr. Matheson intended to achieve his effects by evoking primal emotions, by recasting ancient myths in cutting-edge modern form, by putting archetypal characters in contemporary dress with a flair unseen before, and by providing clear-eyed psychological detail that would bring a gritty realism to stories of the fantastic.

When these tales are evaluated on the basis of how well the author fulfilled his true intentions, they are obviously smashing successes. Likewise, I would not always argue for the superiority of Richard Matheson's style; when he cares to be, he is a fine stylist and a master of quirky viewpoint—as witness "Born of Man and Woman"—but often he is content to write in crisp, fast-moving prose with little concern for vivid imagery or the striking turn of phrase. What his rare critics fail to understand is that his style is always ideally matched to the story he's telling, and that both the energy of his writing and the powerful emotional content hammer home his point better than any tricks of language he might have used to embellish the narrative. Interestingly, while Mr. Matheson's short stories and novels are regularly in print and still inspire legions of young writers, most of the works by that long-ago critic can be found only in old, moldering editions in used book stores. Richard Matheson's work—from science fiction to horror to the western genre—survives because it is dazzlingly inventive, but primarily because it has *heart* and crackles with a passion that too rarely enlivens the work of other writers.

Mr. Matheson's great heart, his empathy and compassion, his clearly conveyed certainty that life has purpose and meaning and dimensions beyond the visible, make it possible for him to take a step that few other writers of the fantastic seem capable of taking: he is not afraid to step up to metaphysical themes. Hundreds of supernatural novels are published every year in which the authors write with great glee about ghosts and vampires and werewolves and demon-possessed children—without once hinting that there might be a light side to the supernatural world as well as the alluring dark side that is so much fun to write about. They can't seem to admit that the existence of demons requires the existence of God. Their omission of God is understandable, because they are not believers, but I can't find their work either convincing or scary, because its use of colorful antagonists based in a religious tradition, employed without any respect whatsoever for religious *faith*, is not fine cabinet-making but only crude carpentry. Mr. Matheson, on the other hand, has a respect for the spiritual that allows him to write fantasy/horror with great conviction and to give us singularly fascinating novels, such as *What Dreams May Come*, which few other writers are capable of conceiving let alone executing with grace.

And *Hell House*. I read this novel thirty-eight years ago, when it was first published, read it again about fifteen years later, and read it for the third time last week. I'm confident that people will be reading it twenty-five years from today and twenty-five years after that and twenty-five years after *that*. It's scary not just because of the poltergeist effects and the vileness of Belasco's spirit, but because it's full of solid psychological insights, empathy for the suffering of others, compassion, and conviction equalled in this genre only by that in William Peter Blatty's *The Exorcist*. I'm not going to analyze *Hell House* as I did "Born of Man and Woman," because that would get between you and your reading—or rereading—of it. I will tell you, however, that you will be scared witless but, in spite of the horrors, will reach the end with an awareness of what a good man Richard Matheson is, what a nice man; his great heart, as always, comes shining through the page.

Although he probably doesn't remember this, I met Mr. Matheson at the only World Fantasy Convention I've ever attended, many years ago in Tucson. It was a brief encounter, but I was impressed by his graciousness, his kindness, and his self-deprecating wit. He was a legend who didn't choose to walk like one. In my hard experience, too many writers are self-centered and petty, eager to enhance their own reputations by tearing down those of their peers. I've even seen best-selling and acclaimed writers, with nothing to prove, being so viciously vindictive toward other novelists that they give deeper meaning to the word "envy." What a pleasure it was, then, to learn that Richard Matheson was not only a good writer but a good person, as his work had always indicated. My memory of meeting him is the best memory I carried away from any of the five such fantasy/science-fiction conventions I've attended over the years. *Hell House* shines because Richard Matheson shines, proof that the essence of a writer's work is always a reflection of his soul.

# My Soul Father

## by Stephen Simon

In the fall of 1975, I was twenty-nine years old and colossally bored.

I had graduated from Loyola Law School and passed the California Bar in 1974, but I had already dispensed with any thought of practicing law. No offense to lawyers here. I love watching great lawyers at work. I just knew I could never be one of them. I felt increasingly edgy.

Remember the Phil Collins song that has the refrain about feeling something "comin' in the air tonight" and how he's been "waiting for this moment all my life"? That was me. The proverbial long-tailed cat in a room full of rocking chairs. I was ready. "It" was coming but I had no idea what "it" was, where it was coming from, or how to know it when it arrived.

I read a lot at that time. I had always loved reading, dating back to the years in which I had proudly read every single Hardy Boys and Tom Swift book that was published. There was a bookstore in Beverly Hills at that time called Martindale's (La Scala is in that location now), and I was there all the time, browsing and getting to know all the clerks.

One day, I walked in and a clerk who knew me well said that they had just received a book that he thought I would love. He knew I loved all fantasy and science fiction, so a new book by a renowned author in that field seemed perfect for me. He handed me a copy of *Bid Time Return* by Richard Matheson and I took it home to read it.

My life was changed forever that night.

By the book, yes.

I read the book in one sitting and was just mesmerized. Through my lifelong passion for movies, I was aware that the hallmark of any great love story is the obstacle between the lovers, dating back to *Romeo and Juliet*. *Bid Time Return* had the very barrier of life itself as that obstacle, so I knew there was something powerful at its core. I also knew that this was the sign for which I had been looking. It was time to get out of law and into the film business so that I could make this book into a film.

Three years later, in 1978, Richard gave me the galleys of his new novel, *What Dreams May Come*.

It took me three years to get *Somewhere in Time* produced and almost twenty years to get *What Dreams May Come* produced. The details of those journeys are available elsewhere.

Yes, my life was changed forever that night in 1975.

By the book, yes.

But more by the man.

Much more by the man.

My father died when I was very young. I never really knew him. My mother remarried and my stepfather was a wonderful, decent man . . . but we didn't connect on an emotional basis until much later in life, nor, most importantly, on a spiritual level. I had a deep curiosity about spirituality but didn't really know what it was or how to access it within myself.

Until I met Richard Matheson.

We met for the first time at a restaurant in Burbank called Sorrentino's. I was so excited to meet him!

The man was already a living legend—all those *Twilight Zone* episodes, *The Incredible Shrinking Man*, *I Am Legend* (HE certainly was). It's been more than thirty years since that moment, but I remember it as if it were yesterday. In he walked. The 1975 version of Gandalf from *The Lord of the Rings*. Wisdom, wit, love, compassion, vision, kindness, patience—and SOUL like in no one I had ever met before.

Yes, we agreed to pursue *Bid Time Return* as a film together but, most importantly, Richard became, at that lunch, my soul father and spiritual mentor.

Over the next twenty-five years, we worked together on the two films that became sources of pride for us both. We worked on a couple of projects that never saw the light of the silver screen. We had our ups and downs as professional collaborators.

Through it all, Richard patiently and lovingly educated me about spirituality. He gave me books to read, concepts to ponder, and ideas to contemplate. More than anything, he inspired and encouraged me to be myself. To pursue my dreams no matter what anyone said. To never let anyone else define me. To always act with integrity. To push beyond the next hill to see what was there. To dream the big dreams and always know in my heart that I was here for a reason. We talked for hundreds, perhaps thousands, of hours about movies, spirituality, love, and life. He was there for me through incredibly painful personal moments (as was his wonderful wife, Ruth).

He always made me feel loved and respected, even when I did things with which he may have disagreed. He never judged me.

When I became a father, I learned at his knee about raising kids and making them feel loved and respected.

He was my constant companion in every aspect of my life.

He quite literally helped me become an adult. A man. A father. A filmmaker. A spiritual being.

Whatever good there is in me in those areas can be traced "Somewhere in Time" to a Richard Matheson moment in my life.

Our relationship is now in its fourth decade.

When I wrote my first book about films and spirituality in 2002, Richard wrote the afterword.

I have celebrated my sixty-second birthday. I have four extraordinary adult daughters. I have finally found my niche in the world. My company, The Spiritual Cinema Circle, is the manifestation of everything Richard and I envisioned over the decades. I have finally become the director/producer I have always dreamed of being. I have married my wonderful Lauren, the woman for whom I have always been searching.

Life is not just good. It is wondrous.

And, deep at the core of all that is my dear Richard.

I have told him this often over the years, but it is high time to put it in writing.

Thank you, Richard.

For taking a clueless, spoiled, immature child-man under your wing that day in 1975.

For guiding and molding me into the person/filmmaker/spiritual being that I am today.

For the gift of my spirituality. You found that in me and brought it out into the light.

For providing me with the role model I have tried to emulate in my adult life.

For being an original, one-of-a-kind visionary.

The world is a much richer place because of your contributions to it.

And my world simply would never have *been* without you.

I honor you.

I respect you.

I love you with all my heart.

And I look forward to the next Richard Matheson book . . . and the next . . . and the next.

# A Speech by Richard Matheson

*Delivered at the World Fantasy Convention III,*
*Los Angeles Biltmore, October 1977*

When I was asked to be the guest of honor at this year's convention, my first reaction, naturally, was one of pleasure. It was gratifying to win the World Fantasy Award last year for my novel *Bid Time Return.* It was equally gratifying to be chosen as this year's guest of honor.

My second reaction was an automatic stipulation that I not be expected to give a speech. Not because I believe that guests of honor shouldn't give speeches, but because I have no talent for it.

I stand in awe of writers like Ray Bradbury, Robert Bloch, Harlan Ellison, Isaac Asimov, the late Tony Boucher, and Gahan Wilson. Men who can not only write but speak to people by the hour and captivate them.

I don't know how to do that. As you've probably noticed, I'm reading this word for word—the only way I can handle it.

It isn't that I *never* give speeches. As a matter of fact, I gave one only nineteen years ago at the World Science-Fiction Convention here in Los Angeles. And I wasn't even an authentic guest of honor then. The man they wanted—I forget who he was—became sick and I filled in for him.

At any rate, when I received the letter from Dennis Rickard asking me this year, I told him I'd be glad to sit on panels and answer questions and do anything I could to be a proper guest of honor . . . but I couldn't give a speech.

Then I started thinking that this might be the one chance in my life I'd have to make a public statement about the people who have been a part of my life in fantasy, and about my feelings in regard to fantasy itself.

So—inner tremors and all—after almost two decades—here I go making yet another speech. I trust you won't regret my rash decision.

To begin with, I would like to mention the years of enchantment, thrills, and delight I've received from the many writers who've contributed their talents to the world of fantasy. Writers like Poe, Kafka, Lovecraft, Dunsany, Machen, Blackwood, Stoker, James, Walpole, Merritt, T.H. White, Bradbury, Bloch, Kuttner, Sturgeon, Leiber, Moore, Kersh, Tenn, Finney, Miller (Ward and Walter), Brown, Bester, Van Vogt, Beaumont, Neville, Russell, Nolan, Ellison et al. They've provided me with days of spellbound joy and nights of delicious insomnia. I thank them all.

I thank, too, the creative minds behind the many fantasy films which transfixed, excited, and often scared the living hell out of me when I was growing up. Men like Browning, Whale, Mamoulian, the Korda brothers, Lewton, Tourneur, Robson, Wise, and others. Films like *Frankenstein, Dracula, The Mummy, Dr. Jekyll and Mr. Hyde, Cat People, Isle of the Dead, The Body Snatcher, King Kong, The Wizard of Oz, Dead of Night, The Thief of Bagdad, The Jungle Book*, and too many others to mention—though I *will* mention some of their too-often forgotten writers: Langley, Florey, Bodeen, MacDonald and Keith, Stallings, Butler, Day, Baines, Clark, MacPhail, Fort and Murphy, Hoffenstein and Heath. To these men, too, I give my thanks.

I am grateful, too, for the many years of knowing kindred souls like Charles Beaumont, Ray Bradbury, Bob Bloch, Bill Nolan, Ray Russell, Ted Sturgeon, Jerry Sohl, Kris Neville, John Tomerlin, George Clayton Johnson, Forry Ackerman, Harlan Ellison, and so many others.

I have warm memories of Ray Bradbury answering my letters when I had sold just a few short stories. Encouraging me as he has encouraged so many beginning writers. I thank him for his time, his kindness, and his inspiration.

I have the warming memory of Bob Bloch actually taking the time to write a praising article about my writing when I had barely begun.

We didn't know each other at the time and I was positively dazzled that a writer of his experience and stature would do such a generous thing. Later, he took even more time to revise and expand the article so it could serve as an introduction to my first collection of stories. I thank him for doing that and for his genial friendship these many years.

I have the memory of Tony Boucher and Mick McComas being so supportive of my writing in my early years. Buying the first story I ever sold and helping me repeatedly to improve my work. Acting as concerned teachers. As Howard Browne did. As Horace Gold did after he bought my second story. I have memories of long telephone conversations with Horace when I lived in Brooklyn and he in Manhattan. Constructive and reassuring conversations which I still recall with affection and gratitude. I thank all these men for their cordial assistance and for the privilege of being published in their magazines. They made my formative years as a writer so much nicer, so much less lonely.

I have the memory of Harry Altshuler writing me after my first story was published and asking if I had an agent. I didn't, and he became my agent and served me faithfully for seven years. I give my thanks to him.

I have memories of Don Congdon serving as my literary agent so well and understandingly for the past twenty-one years. My thanks and gratitude to him as well. And to the varied men who've served as my agents in my film and television work, currently Rick Ray, Sam Adams, Lee Rosenberg, Shelly Weil, and Mark Rosenberg. I thank them all.

My thanks, too, for the considerate editorial attentions of Alan Williams of Viking Press—and to my editor, Ms. Page Cuddy of Berkley Books who, with Putnam, will be publishing my new (*perhaps*, fantasy) novel next year as well as reissuing nine of my past science-fantasy novels and story collections.

I have happy memories about my first book sale to Hollywood. And of seeing what a splendid job Jack Arnold did directing *The Incredible Shrinking Man.*

Happy memories of the years I wrote for *The Twilight Zone.* Memories of the always kind and liberal support of Rod Serling.

I have memories of being overjoyed at how magnificently Steven

Spielberg directed my script for *Duel*. And how rewarding it was to work with its producer, George Eckstein.

Pleasant memories of viewing, for the first time, *The Night Stalker*, *The Night Strangler*, *Dracula*, *Trilogy of Terror*, and *Dead of Night* (the second). For those memories, I thank Dan Curtis and all the talented people who contributed to these productions.

I have happy memories of the years I worked with Jim Nicholson, Sam Arkoff, and Roger Corman at American International. Memories of the delight it was to meet and see my scripts performed so well by Vincent Price, Peter Lorre, Boris Karloff, Basil Rathbone—what a *marvelous* quartet of actors—and the many other artists who contributed their skills to *those* productions.

Happy memories of faces and voices, some of them gone. Memories which I will always treasure. Gratitudes which I will always feel.

I would also like this speech to be an expression of thanks for what fantasy itself has done for my life.

It caught me young and caught me permanently. No matter what other interests I have found creatively and socially, fantasy has always been—and will always be—integral to my life.

Whatever the reason may be, I don't believe that it was simply heredity and environment that drew me to fantasy. I believe that certain people enter this world with a predisposition toward fantasy which goes beyond the influences of parentage, home, and society. I know I've been enamored of it for at least forty-four years and I think that feeling was there when I showed up.

When I joined the library as a young child, the first book I borrowed was *Pinocchio in Africa*. (I *know* it exists though I've never met another person who's read it.) This was followed by a quick devouring of *The Yellow Book of Fairy Tales* (pre-Anita Bryant, of course), *The Red Book*, *The Green Book*, *The Blue Book*, all of them.

It *is* true that my first published work—a poem in *The Brooklyn Eagle* when I was eight—began as follows: "When Columbus sailed, he said 'at least/I'll find a short route to the East.'" Strictly realism—unless you consider my quoting Columbus as fantasy. My next work, however, a short—*very* short—story had to do with a sparrow befriending a little boy and defending him miraculously against a bully.

The fantasies had begun.

Fantasies which have, often, given me the wonder of *living* them even as I created them.

One of the times this happened was in the writing of *The Shrinking Man*. My family and I were living on the north shore of Long Island in a small rented house and every morning, for two months, I would descend into the cellar, sit in an old rocking chair, and, in longhand, describe my tiny hero as I "watched" him move around the cellar. It was easy to keep the environment straight in my mind since it was immovable in front of me, complete to my villain spider in its web. But it also gave me the excitement of living through Scott Carey's miniscule adventures as *he* did.

I did this again in writing *Bid Time Return* . . . living in the Hotel Del Coronado while I wrote part one. My main character walked around the hotel with a cassette recorder, describing what he saw and speaking his thoughts aloud. I did the same. His observations and feelings were mine, as I imagined myself to be Richard Collier. I found the experience intriguing and exhilarating. It engrossed me completely.

These were obvious creative pleasures bestowed on me by fantasy, but there have been many others—moments of bewitched escape into a world from which I have always returned re-created and rehabilitated— my own version of the Medical Corps' R&R leave.

I had the thought recently that perhaps my entire creative life has been an attempt to escape from reality. Perhaps that is the essential motivation for *all* fantasy writers—perhaps all *fiction* writers.

Not that the reality of my life was or is anything to be escaped from. I had a lovely and attentive mother and an older brother and sister who were always sympathetic to me. I have a lovely, loving, and supportive wife, marvelous children, a comfortable home, an acceptably successful career. Still, the "fantasy being" within me searches, looking in all directions—mostly inward, of course—for that strange and moving *offbeat* which characterizes the music of my writing and the lives of all those gripped by fantasy.

In the book *Neurotic Styles*, author David Shapiro has a section entitled "Hysterical Romance and Fantasy." People he describes in this section "see things *differently*. The subjective world that emerges is a colorful, exciting one."

This type of hysteric, according to Shapiro, is carried away by the immediacy of his responses, "his awareness captured by the vivid impressions, romantic provocations and transient moods of his own or of the fantasy characters that, for whatever reason, appeal to him."

I can only respond that if this is mental illness, I must count myself—and *happily*—among the ranks of the hysterics.

I think all of us here know the background of our obsession. Adolescent daydreams. Substitution for painful emotions. Retreat for refuge to a netherworld of make-believe.

We've fantasized to escape the traumas of reality. Diverted our professional terrors into terrors of imagination. Walked a tightrope of narrow adjustment across the pit of actuality, or should I say—the snake pit? In the long run, does it all really matter? Why not, instead, paraphrase John Donne and counter psychology's observations with the words, "these are themes for reason, much too strong for fantasy"?

Perhaps the essence of our long and sweet relationship with fantasy is what part of that relationship we play "for fun" and what part we play "for real." I believe that all of us have built-in instrumentation which enables us to differentiate one from the other. We know "what counts" and what doesn't. Somehow, we manage the schizophrenic zest of enjoying the unreal while still recognizing it for what it is. And, when we choose to fantasize, we choose to regard reality with what they used to call in psychology, *la belle indifférence*.

When we're in the mood, we can take reality or leave it.

*The American College Dictionary* defines fantasy as "imagination, especially when unrestrained." How enviable a quality. How many *other* aspects of our lives can hope to achieve this lovely state of unrestraint? Yet all of us here enjoy that riveting albeit periodic state. That gift for wandering down off-center paths to magical, entrancing realms—and coming back a little happier, a little more enriched.

In an introduction to the second volume of Walt Lee's massive and meticulous *Reference Guide to Fantastic Films*, the superb actor Christopher Lee speaks of fantasy in this way: "What a joy it is. We are, in a literal sense, enchanted. The necromancer waves his hand before our dazzled eyes and immediately we are in a world of mystery, magic and the unknown."

I have very much enjoyed living in that world for more than fifty years. It is a world which has adorned my life. Given me excitement—happiness—delight—blissful terror—and extreme, unending satisfaction. In a very real sense, it has been one of the great romances of my life. What higher praise can I give it? If I had a drink in my hand right now, I would raise it and deliver this toast . . . "To *fantasy*—with *love*." Thank you.

# My Dad and the Dodgers

## Chris Matheson

I'm not sure many people know this, but my dad is a baseball fan. Has been since childhood, a Dodger fan, specifically. First in Brooklyn, then in L.A.

It's something he and I shared while I was growing up. We went to lots of games together. In 1978, Dad and his producing partner at that time, Stan Shpetner, bought season tickets. We went to many games that year, which was great because the Dodgers ended up going to the World Series. (They lost to the Yankees in six.)

Sometimes I'd bring friends, sometimes my mom and sister Ali would come. (Mom wasn't a big baseball fan. She'd mainly sit and watch the birds flying around Dodger Stadium.)

But more often than not, it was just Dad and me. We talked about all kinds of things, but probably mostly baseball. Dad had a sort of philosophy about the Dodgers, developed, I guess, after having had his heart broken by the team his entire childhood and then having had them "follow" him out west five years after he arrived in L.A. The philosophy was something like this: Enjoy the games, appreciate the beauty and complexity of the sport (far more interesting than football or basketball, Dad would say), be happy when the Dodgers win . . . but be prepared, always be prepared, for the last minute, end-of-the-season, ninth inning fold. Don't get too upset or mad when it happens because, on some level, you know, that's life.

I'm forty-seven now, I haven't lived in L.A for over a decade, I've drifted away from the Dodgers. So has Dad. Or at least so he says. Sometimes when I call at night to chat with him and my mom, though, I'll hear a game on in the background. And sometimes there'll be a pause on the line and then a low, murmured groan and a sigh. "The Dodgers," he'll say. "The Dodgers . . ."

# Journal of the Matheson Years

*Gary Goldstein*

As childhood memories go, this is one of my fondest:

I was eleven—the year was 1965—when I opened the *TV Guide* and saw that Channel 7, our local WABC affiliate in New York, was having Monster Week on their daily *4:30 Movie*. The lineup included *The Incredible Shrinking Man*, a flick I'd been dying to see, having read about it in Forrest Ackerman's *Famous Monsters of Filmland* a year or two earlier.

My mother, God bless her, indulged me this one time, making me a Swanson's turkey TV dinner and allowing me to watch the movie in the den while the rest of my family dined in the kitchen. Ah, I still remember the taste of that cardboard turkey, the pasty mashed potatoes, and those shriveled little green peas. I was just dipping into the chemical cranberry as Scott Carey plunged the sharpened pin into the spider's belly. To this day, I never miss *The Incredible Shrinking Man* when it pops up on TV. It's one of those movies you never get tired of. Years later, Richard told me an X-rated and hysterically funny story about his first meeting with *Shrinking Man*'s flamboyant producer, Albert Zugsmith, who also gave the world Orson Welles's awesome *Touch of Evil*, and the great sleaze classics *Sex Kittens Go to College* and *High School Confidential*! Though I'll spare Richard the embarrassment of repeating it here.

When you think of Richard Matheson, it's generally in connection with *The Shrinking Man*, or his kickass *Twilight Zone* episodes (including Richard's "Nightmare at 20,000 Feet," which sent an entire generation of baby-boomers to bed with the lights on for weeks), or the Roger Corman/American International Pictures adaptations of Edgar Allan Poe, like *The Raven, Tales of Terror*, and *Pit and the Pendulum*. And, of course, 1972's *The Night Stalker*, which at that time was the highest-rated made-for-TV movie in broadcast history. Richard Matheson was, among other things, the king of TV movies around that time, with one high-rated hit after another, like *Trilogy of Terror* (1975), *Dying Room Only* (1973, with Cloris Leachman at her hysterical best), *Scream of the Wolf* (1974), and, of course, the 1971 classic *Duel*, which was Steven Spielberg's first full-length directorial effort. Richard also wrote a different kind of horror movie, 1974's *The Morning After*, with Dick Van Dyke giving one of his best noncomedic performances as a middle-class businessman sinking deeper and deeper into the throes of hopeless alcoholism.

The one genre his fans don't associate Richard with is the western—and I was no exception. So it was with a great deal of bewilderment one day in February 1991—when I toiled as the westerns editor at Berkley Books—that I opened the box from his longtime literary agent Don Congdon and gazed down on the typewritten title page and saw *Journal of the Gun Years*, with the subtitle "Being Choice Selections from the Authentic, Never-Before-Printed Diary of the Famous Gunfighter-Lawman Clay Halser." Below that: "By Richard Matheson."

I did a double take—who wouldn't?—and called Don Congdon. *The* Richard Matheson? Yes, said Don. *That* Richard Matheson.

After slogging through manuscripts like *Fifty Guns to Cheyenne Pass, Texas Town Tamer*, and *Cattle Drive Massacre* (in which the author, a New York City resident who'd never been any farther west than Tenth Avenue, inconveniently put a mountain range in the middle of Kansas), reading *Journal of the Gun Years* was sheer pleasure. Taking to heart the old newspaper credo, "When the legend becomes fact, print the legend," *Journal* told the story of thirty-one-year-old Clay Halser, a gunman who ultimately becomes the victim of his own fastest-gun-in-the-West reputation, along the lines of Wild Bill Hickok or Doc Holliday. Written in the style of an old-time dime novel (complete with the profanity intentionally blanked out), *Journal of the Gun Years* was one of the finest pieces of writing I'd ever laid an editor's eyes on. Not a pretty story by any means—it was downbeat and the hero sure as hell didn't ride off into the sunset on the last page. And it was a far cry from the standard shoot-'em-up horse operas Berkley was publishing in the 1990s.

Berkley Books at that time was fortunate enough to have Roger Cooper as its publisher. Roger was (and still is) a man of vision and boundless enthusiasm who possessed a talent unique in publishing: he loved books, but he loved authors even more. And, as it turns out, he was a bigger Matheson fan than I was. It was Roger's excitement for *Journal of the Gun Years* and for Richard Matheson that made it all happen. We closed the deal with Don Congdon that same week. Veteran editor Pat LoBrutto, who was acquiring westerns for M. Evans and Co. at that time, bought the hardcover rights and published his edition in December 1991. (The Berkley mass market edition would come out in March 1992.)

*Journal of the Gun Years*, not surprisingly, got excellent reviews in the trades. *Publishers Weekly* gushed, "The author gives his story a credibility and honesty unusual in the (western) genre." *Library Journal* said, "A wild western . . . very readable."

Later that year, the book got a gift from the gods: writing a piece in *The New York Times Book Review* bemoaning the whole distribution end of book publishing, Stephen King—who has never made any bones about being a huge Matheson fan and being inspired by his work—said, "The best book I read last year was *Journal of the Gun Years*." We hastily sent the paperback edition back to press with the King quote on the cover. Then came more good news: *Journal* was chosen as the 1991 Golden Spur Award winner for Best Western Novel by the Western Writers of America. It was a triumph for Richard and for the book, and Berkley's first Spur winner in thirty-five years of publishing westerns.

Richard and his wife, Ruth, flew into Jackson Hole, Wyoming, in June 1992 for the Spur Awards banquet. I went to the airport to fetch them and bring them back to the hotel. The airport in Jackson Hole, nestled as it is between two mountain ranges including the Grand Tetons, made for a pretty bumpy descent. Richard and Ruth both looked a little pale when they got off the plane. I asked, "What's wrong? Was there a gremlin on the wing?" (It occurs to me now I must have waited almost thirty years to ask him that question.)

The Spur banquet that night was pretty insane. Some genius on the Western Writers of America board of directors brought in radical liberal lawyer Gerry Spence to give the keynote address. Spence was supposed to give a speech about the famous western gunfighters. The problem was, he showed up totally drunk and started preaching about the evils of the death penalty—to a roomful of western writers no less, which today would be the equivalent of Rosie O'Donnell addressing the NRA. Most of the old-timers, and a lot of new-timers, got up and walked out in protest.

Richard, always the model of graciousness, took it all in stride. He went up to the podium to accept his Spur Award clad in a jacket and a bolo tie, and said, "One of the reasons I wrote *Journal of the Gun Years* was because I've had this bolo tie for twenty years and always wanted a chance to wear it."

Richard would publish four more books with Berkley: *The Gun Fight* in September 1993 (which he dedicated to yours truly; the dedication page from that manuscript is framed and hanging on the wall of my home office); *By the Gun* in January 1994, an excellent collection of short stories he wrote for the western pulp magazines in the 1950s; *Shadow on the Sun* in November 1994, a horror novel set in the West about a Quetzalcoatl-type creature who flaps around the Arizona Territory ripping people's heads off (I loved it, though it was definitely a challenge packaging it for the diehard western readers); and *The Memoirs of Wild Bill Hickok* in January 1996.

During this time, I looked for any excuse to call Richard—he was full of awesome stories about Hollywood and working with the likes of Roger Corman and Rod Serling and Vincent Price and Dan Curtis, stories he loved to share. Richard was also a joy to work with and I like to think we made a good team. He wrote them and I published them. (I won't say "edited" because you didn't have to edit Richard Matheson; even the copyeditors were hard-pressed to find anything wrong in his manuscripts.)

What is it, I often asked myself, that has placed Richard Matheson in the pantheon of the great storytellers, as one who has inspired several generations of writers and filmmakers from Stephen King to Steven Spielberg? His vivid imagination? Well, duh. His plotting? Sure—the best. His characterizations? Second to none. His dialogue? Nary a false note in any book, screenplay, or short story.

I was rereading *Journal of the Gun Years* not long ago when it struck me, and the answer was so simple: *drama*. Richard understands the rudiments of drama and how to use them, no matter what genre he's working in, whether it's horror or science fiction or suspense or, in this case, westerns.

By my estimation, in more than twenty years of book publishing, I've acquired and edited close to a thousand books. I've paid anywhere from $2,500 to $400,000. I've published a couple of bestsellers and have even seen a couple of them turned into movies. But I've never been prouder than I was of those five Richard Matheson books, especially *Journal of the Gun Years*. Authors like Richard Matheson come along, if you're lucky, once in an editor's career. I'll always be fortunate that Richard came into mine.

# The House of Matheson

*Barry Hoffman*

By the time this book is released, Gauntlet Press will have published twenty-five volumes of Richard Matheson's work (which doesn't include introductions he wrote for *Psycho*, *As Timeless as Infinity: The Complete Twilight Zone Scripts of Rod Serling, Vol. 1*, and *The Twilight Zone Scripts of Charles Beaumont*; a short story for the *Masques V* anthology; and twelve chapbooks of previously unpublished short stories and scripts). It has been a deeply satisfying eighteen years with, hopefully, many more to come. Even more than any of his trade publishers, we are The House of Matheson.

Gauntlet is a specialty press, which allows us far greater flexibility than a trade publisher. For the most part, we publish signed editions limited to five hundred copies. And our trade paperbacks (we've published two volumes of Richard's *Twilight Zone* scripts and three of his collected short stories) can be profitable with fewer sales, because we don't have the staffing of a trade publisher. The bottom line isn't what we look at. If we can break even, we're satisfied. We also have the opportunity to work hands-on with the author far more than a trade publisher (Richard, for instance, has approval of all cover art, and, as you'll see later, actively suggests images for his books).

My association with Richard began in 1991 with a request that he write an introduction for Robert Bloch's *Psycho*. Bob Bloch, very much like Richard, was humble almost to a fault. When asked to suggest who might write an afterword to his classic novel, he responded, "I can't begin to tell you who might think my work worthy of an introduction or afterword." He was obviously wrong. I queried his good friends and contemporaries, Ray Bradbury and Richard Matheson, and both immediately agreed to contribute to the book. Richard, though, had one caveat. "I've never written an introduction," he told me. "Do you still want me to write one for Bob?" Like I might say no! They provided the two best tributes I've ever received for a Gauntlet Press book. Bob received the galley with the material Ray and Richard had written, on the day he found out he had terminal cancer. "You've made my day," he told me over the phone. Ray and Richard had not only written about Bob Bloch the author, but also lauded Bob Bloch the man—both referring to him as a gentleman in every sense of the word. Yes, Richard Matheson could write an introduction.

Little did I know that this one introduction would lead to a long and ongoing relationship with both living legends. Bob Bloch's passing (six weeks after receiving the galley for *Psycho*) led me to reexamine Gauntlet's direction. I was stunned that only one of Richard Matheson's books had been published as a signed limited edition (*Richard Matheson: Collected Stories*, by Dream/Press). Most specialty presses were publishing the flavor of the day, ignoring the work of far more enduring authors like Bloch, Bradbury, and Matheson, to name just a few. It was a void I intended to fill.

When I first approached Richard about publishing *I Am Legend* as a signed limited, he seemed leery. I didn't learn until much later that Richard's experience with Dream/Press had been less than satisfying. "I received one beautiful copy of the book, but *no* money," he told me just this past fall. Dream/Press (also known as Scream/Press) would soon close up shop, owing authors and customers a good deal of money for books never published. Richard had every right to be concerned that he would fall into a similar trap a second time. Before he would agree to allow us to publish *I Am Legend*, he had some conditions.

"I can't sign five hundred tipsheets at once," he told me. (A tipsheet, or signature sheet, is the first page of the book, signed by the author. It would be impractical to send an author five hundred books to sign, so the author signs five hundred sheets for a book that will have five hundred copies, and the printer binds the sheets into the books.) Richard had written first drafts of *all* of his manuscripts in longhand and it had taken its toll. I told him we'd send the tipsheets to him six months in advance and he could sign a few at a time.

"I won't write introductions to my books," he then told me. I suggested we have someone (it turned out to be the co-editor of this book, Matthew R. Bradley) interview him and incorporate his comments into an introduction. He agreed, but I could almost hear a sigh in his voice.

Lastly, "If you ask someone to write an introduction or afterword, it has to be a request from the publisher, not me," he said. Richard felt those who admired his work would feel obligated to say yes if they thought the request was coming from him. Being the person he was, he never wanted to put anyone in such an awkward position. No problem, I told him.

"Oh, and no dustjacket or artwork on the covers." He wanted just a bonded leather cover with his signature embossed on the front. I told him we could live with that, too.

Happily, Richard was ecstatic with our edition of *I Am Legend* (with a bonded red leather cover and blue slipcase). I suggested *Hell House* as our second "classic revisited." He wanted the same red cover and blue slipcase as we'd used for *I Am Legend*. By this time, I'd struck up a friendship with his son, Richard Christian Matheson, who also happened to be an extraordinarily gifted writer in his own right. When I told him about his father's request for *Hell House*, R.C.'s response was, "No, no, no! *Hell House* is a much darker novel. It should be black, housed in a black slipcase." He said he would talk to his father, and did convince him to go with the black. When Richard called to tell me his decision, he quipped, "What color will my next book be . . . *pink*?"

Limited editions of *What Dreams May Come*, *Somewhere in Time*, *The Shrinking Man*, and *A Stir of Echoes* followed (and no, we never used pink for the cover). At this point, my philosophy regarding books I would publish by Richard and by Ray Bradbury changed. Other publishers were *now* reissuing their classics. I wanted to make previously unpublished material available to enhance both authors' legacies. Richard, in particular, had a treasure trove of work that had never seen the light of day in print—short stories, scripts, and novels. Space doesn't allow for a discussion of each, but some posed unique challenges that merit mention.

*Hunger and Thirst*: This was Richard's first novel as an adult, written after he graduated from college—a manuscript of more than seven hundred pages. His agent at the time told him it was too long to get published, especially as a first novel, so Richard put it away for fifty years. After he sent me the manuscript, it was difficult for me to contain my enthusiasm. While not as polished as Richard's other works (when I asked him if he wanted to edit the book, he cut two short paragraphs and that was it; I agreed that as his first novel, it should appear as he had originally written it), it was a fabulous read. I especially remember the main character walking from Greenwich Village to Central Park in New York City. A native New Yorker, I had made the same trip, and felt I had been in the shoes of Richard's protagonist. I read that section over a number of times. Richard was astute enough to realize that a dustjacket was necessary (complete with the dreaded cover art) so the dustjacket flap could inform readers this wasn't a *new* Richard Matheson novel, but his first. Fortunately the talented (and underappreciated) Harry O. Morris had provided a number of covers for Gauntlet books, including Richard Christian Matheson's short story collection, *Dystopia*. (You can read Harry's essay on illustrating Richard Matheson elsewhere in this book.) Suffice it to say Richard was so taken with Harry's final cover, he requested we have no lettering on it that might obscure some of Harry's details. The title of *Hunger and Thirst* appeared only on the spine (as a specialty press, we could more easily accommodate such a request than a trade publisher could). And, for the first time, Richard asked to write his own introduction. He would do this with all future books Gauntlet published.

*Come Fygures, Come Shadows*: Richard was obsessed with writing epic novels of more than a thousand pages, though he never completed either of the two he started. *Come Fygures, Come Shadowes* and *The Link* were to be his epics, both dealing with the paranormal. He showed portions of the manuscripts to his editors, and in each case the shortsighted response he received was that if it was going to be a thousand pages, it was too long to be published. With a growing family to feed, Richard shelved both projects. He told me that from then on, he never showed a novel to an editor until he'd completed it. No one, for instance, knew he was writing his most recent novel, *Woman*, until he sent it to his agent. *Come Fygures, Come Shadowes* may be Richard's best work that has never been available in a trade edition. Fortunately, what he wrote was a self-contained novel (one-fourth the length he had intended) with a satisfying beginning, middle, and end. It certainly could stand on its own. A novel of the paranormal, *Come Fygures, Come Shadowes* would make a wonderful film—special effects à la *Poltergeist* or *The Omen* (to satisfy the 18–24 demographic studios seem to crave), with a message of child abuse that would make the film even more enduring for adults. We included Richard's outline, which mapped out the plot for the other three-fourths of the originally proposed novel. Sadly, reviewers focused on the gem the fully written book would have been, rather than appreciating what Richard had written. I'm convinced that had we not published Richard's afterword, the book would have been viewed as yet another Matheson classic. At the same time, not publishing the outline for the rest of the book would have been unfair to the reader.

*Pride*: After "Duel" appeared in *Playboy* in 1971, Richard had had his fill of short fiction. The decision was classic Matheson: he later wrote five westerns and felt that with the last, he'd said everything he wanted to say about the Old West. He would never write another western. Money also played a part in his decision to stop writing short fiction. Richard was a hot commodity as a film and television writer at that time. "Why write a short story for a hundred fifty dollars when I could write a script for several thousand dollars?" he told me. In 2002, I suggested to Richard Christian that he and his father collaborate on a short story. Each would write his own version, centered around a theme they both agreed upon, then combine them into a single story. They wrote their stories, and then the project almost fell apart. They simply couldn't combine each other's stories into one. Over the years, their styles had become incompatible (they had collaborated on the short story "Where There's a Will" in 1980). While Richard was a minimalist, as was his son, his story was still two to three times longer than Richard Christian's. R.C. had become adept at what is called the "short-short". In two to four pages, he could craft an emotionally wrenching tale of horror. Not wanting to give up on the project, I suggested they use their short stories as the basis for a teleplay collaboration. Richard Christian had told me that he and his father had recently collaborated on a number of screenplays, several of which had been purchased. Thus *Pride* saw publication with short stories by father and son, and a teleplay collaboration.

One of Gauntlet's hallmarks is bonus material we add to our books to give the reader further insight into how an author approaches his or her work. Richard, as mentioned before, hand wrote all of his work. Shockingly, he tossed the handwritten draft away after it was typed. I began begging Richard to *save everything* he wrote. With *Pride*, we were able to include his handwritten draft of the short story, complete with changes he made as he wrote. It soon became a running joke between us. "Yes, I've saved the handwritten introduction to (fill in the blank)," he'd tell me before I asked.

*Duel & The Distributor* and *Richard Matheson's Kolchak Scripts*: Scripts are work for hire, sold to a studio or television network with all rights usually residing with whoever purchased the script. Few acclaimed authors—that is, legendary authors, not just popular writers—are prolific screenwriters. You can't have a discussion about Richard Matheson's work without mentioning *Duel*, his Kolchak scripts, the Edgar Allan Poe scripts he wrote for Roger Corman, or the *Dracula* script, which he wrote for Dan Curtis; there are also the fourteen scripts he wrote for the original *Twilight Zone*. They're very much a part of Richard's legacy, and begged publication. With *Richard Matheson's Kolchak Scripts*, I first had to get permission from Jeff Rice, the creator of the Kolchak character. Fortunately, the editor of the Kolchak book was his good friend Mark Dawidziak. Rice had (as he often did) gone underground, leaving no one an address or phone number in case he had to be reached. When he resurfaced, Mark negotiated permission to publish the scripts . . . almost. We needed permission from Jeff, as he owned the rights to the character, but ABC Television owned the rights to the scripts themselves. ABC-TV initially rejected our request, but I'm persistent. I spoke to someone at the network who was more sympathetic and we were granted permission to publish the scripts as a hardcover signed limited. Our last problem was actually getting a copy of the *Night Stalker* script. Incredibly, Richard didn't have a copy. ABC-TV didn't have a copy. Dan Curtis (who kept everything) didn't have a copy. We finally found a fan in Australia who had the script. With a bit of negotiating, we acquired it and published the Kolchak scripts.

We encountered a similar permissions problem with Duel. Steven Spielberg's company graciously granted permission to publish Richard's script, *but* we also needed the permission of Universal Studios. I had approached Universal years before, and after two weeks of deliberation they categorically said no. I approached them again when we decided to publish *The Distributor*. The two scripts were similar in tone and would make a wonderful book. The spokeswoman I talked to told me she had to check the contract. Weeks passed and finally she called. Because *Duel* first aired as a made-for-TV film, Universal retained all rights *except* for a hardcover edition. Universal couldn't deny us permission to publish a signed limited hardcover of *Duel*. It's obvious that the first person who rejected our request out of hand had done so without having looked at the contract. I'm especially persistent when it comes to publishing Richard's work.

*Abu and the 7 Marvels*: As a teacher, I was enchanted with the novel, Richard's only book for young adults. The problem was finding a children's artist to Richard's liking. We ended up sending him the work of several artists and he loved the style of William Stout, an acclaimed artist of children's books. Bill readily agreed to illustrate *Abu* and, other than a few suggestions regarding the cover, Richard let Stout do his thing. *Abu* has been considered our most beautiful book, and won the Ben Franklin Award for small press publishing. Richard's longtime agent, Don Congdon, told me that when his other current publisher, Tor, saw the book, an editor there asked why it hadn't been submitted there. Congdon replied that it *had*—fifteen years earlier—and was *rejected*.

I could go on and on. Richard located some short stories and novellas in his files that he didn't want published because he felt they were too "dark." Now, as he looked at them, he changed his mind and we published *Darker Places*. There are many scripts Richard wrote that have not been produced. We decided to publish three of them in a book entitled *Unrealized Dreams*: a sequel to *The Incredible Shrinking Man*; a script written expressly for Clark Gable, who died before it could be filmed; and a follow-up to *The Comedy of Terrors* in which Richard would use the same actors, but they would be given different roles. He was enthralled with the combination of comedy and horror. Sadly, as Richard said in his introduction to the book, the wonderful character actors he had written for began dying one at a time before his script could be filmed. And, in *Bloodlines*, we've included his script for *I Am Legend*, which was banned from production by the British Censor Board, and revised by another screenwriter before finally being filmed (disappointingly) as *The Last Man on Earth*. At least Richard's fans can see his vision for the screen version of what might be his most enduring novel.

It's been an incredible ride, and we're certainly not finished. Still to be published are a second volume of uncollected stories and unfinished novels; "classic-revisited" editions of *The Beardless Warriors* and *Earth-bound*; and an omnibus collection of his westerns. *The Years Stood Still*, a novel he wrote when he was fourteen, appeared in Gauntlet's limited edition of this book, *The Richard Matheson Companion*. *Conjure Wife*, a screenplay he wrote with his good friend Charles Beaumont that was filmed as *Burn, Witch, Burn* (a.k.a. *Night of the Eagle*), will appear in an anthology. And, as always, Richard will find additional material. There's gold in them there files of his, and it's been my pleasure to provide his many fans with books that would have remained buried in his "archives" if I hadn't asked him to write an introduction for *Psycho*.

# Editing Matheson

## Greg Cox

For the last eighteen years, I've been Richard Matheson's editor at Tor Books. The fact that Tor (an imprint of Tom Doherty Associates) has published at least three original books by Matheson, and brought several of his classic works back into print, remains one of my proudest editorial accomplishments.

My professional involvement with Richard began in the fall of 1991, when his longtime agent, Don Congdon, submitted a brand-new Matheson novel, *7 Steps to Midnight*, to Bob Gleason, who was then Tor's editor-in-chief. As is usually the case, especially where overworked senior editors are concerned, Bob handed the manuscript over to a more junior editor for a preliminary read. (No disrespect to Matheson should be inferred here; this was simply standard procedure.) This associate editor, John Ordover, knew that I was a huge Matheson fan and suggested that I should take a look at it instead. Needless to say, I jumped at the chance.

To my delight, *7 Steps* turned out to be an engrossing, Hitchcockian thriller along the lines of *North by Northwest* and *The 39 Steps*. It also seemed to me that Matheson would be a distinguished addition to Tor's list, which already included such celebrated authors as Robert Bloch, Brian Lumley, and Andre Norton. Although the company has since branched out into other genres, Tor was built on science fiction, fantasy, and horror. Richard Matheson fit right in.

I enthusiastically recommended *7 Steps* to Bob Gleason, Tor acquired the book, and I soon found myself assigned as the editor on the project. Somewhere along the way, we also acquired the reprint rights to both *I Am Legend* and *The Shrinking Man*, which proved to be a shrewd move on Bob's part. (*Legend*, in particular, has been a remarkably strong seller over the years . . . and that's *before* the third movie version.)

At this point, it might be worthwhile to explain what exactly an editor does at a publishing house like Tor. Technically speaking, I've only actually edited three original novels by Richard, but an editor's job involves a lot more than just scribbling with a red pencil all over a pristine manuscript. An editor serves as the point person, chief advocate, and number-one cheerleader for the various books and authors under his or her purview. The editor works closely with the marketing department, the art department, the sales force, and publicity to make sure that each new book gets the tender loving care it deserves. In my case, that means preaching the gospel of Richard Matheson to anyone who will listen, while also keeping a close eye on any upcoming movie or television adaptations that Tor might be able to capitalize on. Editors also do their best to keep the author and his or her agent both informed and happy.

Fortunately, Richard has always been a pleasure to work with. In eighteen years, I can only think of one serious disagreement (regarding the title of one of his later books), and even then Richard was remarkably courteous and patient, despite his disappointment with the way things turned out. (More about that later.)

I confess, however, that I found the prospect of editing *7 Steps* somewhat intimidating. After all, Matheson was a living legend, who had been writing world-famous books, stories, and screenplays since before I was even born. Who was I to tinker with his prose and suggest the occasional rewrite?

Fortunately, *7 Steps* was in pretty good shape from day one. Despite a diabolically twisty plot, the whole thing held together ingeniously. In the end, I just asked Richard to clarify a couple of the more confusing plot points and passed the book on to production. Then it was time to go to work on the marketing. . . .

One of the most gratifying aspects of the *7 Steps* experience was the way Richard's peers and colleagues rallied to support the book, Richard's first in many years. I sent out advance copies of the manuscript to various big-name authors and soon found myself swimming in laudatory quotes from Ray Bradbury, Robert Bloch, Brian Lumley, Loren D. Estleman, Warren Murphy, and Ramsey Campbell. It says a lot about their high regard and affection for Richard that so many busy writers took time out of their schedules to write me notes about how much he had inspired them. (I never bothered to bug Stephen King for a quote, incidentally, because I already had a stack of interviews and articles in which King had generously praised Richard. "The author who influenced me the most as a writer was Richard Matheson," King once wrote, and how could I possibly ask for a better quote than that?)

A bibliographical note: 7 *Steps to Midnight* ended up being one of the very first books published under Tor's new Forge Books imprint. The reasoning behind the new imprint was simple: we had discovered that Tor was so associated with the best in science fiction, fantasy, and horror that it had become difficult to market, say, a spy novel or a historical romance under that label. No matter what we put on the cover, critics and booksellers just assumed it was sci-fi! Hence, the invention of Forge. Since 7 *Steps* was a straight thriller, with only minimal supernatural elements, it was exactly the sort of book for which Forge was devised.

7 *Steps* was only the beginning. Not long after, I received the manuscript for another new thriller by Richard, titled *Magician's Choice*. This eventually became the novel published as *Now You See It . . .* (the ellipsis is part of the title), but not until after a bit of a struggle on the part of everyone concerned.

*Magician's Choice* presented an intriguing challenge. The project had begun life as a theatrical production that never quite got off the ground. The story, which involved a retired stage magician's elaborate revenge on his enemies, took place in one afternoon, in a single setting, with a cast of only a few characters, none of whom was quite what they appeared to be. Disguises and deception were the order of the day.

The plot was ingenious and full of unexpected twists. Unfortunately, because of its theatrical origins, the original manuscript read more like a detailed treatment for a movie or stage play rather than a full-fledged novel. It was written in present tense, with descriptions that read like stage directions, and was told entirely from an omniscient point of view, as opposed to that of a central character. It was a fascinating story, but it needed to be fleshed out more to work as a novel. And by now I felt confident enough in my relationship with Richard to point this out.

The biggest problem was figuring out whose point of view to tell the story from. As it happened, every one of the characters in the original manuscript had some sort of hidden agenda or secret. There was no way to go inside any of these characters' heads without giving away a major twist or two.

Eventually, Richard, Bob Gleason, and I came together on a snowy night in Stamford, Connecticut, to wrestle with this dilemma. Richard was the guest of honor at the 1993 World Horror Convention, a blizzard was blowing outside, and the three of us sat in front of a hotel fireplace until well past midnight, throwing ideas at one another. Sixteen years later, I can't remember who finally came up with the idea of adding a new character to the mix, an innocent bystander who knew nothing of the various intrigues simmering beneath the surface. But Richard ultimately went back to California and retold the entire story from the point of view of a paralyzed stroke victim, forced to watch the deadly drama from the confinement of his wheelchair! Richard also retitled the book *Now You See It. . . .*

In the end, the book got stellar reviews and went through multiple printings in hardcover. Meanwhile, there have been periodic attempts to bring the theatrical version to the stage. Maybe one of these days. . . .

Beginning with *The Incredible Shrinking Man* and *I Am Legend,* Tor embarked on an ongoing program to bring Matheson's previous works back into print. We started out publishing them as mass-market paperbacks, but eventually discovered that it made more sense to issue them as quality trade paperbacks, which secured them a much longer shelf life. Not much actual editing was involved with these reprints, but a few interesting issues arose.

I'll take the rap for using the movie titles, as opposed to the original book titles, on the Tor editions of *The Incredible Shrinking Man* and *Somewhere in Time,* even though those books were initially published as

*The Shrinking Man* and *Bid Time Return*. Purists may cringe, but, to my mind, I was simply recognizing the reality that the movie titles are the ones everybody recognizes. Like it or not, most of the world remembers the Shrinking Man as Incredible. (I drew a line at publishing *I Am Legend* as *The Omega Man*, however. I do have *some* standards.)

The 1994 Tor edition of *Earthbound* was notable in that it was the first American publication of Matheson's preferred text for the book. An earlier version, published by Playboy Press in 1982, had been so severely edited that Matheson insisted it be issued under his pseudonym of Logan Swanson. Finally, after a dozen years, Richard got to put his own name on an *Earthbound* he could be proud of! The cover illustration for a new 2005 edition won a Silver Award in the prestigious Spectrum Awards for Fantastic Art.

Over the years, in fact, Tor's talented art department (headed first by Maria Melilli and later by Irene Gallo) has come up with a number of outstanding covers for our Matheson titles. I believe that Richard's favorite is the beautiful Michael Deas painting on the cover of *Hell House* (Tor, 1999). Me, I'm perversely proud of the horrific zombie-packed cover for our edition of *I Am Legend*, even though I know it's a bit too grisly for Richard's taste. We still get queries from foreign publishers wanting to use that artwork on their own translations of *Legend*. (None of which stopped me, of course, from slapping Will Smith's image on the movie tie-in edition.)

Speaking of movies, an opportunity arose when PolyGram started filming a big-budget screen version of *What Dreams May Come*. Although the original novel had been out of print for years at that point, Tor rapidly acquired the book rights from Don Congdon, then worked out a deal with the studio to use their poster art on a new paperback edition. To their credit, the movie folks were remarkably cooperative, which isn't always the case. (I could tell you stories. . . . ) The movie itself got a mixed reception, but it succeeded in at least one respect: the book sold extremely well, even hitting the lower reaches of the *New York Times* bestseller list. Which just goes to prove that a movie doesn't have to be a big hit to bring new readers to the original novel.

A similar scenario played out with the 1999 film adaptation of *A Stir of Echoes*. Tor again published a movie tie-in edition, albeit to more modest results. Alas, the movie version (which is worth checking out on DVD) had the bad luck to open a few weeks after the similarly themed *The Sixth Sense*, which proceeded to eat our lunch. Oh well. If nothing else, the movie inspired me to add the novel to our Matheson program, where it remains to this day.

I also got to attend the New York premiere of the movie, which was seriously cool. . . .

Another direct result of *What Dreams May Come* hitting the bestseller list was Tor's publication of *The Path*, a slim volume of metaphysical musings reflecting Richard's spiritual beliefs. I had passed on *The Path* when it was first offered to me. Although it was an interesting book, it didn't seem right for Tor, which mostly publishes commercial fiction. *The Path* struck me as better suited for a publisher that specialized in metaphysical-type books.

Then *What Dreams May Come* sold umpteen thousand copies. . . .

Suddenly, it occurred to me that, if ever there were a time to try publishing *The Path* to a mass audience, this was it. Thanks to the movie, there were hundreds of thousands of new readers out there who might be interested in learning more about Matheson's views on the afterlife. I called Don Congdon and told him that I had changed my mind about *The Path*. Was it possible that, pretty please, the book was still up for grabs?

Tor's edition of *The Path* never hit the *Times* bestseller list like *What Dreams May Come* did, but it's remained in print ever since.

The book that eventually became *Hunted Past Reason* took me by surprise. At that point, the double whammy of *7 Steps to Midnight* and *Now You See It . . .* was several years in the past and I had pretty much resigned myself to simply reprinting Matheson's older books from now on. As far as I knew, Richard was busy with various theatrical projects, including the much-delayed stage version of *Now You See It.* . . . Then a manuscript titled *To Live!* landed on my desk.

*To Live!* was a brutal suspense novel about a life-or-death chase through the California wilderness. Like *7 Steps*, it required very little editing. My only major suggestion involved a rather nasty rape scene near the end of the book. An earlier rape scene had served the legitimate purpose of establishing just how disturbed and dangerous the villain was, but this second rape struck me as unnecessary; we already knew the villain was bad news. At my request, Richard graciously agreed to tone down that final scene, allowing the hero's wife to narrowly escape being raped.

But with the book ready to go to press, there remained the issue of the title. This turned out to be a matter of some controversy. Richard has made no secret of the fact that he dislikes the title under which the book was ultimately published: *Hunted Past Reason.* I regret that he's unhappy with the title, but let me try to explain how this came about.

I'll admit that I never liked *To Live!* as a title. Among other things, I was concerned that the book might be mistaken for another spiritual guide like *The Path.* I also ran *To Live!* past some of my colleagues at Tor, just in case I was missing the boat somehow, but didn't encounter a great deal of enthusiasm from them for that title. This was a problem, since Tor wanted to make a big splash with this novel, Richard's first new book after years of reprints, and I really wanted to put our best face forward. Having a strong title to sell with was part of that.

Richard and I went back and forth for a while, but never managed to come up with a title we both liked. Finally, with catalog deadlines looming, I dived into *Bartlett's Book of Familiar Quotations* looking for an appropriate Shakespearean quote along the lines of *What Dreams May Come* or *Bid Time Return.* (Hey, if it worked before. . . . ) I quickly latched onto a quote from the sonnets:

Past reason hunted; and no sooner had,
Past reason hated, as a swallowed bait. . . .

Touching on the themes of hunting and madness, *Hunted Past Reason* seemed a good fit for the new novel. When I pitched the title to Richard over the phone, he seemed a bit bemused by the notion, but grudgingly agreed to go with *Hunted Past Reason*.

Problem solved, I thought.

In my defense, let me point out that Richard *did* agree to the title during that initial discussion. On the other hand, I obviously failed to appreciate just how reluctant he had been to do so. In retrospect, I wish that I had been a little more perceptive there. Who knows? Maybe we could have gone back to the drawing board one more time before settling on the final title.

Unfortunately, by the time I belatedly figured out just how much Richard truly hated the new title, *Hunted Past Reason* had acquired a life of its own. Catalogs and book jackets had been printed, orders had been solicited; any attempt to switch titles in midstream might have had a negative effect on sales. Frankly, everything was going so smoothly on the marketing front that I didn't want to do anything that might derail the book's momentum.

And that's how a terrific novel got stuck with a title that the author can't stand. Obviously, I wish things had turned out differently.

It's still a great book, though.

As of this writing, Tor has almost a dozen books by Richard Matheson in print, including three short-story collections and an omnibus volume containing three of Richard's early suspense novels. The recent movie tie-in editions of *I Am Legend*, featuring Will Smith on the cover, spent multiple weeks on the *New York Times* bestseller list, getting as high as number two; and the mass-market edition was the 72nd best-selling book in the country that year, according to *USA Today*.

Coming up next is a feature-film version of Richard's story "Button, Button," which is also the title story of our most recent collection. (No, that is not a coincidence. I put the new collection together the minute the movie was announced.) The title of the new movie, which stars Cameron Diaz and James Marsden, remains undetermined, but I'll definitely have a movie tie-in edition of the collection out in time for the film, which is tentatively scheduled for winter 2009. Movie versions of other Matheson books and stories are also in the works, which may inspire more publications in the future. In addition, Forge will be reprinting four of Richard's western novels, beginning with *Journal of the Gun Years* in spring 2009.

Could another unexpected new manuscript show up in the mail? Well, you'll have to ask Richard about that. I can only hope.

In the meantime, I derive great satisfaction from the fact that one can now wander into any large bookstore and find an impressive selection of Richard Matheson books on sale. Classics like *I Am Legend* and *Hell House* deserve to be available to the largest possible audience, and I'm proud that Tor/Forge has played a part in making this happen.

It's been a great eighteen years.

1943

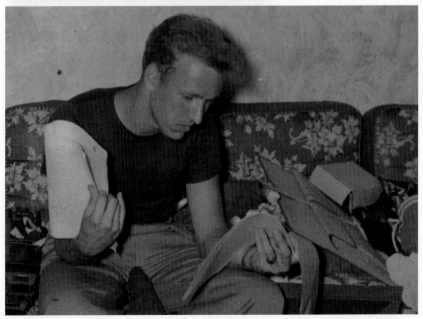

"1950. Taken in Brooklyn, N.Y., after I graduated from the University of Missouri with a Bachelor of Journalism degree."

"1951. Taken in Bay
Shore, Long Island,
N.Y., shortly before I
left for California."

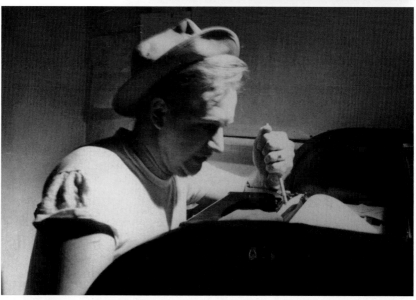

"'Work' shot—1954. Bay Shore, Long Island apartment. Maybe starting
*The Shrinking Man*."

"1954. The house we lived in in Sound Beach on Long Island, N.Y. In the cellar of this house, I wrote *The Shrinking Man*, my novel."

"Disneyland, 1957."

"1960. With wife Ruth, daughter Tina, son Richard and [producer] Jim Nicholson on the set of *Master of the World*."

"1972. I am given an award by the Count Dracula Society. My wife [Ruth], Forry Ackerman, and me." (Forrest J. Ackerman is the legendary editor of *Famous Monsters of Filmland*.)

"Early or mid-1980s Academy gathering during which *Burn, Witch, Burn* and *The Incredible Shrinking Man* were honored. With Jack Arnold, Janet Blair, and George Pal's widow." (Arnold directed *The Incredible Shrinking Man*; Blair starred in *Burn, Witch, Burn*; Pal was a famed SF/fantasy filmmaker.)

"Somewhere in the 1980s. Forry Ackerman and I posing for a silly photo."

"Taken in Paris [with son Richard Christian Matheson]—1990s."

"1993 (or thereabouts). Taken at the Academy of Motion Picture Arts and Sciences. My wife [Ruth], Vincent Price, and me, chatting." (Price starred in seven of Matheson's films.)

2005. Matheson chats with Roger Corman at the book release party for *Woman*. Corman directed four of Matheson's films. (Photo courtesy Paul Stuve)

2005. Richard Matheson and family at the book release party for *Woman*. (Photo courtesy Paul Stuve)

# Richard Matheson: A Living Legend

*Brian Lumley*

With regard to the title of this piece: I really don't know if there's any
such rank or position among the horror writer hierarchy. I am aware of
a list of so-called Grand Masters because I myself was knocked out, left
literally speechless at the 8th World Horror Convention in Phoenix,
Arizona, when my name was added to the list. But as for "Living Legends," well—

—I feel I can definitely state that if there was such an honor, it would
be long overdue in the case of Richard Matheson. How else may we
consider an author working in horror fiction (among many other genres)
who Stephen King has credited as being his biggest influence when he,
King, was coming up? Only as a Living Legend, surely. And years before I knew of Stephen King's regard for Matheson's work—indeed long
before I wrote my own first story—I was very much in awe of this same
man's talent. I knew that when I bought a book by Richard Matheson,
I was going to be entertained—totally immersed, in whichever of his
worlds—from the first word of the very first sentence to the last. Only
one other living author of fantastic fiction has the power to affect me that
way, and that's Jack Vance. Vance's and Matheson's styles are as different
as chalk and cheese, but to my mind they are both on a level so high that
it's almost inaccessible to the great majority of their contemporaries.

And so it's not difficult to imagine how delighted I was in 1992,
and how honored, to be acting as toastmaster at the 2nd World Horror
Convention in Nashville, Tennessee, where Richard Matheson was the
guest of honor, and to be called upon to introduce him (as if Mathe-

son needed an introduction) to a most appreciative opening-ceremonies audience. I recall announcing (as if it were necessary, since he was the main attraction for most of those people) to the crowded ballroom that the convention's principal guest was "the man who wrote *I Am Legend*," and that it was "now my pleasure to welcome to the podium the literally legendary Richard Matheson . . ."

And what do you know. Before he'd even reached the microphone or said a word, the man was receiving a standing ovation from a crowd made up of people who were at least as much Matheson fans as I was; and you can believe me when I say that like with most conventions of that sort, there were plenty of well-established professionals among them.

And so was I well established; at that time, the first five books in my *Necroscope®* series were still flying off the bookstore shelves. But standing there beside Richard Matheson I felt just like a fan! Because I could remember what it was like when I was coming up, and how much I had enjoyed his work. . . .

I didn't get a foot on the literary ladder, didn't begin writing and selling my own stories, until 1967–68 when I was only halfway through a twenty-two-year military career. So maybe I can be excused when I admit that in those early days when I was new to the game I had failed to connect the author of *I Am Legend* with something else that had left a vivid impression on my mind when I was even younger. It wasn't a novel that time, but a movie, a sci-fi fantasy/horror of miniaturization that predated *Fantastic Voyage* and, to my mind, was far superior despite it being filmed in black and white. (At least that's how I remember it, not having seen it for far too many years now. So if in fact it was in color, just put it down to the fact that it's so stark, so sharply etched in my mind's eye that I see it only in monochrome.) I'm talking about *The Incredible Shrinking Man*, of course, after the novel *The Shrinking Man* by who else but Richard Matheson. How I loved that movie—but God, if only it had been scripted more closely to the novel, to the way it had been written!

And since I'm on this movie kick, I may as well mention one more of my infamous failures to connect. Just a day or so ago, when I told my movie-buff American wife that I was about to be writing a brief appreciation of Richard Matheson, she said, "Well, don't forget to talk about *Somewhere in Time*," one of her all-time favorite movies. What? *Somewhere in Time* was a Matheson? Had I seen it? No, I hadn't seen it . . . probably because I had failed to connect its title with that of the original book, *Bid Time Return.* . . .

Damn! So now that one's gone to the top of my list of must-see movies—and I can't wait.

There is just one more thing that I really must say, which I don't think anyone else is going to duplicate. You see, I've always had this warm spot for vampires. No, not the "real thing" (if there ever was any such thing as a vampire), but the fictional fiend, of course. And Richard Matheson's *I Am Legend* had put me off having a go at my own blood-sucking novels, the long-running *Necroscope®* series, for twenty years or more! I mean, I had always known something of what I wanted to do—I had an idea of how my story should go—but in the back of my mind, there was this book by Matheson which I knew I could never equal or get close to. And so, because I seemed to have a knack for Lovecraftian "Cthulhu Mythos" stories, I had written those instead. It was only after I left the army on completion of my twenty-two years—only then, with a handful of books behind me, when I had decided to try and make a living at this writing business—that I felt confident or even competent enough to try my hand at writing in-depth vampire stories.

So really I suppose I should thank Richard Matheson that it was mainly his marvelous novel that caused me to bide my time and wait until I'd honed my craft a little before attempting to write my own version of the vampire myth. And three books into that saga, after I'd found a measure of success, at the end of *Necroscope III: The Source*, finally I had found a way to insert a small homage to the novel which had both inspired and frustrated me. It's the scene where a naked, lustful vamp, the so-called "Lady" Karen, tries to seduce the man who is bent on her destruction, the Necroscope Harry Keogh. And at that point any reader who had also read *I Am Legend* would have known precisely where I was coming from.

It had of course dawned on me by then that pretty much the same thing had happened in Bram Stoker's *Dracula*, and that the selfsame scene had been reprised in (probably) every other vampire novel and movie ever since. Well, that may be true—but it was Matheson's version that lodged itself permanently in my mind.

I have written elsewhere that I can trace my interest in vampires back to E.C. Comics, *Weird Tales*, Christopher Lee, and Richard Matheson, "whose stories in this sub-genre really bit me." All of which is factual—but I reckon it's Matheson who has the biggest stake in this claim . . .

Somewhere in this article's early paragraphs, I've said that in Richard Matheson's presence I felt just like any other fan. And why not? After all—and despite that no such title exists among the horror writer community—Matheson most certainly is a living legend, and I'm just one of a great many fans . . .

# Some Notes on Working with Richard Matheson

## Harry O. Morris
### (with assistance from Christine Morris)

There are certain episodes in most every person's life which stand out—which, in looking back, can even be seen as monumental. One such turning point for me happened when Barry Hoffman of Gauntlet Press offered me the chance to do the cover for Richard Matheson's seven-hundred-page novel, *Hunger and Thirst*. I was alternately elated and terrified. Both of these emotions were due largely to the stature of the writer in question—in two words: unquestionably legendary. I'd had the pleasure of meeting Mr. Matheson and his lovely wife, Ruth, through their son, Richard Christian Matheson. The author of such classics as *I Am Legend*, *What Dreams May Come*, and *The Shrinking Man* seemed human enough—very cordial and charming, actually. Nevertheless, I felt out of my league with the prospect of working with him (Barry Hoffman encourages writer and artist to work together), providing I was able to come up with something he liked to begin with.

The dustjacket blurb for *Hunger and Thirst* provides a concise description of the story:

> Erick Linstrom, paralyzed, lies helpless in his furnished room
> in New York City. As days go by, faced by probable death
> from hunger or thirst, he re-lives his past, recalling the varied
> experiences which brought him to his frightening state.

According to notes I've kept, I mailed Mr. Matheson the piece I came up with on March 7, 2000, and he called me a few days later saying that he liked the picture in general, but there were a few changes he'd like to see. These changes expanded my initial effort, which showed mainly the protagonist against a New York City skyline, to include other scenes that Erick revisits. Here are some of my hastily scribbled notes from that phone conversation:

- *Main front cover—O.K.—suggest subway entrance bottom right (more skyline top?)*
- *Back cover—not so much brick*
- *Replace far left wall with window looking out on NYC*
- *Suggest figure looking out the window (even just a hand on a bed)*
- *Replace army men with couple hand in hand—symbolic of Erick & Sally on campus*

It goes without saying that I was elated on hanging up the phone, because the picture had been accepted as a promising starting point, and glad that if there were changes to be made, they were very specific and clearly defined. An aside—Richard most always knows what he wants in the picture and doesn't have any trouble describing it, unlike some art directors who suggest that "something" about the picture be changed, but cannot describe what they have in mind. I was anxious to get started on the revision.

To make a long story short, these changes led to others, and after four or five mailings and phone calls, we had it nailed—the piece was accepted on April 27, 2000. Richard even paid the piece the ultimate compliment by requesting that the title and his name not appear on the cover, to give more room to the image. This was an unusual and self-assured move on his part, considering the egos and marketing in the field. Happily, Barry was likewise brave and took the chance of leaving the title and author off the cover. The fact that the book was for a specialty market helped make such a dramatic move possible. (Later, Richard Chizmar of Cemetery Dance Publications did the same for Matheson's *Camp Pleasant*, another cover that I'd done at the author's request.)

Working together during the course of *Hunger and Thirst*, there were times when the revision work could be challenging, to greater or lesser degrees. Most often, Richard's observations helped me remove extraneous elements from the compositions. On rare occasions, Richard would see something in the picture that I didn't put there consciously, and would request an explanation. One I remember most clearly was his seeing a witch inside the window-room where the protagonist, Erick, was lying in bed. One other person has reported seeing the witch, even after I had retouched out what I thought was the mysterious sorceress. To be fair, many people have told me that they see things in the more abstract portions of my pictures—chalk it up to Leonardo's old paranoiac wall. (An aside—the Paris surrealists of the 1920s would later celebrate this spit-covered wall and populate their paintings of distant vistas with fighting demons, witches, and other monsters from the hallucinatory realms of the unconscious.)

Back to the present. Whatever trials and tribulations I had in making this picture and others for Richard Matheson, I now get down on my knees and thank whatever art spirits are out there—and Mr. Matheson, for polishing the mirror, allowing the picture to reflect his story and words so much more clearly. I can honestly say that the *Hunger and Thirst* cover is one of the accomplishments I'm most proud of.

Richard requested that I mention that the portrait displayed on the cover of Gauntlet's limited edition of this book—*The Richard Matheson Companion*—is not a straight photograph. It did start off as a standard black-and-white publicity photograph, but I like to think that, as the author believes, it has gained another dimension—somewhere closer to the soul—through computer manipulation and psychic automatism. I thought it would be a good idea to incorporate some of the author's printed words within the portrait, as this approach was effective on covers for three volumes of *Richard Matheson: Collected Stories* from Gauntlet's Edge Books. Richard Christian saw the portrait at this point and suggested using titles from his dad's most recognized novels. This turned out to be the perfect touch, blending the man and his work together on the same plane.

Other interesting cover anecdotes I might mention are:

For *Duel & The Distributor* (Gauntlet Press, 2004), Richard requested that I put a driver at the wheel of the semi for the cover (which illustrated *Duel*), after seeing the first version, which had no driver. He explained that he intended a human presence to be responsible for the harrowing events, not a supernatural machine. On the endpaper, which illustrated *The Distributor*, he suggested that the moving van be placed in a more pleasant neighborhood, after I presented him with a version he described to me as looking like "the House of Usher." The early version was photographed around my own neighborhood. I quickly found a more upscale area for the final version! I understood the concept of the story, but didn't make it clear at first. This lesson in clarity is one of many I've learned from Richard. I won't comment on all of the covers I've done so far for books by Richard Matheson, but do want to mention that the most recent one, *The Link*, went smoothly, without any revisions. Ah, we were connected.

Whenever someone new I've been introduced to asks me, "What authors have you done covers for?" Richard Matheson is usually the first name I reply with. I must admit that this is sometimes met with a blank look (the same would probably apply if I'd said Charles Beaumont or Shirley Jackson). At this point, I usually continue by describing Dennis Weaver being pursued cross-country by that unrelenting eighteen-wheeler, and this almost always evokes a response of "Oh, yeah—I remember that!" Then I mention the *Twilight Zone* episodes and some of the better-known novels and screenplay adaptations, and most everyone's face brightens up with renewed memories and awareness. I feel privileged to consider myself a friend of this writer who has made such a lasting mark on the collective consciousness of an entire culture.

# A Speech by
# Richard Christian Matheson

*Delivered at the Peninsula Hotel,*
*Los Angeles, June 25, 2005*
*(for the release party of*
*Richard Matheson's novel* Woman)

Good evening. I'm Richard Christian Matheson and, on behalf of my family and Gauntlet Press, I'd like to welcome you to the beautiful Peninsula Hotel and the debut of *Woman*, the controversial new novel written by my father, Richard Matheson. It's an honor to have you all here.

Tonight we are joined by old friends, new friends, directors, novelists, actors, producers, journalists, and many who have worked with my father on various projects. We all know how remarkable he is—but I'd like to brag about him a bit because he's too modest and you'll never hear it from him.

I guess you could say he started young, since he wrote his first novel, *The Years Stood Still*, when he was fourteen. Its story involved international intrigue and romance, and centered on a young woman who fell down a flight of stairs, hit her head violently, and never aged. The book included, among other precocious subplots, the Zulu uprisings in Africa, the blitz during turn of the century England, a plague which broke out on a commercial steamship in London Harbor, and an intrepid hero who works as a policeman in Johannesburg.

And *that* was chapter one. He was off to quite a start.

With his usual modest aplomb, he moved to short stories and, from the start, was the envy of any writer who ever rubbed a noun against a verb and tried to make fire.

With a tightrope style that blended hypnotic anarchy and exquisite formalism, his stories were miniature worlds of dread, hope, and paradox that took your breath away. Like ships in a bottle, they were delicately assembled, precise, and *impossibly* cool.

His prose and ideas consistently broke rules, blurred past speed limits—made it all look easy. His rhythms were pure seduction: acrobatic, eloquent, deceptively minimalist.

The work used language and ideas like they were freeform jazz and, with fellow players who burned just as white-hot, they tore down the joint: Ray Bradbury, Charles Beaumont, Theodore Sturgeon, to name a few. They were gunslingers of the surreal and the English language didn't know what hit it when they blew into town.

And my father could do it all. Whether writing science fiction, horror, or fantasy, he was a swaying cobra.

Inevitably, he concentrated on novels and, to no one's surprise, except likely his, they became watermarks; tours de force of elegance and sheer nerve.

And without any plan to do so, along the way, he reinvented modern horror.

His pragmatic, suburbanized reexaminations of terror brought it into the subdivisions of Southern California where, in his novels, dark intentions dwelled behind manicured lawns, in stucco haunted houses. In these cul-de-sac purgatories, friendly neighbors had sociopathic, even, at times, monstrous agendas and the reassuring rules of neighborly etiquette and even physics protected none.

With his uncanny talent for weaving original ideas into modern myth, Hollywood began to notice him in a big way. He wrote countless scripts for TV and movies, each a lucent study of magic and/or edge, his alchemy soaring in these new venues. *The Twilight Zone, The Legend of Hell House, Duel, The Night Stalker, Somewhere in Time*—it's a long list.

Because he always understood that life and death were codependent, not just in the narrative of horror, but in cycles of the soul, his creative path grew deeper and his need to explore divine meanings, yet to come, drew him no longer toward matters of the occult or paranormal—but of the spirit. He immersed himself and became a self-taught scholar of the soul's journey into afterlife.

I prefer to call him a *metaphysical astronaut.*

Now, he's added playwriting to his dizzying résumé and, along the way, also wrote a few western novels. FYI: his very first one, *Journal of the Gun Years*, was nominated by the Western Writers of America as best novel of the year.

It won.

One of my favorite photos of my father is when he was a teenager, seated happily in a rowboat that's dry-docked in a meadow of flowers. He's in a straw hat, gripping the two oars and drifting through the daffodil sea, as if rowing through his own subconscious, into a perfect dream.

In five decades, he's staked vampires, exterminated haunted houses, introduced us to the seersuckered madness of Carl Kolchak, explained Captain Kirk's really bad moods, pissed off a ton of truck drivers, time traveled to find perfect love, and safaried into hell itself. He has allowed us to see the wondrous contradictions of this life and peer into the mystic precincts of what comes next.

He's always been the rarified summit where only the hip and fearless dwell. Imagine dreaming up brilliant ideas for decades, writing them so well they became classics. Imagine remaining true to your art and your vision, undaunted by trend or fortune. My father has gone one further. He still does it.

With pristine economy, impassioned audacity, and no fear of heights, he has given imagination and us a run for our money for over sixty years.

He is what used to be called a sorcerer. Now they say of such writers, *they remind me of Richard Matheson.*

He grew up in Brooklyn, the introspective son of Norwegian immigrants. And with his singular talent leading the way, he's become one of the most daring authors of our time.

He's a sinister poet, perceptive cynic, hopeless romantic, and humble maestro.

And on a personal note: he's also the best father a son could dream of having.

Please join me in a round of applause for Richard Matheson.

# Richard Matheson–A Subjective Assessment

*Ed Gorman*

Mention Richard Matheson and the conversation shifts quickly to *I Am Legend* and *The Shrinking Man* and "Duel." And rightly so. Each is a true masterpiece.

But there are moments in each of these pieces that get overlooked, and one example is in *The Shrinking Man*.

*Shrinking* is invariably and deservedly praised for its action set-pieces, especially the extended scene with Scott Carey battling the black widow spider. But I'll tell you, for me the most difficult scene to write may well have been when Carey, now forty-nine inches tall, attempts to make love to his wife. Because what you have here, friends and neighbors, is a dirty joke. Think about the kind of bar patter this situation would inspire in any other hands. *Seinfeld*'s George and his "shrinkage" problem (yes, ladies, they really do shrink when we've been in cold water) was nothing compared to what Carey experiences. But Matheson makes this one of the most tender, emotionally compelling scenes in the book. It could have been lurid and freakish, and yet it defines Carey's love for his wife, Louise, in a way no other scene in the book quite matches.

If you don't believe me, try writing it yourself.

But where Matheson is concerned, it isn't just moments that get overlooked, it's entire books.

So I'd like to remind you of some of Matheson's lesser-known books that, on reading, deserve full mention in any listing of his important works.

*Earthbound* is usually dismissed as minor Matheson, and I've never quite been able to figure out why. The best-selling author Stuart Woods did a book called *Under the Lake* that used many of the same tropes and tricks. He didn't copy the Matheson book—he may not have even read it—but he did show us how *not* to write a novel about being possessed by gorgeous erotic supernatural women (though, to be fair, there are some nice long stretches of writing in it). Matheson takes what is essentially the material of another dirty joke—humping lady spooks—and turns it into a serious and moving look at a marriage that is beginning to fail, and a man who has begun to question some of his key values. The use of barren winter seashore images to contrast with the heat of the ghost is remarkable, as is the sorrow of the wife who can't understand—or quite face—what her husband is going through. It's one hell of a good, solid, eerie read. This is one of the few supernatural stories I've ever found believable, by the way.

*Shadow on the Sun*—Here's one for you, a horror-western, the only good horror-western I've ever read/seen/heard of, in fact. This was originally a screenplay but it adapted just fine, thank you, to prose. Would've made a really nice TV movie back when the networks were pushing that long-lost breed of cat (I don't count all those current Sunday- and Monday-night weepies as TV movies—they're just long-form soap-opera installments). This would also make an especially fine graphic novel, should anybody be interested. Here, atmosphere and plot trump character, though Matheson gives us some really nice glimpses into some really not nice people. His mixture of Indian supernatural lore with the spur-jingling realism of traditional western tropes works very very well.

*The Beardless Warriors* is another one of those Matheson novels that disappeared for decades after a successful first appearance. This is likely one of his three or four most accomplished novels for two reasons—it is (for me, anyway) his most ambitious in terms of the writing problems he sets for himself. The first difficulty is to shape a fast-paced drama about a group of young draftees coherently. A group, mind you; the challenge is to present a group but make them each individual enough to be re-membered as separate people. Second, this is no simple drama. He must describe a war, Pvt. Everett Hackermeyer's place in that war, and the young man's reaction to the numerous small dramas all around him. I love this book, and I generally hate war novels. But Matheson plays the entire symphony here—action, tragedy, poignance, humor, the lore of epic battle, and a stunning portrait of a young man's feelings about the requirements of war. No John Wayne crapola here. This is much more in the mode of Samuel Fuller's *The Steel Helmet*, reporting the tedium and terror and ambivalence of young soldiers in battle. I can't overestimate the grace and power of this novel. (This is one of the many recent reissues in handsome trade paperbacks from Tor/Forge.)

*What Dreams May Come*—My wife, Carole, read this shortly after she was diagnosed with multiple sclerosis. (Not to worry; she's symptom-free now.) The book changed her life, as she always tells people when urging them to read it. She found in it elegance and beauty, the kind of spirituality she'd never been able to find in churches, a sense of spiritual well-being unfettered by dogma or doctrine. While my reaction was less dramatic, I was struck by how similar my own vague religious feelings are to Matheson's. This is the ultimate love story, of a husband who seeks, and ultimately saves, his wife even though he has died and exists on another plane of reality. I'm not drawn to novels of spirituality, but this one works as both a spellbinding fantasy and a serious speculation about life after death.

*Bid Time Return*—In gentler times, there was a fine fantasy writer by the name of Robert Nathan. His most famous book was *Portrait of Jennie*, which is one of the finest romances I've ever read. Then came Jack Finney who, after scaring the hell out of us with *The Body Snatchers*, spent the second part of his considerable career reimagining his beloved town of Galesburg, Illinois, in two excellent historical novels. I'd say that Matheson, in *Bid Time Return*, demonstrates that he is their equal in matters of time travel mixed with romance. What an enormous accomplishment this novel is—a quicksilver story of a man and woman of different centuries who not only fall in love, but also transcend the problems of time. It's hard to imagine any kind of reader not liking this book. The word "fetching" could have been created to describe it.

*Richard Matheson's Kolchak Scripts*—Gauntlet Publications is in the midst of a major Matheson publishing and republishing program. That excellent journalist and reporter Mark Dawidziak has put all three Kolchak scripts (the third being a collaboration between Matheson and William F. Nolan), plus extensive—and excellent—essays on the entire Kolchak saga, into a huge volume that is certainly the definitive book on the subject. If *Psycho* forever changed suspense movies and novels, the first Kolchak movie, *The Night Stalker*, forever changed horror movies and novels. Yes, there had been gritty newsroom horror films before; and yes, there had been wry, even comic horror flicks before. But using Jeff Rice's clever novel as a basis, Matheson brought his own shrewd take to this new form. Instead of using humor as farce or slapstick, he used it to make the realistic elements all the darker and more believable. I just watched it again, and it's as fresh, sassy, and spooky as it was three decades ago. It's a gloriously lurid and nasty piece of work, glitz played off just the right amount of gore, a true classic.

Chris Carter has always said that *The X-Files* was directly inspired by *The Night Stalker*, and when you think about it, it sure was. What is odd is that *X-Files* was imitative in many ways, but there were few *Night Stalker* homages (as we call them in the land of litigation). Maybe this is because the duo of Matheson and Darren McGavin, who played Kolchak, brought a unique insolence to the respective parts they played. In places, *The Night Stalker* teetered right on the brink of parody, both in the writing and in McGavin's acting. But it never crossed the line, remaining mostly dark and surprisingly realistic, because Matheson gave the whole journalistic angle the world-weariness (if not cynicism) one finds in most real newsrooms.

Gauntlet also published Matheson's award-winning and beloved children's book *Abu and the 7 Marvels*, a bracing adventure that your kids and grandkids will love (mine sure do). You've got your princess, you've got your hero, you've got your wizard, and you've got your quest. You might think you know what Matheson does with these familiar elements, but you'd be wrong. Matheson never gives us same old, same old. Never.

*Camp Pleasant*—Cemetery Dance Publications is another small press that has produced several beautifully made and important books by Matheson. *Camp Pleasant* is a superior short novel about a summer camp that is turned into a concentration camp of sorts by the man who runs it. The writing here is outstanding Matheson, outright poetic in places, mixing humor and terror as the bully intimidates virtually everybody in the camp. This is a real page-turner with plenty of suspense, but best of all there is Matheson's compassion for the weak who must suffer at the hands of the ruthless. A fine, quiet addition to the Matheson library.

And now the crime stories that have become widely available again, thanks to the Tor collection, *Noir: Three Novels of Suspense.*

The year is 1953. Family values besiege the surface lives of Americans. As do the Cold War and Mr. Joseph McCarthy. Bishop Sheen is a network prime-time winner. Richard Nixon is sharpening his knives.

Of course, beneath the surface, things aren't quite as tranquil as Ozzie and Harriet would have you believe. Chuck Berry makes his first record. Allen Ginsberg begins publishing poetry. Bettie Page is an underground success. Marijuana spreads across the United States. White teens begin listening to "race" music. And in New York City, a small paperback house called Lion Books begins to publish Jim Thompson, David Goodis, David Karp, and some new guy named Richard Matheson.

Now, if I told you that Matheson opened up his suspense novel *Fury on Sunday* with a scene more shocking than any rendered by Thompson or Goodis—well, it would be true. *Fury on Sunday* opens with a brutal homosexual scene in which one of the participants is murdered. In 1953.

*Fury on Sunday* portrays concert pianist Vincent as he escapes from a mental hospital after letting a sadistic guard have sex with him. And then murdering the guard. Vincent is on a murder streak with one aim, to find his lost love, who he believes still loves him—even though she's married to a man she deeply loves. This all ends in a vicious and bloody confrontation in a Manhattan apartment, where the wily Vincent has arranged to lure his true love's husband. The wife comes along soon after.

*Fury* followed Matheson's first published novel, *Someone Is Bleeding,* that same year. *Someone Is Bleeding* is the story of a struggling writer in Los Angeles who meets a fetching but strange and very secretive girl at the beach one day, and falls obsessively in love with her. The book anticipates by many years the subgenre of the mysterious girl who may or may not be a killer. It outdoes Mickey Spillane in that Matheson pays it off brilliantly in the very last line.

*Ride the Nightmare* concerns a man with a past—in this case, a man who went straight, and whose life and family are now threatened by the appearance of his old hoodlum friends. This is one of the most brilliantly structured suspense novels I've ever read. It should have won an Edgar Award for best paperback original. Nothing else that year came close.

It's been said that most of Matheson's stories concern a man fighting against a much greater force than himself. And while that's certainly true in such masterpieces as *I Am Legend, The Shrinking Man*, and "Duel," in these noirs we have a man struggling to save not just himself but his loved ones as well.

Each of these books is about love—the twisted love of Vincent for the married woman he imagines loves him; the love the young writer feels for the strange woman he wants to marry; and the love of the man whose past threatens his entire family. Here we see the Matheson protagonist as not simply warrior but protector, and I think this adds an interesting dimension to each book.

The strongest of the novels, for me, is *Ride the Nightmare*. This is one of the novels I recommend to people who say they want to try a suspense story. It is relentless in its traps and tension. Edge-of-the-seat all the way. Published in 1959, it also represents the mature Matheson, with *I Am Legend* and *The Shrinking Man* and so many classic stories behind him at this point.

This omnibus edition of three novels should be a staple in any serious Matheson collection. Each book offers rich pleasures. Each book shows different aspects of the Matheson talent. And each book demonstrates why, at least for me, Richard Matheson is the best storyteller and artist of his generation.

# The Incredible Scripting Man: Richard Matheson Reflects on His Screen Career

*Matthew R. Bradley*

Richard Matheson was a critically acclaimed but financially struggling author with a job cutting out airplane parts at Douglas Aircraft when he returned to the East Coast, where he had been born and raised, and rented a house on Long Island to write his fourth novel, *The Shrinking Man* (1956). The sale of the film rights to what was then Universal-International not only enabled him to settle permanently in the Los Angeles area, to which he had first moved from Brooklyn in 1951, and support his growing family as a full-time writer, but also began his successful screenwriting career, because the book was sold on the condition that he be allowed to adapt it. "I think that was the only way you *could* do it unless you got hired, through some means that I was never privy to, as a contract writer. I had a friend named William R. Cox, who was a western writer, and when I joined a group out here called The Fictioneers in 1951, he was working at Universal. He was making like $375 a week, you know, doing any kind of assignment—we just thought he was like a god, with the kind of position he had."

While producer Albert Zugsmith added the adjective to the title, and the studio insisted on scrapping the novel's intricate flashback structure, Jack Arnold's *The Incredible Shrinking Man* (1957) is otherwise quite faithful to the novel. Embodying Cold War–era anxieties and the paranoia that is Matheson's frequent theme, it depicts the plight of Scott Carey (played by Grant Williams), an ordinary man trapped in his own cellar after a chance combination of insecticide and a radioactive mist causes his body to dwindle down to mere inches. "Jack did a wonderful job. . . . Richard Alan Simmons did a revision and then I—I thought at the time brilliantly—prepared my argument against [Simmons] having any kind of credit. Years later, getting to know him a little better, I think he just was nice to me and backed off, and said, 'Yeah, let him have his own credit.' He did a number of major scenes in it, like the paint can scene and everything, that was all his. I mean it was still pretty much the same story, it was just altering one scene, one setup for another." An enduring classic, the film won the Hugo Award for Best Dramatic Presentation.

After writing *The Incredible Shrinking Man*, Matheson was hired to expand his short story "Shipshape Home" into a feature film. While his screenplay was never shot, an earlier version had been produced as a 1955 episode of *Studio 57*, an anthology series sponsored by Heinz 57 Varieties that aired briefly on the short-lived DuMont network before being syndicated. Adapted by veteran screenwriter Lawrence Kimble, "Young Couples Only" is almost certainly the very first Matheson dramatization of any kind, featuring Barbara Hale (*Perry Mason*'s Della Street) and her real-life husband, Bill Williams, as the residents of a suspiciously affordable apartment building, part of an entire city block that turns out to be a gigantic disguised spaceship. Their sinister janitor, who has a third eye in the back of his head, has been collecting "perfect physical specimens" that he then whisks unwillingly off into space. In an inspired bit of casting, Peter Lorre (to whom the janitor is compared in the original), who would later appear in three of Matheson's movies, played the part.

Around this time (c. 1958–60), Matheson also wrote "Thy Will Be Done," the unaired pilot episode for another anthology show entitled *Now Is Tomorrow*. "I think they just did the one pilot," Matheson recalled. "It was supposed to be about what happens in the near future, various stories. I don't know whether they had any kind of series bible or anything." Directed by Irvin Kershner, best known for such sequels as *The Empire Strikes Back* (1980) and *RoboCop 2* (1990), the pilot has been cited by Matheson as a rare case in which his script was filmed exactly as he envisioned it. "I don't blame [Kershner], he did a good job," he said after seeing it again for the first time in forty years. "I think the script just wasn't as good as I remembered it." Robert Culp and future Oscar-winning producer-director Sydney Pollack played characters who were part of a group of military officers gradually unhinged by the heavy responsibility of their daily two-hour watch, in which each man must be prepared to launch atomic missiles against "the enemy" at any moment.

Matheson had better luck with more established series and genres, often working with Charles Beaumont, who was at the center of a close-knit circle of fellow fantasy writers, many of them accomplished authors also breaking into film and television at that time: Robert Bloch, Ray Bradbury, Harlan Ellison, George Clayton Johnson, William F. Nolan, Ray Russell, and Jerry Sohl. "We were very close friends," he said of Beaumont. "When we joined this agency [Adams, Ray, and Rosenberg], it was such a strange new world out there that we decided to work together. We collaborated on a lot of different shows. . . . We knew each other, our families knew each other, our kids knew each other." Alone or with Beaumont, Matheson received story and/or script credit on episodes of detective series such as *The D.A.'s Man* ("Iron Mike Benedict"), *Markham* ("The Marble Face," which they apparently drafted as "Spirit Unwilling"), and *Bourbon Street Beat* ("Target of Hate"); no information is available on Matheson's work, with or without Beaumont, on the series *Philip Marlowe* or *Richard Diamond, Private Detective*.

He also found fertile ground in the westerns then dominating the airwaves, sharing credit with Beaumont on episodes of *Buckskin* ("Act of Faith"), *Wanted: Dead or Alive* ("The Healing Woman"), and *Have Gun—Will Travel* ("The Joust" [apparently unfilmed] and "The Lady on the Wall"), as well as writing a solo script for *Cheyenne* ("Home Is the Brave") and six scripts for *Lawman*. Matheson contributed more teleplays to the latter than to any series except *The Twilight Zone*, due to an unusually harmonious relationship with producer Jules Schermer, who ensured that his work was left unchanged. They were directed by the likes of Hollywood veteran Stuart Heisler, including "Yawkey," for which Matheson earned his first Writers Guild of America Award, and "Samson the Great." He adapted "Thirty Minutes" and "Cornered" from "Of Death and Thirty Minutes" and "Little Jack Cornered," respectively, hitherto unsold stories later published in his collection *By the Gun* (1993). Actor Marc Lawrence directed "Cornered," and then guest-starred in "Homecoming," while "The Actor" offered John Carradine a plum role, appearing in his first of three Matheson teleplays.

Matheson continued his association with Albert Zugsmith, but most of the material he wrote for the producer remained unfilmed, including *Adam and Eve* (filmed as *The Private Lives of Adam and Eve* in 1961 from a script by another writer) and two adaptations of *Gulliver's Travels*, one of which was to have reunited David Niven and Cantinflas from *Around the World in 80 Days* (1956). A proposed sequel to *The Incredible Shrinking Man*, originally entitled *The Fantastic Shrinking Girl* (with the adjective again added by Zugsmith), *The Fantastic Little Girl* would have followed Carey's wife on a similar odyssey into their cellar, utilizing some of the oversized sets and props left over from the original; the screenplay was published in Matheson's collection *Unrealized Dreams* (2005). Their only other effort to reach fruition, *The Beat Generation* (1959), had less in common with *The Incredible Shrinking Man* than with Jack Arnold and Albert Zugsmith's juvenile delinquent classic *High School Confidential!* (1958), whose eclectic cast included Mamie Van Doren, her sometime husband, bandleader (and *Shrinking Man* trumpet soloist) Ray Anthony, and former child star Jackie Coogan.

All three appeared in *The Beat Generation*, which was inspired by a true-crime article in *Cosmopolitan* about a serial rapist (played by Ray Danton, the star of Matheson's *Lawman* episode "Yawkey") who insinuated his way into his victims' homes by pretending to be acquainted with their husbands, using personal details that he had gleaned from chance meetings while hitchhiking. Exemplifying Zugsmith's ensuing career as an exploitation filmmaker, producing and later directing Van Doren vehicles like *Sex Kittens Go to College* and *College Confidential* (both 1960), it was released by MGM and starred Steve Cochran as a cop betrayed by his first wife, whose mistrust of women is exacerbated when his second wife learns she is pregnant after being attacked by Danton. Zugsmith insisted on setting the story against a trendy backdrop of the beatnik coffeehouse culture, filled with a wide variety of "colorful" characters, and had Matheson's script so heavily revised by Lewis Meltzer—a veteran of *High School Confidential!*—that Matheson had to fight to retain his credit, although ironically he disdains the result.

That same year, 1959, Matheson began a decidedly more harmonious and productive relationship with acclaimed writer and executive producer Rod Serling, when he and Beaumont became the most prolific contributors—after Serling himself—to one of television's most beloved anthology series, *The Twilight Zone*. He wrote fourteen teleplays, published as *Richard Matheson's* The Twilight Zone *Scripts* (1998), for the first of the show's many multimedia incarnations to date, running on CBS from 1959 to 1964. Serling adapted Matheson's work into two additional episodes, "And When the Sky Was Opened" and "Third from the Sun." The former took little more than its central premise of a person's life slipping away, piece by piece, from Matheson's "Disappearing Act," which later reportedly became the uncredited basis for a segment of the Brazilian anthology film *O Impossível Acontece* (a.k.a. *Believe It or Not*, 1969). "I'd never heard of that. I'll have to tell my agent—they probably cheated me out of some money," Matheson laughed when he was apprised of the pirated adaptation.

"I think if it was filmed as written, it would be great, [but] there was no point [in trying to adapt it personally], because I didn't own it. I sold the story to *The Twilight Zone*. I would have liked to. I didn't know at that time—I'm not sure, but it seems like they bought those two [stories], maybe before Chuck Beaumont and I even went in [to work on the series]. Actually, those are the only two stories I sold them for many years, because I wanted to just do original [teleplays] and hold onto my stories. . . . [L]ater on I sold some of the stories, because all my early ones, if you notice, are originals. . . . [Serling's adaptation of "Third from the Sun"] was okay. That was closer to my story. I mean, it was a very short story. They had to expand it. . . . I got all of fifty dollars for it [when it originally appeared in *Galaxy* in 1950]. I was thrilled. I remember walking on Third Avenue with a friend of mine, and he just couldn't believe it. 'Fifty dollars for a short story! Whoa!' " His second published story, it concerned two families fleeing to another planet—eventually revealed as the Earth—to avoid an impending nuclear war.

Already established in the field, Matheson and Beaumont saw no need to collaborate on the series. "Chuck Beaumont and I had a similar take on fantasy, I think. It's been mentioned before, but I never made any social commentary in my [episodes of *The*] *Twilight Zone*. They were all just stories and character studies, whereas very often [Serling's] had a social commentary, and I don't think Chuck Beaumont did that, either. I think his were just plain stories, too, because when we were in print, with the stories we wrote for magazines, that's what they were. Once in a blue moon: I wrote a story once ["Full Circle"] about a reporter who covers a puppet show, but it isn't a puppet show, it's little Martians doing 'Rip Van Winkle.' [Larg, the leader of the "living marionettes"] is an older man and very wise, and very tired and exhausted, and [the reporter] writes this real harsh story about the terrible plight of this little Martian, and his editor doesn't print any of it, so that was obviously social commentary. But I didn't do too many of those [stories], and unless I'm wrong, none for *The Twilight Zone*."

Although the styles of their scripts differed somewhat, Matheson and Beaumont were in many ways the ideal contributors to *The Twilight Zone*. "We both thought similarly about fantasy. We were both already well established in the magazine field, we knew how to write that kind of story, and we were very adaptable. We could fit the *Twilight Zone* pattern almost instantly, which as I've said many times was a very specific pattern. The pattern is: a teaser that gets your interest, and then Rod making a comment, and then your first act with a cliffhanger, and then to your ending, which hopefully [is] a surprise. Most [magazine stories don't fit that pattern, but] . . . just sort of start out gradually. You know, very often it's like, 'I met this man on a train, and he told me a story about how his Uncle Dudley had something horrible happen to him,' and the last line is, 'and there was Uncle Dudley with a moth's face,' or something. But they didn't do that approach [in magazine stories], where you just [start out with a] bang, and I didn't do it, either. You have a little more time when you're writing a short story."

Matheson enjoyed the confidence of both Serling and Buck Houghton (who produced the show's first three seasons), and found them receptive to the ideas he pitched. "I don't know how many [times] I actually went in. I know I had to go in and pitch the first one ["The Last Flight"], which was extremely simple. . . . 'World War I pilot gets lost, lands, and he's in a 1959 SAC base.' That was enough. I didn't have a story, I didn't know where it was going to go. I had to figure that out, but just the image was so vivid that they said, 'Yeah, go ahead.' Of course, since I had been published and they knew more or less what I could do, it wasn't as if they were taking that big a chance. Well, that idea certainly grabs you right out of the gate. [Kenneth Haigh, who played the pilot], did a very good job." Matheson's *Twilight Zone* debut marked a rare case in which his original title, "Flight," was changed against his wishes. "I liked 'Flight' better. It was his flight from his cowardice, and a flight from the past to the future, and so on. 'The Last Flight' sort of narrows it down. That's always fun to do," that is, creating titles with multiple meanings.

Matheson also contributed "A World of Difference"—in which Howard Duff's character, an actor, escapes an unhappy marriage by slipping completely into his role of a businessman—and then ended the first season on a whimsical note with "A World of His Own," in which a playwright (played by Keenan Wynn) conjures up characters by describing them on audiotape, and banishes them by burning the tape. Actually inspired by Matheson's much more serious (and hitherto unpublished) story "And Now I'm Waiting," it concludes with Wynn zapping Serling, in the first of his trademark on-camera appearances after narrating the series offscreen, out of existence. The second season's "Nick of Time" was one of two episodes—both written by Matheson—that starred an up-and-coming William Shatner, playing a newlywed trapped in an Ohio diner by his obsession with a devil-headed fortune-telling machine. "When I lived in Brooklyn, before I came out to California, I used to go out of my way to watch [Shatner] when he was on television programs, so I think he'd been in it quite awhile. Certainly he didn't have the scope of a career as when he did *Star Trek*.

"My wife and I were in a coffee shop in the San Fernando Valley, and there was this little answer machine that answered yes or no," he added of its real-life origins. "And so I just thought, 'Oh, that's an interesting idea.' You know, most ideas come from . . . something you read. Or something I see in the movies. If it's a lousy movie, I don't leave, which I should, but my mind drifts, and something that I see may just trigger an alternative idea." The sight of Ray Milland donning Aldo Ray's huge hat in *Let's Do It Again* (1953) gave Matheson the idea for *The Shrink-*

*ing Man*, while a 1940s revival screening of *Dracula* (1931) eventually resulted in another classic novel. "I thought, 'Gee, one vampire is scary, a whole world full of vampires would really be scary.' I was only seventeen, and it took me a long time before I wrote [*I Am Legend* (1954)]." Agnes Moorehead's performance as a mute woman pitted against tiny spacemen, ultimately revealed to be from Earth, helped make his other second-season episode, "The Invaders," a classic, but again, Matheson had his reservations.

"What's there is good, because I have said many times that I would have liked it if it had gone faster . . . I had a lot more material—more going on between her and these little critters, because the opening I find, to this day, unbearably leisurely. It just takes forever before she hears the noise on the roof, and then it takes forever for her to get up there. I think [the opening scene] probably could have been cut in half, or by a third. . . . And I didn't like the little [spacemen], those little roly-poly things. . . . I had them flying past your eye or your attention. They had little space things that made them fly, and you would just see them and then they'd be gone. They weren't just wobbling around." Matheson had similar regrets about his comedic episode "Once Upon a Time," with silent film star Buster Keaton (whom he had met through his friend William R. Cox) as a janitor dissatisfied with the fast pace of life in 1890, who uses his employer's experimental "time helmet" to travel to 1962, but finds it no better. Matheson's script was filled with chase scenes and sight gags that were never shot.

Dramatic deficiencies diminished another third-season episode, "Young Man's Fancy," in which it appears that a thirty-four-year-old bridegroom (Alex Nicol) is being pulled into the past by his dead mother. Yet when his new bride (Phyllis Thaxter) confronts her spirit, it is revealed that the son has not only brought about her ghostly manifestation but also, through force of will, returned to his boyhood self. "I liked all of that [one] until the last few minutes. . . . Alex Nicol could have been a little better, but Phyllis Thaxter was a wonderful actress. I don't know whether she's still alive or not, but she was wonderful in it. . . . [The mother] looked like Stella Dallas. She should have been scary looking. You know, she's a ghost. It should have been like *The Uninvited* [1944]. I still get chills when I watch that." Curiously, despite the casting of the forty-something Nicol, the reference to his character's age in Serling's opening narration was neither altered to suit the actor nor omitted. "They should have upped his age. It would have been a better point, that he had waited so long to marry. I never thought of that."

With the third season's "Little Girl Lost," Matheson began adapting episodes from his stories rather than writing original scripts. "I don't know why I didn't do it [before], except I guess I figured maybe it was easier to do an original, because you could impose the structure of *The Twilight Zone* on it immediately, where with a short story, you had to sort of finagle around." The episode, which concerned a sleeping child who falls through a portal into the fourth dimension, was once again inspired by real-life events. "Our older girl, Tina—the same name as in the story—was crying, and I went into the room. Actually, the apartment was so small, it was just a wooden army cot that she slept on at that time. I felt around the bed and she wasn't on the bed, and I thought, 'Oh, my Lord, the poor kid fell on the floor,' then I felt on the floor, she wasn't there. When I felt under the bed I couldn't find her. She had gone under the bed and rolled all the way to the wall, and that's where I found her. Then of course, given the diabolical writer's mind, you know, after the kid stops crying you think of a story."

For the fourth season, Matheson adapted two of his stories, "Mute" and "Death Ship," but added material to the latter to accommodate the show's short-lived sixty-minute format. "You had to make it an hour, which was really a terrible idea for a *Twilight Zone* season, because that just was not the flavor of *The Twilight Zone*, and we were all glad it went back to a half-hour for the last season. . . . I did some of my best work in the last season." In "Death Ship," the crew of an interstellar Flying Dutchman is confronted with the wreck of a duplicate ship that contains the corpses of their own doubles, while "Mute" concerns a young girl who is raised in isolation to communicate only by telepathy, and then finds it acutely painful when, after being orphaned by a fire, she is forced by an uncaring teacher to adjust to using speech instead. "I kind of like ["Death Ship"], because it had such a good cast, and it had a lot of honest emotion in it. The other [hour-long] one wasn't too bad, but that one, 'Mute,' was a long story [to begin with]. Why they turned [the child] into a girl instead of a boy I don't know." A feature-film version of "Death Ship," entitled *Countdown*, is currently in development.

Matheson's four contributions to the show's fifth and final season included his personal favorite, "Steel," with Lee Marvin as a manager who, in desperation, takes the place of his robot prizefighter. "'Steel' refers to the strength of his personality plus the fact that these [robots] are made out of steel. . . . I love titles like that. Usually, if you can think of a title, you can do it right away, and you're very happy with it. If you have to spend a lot of time thinking about it, you never get it right." He also successfully advanced Jacques Tourneur, whose work with producer Val Lewton he had admired as a teenager, as the director of "Night Call," in which a crippled spinster receives mysterious phone calls from beyond the grave. "I talked them into hiring Tourneur, because I said, 'You know, he's a great director,' and my recollection is they were very dubious, because they thought, 'Well, he's a *movie* director, he's going to take forever to do it.' And to my knowledge—maybe I'm wrong—but my memory is that he shot the shortest *Twilight Zone* schedule that anyone had ever done. It was like twenty-eight hours or something."

"Spur of the Moment" was Matheson's only original teleplay that season, in which a girl is pursued on horseback by a terrifying figure revealed as herself, traveling back from the future in a failed attempt to stop her from marrying the wrong man. "I like that kind of story, and the only thing I didn't like was that I thought in the beginning they gave it away. You should not have seen her face when she was chasing the young girl. It should have just been a scary figure in black in the background."

William Shatner made his only other *Twilight Zone* appearance as a mentally unstable passenger, who alone sees the gremlin tearing at the wing of the plane, in "Nightmare at 20,000 Feet," which is undoubtedly the best-known episode, spoofed in everything from a Looney Tunes comic book to *3rd Rock from the Sun*. It also gave Shatner's character a wife who did not accompany him in the original story. "I must have cut about five thousand words out of it [before it was published]. The story [originally] starts a [while] before [he boards the airplane]—he's in his office, he's in the cab; it goes on just establishing the mental state he's in."

Still hugely popular after almost fifty years, *The Twilight Zone* featured a mix of veteran and rising talent on both sides of the camera. "The guy who [directed] 'Steel,' Don Weis, he did a very good job. . . . I thought [Richard] Donner did an excellent job on 'Nightmare at 20,000 Feet,' and Douglas Heyes, who did . . . 'The Invaders'. . . . [And] the acting was very good. I cannot recall anybody in [the series] who I thought was not good, and some of them very good indeed. . . . [But] they're interesting stories. That's my answer, there's no other reason. If they put 'Richard Matheson—Storyteller' on my tombstone, that's okay with me. . . . I would say it was more of a fantasy series than science fiction. I mean, just because we had a rocket ship now and then, and time travel— that's just like Ray Bradbury being called 'Mr. Science Fiction,' or 'the greatest science-fiction writer in the world.' He is probably one of the greatest *fantasy* writers. Just because he had his story on Mars, it was not science fiction. I mean, if you want to read science fiction, you read [Isaac] Asimov, you read Arthur C. Clarke."

During his *Twilight Zone* tenure, Matheson formed a fruitful association with American International Pictures (AIP), founded by James H. Nicholson and Samuel Z. Arkoff. He recalls that Arkoff "was strictly a very good businessman, but any creative contact, I had with Nicholson. Not that I disliked Arkoff, it's just that he was a businessman and nothing else. I had a percentage of the net on all the pictures, and I was getting nothing, and I knew I would never get anything. And so [AIP] finally talked me into selling all my percentages to them for ten thousand dollars . . . which at the time was ten thousand dollars more than I'd have made anyway. But when all this residual stuff started, if I had held on to them, I would have done much better." His first film for AIP, *House of Usher* (1960), was based on Edgar Allan Poe's "The Fall of the House of Usher," and achieved a new level of commercial and critical success for the studio and for director Roger Corman, also consolidating the position of Vincent Price (who enjoyed one of his best roles as Roderick Usher) as an American counterpart to British horror stars Christopher Lee and Peter Cushing.

"There are some writers who are very visual, and it's easy to adapt them to a screenplay form; others are not—some writers do a lot of introspection, interior monologues and that's difficult, too. . . . Poe was difficult . . . 'cause his stories were not exactly page-rippers. . . . ['Usher' is] very brooding and ruminating, and not too much plot, not too much movement or dialogue. . . . I wrote an extremely complex outline for it, I analyzed Poe, and it turned out very well. AIP were totally floored by the success of it, they didn't expect it at all. It ran all summer, [and] on a double bill with *Psycho* [1960]. It made all kinds of money, and they were just going to do it as a one-shot, and then they started doing the whole cycle of [Poe] pictures because of that." Corman continued to mine this lucrative (and, thanks to his work being in the public domain, economical) vein with seven more films that were at least nominally based on the stories and poems of Poe, three of which were scripted by Matheson: *Pit and the Pendulum* (1961), *Tales of Terror* (1962), and *The Raven* (1963).

But first, Matheson was reunited with Vincent Price on *Master of the World* (1961), with which AIP clearly hoped to duplicate, on a smaller budget, the success of the Jules Verne adaptations *20,000 Leagues Under the Sea* (1954) and *Journey to the Center of the Earth* (1959). Matheson expertly conflated Verne's novels *Robur le Conquérant* (*Robur, the Conqueror*, a.k.a. *The Clipper of the Clouds*) and its eponymous sequel, *Maître du Mond* (*Master of the World*), which feature a kind of airborne variation on his own character of Captain Nemo in the form of Robur. "I did two of them," Matheson noted of the novels. "I don't remember whether they were hard [to adapt] or not. I remember reading a translation of *Journey to the Center of the Earth* which was so fast moving and so clean that it would have been simple to do an adaptation." Played by Price in the film, who's opposed by the young Charles Bronson, Robur endeavors—like Nemo with his submarine, the *Nautilus*—to banish warfare with the use of his revolutionary airship, the *Albatross*.

Its onscreen title dropping the initial article from Poe's tale of torment by the Spanish Inquisition, *Pit and the Pendulum* otherwise added to, rather than subtracted from, the virtually plotless original, recombining many of *House of Usher*'s story elements with Price as the unstable son of an Inquisitor, and rising genre star Barbara Steele as the wife who comes to regret deceiving him. *Tales of Terror* was an anthology film featuring Price as an embittered recluse doomed by the spirit of his late wife in "Morella"; an adulterer walled up alive by the inebriated character played by Peter Lorre, after they have engaged in a hilarious wine-tasting contest, in "The Black Cat"; and a man forced to remain at the point of death by an evil mesmerist played by Basil Rathbone in "The Case of M. Valdemar." Expanding on the comic tone introduced in "The Black Cat," which incorporated Poe's "The Cask of Amontillado," *The Raven* added another aging horror star, Boris Karloff, to AIP's roster as a master magician who steals Price's character's wife (played by Hazel Court) and turns Lorre's character—with neophyte Jack Nicholson as his hapless son—into the titular bird, before facing Price's character in a sorcerous final battle.

Matheson's artistic dissatisfaction increased as the series progressed. "I kind of faked on the Poe things. In the first one . . . I put in a romance with the guy who comes to the house, whereas I don't think that was the case at all in the story. And the others, I mean *Pit and the Pendulum* was ridiculous, 'cause we took a little short story about a guy lying on a table with that razor thing going over him, and had to make a whole story out of it. I had a plot for an old suspense mystery, which I just imposed on that. [*Tales of Terror*] was easy—I combined a couple of stories [in one segment], but the others were pretty much the way the stories were. . . . Then after that . . . it got further and further away from Poe. I mean, we did *The Raven*, which is a poem, which I turned into a comedy. But they always say 'Edgar Allan Poe's *The Raven*'. . . . Then they would do a book adaptation of the screenplay, so it would be '*The Raven*, by Edgar Allan Poe,' and it would be a story that had nothing to do with the poem. And nobody ever knew it . . . unless they were familiar with literature, they wouldn't even know it was based on a poem."

The cycle continued without Matheson, who complimented Corman's efforts. "Roger did some very good work on the Poe stuff. . . . I think [the others] turned out quite well. I know Chuck Beaumont did several [including *The Premature Burial* (1962), written with Ray Russell, and *The Haunted Palace* (1963)]. *The Masque of the Red Death* [1964] was quite artistic, I thought. Then there was [*The Tomb of Ligeia* (1964), written by Robert Towne]. . . . They got pretty arty and did quite a nice job of it. I could never have done it. After [*Tales of Terror*] I couldn't take them seriously, that's why I made one of the stories a comedy with Peter Lorre in it, and after that I couldn't take it seriously at all." Matheson, meanwhile, let his lighter side run riot with *The Comedy of Terrors* (1963), a horror spoof that teamed up Price, Lorre, Karloff, Rathbone, and Joyce Jameson (also seen in "The Black Cat"), with a funeral-parlor setting, droll dialogue, and—to Matheson's delight—the direction of Val Lewton veteran Jacques Tourneur. "I loved his early work, and I thought he did a very amusing job with *The Comedy of Terrors*. . . .

"I had a good relationship with James Nicholson of American International, and he responded to my ideas. I gave him the idea of a couple of rascally undertakers, and when business was slow they just went out and killed people, and provided their own customers. And he liked that, so I think that was all I had at the start. I knew I had Price, I knew I had Lorre, and I think I knew I had Rathbone. I didn't know that Karloff was going to be in it. Actually, [he and Rathbone] were supposed to play the opposite parts. Karloff was too ill to play the bigger part of the landlord . . . so he himself suggested that they switch. What's amusing is Rathbone was older than Karloff. The man had so much energy, God, that man was full of energy. I remember talking to him. We spent a whole fascinating day with him telling me about [*The Adventures of*] *Robin Hood* [1938], which is one of my favorite pictures, and how they spent three days filming the duel. Here we were doing a picture that we were shooting in ten days, and he was telling about doing the duel in *Robin Hood* and taking three days just to do that."

Given their reputations as horror heavyweights, the leads showed a surprising affinity for comedy (especially Rathbone, with his deliberately flowery dialogue), doubtless enjoying the change of pace, while Matheson, who also served as the film's associate producer, found them equally delightful offscreen. "They were all just absolutely charming people, they couldn't have been nicer. Lorre was so sweet and so funny. And the fact that he mangled all my dialogue, and just came out with some approximation of what I'd written—ordinarily that infuriates me, but with him, you just sort of let it go. He would tell me how [his frequent screen partner] Sydney Greenstreet used to go absolutely ape over it, because he'd had stage training, and every line was exact. And even Price told me—he would always do my lines word for word; that was the thing about AI's pictures, although they weren't usually brilliantly done, they always did my dialogue word for word, except for Lorre—he said that he had to learn to adapt to Lorre's unexpected rejoinders. . . . Karloff didn't like it either. It drove him nuts."

A follow-up film that was written to reunite the same stars sadly never materialized. "There was one I was going to do after *The Comedy of Terrors*: AIP wanted to do a picture with Tallulah Bankhead. I wrote a movie called *Sweethearts and Horrors*, about the Sweetheart family, where Vincent Price was an alcoholic ventriloquist, Peter Lorre was a magician with a great fire act who burned down every theater he ever performed in, Tallulah Bankhead was a terrible aging movie star with a drinking problem, Basil Rathbone was an old musical comedy star going to pot, and Karloff had a children's program called *Dudley's*, where he just hated children. And then they're all called home for the reading of the will of their father, who had one of these companies that made novelties and gags and everything, so the whole house is gimmicked up, and there are murders—it was a charming, very funny script, but they never did it." The project fell apart as all but Price began to die off, one by one, between 1964 and 1969 (although the script saw the light of day when it was published in *Unrealized Dreams*).

Between Poe films, Matheson collaborated with Beaumont on their only feature, Sidney Hayers's *Night of the Eagle* (a.k.a. *Burn, Witch, Burn,* 1962). "We just went to a bar one night, we were chatting, and we decided, 'Let's write a movie together.' We both loved [Fritz Leiber's novel] *Conjure Wife*, and we knew that it had already been filmed, but we ignored the fact and did it anyway. We were both working for American International at the time, and they liked the script very much. But since they had to buy the rights from Universal, who had made *Weird Woman* [1944], the one with Lon Chaney, Jr., I think we split ten thousand dollars between us for the script, that's all we ever made. . . . They did a very nice job on it. I thought it turned out extremely well. . . . I wrote the first half, and Beaumont wrote the second half. We just each looked at it and made suggestions on each other's half. Actually, it doesn't seem like it when you read our short stories, but when it came to scripts we wrote pretty similarly." George Baxt, who had worked with Hayers previously, shared the scriptwriting credit only in England, where the film was shot.

Matheson continued contributing scripts to anthology series such as *Thriller*, for which he adapted "The Return of Andrew Bentley" from a story by August Derleth and Mark Schorer. Derleth was a disciple of H.P. Lovecraft, of whom Matheson stated, "He wasn't my kind of writer—too heavy. Heavy stuff. You know, how he'd spend fifty pages talking about some Eldritch horror that is so horrible to describe that he can't possibly do it, and then in the last ten pages he describes it. I mean obviously the man was brilliant, I just don't care for that kind of writing." John Newland doubled as director and star of the episode. "I spoke to him a lot of times about some scripts for *One Step Beyond* [also directed and hosted by Newland], which I would have enjoyed doing. He was a very good actor . . . [but] I didn't like what was done to the *Thriller* script. They redid it. There was a lot more humor in my script. The attitudes [of the protagonists] were sort of like those of [the characters of William Shatner and his wife] in 'Nick of Time,' and then little by little they became frightened, because something really scary was going on."

His work was revised even more drastically in "Forgotten Front," the premiere episode of the World War II series *Combat!*, resulting in the first onscreen appearance of his Logan Swanson pen name. "When they sent me the [final] script, I first thought they'd sent me somebody else's script. Then the funny thing is that Robert Blees, the producer, was so full of praise when I went in to be introduced to people, and I guess he must have done it, since he was a writer. It was just changed so much, I really thought it was somebody else's script, and that's why I put the [pseudonym on]. . . . But then I met Blees at a party many, many years later, and for the first time said, 'Why did you do that to my script? Why did you change it so much?' And he said, 'We didn't change it.' It was like George Orwell at work." Combining his mother-in-law's maiden name with the American version of his own mother's maiden name, Svenningsen, the pseudonym dates back at least as far as the March 1957 issue of

*Alfred Hitchcock's Mystery Magazine,* which contained two of Matheson's stories, but he could only use his real byline on one of them.

The Master of Suspense was reunited with "Swanson" soon after when Matheson wrote two scripts for *The Alfred Hitchcock Hour,* the second of which, "The Thirty-first of February," was based on the novel by Julian Symons and, again, rewritten so heavily that he substituted his pen name. William Conrad played an overzealous detective who drives an innocent man insane. The first was an altogether happier affair, a necessarily truncated but otherwise faithful version of Matheson's noir novel *Ride the Nightmare* (1959), with Hugh O'Brian and Gena Rowlands as a couple placed in jeopardy, and in the typically Hitchcockian dilemma of disposing of a corpse, when the husband's long-buried criminal past resurfaces in the persons of three escaped convicts. Matheson considered the feature-film remake, *Cold Sweat* (1970), which he did not adapt, to be a disappointment despite its relative fidelity—even restoring some plot elements eliminated in the televised version—and impressive pedigree: it was directed by Terence Young (as were three of the first four James Bond films), and featured Charles Bronson, Liv Ullmann, and James Mason.

The only feature-film credit under the name of Logan Swanson is *The Last Man on Earth* (1964), the first official adaptation of *I Am Legend,* which also inspired George A. Romero's seminal *Night of the Living Dead* (1968). After spurring the Gothic horror revival with *The Curse of Frankenstein* (1957), England's Hammer Films acquired the rights and hired Matheson to adapt the novel, in which the sole survivor of a plague that has turned everyone else on Earth into vampires leads a lonely existence, staking the dormant bloodsuckers by day and barricading himself against their attacks by night. "I lived [in London] for about two months doing the screenplay on it [retitled *Night Creatures,* with the late Val Guest slated to direct]. I went over on the *Queen Elizabeth,* and I lived in the Green Park Hotel, and I walked all over London. It was really nice. . . . I always thought that they were kidding me when they said the censor wouldn't pass it, but then I read an interview with [the late AIP writer-producer Louis M.] 'Deke' Heyward, and he said that that *was* the reason—that the censor wouldn't allow them to make it, which seemed kind of odd."

Faced with an outright ban in England, Hammer was forced to sell the property to its sometime U.S. distributor, producer Robert L. Lippert, who had the script rewritten by William F. Leicester—prompting Matheson to substitute Swanson for his screenwriting credit—and shot it in Italy for budgetary reasons. "I remember [Lippert] telling me . . . 'I think we're getting Fritz Lang to [direct] this,' and I thought, 'Oh, my God, Fritz Lang!' And then one day he said, 'Well, we're going to go with Sidney Salkow,' and I thought, 'Oh, gee, that's a bit of a comedown from Fritz Lang.' It doesn't look like the United States, there's something about the architecture of the buildings. At least it's closer to the book. The second [version] had no relationship to the book whatever. [Vincent] Price was totally wrong for it. I mean, he was marvelous in many of the pictures I wrote, but that really wasn't his kind of thing." Charlton Heston starred in the remake, *The Omega Man* (1971), which supplanted vampires with albino mutants; the novel was reportedly also adapted as a short Spanish film, *Soy Leyenda* (*I Am Legend*, 1967).

However, the *Night Creatures* fiasco did have one positive result: "That's how I got to meet [Hammer producer] Tony Hinds. Because he liked my work, later on he gave me [Silvio Narizzano's] *Fanatic* [a.k.a. *Die! Die! My Darling!*, 1965]. It was quite well done, I thought, though it got a little heavy on the melodramatics toward the end. I didn't know Tallulah Bankhead was going to be in it, I had no idea. In the book [Anne Blaisdell's *Nightmare*] she's a dumpy little lady with pulled-back gray hair, and then it ended up as this flamboyant ex-actress with a drinking problem. . . . Stefanie Powers was quite good [in the lead], although someone told me that, in an interview, she said that it had been a terrible script, and she'd managed to save it, and I thought, 'Here we go again, another one of these egomaniacal people.' Actors and actresses talk about how they 'saved' the picture. And the directors, of course, have monstrous egos where they believe they've done it all themselves—you know, the *auteur* theory, which started in France, but has reached absurd depths in this country."

The year 1966 saw three more Matheson teleplays hit the screen, beginning with "Time of Flight," an episode of *Bob Hope Presents the Chrysler Theatre* that served as the pilot for a proposed series, *Race Against Time*, and concerned time travelers who help a private detective protect an informer. "They did a nice job on that. [Jack] Klugman played the guy from the future, but then the lead was Jack Kelly. He had a sister, Nancy, who [earned an Oscar nomination] in *The Bad Seed* [1956]. I liked him, and I liked Juliet Mills, and they kept the humor in it. I thought [director Joseph] Sargent did a nice job. I don't know whether they kept [that series] on tape, or burned them afterwards. They destroyed so many wonderful television shows." He also scripted "The Atlantis Affair" for *The Girl from U.N.C.L.E.*, a short-lived spy spin-off series starring none other than Stefanie Powers, but his teleplay "was much more ambitious [than what was shot]. It had to do with Atlantis and everything, [that] obviously they could not afford to do, and [producer] Doug Benton had to sort of prune it down to size to fit [the budget], so I don't even remember it."

Easily the most enduring was "The Enemy Within," his sole episode of *Star Trek*, which, like *The Twilight Zone*, recruited genre authors with mixed success. "Gene Roddenberry had the same idea, and it didn't work out, because to be able to write prose is not the same. Television is a specific form, and you've got to be able to adapt yourself to it. Script form—it should be obvious, but I guess it isn't to a lot of people—is very different from prose. The reason that Chuck Beaumont and I were able to do that is we both wrote visually to begin with, so we knew about that, and it was not that hard to shift over into script form. In fact, it was easier, because you didn't have to describe anything as much as you did in a story." Matheson disliked the addition of a B story, concerning a survey team stranded on a frigid planet, to his teleplay about a transporter malfunction that divides Captain Kirk (William Shatner) into two opposite beings. "It was just the split personality, the good side versus the evil side, the positive versus the negative, and the idea that you needed them both . . . I don't like B stories."

Matheson, George Clayton Johnson, Jerry Sohl, and their colleague Theodore Sturgeon were writing scripts for the first season of *Star Trek* when Sohl suggested teaming up to create an anthology series similar to *The Twilight Zone*, borrowing the title of Sturgeon's 1958 collection *A Touch of Strange*. (Beaumont's earlier attempt to launch a series entitled *Out There* around 1960 had failed despite a score of scripts by Matheson, Sohl, Bradbury, Ray Russell—who, as an editor at *Playboy*, acquired many of Matheson's stories—Robert Bloch, and others.) So the four friends formed a corporation called the Green Hand, intending to create new series for various networks, but according to Johnson, who served as president, *A Touch of Strange* was turned down by Michael Eisner, who was then a vice president in charge of development for ABC. "Oh, my God, well that's a whole damn story in itself," Matheson said. "I mean, we got together, we incorporated, we had this big, beautiful suite of offices in Beverly Hills, we had an office at Metro-Goldwyn-Mayer, we were meeting with the top bigwigs in all these studios, we had some wonderful ideas.

"Unfortunately, Jerry Sohl and I were the only ones who did much writing. The other two—you know, Ted Sturgeon [was] one of the really great writers in the field, science fiction *and* fantasy, but he didn't really do that much for the Green Hand, and so we never got anything down on paper that went anywhere, and finally I just backed out of the whole thing. We had a manager and we were paying him $250 a week at that time, which was quite a salary, and then later, after I had backed out, they found themselves in trouble with the IRS and found out that this guy had been continuing to pay himself, even though the whole thing was kaput. But it was fun; we used to meet at each other's houses, and they would smoke pot. I didn't, but I probably got high just on the fumes. We had some wonderful ideas. I remember one day walking from Metro to a coffee shop and back with George, and before we had gotten back to the studio he and I had plotted out an entire movie, which would have been very fascinating, but we never wrote it." Sadly, none of the Green Hand projects were ever produced.

Matheson, who saw action in Germany with the 87th Division of the U.S. Infantry during World War II, and later received a medical discharge after sustaining a combat-related injury, drew upon those wartime experiences in his critically acclaimed seventh novel, *The Beard-*

*less Warriors* (1960), which he adapted into John Peyser's now little-seen film, *The Young Warriors*. Rarely televised, and apparently never released on home video in any format, it was cast largely with Universal contract players, supplemented with combat footage from the studio's hit Audie Murphy biopic, *To Hell and Back* (1955); according to cast member Hank Jones, shooting was completed in the spring of 1966, yet the film was reportedly not released in the United States until 1968. That same year, Matheson's "No Such Thing as a Vampire" (bought by Ray Russell for *Playboy*) was adapted as an episode of the BBC-TV anthology series *Late Night Horror*, with Hammer mainstay Andrew Keir as the cuckolded doctor with a macabre method of disposing of his rival. Contrary to some sources, Matheson did not write the teleplay, which was done by Hugh Leonard.

His second script produced by Hammer, *The Devil Rides Out* (a.k.a. *The Devil's Bride*, 1968), is one of the finest efforts from all concerned, with studio regular Christopher Lee in a rare heroic role as Dennis Wheatley's Duc de Richleau. But, as was often the case, Matheson was initially disappointed at how his work was interpreted on the screen. "I like it better now. I didn't like it in the beginning at all, but I finally recorded it for myself one night on television, and even the casting, which I initially thought was offensive, isn't too bad. Of course, I never thought Christopher Lee was anything but good, and Charles Gray I thought was excellent [as the Aleister Crowley–inspired Satanist, Mocata]. It was some of the others I didn't like. It's got a great plot, and it never slows down—that's what Dennis Wheatley liked about what I did, I kept it rolling along. He wrote me a very nice letter, telling me how pleased he was and thanking me for having done a good job on it. [He] just had a lot of material, so that you had to cut it down a little."

Matheson praised director Terence Fisher's work on the film, and was approached about adapting Wheatley's *The Haunting of Toby Jugg*, also for Fisher, whose declining health soon derailed his career. "I think I even read it, and I guess I said, 'Yeah, sure, I'll do it,' and then nothing came of it. Who knows what happens with these things? One day they're full of enthusiasm, and everything's a go, and then you don't hear anything for a year, and you finally ask, 'Whatever happened to that?'

and they just sort of shrug and look embarrassed." His final connection with Hammer was an indirect one, an adaptation by Robert Bloch and Michael J. Bird of his story "Girl of My Dreams" for the anthology series *Journey to the Unknown*, which the studio produced in association with 20th Century-Fox. American actor Michael Callan played an opportunistic photographer who uses information gleaned from his wife's precognitive dreams to extort money from people wishing to avert catastrophes. "I really don't remember it. I don't know why they didn't let me [write the teleplay], because it was easy to adapt."

Problems on the set of Matheson's last AIP film, the unconventional and originally X-rated (though conspicuously tame by today's standards) biopic *De Sade* (1969), sent Roger Corman to Berlin to lend an uncredited hand. "Roger went over there because [director] Cy Endfield was having a mental breakdown, they told me. He shot the picture as though it were a straight story and not a fantasy, which I found bizarre, because my idea was like that film *Jacob's Ladder* [1990]. It was a strange, fantastic horror story that jumped time and jumped place and everything, and it turned out at the end it was all going through De Sade's mind as he was dying in prison. But Endfield took out the fact that it was a dying hallucination in his brain, so it made no sense whatever. And then Roger told me that [Endfield] would put red X's through the pages, which indicated they were shot, and they weren't shot, so [Corman] had to go over there to shoot a lot of orgy scenes, which did nothing for the picture." Keir Dullea, who has disputed the reports of Endfield's breakdown, played Matheson's heavily researched character.

"I read all about De Sade. As a matter of fact, it was the only script I ever did for them where I didn't have to change a word. And then Samuel Arkoff, you know, called me and said, 'Don't forget, you owe us a rewrite.' But he didn't ask me to rewrite it. I didn't write the interminable orgy scenes at all, but the dialogue is mine. And then what killed me was that Nicholson said that [John] Huston, who was in it, said, 'Why didn't you ask me to direct it?' That made my day." *De Sade* was envisioned as the flagship production of AIP's European division, run by Deke Heyward, and the first in an ambitious slate of films that would raise their critical and commercial status, but its failure scuttled several Matheson screenplays, including an adaptation of H. G. Wells's *When the Sleeper Wakes*. "I did some really good scripts the last couple of years with American International: They had me doing some really high-toned projects they were going to make in England. And whereas [with] the earlier ones, the ink was barely dry on the paper and they were shooting them, with these nothing ever came of them. And some of them were quite good.

"One of them was very good. It was called *Implosion*, based on a book [by D. F. Jones] about something getting in the water, I don't know whether it's put there by an enemy or not, but all the women in England except for a small handful become barren, and they can't have children. So in order for civilization not to disappear, they create these breeding camps. And the protagonist, this guy who's high in the government—his wife is one of them. It's a very strong story, and it turned out to be a very good script. Again, the British wouldn't allow it to be shot, because it reflected badly on their government. And then I did another one which I kept turning down, it was called *Private Parts in Public Places*, about the pornography business in England—just an insane, dark, savage humor type of thing. It's very serious for a movie, and I turned it into an out-and-out bizarre comedy, and they never made that, either. And I took my story 'Being,' and made a long script about that—although they had [also adapted it] earlier, this was a different version of it—and saw nothing. I don't know, there may have been others, too."

This adaptation of "Being," titled *"It's Alive!"* (1969), was one of several microbudgeted efforts (which included remakes of various AIP genre films) from Dallas-based Larry Buchanan to beef up two packages of films for American International Television. It substituted a shoddy amphibian for the gelatinous alien in Matheson's story, which was mercifully uncredited. "I don't even know whether I ever saw it," admitted Matheson, whose produced scripts of the 1970s were mostly confined to the small screen. The burgeoning TV-movie format, however, soon eclipsed his work in episodic television, which included adaptations of his stories "Big Surprise" and "The Funeral" for Rod Serling's second anthology series, *Night Gallery*. "I think I did several others, but they didn't get made. They were adaptations of other writers' stories. They did that—all of their stuff was adaptations, except for the little five-minute segments which I guess were comedies. I had nothing to do with those. There were certain producers who just really didn't like what I did. I don't think [producer] Jack Laird cared for what I did."

"Big Surprise" starred John Carradine as a sinister old man who urges a young boy to dig a hole in a certain spot. The boy complies, hoping to find a fortune in gold, but uncovers a coffin-shaped box from which the grinning Carradine emerges. "In *Ellery Queen's Mystery Magazine* [where the story was first published], they didn't have the ending. They called it, 'What Was in the Box?' and they asked readers to write in: 'What do you think the kid found when he opened up the box?' It just seemed like an interesting idea. I guess if you had to explain it, you'd say it was the guy's ghost." *Night Gallery*'s original hour-long incarnation included stories of varying lengths, many of which were butchered or, like "Big Surprise," padded with stock footage to fit a half-hour time slot when the show was syndicated. "The other one they sort of did the way I wrote it," Matheson said. "The Funeral" featured sitcom veterans Werner Klemperer (*Hogan's Heroes*) and Joe Flynn (*McHale's Navy*) in his humorous tale of a dapper vampire who buys himself a "tasty" send-off, attended by all manner of gruesome guests.

In 1975, Serling died at age fifty after heart surgery, outliving the series by only two years. "Rod's father died of the same thing at the same age. My heredity is basically good, and I have a good marriage, a good family, and writing just tended to enrich my life, not make it nervous and short. And also, [Rod] had this terrible pressure from [*The Twilight Zone*]. He was always working so hard. He had to write eighty percent of the scripts. He just was under terrible stress, and then after *The Twilight Zone*, they kind of stuck him with that, and they had him doing *Night Gallery*. But he didn't have the control at all over that one he did on *The Twilight Zone*. . . . [And] Chuck Beaumont, I think, had been ill, really ill, from the day I met him, and it just made him pass away at an extremely early age." Ravaged by a degenerative disease, most likely Alzheimer's, Beaumont died at thirty-eight in 1967, followed four years later by his wife, Helen. The struggle of their eldest child, Chris, to obtain guardianship of his three siblings was fictionalized in the TV movie *All Together Now* (1975), to which Matheson's uncredited script revisions may or may not have been used.

Matheson also had a "developed for television by" credit on another anthology series, *Ghost Story* (later known as *Circle of Fear*), although his involvement was limited to adapting the pilot episode, "The New House," from Elizabeth Walter's story. "I don't have a copy of it, I don't even remember it. . . . It's about some couple, I guess it has a house, and it turns out that they hanged witches on this property. I told [executive producer William] Castle, 'You know, a great place for you to have your series would be the Coronado Hotel down in San Diego.' And at the time I was just starting to work on my novel *Bid Time Return* [1975], which became *Somewhere in Time* [1980], and setting it there. He just picked up on it immediately, and shot his openings to the series down at the Coronado, and I thought, 'Oh, God, I've screwed myself!' . . . I think I first met him because I was up for writing *Rosemary's Baby* [1968], and then he hired [Roman] Polanski to direct it, and of course Polanski, being a consummate writer, insisted on writing it. That was fine with me. He made a masterpiece."

Matheson's first TV movie, *Duel* (1971), starred the late Dennis Weaver as a motorist caught in a deadly cat-and-mouse game with a psychotic trucker, and marked Steven Spielberg's feature-length screen debut after directing episodic television and a segment of the 1969 *Night Gallery* pilot. "I was flabbergasted at how good it was. Actually, when I first saw it, they had a huge screening party at Universal. They showed it to all these critics in about six or seven screening rooms. When it started out, I didn't realize that what they had done was buy a recent broadcast from some well-known guy on the radio. When I heard that, I thought, 'Oh, my God, they've rewritten my entire script!' And then as soon as that was over, there was the script, intact. . . . [Spielberg] took my script—and it *is* my script—and added his own incredible touch to it, but they didn't make big changes. All they did was cut some of my narration." Matheson adapted the film from his short story of the same title, published in *Playboy* that year and inspired by a real-life incident that happened as he and Jerry Sohl drove home from a golf game the day President Kennedy was shot in 1963.

His sophomore outing, *The Night Stalker* (1972), was the highest-rated TV movie of its time, with seventy-five million viewers, and remains among the top ten. It spawned a sequel, two weekly series, comic books, and several volumes of fiction and nonfiction, as well as winning a Writers Guild of America Award and the Mystery Writers of America's Edgar Allan Poe Award. It was faithfully adapted from Jeff Rice's *The Kolchak Papers*, a then-unpublished novel about a reporter tracking a vampire in modern-day Las Vegas, but Matheson deserves much of the credit for shaping the screen character of Carl Kolchak. "Actually, I don't know if you've read the original book, but in it he's sort of a heavyset Hungarian who believes in vampires right from the start, at least that's what he was in the manuscript that I saw, and I just turned him into something out of *The Front Page*—you know, a wisecracking reporter with a love-hate relationship with his editor." Sadly, star Darren McGavin, who seemed born to play Kolchak, and producer Dan Curtis, the creator of *Dark Shadows*, both died within weeks of each other in 2006.

When approached to adapt the novel, Matheson was unfamiliar with Curtis, who later became a frequent collaborator. "The only thing I knew about [him] was that some editor had given him a galley of *Hell House* [1971] before it was published, which he wasn't supposed to have, and they were trying to buy it from me for ten thousand dollars, all rights to it. So when I met him, I hated him before I even knew him. I found out later it was like taking my life in my hands, 'cause he had a violent temper, and I treated him rudely and impolitely. I'm surprised he didn't rip my throat out. Just a tremendous temper. But once I got to know him, he was a lot of fun. The guy's got a marvelous sense of humor, which helps to balance it out. [But he] is a very talented man. He did some wonderful things with stuff that I wrote. . . . That was the only one I ever did with Dan where he didn't direct it." That task fell to John Llewellyn Moxey (who soon followed it with Matheson's *Ghost Story* pilot). "It was pretty astonishing. It was awfully well done. It had a great character to it, it was very fast and sharp, and Moxey did a great job."

The character of Kolchak returned in *The Night Strangler* (1973), with Curtis assuming the director's chair this time, but Matheson had trouble coming up with his new antagonist, a 144-year-old alchemist who requires human blood to rejuvenate himself every twenty-one years. "I remember sitting up at ABC with Jim Greene—he and Allen Epstein have their own production company now—and Dan Curtis and several other executives, and we were just talking about it: 'Well, what'll we do, shall we make it a werewolf? Shall we make it a vampire?' And I remember saying, 'This is insane, we're a bunch of grown men sitting up here talking about this nonsense!' Actually, I wanted to make the guy in the second one Jack the Ripper, who was still alive and had come over to this country, but I'm a friend of Robert Bloch's, and I called him and asked him if it would disturb him if I did that [because of the similarity to his classic short story "Yours Truly, Jack the Ripper"], and I could sense that he felt that it would, so I didn't do it. Then of course right afterward, on the TV show *The Sixth Sense*, they did the same thing anyway, but at least I didn't do it."

Darren McGavin "was marvelous. As a matter of fact, William F. Nolan and I wrote a third [movie] called *The Night Killers*, which took place in Hawaii, and which was a wonderful script. The idea, I think, has been used now, but at the time it was a new idea, and I'm surprised that it was never made. The concept was that they—I forget who, aliens or something—were making android duplicates of high political figures and then killing off the real ones. They were going to try and take over the government of Hawaii, and then little by little the governments of the world. That idea's been used a number of times since, but at that time it hadn't. . . . It was a very funny script." Published in *Richard Matheson's Kolchak Scripts*, it was abruptly cancelled in favor of the weekly *Night Stalker* series, sans Matheson or Curtis. "I just don't know whether I'd have been involved. . . . I might have, if Dan was going to be able to, then I guess they didn't work out a deal that was satisfactory to him, so he backed out. I don't know, it was trouble enough for me to think up an idea for the second movie, much less an idea every week."

Accounts vary as to the reason for the decision not to produce *The Night Killers*, ranging from a concern that the script was too similar to the first two—making the decision to do a weekly series somewhat odd—to tensions between Curtis and McGavin. Matheson revealed his own contretemps with the actor: "I saw comments through the years by McGavin, because when I went to the shooting of *The Night Stalker*, I saw all these colored pages, the change pages [author Jeff Rice reportedly made uncredited revisions], and I thought, 'Oh, my God, there's nothing left of my script,' and I got infuriated. I was there with my wife and my kids, we were passing through Las Vegas, and I left in a rage, and I didn't express it to anybody, but I guess Darren heard about it, and thought there was something wrong with me. Then, when I saw the picture, I saw that they hadn't changed it that much. Finally Darren and I were talking on the phone, and we sort of made peace when I explained it to him. He didn't know what had happened, what I felt. So, it worked out well."

In an ironic twist, Rice—whose novel *The Kolchak Papers* was finally published as the *Night Stalker* after the first film's success—then novelized the *Night Strangler* teleplay. "I don't know whether they still do them," Matheson said of novelizations. "I guess they do, I don't think they're as big as they used to be. It's kind of silly, it's like merchandising, like making a toy of a Ninja Turtle, that's all. You're making a book, and you hope you make a few extra bucks out of it. I would think it would be pretty easy, because you have the whole script there, you would just sort of put yourself on automatic and turn it into past tense and get the novel. But most writers really want to turn it into a novel, which to me is a waste of time. You might as well just do the script in past tense." Other adaptations of Matheson's scripts include Albert Zugsmith's hackneyed *The Beat Generation* and James Blish's version of "The Enemy Within" in *Star Trek 8*, while Lancer Books issued novelizations by various authors of his AIP films *Pit and the Pendulum*, *Tales of Terror*, *The Raven*, and *The Comedy of Terrors*.

Matheson adapted his only feature film of the 1970s, *The Legend of Hell House (1973)*, from his novel *Hell House*, which was in its own way a response to Shirley Jackson's *The Haunting of Hill House* and the screen version directed by Robert Wise, *The Haunting* (1963). "I saw their film, so I'm sure it was in my mind to write a haunted house story.

I think . . . *The Haunting* is a marvelous film, very scary, but I didn't like the idea that you never really knew what did it—was it Julie Harris's hallucination, was it really her? And I thought, 'I'm going to do a haunted house story where you damn well know it's haunted, and there's no question in your mind.' And I'd always wanted to write a haunted house story anyway. But I wasn't trying to parody *The Haunting* or anything. [Wise] had two female psychics, and I don't know who the young guy was [a relative of the house's owner, played by Russ Tamblyn] . . . and one parapsychologist. I had the parapsychologist's wife, who was sort of an innocent, and then the male and the female psychic, who were supposed to be much older [than they were in the film].

"Later on, my dream casting at the time might have been feasible. Right after this film came out, *The Exorcist* [1973] was made, and all of a sudden the horror film became an 'A' product, I think, which would have reflected well on *Hell House*. Not that it was done badly, but I would have liked to have seen Elizabeth Taylor and her [then] husband, Richard Burton, as the two psychics, and Claire Bloom and her [then] husband, [Rod] Steiger, as the parapsychologist and his wife," roles played by Pamela Franklin, Roddy McDowall, Clive Revill, and Gayle Hunnicut, respectively. Initially disappointed once again, Matheson later came to appreciate John Hough's film, despite their having had to tone down the violence and depravity required of "the Mount Everest of haunted houses" in his relatively graphic novel. The following year, writer-director Georges Launter also adapted his first novel, *Someone Is Bleeding* (1953), as *Icy Breasts* (*Les Seins de Glace*, 1974), a French-Italian coproduction starring Alain Delon as a lawyer who shares the protagonist's dangerous obsession with a frigid, man-hating, psychopathic blonde.

Matheson, meanwhile, returned to his series of successful TV movies with *Dying Room Only* (1973), featuring an effective performance by Cloris Leachman as a woman whose husband mysteriously vanishes from a seedy roadside café during a cross-country road trip. "Philip Leacock . . . did a fantastic job. I've been quoted many times as saying that was the one time where I thought the show was better than it deserved. He did it so well. He's a marvelous director. Well, he *was* a marvelous director, I don't know if he's still alive. You have to keep saying that nowadays." (He died in 1990.) Having authored *I Am Legend*—plus such stories of the undead as "Blood Son" and "Dress of White Silk"—as well as scripting *The Night Stalker*, Matheson was clearly a natural to adapt the ultimate vampire novel, Bram Stoker's *Dracula*, for Dan Curtis. Their version, starring Jack Palance, was scheduled to air on October 12, 1973, but was preempted by President Nixon's historic speech regarding the resignation of Vice President Agnew; it was eventually broadcast the following February and, like *Duel*, released theatrically overseas.

"You can do *Dracula* so many different ways. I think my script was closer to the book than anybody's had ever been, which I found kind of amazing after all the number of times the story was filmed. [It] started out based on the Broadway play, which was kind of a remove from the novel, and I don't think anyone had ever just started out the way the book did. I never had seen one that I thought was worthy of the book, really, and I still haven't. When they said that [Francis Ford] Coppola was going to make it, and Anthony Hopkins was going to play Van Helsing, I thought, 'Oh, wow,' and then I read the script, and it's like it's a porno version of *Dracula*. It's unbelievable! It's just nothing but sex. Dracula walks around in the daytime, it's all young people, and all they're doing is screwing all the time. When Jonathan Harker goes to the castle, it's just one orgy scene after another, with him and Dracula's wives. I was stunned. So as of today they're still not going to make *Dracula* the way [Stoker wrote it]." Matheson, it should be noted, did respond favorably to Coppola's finished film, *Bram Stoker's Dracula* (1992).

However, "I remembered that when they did it on PBS with Louis Jourdan [as *Count Dracula* (1977)], I was thinking, 'Well, that's great casting, Dracula should be attractive, he should be extremely attractive.' But then I saw it, it was not good at all. . . . I mean, why don't they give up on vampires? I think they've done it to death. You would think they'd come up with something new—they have Dracula, they have Frankenstein, they have the mummy, the wolfman, and that's it." He and Curtis next attempted their own take on the werewolf theme with *Scream of the Wolf* (1974), which was based on David Case's story "The Hunter" (also the film's working title), but with less satisfying results. Clint Walker, for whose series *Cheyenne* Matheson had written one episode, starred as a big-game hunter who tries to lure his friend and former colleague (played by Peter Graves of *Mission: Impossible* fame) out of retirement by committing a series of murders that appear to be the work of a werewolf, then forces Graves's character to hunt him to the death, *mano a mano*.

Based on the novel by Jack B. Weiner, *The Morning After* (1974) earned comedian Dick Van Dyke an Emmy Award nomination for his television dramatic debut, playing a public relations writer whose drinking costs him his self-respect, his career, and his family; unknown to Matheson, the star himself was privately battling alcoholism at the time. "That I thought was moving. Director Richard T. Heffron did a wonderful job. I've had more success in television than I've had in films by far. [With a film], you know it ahead of time when you go into it, you know you can't do certain things, so you don't even think about it. But you can do things that *say* something on television; the 'message' film in theatricals today is almost unheard of . . . unless you get a star to do *Silkwood* [1983] or something like that." Rounding out a busy year, *The Stranger Within* (1974) featured Barbara Eden as a woman impregnated by aliens as part of a proxy invasion—a new idea when his story "Trespass," which once again served as the film's working title, was first published in 1953 as "Mother by Protest," though it was later used by others.

Curtis's *Trilogy of Terror* (1975) cast Karen Black in three Matheson stories. "I was kind of cruel to Bill Nolan and gave him the two other stories [to adapt], because I didn't want to do them. I was amazed that he was able to make anything out of them. One of them, with the girl who had a double personality, was a page-and-a-half short story, and he did a remarkable job with them. But I kept the good one ['Prey'] for myself." That gave Black what may be her best-known role as the title character in "Amelia," a woman pursued by a lethal Zuni fetish doll, while Nolan adapted "The Likeness of Julie" and "Therese" (originally published as "Needle in the Heart") as "Julie" and "Millicent and Therese," the film's first two segments. "I couldn't do it. I wouldn't even try it, because if the story's a page and a half, that's the length it demands, but Bill did a very good job. I don't know how he did it. It was an excellent adaptation. It kept the flavor of the piece, and it's easier, I think, to do that with somebody else's short story. I could never do it with one of my own. I would just say, 'Now what am I going to do? How can I make this a half-hour?' "

Directed by genre veteran Gordon Hessler, *The Strange Possession of Mrs. Oliver* (1977) played like an extended version of the split-personality middle segment in *Trilogy of Terror*, an impression only strengthened by putting Black in the role of an amnesiac whose "possession" is really just her original persona reasserting itself. Matheson was then reunited with Curtis for *Dead of Night* (1977), which, like its classic 1945 namesake from England's Ealing Studios, was another anthology horror film, and became their final collaboration of the '70s. "We tried to use *Trilogy of Terror* as a pilot for a series, and that didn't work. Then we decided together to create this other series, and we prepared an opening, which was very similar to what they did later in *Tales from the Crypt*, you know, moving toward this old house and going into it, and then using these three stories. I guess [ABC] just didn't like the idea. At that time, I think anthologies were sort of persona non grata. They preferred just one story, and Curtis couldn't sell that, either. So there were two pilots, for two series like that, and neither one of them sold.

"They're usually based on short stories, so if you tried to extend [the stories] into full-length films, it wouldn't work. They never did well as motion pictures. They used to do that back in the '40s, they did *Tales of Manhattan* [1942], and things like that. [The original *Dead of Night*], that's a dandy. . . . But I don't think they were ever really big successes. People seem to prefer one story." Based on Jack Finney's "Second Chance," the first segment "was about a guy who makes an old-fashioned car and drives back through time. . . . It's a fascinating theme—not time travel per se. I don't know how many time-travel stories have gone into the future; I know the H.G. Wells one. That doesn't interest me. It's going into the past that is interesting. I don't know why, it just seems more romantic . . ." The second was Matheson's own adaptation of "No Such Thing as a Vampire," while the third, "Bobby," was an original script about a woman tormented by the drowned son she brings back from the dead, in which "we tried to recapture the same pace and mood of the one with the doll chasing Karen Black."

Matheson noted that Finney, also the author of the frequently filmed science-fiction classic *The Body Snatchers*, "was the master of the time-travel story, and ['Second Chance'] was one of them. I love his time-travel stories, [like] 'The Love Letter.'" As early as 1973, Matheson had adapted "The Love Letter" into a half-hour script for the abortive *Dead of Night* series, but it was never filmed, and a quarter-century later, Curtis and screenwriter James Henerson expanded the story into a two-hour *Hallmark Hall of Fame* presentation. "As I said, I couldn't take a story that to me is perfection at its length and then try to stretch it out to fit a time period, but you know, [Finney has] written so many wonderful stories. His novel *Time and Again* is just marvelous, and I have said before that when I was going to do *Bid Time Return*, which became *Somewhere in Time*, I asked Jack if he minded if I wrote a time-travel novel, and of course he didn't. That's why there's a 'Professor Finney' in [the film]." *From Time to Time*, Finney's long-awaited sequel to his classic 1970 time-travel romance, *Time and Again*, was published just before he died in 1995.

Matheson's "The Test" was apparently adapted by Italian director Alessandro Blasetti for his series *I Racconti di Fantascienza di Blasetti*, as were several stories by Ray Bradbury, whose work was also the basis for Matheson's most ambitious script produced to date. But the six-hour NBC miniseries of Bradbury's *The Martian Chronicles* (1980) was hampered with a low-rent look and leaden direction by Michael Anderson. "I know we were both unhappy with the final product. I tried to be faithful. [The producers] actually wrote one in there themselves ['The Long Years'], about the guy who's got a robot wife, and he's out in the desert or something; I didn't write that one. I had done 'Usher II,' one of the [other] stories, rather than that, and it turned out quite well, actually. I had [set] 'There Shall Come Soft Rains' back on Earth, where the Rock Hudson character goes to his brother's house after the atomic war, and sees this house in operation, so that it's more or less identical to the story, except that he's there observing it, which Ray liked a lot. But then, because they'd put so much money in the space center [set], they stuck the story in that. Lost it entirely."

Matheson developed a warm rapport with Stephen Deutsch (a.k.a. Simon), who produced the film version of *Bid Time Return*, winner of the

World Fantasy ("Howard") Award for best novel. "I think on *Somewhere in Time*, because I had a closer relationship with the producer, it was the only time I had ever been *asked* to come on the shooting and stay there, and have transportation provided, a room provided, and my presence *desired*. Hollywood doesn't do that. There's nothing more of a pariah in this business than the writer after the script is written; they just want him out of the picture. They don't want to see him, they don't want to be reminded of how beholden they are to him. So they'd just as soon have him disappear, and then they can act like it's theirs entirely. Which they usually do." The late Christopher Reeve starred as a successful playwright who visits Grand Hotel on Michigan's Mackinac Island, where he falls in love with a 1912 photo of actress Elise McKenna (played by Jane Seymour) and wills himself back in time to join her. But after their brief romantic interlude, a mishap wrenches him, brokenhearted, into the present.

Poorly released and received at the time, the film grew into a cult classic after endless screenings on cable's famed Z Channel in Los Angeles, and inspired one of only three fan clubs devoted to a single motion picture, the International Network of *Somewhere in Time* Enthusiasts (INSITE), which has held a weekend at Grand Hotel every October since 1991. "That certainly seems to have worked out incredibly. . . . People are going back there and bringing all their own costumes and everything, and a man out here [Bill Shepard] started a newsletter [also called *INSITE*] a couple of years ago based on that one film, which is very successful. They've got more than [a thousand] subscribers to it." Jo Addie, who since 1999 has run INSITE and edited its journal, updated Shepard's book *The* Somewhere in Time *Story: Behind the Scenes of the Making of the Cult Romantic Fantasy Motion Picture* for the twenty-fifth anniversary of the film's release. John Barry's beautiful score, incorporating Rachmaninoff's *Rhapsody on a Theme of Paganini* (op. 43), variation XVIII), has also become a best-selling soundtrack album with several different recordings.

The film marked Matheson's only onscreen appearance to date in his own work, making a cameo as an "astonished man" who encounters Reeve outside a hotel men's room, but it was not his professional screen debut. "I was in a drama group [The Hidden Hills Players] out here where I live, and I did a lot of plays, and this producer we knew [Jo Swerling, Jr.] saw me in it, and had me do a part in *Captains and the Kings* [1976], the miniseries [based on Taylor Caldwell's novel, which also featured Jane Seymour]. I played President Garfield. There's a funny story about me finding out I was going to do a scene with Henry Fonda, which chilled my blood. [Later] another guy [Bernie Willits] saw me act out here and he had me do a whole educational film [*Jefferson and Hamilton*]—as a matter of fact, Ray [Bradbury] has seen it—where I play this sort of diabolical master of ceremonies who brings Alexander Hamilton and Thomas Jefferson back from the grave to debate—not only their period and the industrial revolution, but the Civil War and Vietnam. It was quite imaginative. I had a big part in that.

"I had a lot to learn, but my one word in *Somewhere in Time*, I memorized that pretty easily." Reminded that he actually says two words, he added, "I was padding my part. I tried to talk Jeannot Szwarc [also the director of Matheson's 'Big Surprise'] into letting me say something else, but he said no. . . . As a matter of fact, I remember they had a scene which I had written, it was in the book and in the movie, where this guy is talking to Chris Reeve in the elevator while he's coming downstairs to the lobby, and everything he says is totally incomprehensible to him, because of the [changes in the] language and what he's talking about, and the guy did it so badly that they cut it out. And Chris said, 'They should've let you do it.'" Matheson's daughter Ali Marie was also cast in the opening party scene, but "got excised. She had a lot more footage. She was going to be Chris Reeve's girlfriend in it, and then they edited it down so much I don't know whether you can even see her. She had no lines left. She was only around for like three weeks or a month."

Originally developed by director John Landis as a vehicle for Chevy Chase, a comedic version of *The Shrinking Man* was scaled back due to budgetary concerns and retooled into Joel Schumacher's disappointing distaff remake, *The Incredible Shrinking Woman* (1981), written by Jane Wagner for her partner, Lily Tomlin. Matheson's work fared less well in this social satire than on *The Simpsons*, which has variously— and hilariously—spoofed "Nightmare at 20,000 Feet" (as "Terror at 5½

Feet"), "Little Girl Lost" (as "Homer³"), and *The Omega Man* (as "The Homega Man") in its annual Halloween specials. "I love 'em, that's great. If they had made *The Incredible Shrinking Woman* into a really funny picture, you know, like the Zuckers [did] with *Airplane!* [1980], I wouldn't have said a word. It would have been great. Not that I said a word anyway, but I would have enjoyed it. I just didn't think they did a good job on it. I would have been happy to turn it into a comedy myself, and I think it would have been funnier. It turned out pretty poorly." A second comedic remake, possibly starring Eddie Murphy, has been announced.

It was not until twelve years after *Duel* that Steven Spielberg once again worked with Matheson, although in the interim, "one time [producer] Julia Phillips and her husband, Michael, had asked me if I wanted to write a movie about flying saucers, and I said no. And I gather that's what turned into *Close Encounters* [*of the Third Kind*, 1977]. . . . And it seems to me that I was even asked to do a rewrite on *Jaws* [1975], though I'm not positive of that, and if I was, I turned that down, too. I've got great judgment." But many saw a similarity between his work and the Spielberg-produced *Poltergeist* (1982), with its disembodied voice of a child trapped in another dimension. "If I'd sued, I would've gotten clobbered. It was too much money on the other side. Spielberg [had] asked me if he could see a cassette [of] . . . 'Little Girl Lost,' and I sent him one. This was some old Beta type of cassette. . . . He looked at it and then sent it back, and I never heard until someone said, 'Hey, I see they made your *Twilight Zone* into a movie.' Of course, there was a lot more to the movie than just that, but certainly that was part of it," he said.

"I think maybe Spielberg knows this and always came to me with some kind of offer that would sort of compensate. You know, to repay me or something like that, like writing the script for *Twilight Zone—The Movie* [1983], or having me as a consultant on *Amazing Stories*." The former (which was novelized by Robert Bloch) included Matheson's rewrites of three episodes, each with a different director, while John Landis (who also produced the film with Spielberg) wrote and directed the prologue and a fourth segment, during the filming of which actor Vic Morrow and two child actors died as the result of a helicopter crash. "It was horrible. I remember when I had lunch with Steven and Joe Dante [who, along with Australian director George Miller, helmed the other three segments] and John Landis, that Steven was kind of horrified by the [Landis] script. I mean, it had nothing to do with the accident, but it was so dark and foul and profane. Especially if you compared it to the second story, [a remake of George Clayton Johnson's classic] 'Kick the Can,' about the old folks' home.

"I did the script on that, too, but Steven had Melissa Mathison—who wrote under a pen name of Josh Rogan, which I guess was a joke about how a Japanese would say Josh Logan—redo it and they made it kind of mushy; mine was a lot harder edged, I thought." Matheson was also displeased with changes made to his script for the remake of "Nightmare at 20,000 Feet," with John Lithgow as the terrified passenger who, in this case, is already frantically afraid of flying. "That was George Miller's doing. He rewrote the script and, you know, [if] you turn the guy into a raving maniac from page one, where do you have to go? You can't build him up; if he's absolutely 125 percent terrified, you don't have that much area to work with. That's why I liked the one with Shatner so much, in that he had had a mental breakdown, and he was holding himself in real tight check, because he was afraid it was starting to happen again. Much more interesting. You know, Lithgow's a wonderful actor, and what he had to do he did as well as you could do."

The remaining segment was based on Jerome Bixby's "It's a *Good Life*," which Serling had adapted into one of the most memorable episodes, and was left largely intact by director Dante, but the same was sadly untrue of Matheson's belated ichthyological entry, *Jaws III* (a.k.a. *Jaws 3-D*, 1983). "I always say this, I sound paranoid, but I came up with a really good idea . . . of setting it in a marine park, like Sea World, and I had a really excellent story. And my script was very good. It's just that this guy who had been the art director [on the original *Jaws*], Joe Alves, directed it, and as you notice, he's never directed since. He's a wonderful art director, but he just simply is not cut out to be a director. It was just awful, and then [Carl] Gottlieb [a veteran of both previous films] did a terrible rewrite on it, and it just turned miserable. It was a pitiful piece of work. It could have been very good. Actually, although Jeannot [Szwarc] did a very good job with the second one [the success of which helped make *Somewhere in Time* possible], it could have been better in that [Alves] didn't have to have a carryover from the prior film.

"*Jaws II* [1978] *had* to be a continuation of *Jaws*, in the same location, with the same people, and everything. [With] *Jaws III* you could have completely jumped away from that, which I did. It was [Sidney] Sheinberg, of Universal, who insisted that it be the two sons of Sheriff Brody. I mean, it's ludicrous. The two sons of the sheriff go all the way down to Florida and have troubles with a great white? And he wanted it to be the same damn shark that had been burned in *Jaws II*! In the last one [*Jaws—The Revenge* (1987)], they had Brody's wife being chased—it's like these sharks have been to Oxford or something, they know exactly how to get around, they know where to find people, and they've got terrible, vengeful personalities." Part of the brief early-1980s 3-D revival, the film featured Dennis Quaid and John Putch as Mike and Sean Brody, respectively, the grown sons of Roy Scheider's character from the first two films, who run afoul of a great white and its thirty-five-foot mother inside Sea World, with Louis Gossett, Jr.—who had appeared in another Peter Benchley adaptation, *The Deep* (1977)—as the park's creator.

"Actually, the 3-D was my idea. We went down looking for locations, and we saw this wonderful spot—I recently saw it again at Epcot—called 'Sea Dreams,' which is just incredible, the effects of it. You're surrounded by the noises of underwater, you really feel like you're underwater. And it was so eerie, and I thought, 'Boy, if we could get this effect in the film, and do it in 3-D.' And then Joe Alves put them together and called it *Jaws 3-D*, but what they did with the 3-D was ludicrous. It added nothing, no effect whatever. And it just made the film darker. So that was really bad. . . . [Then] they gave the story credit to some guy who I never met [Guerdon Trueblood], who I didn't know was involved with the story. As far as I knew, I had made up the story myself. . . . But this other guy, they gave him credit for the story. . . . I never saw it, I never met him, I didn't know he was working on it, I don't know who he is to this day. It was just one of those little rulings that the Writers Guild [of America] makes." During the 1970s, Trueblood had written a series of TV movies that featured killer bees, ants, and tarantulas.

Matheson collaborated with James Bond screenwriter Richard

Maibaum on an unfilmed pilot for yet another anthology series, *Galaxy*. Horace Gold—who had published five of his stories, including "Shipshape Home," in *Galaxy* magazine in the early 1950s—was story editor. Aptly, when Matheson did return to episodic television after more than a decade, it was to adapt "Button, Button" from his story for the 1980s revival of *The Twilight Zone*; he hated what was done with his script, and to his relief, a second one, "The Doll," was produced instead on Spielberg's rival series, *Amazing Stories*. "It ['Button, Button'] was crappy, it was a piece of junk. It was just miserable. I wish I had been able to get that one away from the producers, like Spielberg was able to get 'The Doll' away from them. I could have done a much better job on the script, and I'm sure [Spielberg] would have done a lot better job on the production. They revised [my] script, and then did a bad job on it." The story concerns a couple offered a fortune to dispose of a total stranger by remote control; a feature-length version, *The Box*, is scheduled for release in March 2009.

"They were going to do 'The Doll,' and thank God they didn't," added Matheson, who put his Swanson pseudonym on the "Button, Button" script credit. "Finally they gave it up and gave it to *Amazing Stories*, [which] did a lovely job with it. It was a thing I had done for the original *Twilight Zone*. . . . It wasn't filmed because I wrote it for Bert Granet, and then Bill Froug, the producer who took over, didn't like my writing. As a matter of fact, when I was collaborating with Chuck Beaumont, I made the mistake of saying, because I didn't like to go out, 'I'll do the first drafts, and you go out and do the office meetings.' So because of that, everybody got the impression that I was like the retarded country cousin he was supporting out in the sticks. And Froug, the producer who we did *Philip Marlowe* for, was totally convinced of that. . . . I saw him one night on television with George Eckstein, the producer of *Duel*, and [Eckstein] was saying, 'You know, I'm really offended by this idea of [referring to the film as] Steven Spielberg's *Duel*. How dare they give him full credit, when it should be George Eckstein's *Duel*!' "

John Lithgow won an Emmy Award as outstanding guest performer in a drama series for his work in "The Doll" as a lonely bachelor who falls in love with the gift he bought for his niece, only to learn that its model, a spinster schoolteacher, not only matches the persona he has created for it, but also bought a doll in *his* image from the same shop. "I remember at the time talking with the producers before Bert Granet left, and I was thinking of Marty Balsam playing the part. But it turned out very nicely. I mean, I was very happy with it the way they did it on *Amazing Stories.*" Just a week later, the show featured Matheson's adaptation of his story "One for the Books," with Sean Penn's father, Leo Penn, playing a college janitor who inexplicably begins absorbing knowledge. "I just met him on the set, and talked to him briefly. A very nice man. He lived next door to my son Richard the last three or four years, and Richard got to know him quite well. A very sweet man. . . . You know, Sean Penn's mother, Eileen Ryan, was in my Howard Duff episode [on *The Twilight Zone*]." The late Leo Penn had also directed Matheson's "The Enemy Within."

Matheson was hired as a creative consultant for the second and final season. "I enjoyed it very much. My agent called it 'The Gig of the Year.' What I first did was, I would read a bunch of their scripts and ideas and make notes on them, and then we would go to a big general meeting in this big boardroom at Amblin [Entertainment], and Spielberg would be there, and the two guys [Joshua Brand and John Falsey] who created that funny series about Alaska, *Northern Exposure*. They were the story editors [and supervising producers] when I went to these meetings. And [production executive] Kathleen Kennedy would be there, and we would just talk. There was a whole pile of food up on the bar—bagels and cream cheese and all that delicious stuff, and then we would just work for two or three hours discussing, and then we'd go out on the deck and they'd have a big catered meal, so it was great. And I guess they liked what I contributed to these meetings, so they hired me to come and do it on a weekly basis." The series was a veritable family affair, with both Richard Christian and Ali Marie Matheson contributing teleplays.

"She also did an *Amazing Stories* ['Lane Change'], an original. That was her own idea. I helped her a little with the surprise ending, but it was her story, basically," while the final episode, "Miss Stardust," was adapted by R.C. and his sometime writing partner, Thomas Szollosi, from Matheson's story. Tobe Hooper, best known for *The Texas Chain-*

*saw Massacre* (1974), Stephen King's *Salem's Lot* (1979), and *Poltergeist*, directed this comic tale of a vegetative alien ("Weird Al" Yankovic) who demands that the titular beauty contest include entrants from Mars, Venus, and Jupiter. "I got a kick out of what Richard and Tom did with 'Miss Stardust' . . . It was kind of bizarre, with these strange creatures and everything, and I guess that's why [Hooper was chosen to direct]. You know, it's like people associate me with scary stuff. They don't realize I've written a lot of comedies." This was the first produced script for which one of the Matheson children had collaborated with him or adapted his work onscreen.

As early as 1972, Richard Matheson and his son R.C. had joined forces for *PSI*, a one-hour pilot story and script about the work of the UCLA parapsychology lab (R.C. had worked there as an investigative journalist, and related, "they permitted us access to their well-protected files"), which was sold to Lorimar Television and ABC, but never produced. They now embarked on a productive period during which they collaborated on a trio of speculative screenplays (*Face Off, Shifter,* and *Midvale*); the younger Matheson had six under his belt already, the first of which, *Three O'Clock High* (1987), was written with Szollosi and sold to Spielberg, who served as its uncredited executive producer. Ironically, only one of the Mathesons' efforts has been filmed to date, and that in a form far from what they had envisioned. But the experience was uniquely rewarding, both personally and professionally: it brought them closer, both as writers and as father and son, as well as earning them a great deal of money in a relatively short period of time.

Their first screenplay was for a buddy-cop movie—familiar ground for R.C., who had been a writer and/or producer on such shows as *Stone* (featuring *Duel* star Dennis Weaver and his son Bobby), *Simon & Simon*, and *Hardcastle and McCormick*—involving a brilliant but erratic detective whose multiple personality disorder manifests itself in times of stress. Due to various commitments by both Mathesons, it took them a year of working in coffee shops and in their respective homes to write *Face Off,* so titled because the villain was originally a sociopathic hockey player. Their agents at the Creative Artists Agency soon sold it to Tri-Star as a planned sequel to the movie *Cobra* (1986), but star Sylvester

Stallone then dropped out. Reconfigured for CAA clients Gene Hackman and Dan Aykroyd as a variation on the *Lethal Weapon* franchise, the project was given to director Bob Clark, whose holiday favorite *A Christmas Story* (1983) starred none other than Darren McGavin. After being rewritten by Clark and an uncredited Aykroyd, the script was first retitled *The Von Metz Incident* and finally filmed as the critically reviled *Loose Cannons* (1990).

Said Matheson, "It's reached a point now where the director will be hired, and part of his contract is that he gets to rewrite the script, whether he's a good writer or not. My son Richard and I sold a script and the director, Bob Clark, completely redid it. It ended up as *Loose Cannons*. He totally rewrote it, totally. There was almost nothing left of it. Then I did an excellent job on this adaptation of John Saul's *Creature*. Universal said, 'Yeah, let's make it,' and they finally got this director [Frank LaLoggia], and at the moment, as we speak [in 1991], he's rewriting the script. I hope there's enough left so that I'll get a cocredit." *Creature* was never produced, but Matheson's version was published in his collection *Darker Places* (2004). He and R.C. next wrote *Shifter*—a horror comedy about a shape-shifter who is having a nervous breakdown—and quickly sold it to Richard Donner (the director of the original "Nightmare at 20,000 Feet"), but left the project early due to creative differences with Donner's wife and producing partner, Lauren Schuler Donner; having been revised by other writers, it also remains unproduced.

Described by R.C. as "a magical story about death and reconnection," *Midvale* was sought by several prospective buyers, and in 1996 became the first speculative script purchased by powerhouse producer-director Ivan Reitman in the twenty-year history of his production company, Northern Lights Entertainment, which was based at Universal Studios. Reitman noted in a front-page *Daily Variety* article that he was moved to tears by the script, and he so enjoyed working with the Mathesons on minor rewrites that after leaving Universal to start a new company, Montecito, he asked them to pen a second screenplay for an "A" horror film in the tradition of *The Haunting* and Donner's *The Omen* (1976). While Reitman pursued casting options for *Midvale*, most notably Tom Cruise, the Mathesons responded with *The Nature of Evil*, a story about supernatural horror on a college campus, but unfortunately, neither has gone before the cameras to date, and with no time for further screenplay collaborations, father and son have since turned down multiple offers from other studios and producers with whom they felt less in synch.

As with many screenwriters, Matheson's unproduced projects outnumber those that were filmed, a fact he has frequently lamented. "I was paid for them, but they were never filmed. It was the unfulfillment I was regretting. But then, as I think I added and my wife always points out, I was supporting four children at that time, so I really didn't have much choice. But it's too bad. A lot of novels never written." He has occasionally turned unproduced scripts or stage plays into novels like *Earthbound* (1982) and *Now You See It* . . . (1995). The former "would make, I think, a fascinating, almost an X-rated horror picture. . . . Actually, they ripped me off, there was a television film [*The Haunting Passion* (1983)] with, of all people, Jane Seymour, where she was being assaulted sexually by a male ghost. But I still hope something comes of *Earthbound*—or as my good friend Stan Shpetner, a TV producer, insists on calling it, *The Cold and Alien Kiss of Death*. Try to squeeze that onto a twelve-inch screen!"

Matheson returned to the TV-movie format with his next two produced projects, starting with *The Dreamer of Oz* (1990), a warm-hearted biopic portraying both the life of and the fantasy world created by L. Frank Baum (played by John Ritter), who wrote *The Wonderful Wizard of Oz* and thirteen sequels. "The guy who directed *The Dreamer of Oz*, Jack Bender, did a beautiful job," yet Matheson was less satisfied with the misleadingly titled *Twilight Zone: Rod Serling's Lost Classics* (1994), for which he turned a ten-page outline discovered after Serling's death into a half-hour script. "I went in with Carol Serling [Rod's widow] and CBS, and they had this long script that Rod had written ["Where the Dead Are"], and then there were five or six [outlines], and I chose a couple of them. I guess I just adapted the one, 'The Theatre.' The long one was [filmed] exactly as Serling had written it. I did the other one, and I really wasn't crazy about it. It was difficult to do properly, and I don't think what they did was all that good anyway." Because the longer script ran for a full ninety minutes with commercials, it could never have been intended as a *Twilight Zone* episode.

Matheson's work began appearing on cable television when Ali Marie and her husband, Jon Cooksey, adapted his story "First Anniversary," about a man married to an alien shape-shifter, into an episode of Showtime's *Outer Limits* revival. "I thought, how on Earth could they make something out of 'First Anniversary'? It was such a short story. I couldn't understand how they did it, she and her husband. It just baffled me how they could do it so well." Then, more than twenty years after the original, he was reunited with Curtis and Nolan (in a manner of speaking) for *Trilogy of Terror II* (1996), which aired on the USA network, with Lysette Anthony in the multiple leading roles and Nolan and Curtis writing both "The Graveyard Rats" (adapted from Henry Kuttner's story) and "He Who Kills." The latter was a sequel pitting Anthony's character against the eponymous Zuni doll, which like *The Night Strangler* was well made but essentially a rehash, while the second segment was simply a refilming of Matheson's "Bobby," the last episode in *Dead of Night*, with Anthony supplanting Joan Hackett as the ill-fated mother.

It has now been more than a decade since a Matheson script was produced, but his onscreen presence continued with versions of his novels *What Dreams May Come* (1978) and *A Stir of Echoes* (1958), each of which he had also adapted into an unfilmed screenplay. Vincent Ward's *What Dreams May Come* (1998) featured Robin Williams as a man who tries to contact his grieving widow (Annabella Sciorra) after he dies in a car crash, and when she commits suicide, he voluntarily leaves his idyllic afterlife—rendered as a kind of interactive painting with Oscar-winning effects—to follow her into Hell and save her soul. Writer-director David Koepp's *Stir of Echoes* (1999) updated and relocated the story from an L.A. suburb to working-class Chicago, yet remained true to its spirit (eliciting praise from Matheson), with Kevin Bacon impressive as a telephone lineman turned into an unwilling psychic "receiver" by hypnosis. In Ernie Barbarash's Sci-Fi Channel sequel *Stir of Echoes: The Homecoming* (2007), Rob Lowe starred as an Iraq war veteran haunted by visions of the dead, with the son of Bacon's character appearing in one scene; Matheson received no credit.

Matheson was being courted by the producers of various series fairly recently, with an eye toward possible employment, but has been disinclined to accept, and said at the time, "It seems like the anthology type of show is just nonexistent now. Is there anything on television? I don't think so. It's all running stories, running characters. . . . I had been approached by Mel Tormé's son [Tracy] to work on *Sliders*, and I've been in to talk to Chris Carter of *The X-Files* because he has said that he was inspired by the two Kolchak movies on the series. He sent me a bunch of scripts to read, but whether he really wanted me to work on them, I don't know. Of course, he certainly didn't need me. And *Outer Limits*, too. I went in to talk to them, and I just didn't want to do it." Both Carter and J. Michael Straczynski, who created *Babylon 5* and its short-lived spin-off, *Crusade*, have named characters after Matheson in their respective series.

R. C. Matheson was reunited with Tobe Hooper on a second adaptation of his father's work, "Dance of the Dead"—a 2005 episode of Showtime's *Masters of Horror*, in which corpses are utilized for gruesome post-apocalyptic entertainment—and has also scripted a third, "Mad House," which as of this writing may be produced if the cable anthology series returns for a third season. Two shorts based on Matheson's "Blood Son" appeared in 2006, the first of which was an accomplished and largely faithful fifteen-minute adaptation that marked the directorial debut of Michael McGruther, the cowriter of Joel Schumacher's *Tigerland* (2000). Shot in Matheson's home state of New Jersey, where it won a Director's Award at the Trenton Film Festival, McGruther's *Blood Son* concerns Jules (played by Lucas Wotkowski), a teenager who is shunned for being "different" and then, after reading *Dracula*, decides that his ambition—as well as his path to revenge—lies in becoming a vampire. The second version, the eight-minute *My Ambition*, was written and directed by Keith Dinielli, who is now working with producer Michael Phillips to develop the story as a feature.

Clearly, Matheson's influence on a generation of authors and filmmakers is strong, from his own children (three of whom are active in film and television, with Richard Christian enjoying an acclaimed literary career as well) to the likes of Spielberg and Stephen King, both of whom have repeatedly cited the profound effects of Matheson's work on their stunning success. "Stephen, I guess, has said that up till that time, he thought you had to do crypts and graveyards and all that, and he found out that you could do a horror story in a supermarket, and that sort of altered his entire approach to what he was writing. I also got Steven Spielberg started out, too. [*Duel*] was his first film. So, I'm like their creative father. I have a big poster from *Duel*, and Steven Spielberg wrote on it, 'I feel like we grew up together.' . . . He made a speech at the Writers Guild when they gave him a big award, in which he personally read off the names of every writer who had helped create his career, and my name was certainly in it." The third feature-film version of *I Am Legend*, starring Will Smith, was released in December 2007 and propelled the movie tie-in edition of the novel to number two on the *New York Times* mass-market bestseller list—ironically, the best sales of Matheson's career to date.

*Author's Note*: Richard Matheson was the first person I ever interviewed professionally, and that experience led directly to my secondary career as a film journalist and sometime editor; day jobs came and went, but my love for writing about movies, and talking to those who made them to preserve their experiences in their own words, endured and flourished. Over the years, I have had the great good fortune to interview, correspond with, and in some cases even befriend several other members of Matheson's illustrious creative circle—Robert Bloch, Ray Bradbury, George Clayton Johnson, William F. Nolan, and Jerry Sohl (some sadly no longer with us)—yet it is Richard who remains my obsession. I'd always admired and enjoyed his work, even before I started connecting the dots and realized he was at the forefront of a renaissance in fantasy films and television during the 1960s and '70s, his name linked with some of the biggest in the genre: Jack Arnold, Rod Serling, Roger Corman, Terence Fisher, Steven Spielberg, Dan Curtis, and others too numerous to mention.

We finally met face to face at the same snowy World Horror Convention described in Greg Cox's essay (in this book) "Editing Matheson," and I couldn't believe the stroke of luck that brought Richard to my home state of Connecticut, of all places; little did I dream (darkly) that I would one day co-edit this book with the master of ceremonies,

Stanley Wiater—a total stranger to me at the time. I'll never forget my excitement at hearing Richard give what he said was, incredibly, his very first public reading, or how warmly welcome I was immediately made to feel by the Matheson family, who invited me to dine with them and with Peter Straub, and were solicitous of my safety when they learned I would be driving from Stamford back home to Danbury in the blizzard later that night. One of my most cherished memories is of the moment (I believe it was after a screening of *Burn, Witch, Burn*, which I'd heard about for years but never seen, and of course thoroughly enjoyed) when Richard Christian Matheson—who has inherited every drop of his dad's graciousness—took me aside and told me just how much my friendship and my work meant to Richard, Senior.

It was not until 2005 that we all saw one another again, this time at the Horror Writers Association's annual Bram Stoker Awards Weekend in Burbank, where Richard joined George Clayton Johnson (whom I had the pleasure of meeting for the first time that night, years after I'd interviewed him over the phone) for the panel entitled "Meet the Masters of *The Twilight Zone*." Despite working in Manhattan for two decades, I was still pretty much a hometown boy, a little nervous about navigating the notorious freeways of L.A. But thanks to the miracle of MapQuest, I got safely to the Burbank Hilton, and the next day I finally made the long-awaited pilgrimage to Richard's house, a former horse ranch in the hills that seemed a world away from L.A. proper. By then, I was immersed in my magnum-opus-in-the-works, a comprehensive study of his film and television oeuvre (periodically put on the back burner to edit his *Duel & The Distributor* and the volume you are now reading). As he patiently endured endless questions about stuff he'd done almost fifty years ago, he and his lovely wife, Ruth, once again made me feel right at home.

As of this writing, *Richard Matheson on Screen* is nearing completion after more than a decade, and Richard—who has seen quite a bit of the manuscript as I painstakingly polish it to my perfectionist's satisfaction—has paid me the enormous compliment of observing on more than one occasion that it contained information even he had never known. It bespeaks his tremendous stature and influence among those who know his work that, since he made his screenwriting debut with *The Incredible*

*Shrinking Man* in 1957, nearly a hundred films and television episodes have been written by Matheson or based on his work, giving me a steady stream of new material, yet with the side effect of making my own book perennially incomplete. I can only imagine what other Matheson-related projects will have dropped into my lap by the time this one is actually published, but I hope most of all that the object of the exercise continues to approve of what he sees from his self-described "demi-Boswell," and in the meantime, here are eighteen years' worth of grateful thanks to Richard Matheson from his longtime friend and fan.

All quotations by Richard Matheson taken from telephone interviews conducted by the author on August 3, 1991, and January 12, 1999, portions of which were published in *Filmfax* #42 (Dec./Jan. 1994) and #75–76 (Oct./Jan. 2000), respectively.

# Bibliographies, Filmographies, and More

*Compiled and Annotated by Paul Stuve
and Matthew R. Bradley*

The following lists are the result of years of exhaustive research, and we believe they are the most complete and accurate sources of "Mathesoniana" available anywhere. While the careful reader may notice some slight differences between the titles herein and those found in previously published lists of Matheson's work, in nearly all instances the information we cited was obtained by examining the actual item itself (book, magazine, film, episode, etc.), and only rarely was it necessary to rely on other published sources for the details of a particular entry. In this manner, we have been able to correct several errors that previously published lists have propagated. We should note, however, that the exact titles of some books and magazines remain unresolved due to inconsistencies between the cover, spine, title page, and/or copyright page. For example, is the classic magazine called *The Magazine of Fantasy and Science Fiction* or *The Magazine of Fantasy & Science Fiction*? Each appears on the covers of different issues. Similar variations in book titles include *Off Beat* vs. *Off-Beat*, and *The Gun Fight* vs. *The Gunfight*. The most inconsistent item we reviewed was the fifth edition of Frederik Pohl's *Star Science Fiction* anthology, which has three variations in the title on the cover, spine, and title page. When faced with such inconsistencies, we resolved them by using first the copyright page (if any), then the title page, and then the cover. While these minor variations represent a challenge for the bibliographer, we are confident that the wording ultimately selected for inclusion is sufficient for the collector to locate any desired items. Happy reading!

## Books: First and Limited Editions

These are the first hardcover and paperback editions of Matheson's books and chapbooks, as well as all special and limited editions. Most of these are American editions, but some titles were first published in England. The term "first edition" can be confusing at times, and for this list we use the clarifying definitions found on the website of *Firsts: The Book Collector's Magazine* (www.firsts.com). "True first edition" refers to the very first publication of a book or collection. "First hardcover edition" and "first paperback edition" refer to books or collections that were previously published in paperback or hardcover versions, respectively. "First separate edition" refers to a work that has been published previously as part of another book, and is now being published in a separate "stand-alone" volume for the first time. "First edition thus" refers to a book that has been previously published and is being reprinted, perhaps by a different publisher, with a major revision and/or additional material, such as new illustrations, a new foreword or afterword, etc. Many of Matheson's limited editions fall into this category.

*Someone Is Bleeding* (Lion Books, Inc., 1953)
   Novel. Paperback original and true first edition. Matheson's first published book.

*Fury on Sunday* (Lion Books, Inc., 1953)
   Novel. Paperback original and true first edition.

*I Am Legend* (Fawcett Gold Medal, 1954)
   Novel. Paperback original and true first edition. The first science-fiction novel published by Fawcett Gold Medal.

*Born of Man and Woman* (Chamberlain Press, 1954)
   Short story collection. True first edition. Matheson's first hardcover book, issued with dustjacket. Anthology of fifteen previously published and two previously unpublished short stories.
   "Introduction: The Art of Richard Matheson" (by Robert Bloch)
   "Born of Man and Woman"

"Third from the Sun"
"Through Channels"
"Lover When You're Near Me"
"SRL Ad"
"Mad House"
"F—" (originally published as "The Foodlegger")
"Dear Diary"
"To Fit the Crime"
"Witch War"
"Return"
"Dress of White Silk"
"Full Circle"
"Disappearing Act"
"The Wedding"
"Shipshape Home"
"The Traveller"

*Third From the Sun* (Bantam, 1955)

Short story collection. First paperback edition. Matheson's first paperback anthology, it collects twelve previously published stories from Chamberlain Press's *Born of Man and Woman*.

"Born of Man and Woman"
"Third from the Sun"
"Lover When You're Near Me"
"SRL Ad"
"Mad House"
"F—" (originally published as "The Foodlegger")
"To Fit the Crime"
"Dress of White Silk"
"Disappearing Act"
"The Wedding"
"Shipshape Home"
"The Traveller"

*The Shrinking Man* (Fawcett Gold Medal, 1956)

Novel. Paperback original and true first edition.

*The Shores of Space* (Bantam, 1957)
Short story collection. Paperback original and true first edition. Anthology of thirteen previously published short stories.
"Being"
"Pattern for Survival"
"Steel"
"The Test"
"Clothes Make the Man"
"Blood Son" (originally published as " 'Drink My Red Blood . . .' " and also as "Drink My Blood")
"Trespass" (originally published as "Mother by Protest")
"When Day Is Dun"
"The Curious Child"
"The Funeral"
"The Last Day"
"Little Girl Lost"
"The Doll That Does Everything"

*A Stir of Echoes* ( J.B. Lippincott Company, 1958)
Novel. Hardcover, with dustjacket. True first edition.

*A Stir of Echoes* (Crest, 1959)
Novel. First paperback edition.

*Ride the Nightmare* (Ballantine Books, 1959)
Novel. Paperback original and true first edition.

*The Beardless Warriors* (Little, Brown and Company, 1960)
Novel. Hardcover, with dustjacket. True first edition.

*Shock!* (Dell Publishing Co., Inc., 1961)
Short story collection. Paperback original and true first edition. Anthology of thirteen previously published short stories.
"The Children of Noah"
"Lemmings"
"The Splendid Source"
"Long Distance Call" (originally published as "Sorry, Right Number")

"Mantage"
"One for the Books"
"The Holiday Man"
"Dance of the Dead"
"Legion of Plotters"
"The Edge"
"The Creeping Terror" (originally published as "A Touch of Grape-
    fruit")
"Death Ship"
"The Distributor"

*The Beardless Warriors* (Bantam, 1961)
    Novel. First paperback edition.

*Shock II* (Dell Publishing Co., Inc., 1964)
    Short story collection. Paperback original and true first edition. An-
thology of thirteen previously published short stories.
    "A Flourish of Strumpets"
    "Brother to the Machine"
    "No Such Thing as a Vampire"
    "Descent"
    "Deadline" (originally published as "Dead Line")
    "The Man Who Made the World"
    "Graveyard Shift" (originally published as "The Faces," and also as
        "Day of Reckoning")
    "The Likeness of Julie"
    "Lazarus II"
    "Big Surprise" (originally published as "What Was in the Box?")
    "Crickets"
    "Mute"
    "From Shadowed Places"

*Shock III* (Dell Publishing Co., Inc., 1966)
    Short story collection. Paperback original and true first edition. An-
thology of thirteen previously published short stories.
    "Girl of My Dreams"

"'Tis the Season to Be Jelly" (originally published as "Tis the Season to Be Jelly")

"Return"

"The Jazz Machine"

"The Disinheritors"

"Slaughter House"

"Shock Wave" (originally published as "Crescendo")

"When the Waker Sleeps" (originally published as "The Waker Dreams")

"Witch War"

"First Anniversary"

"Miss Stardust"

"Full Circle"

"Nightmare at 20,000 Feet"

*Shock Waves* (Dell Publishing Co., Inc., 1970)

Short story collection. Paperback original and true first edition. Anthology of twelve previously published short stories, one previously unpublished short story, and the first three previously unpublished chapters of a planned novel (*Come Fygures, Come Shadowes*). Published in Great Britain under the title *Shock 4*.

"A Visit to Santa Claus" (originally published as "I'll Make It Look Good")

"Finger Prints"

"Deus Ex Machina"

"The Thing"

"The Conqueror" (also published as "Go West, Young Man")

"A Drink of Water"

"Dying Room Only"

"Advance Notice" (originally published as "Letter to the Editor")

"Wet Straw"

"Therese" (originally published as "Needle in the Heart")

"Day of Reckoning" (originally published as "The Faces," and also as "Graveyard Shift")

"Prey"
"Come Fygures, Come Shadowes"
"The Finishing Touches"

*I Am Legend* (Walker and Company, 1970)
Novel. First hardcover edition, issued with dustjacket.

*Hell House* (Viking Press, 1971)
Novel. Hardcover, with dustjacket. True first edition.

*Hell House* (Bantam, 1972)
Novel. First paperback edition.

*The Shrinking Man* (David Bruce & Watson, 1973)
Novel. First hardcover edition, issued with dustjacket. Published in England.
Introduction (by Kingsley Amis)
*The Shrinking Man*

*Bid Time Return* (Viking Press, 1975)
Novel. Hardcover, with dustjacket. True first edition. Winner of the World Fantasy Award for best novel in 1976.

*Bid Time Return* (Ballantine Books, 1976)
Novel. First paperback edition.

*What Dreams May Come* (G.P. Putnam's Sons, 1978)
Novel. Hardcover, with dustjacket. True first edition.

*What Dreams May Come* (Berkley, 1979)
Novel. First paperback edition.

*The Shrinking Man* (Gregg Press, 1979)
Novel. First edition thus. Hardcover, issued without dustjacket. Part of The Gregg Press Science Fiction Series. Includes previously unpublished storyboards and stills.
Introduction (by Joseph Milicia)
Storyboards (by Jack Arnold)

Stills

Introduction (by Kingsley Amis)

*The Shrinking Man*

*Earthbound* (writing as Logan Swanson; Playboy Paperbacks, 1982)

Novel. Paperback original and true first edition. This edition was heavily edited without Matheson's approval, and was published under his pseudonym.

*The Twilight Zone: The Original Stories* (Edited by Martin H. Greenberg, Richard Matheson, & Charles G. Waugh; Avon Books, 1985)

Short story collection. Paperback original and true first edition. Anthology of thirty previously published stories, including eight by Matheson, that Rod Serling bought for the *Twilight Zone* television series.

Preface (by Carol Serling)

Introduction

"Disappearing Act"

"Third From the Sun"

"Little Girl Lost"

"Mute"

"Death Ship"

"Steel"

"Nightmare at 20,000 Feet"

"Long Distance Call" (originally published as "Sorry, Right Number")

*Earthbound* (Robinson Publishing, 1989)

Novel. Hardcover, with dustjacket. First edition of Matheson's approved text, and first edition published with Matheson's name rather than his pseudonym. Published in England.

*Richard Matheson: Collected Stories* (Dream/Press, 1989)

Short story collection. Originally planned as a two-volume set in slipcase, it was ultimately published in a single 900-page tome. Published in three hardcover states, all issued without dustjacket: a 100-copy deluxe numbered edition in leather traycase, a 400-copy numbered edition in slipcase, and a 500-copy unnumbered edition, all signed by

Matheson. (The publisher reports that the total edition size is 1250 copies, although the nature of the remaining 250 copies is unknown.) The deluxe edition is particularly nice, printed on heavier stock paper and bound in full leather with handmade marbled endpapers, red top-staining, and a red ribbon, and housed in a quarter-leather and cloth clamshell traycase. All of these editions were preceded by a 350-copy paperback "Prevue" edition sold at the 1989 World Fantasy Convention, which is regarded as the true first edition. There are also twenty-five hand-bound leather contributor copies (twenty in brown leather and five in red) made as thank-you gifts for use by the author and publisher. These are printed on 60-lb. stock with red top-staining, a red ribbon, and marbled endpapers that differ from those used for the deluxe numbered edition. Both versions are signed and dated by Matheson. The red version also includes copies of Matheson's handwritten thank-you notes to contributors and a Polaroid photo of him inscribing those copies. The book won the Bram Stoker Award for fiction collection in 1989, and the World Fantasy Award for best collection in 1990.

"To the Reader"

"Born of Man and Woman"

"Third From the Sun"

"When the Waker Sleeps" (originally published as "The Waker Dreams")

"From Ray Bradbury" (by Ray Bradbury)

"Blood Son" (originally published as " 'Drink My Red Blood . . .' " and also as "Drink My Blood")

"Clothes Make the Man"

"Dress of White Silk"

"Return"

"The Thing"

"Through Channels"

"Witch War"

"From Robert Bloch" (by Robert Bloch)

"Advance Notice" (originally published as "Letter to the Editor")

"Brother to the Machine"

"F—" (originally published as "The Foodlegger")

"Lover When You're Near Me"

"Mad House"

"Shipshape Home"

"SRL Ad"

"To Fit the Crime"

"Death Ship"

"From William F. Nolan" (by William F. Nolan)

"Disappearing Act"

"The Disinheritors"

"Dying Room Only"

"Full Circle"

"The Last Day"

"Lazarus II"

"Legion of Plotters"

"Little Girl Lost"

"Long Distance Call" (originally published as "Sorry, Right Number")

"Slaughter House"

"Trespass" (originally published as "Mother by Protest")

"The Wedding"

"Wet Straw"

"Being"

"The Conqueror" (also published as "Go West, Young Man")

"From Jack Finney" (by Jack Finney)

"The Curious Child"

"Dear Diary"

"Descent"

"The Doll That Does Everything"

"The Man Who Made the World"

"The Test"

"The Traveller"

"When Day Is Dun"

"Dance of the Dead"

"The Funeral"

"Miss Stardust"

"One for the Books"

"Pattern for Survival"

"From George Clayton Johnson" (by George Clayton Johnson)

"A Flourish of Strumpets"

"The Splendid Source"

"Steel"

"A Visit to Santa Claus" (originally published as "I'll Make It Look Good")

"The Children of Noah"

"The Holiday Man"

"Lemmings"

"Old Haunts"

"The Distributor"

"The Edge"

"Big Surprise" (originally published as "What Was in the Box?")

"The Creeping Terror" (originally published as "A Touch of Grapefruit")

"Deadline" (originally published as "Dead Line")

"Mantage"

"No Such Thing as a Vampire"

"From Harlan Ellison" (by Harlan Ellison)

"Crickets"

"Day of Reckoning" (originally published as "The Faces," and also as "Graveyard Shift")

"First Anniversary"

"From Shadowed Places"

"Nightmare at 20,000 Feet"

"Finger Prints"

"The Likeness of Julie"

"Mute"

"Deus Ex Machina"

"Girl of My Dreams"

"The Jazz Machine"

"From Stephen King" (by Stephen King)

"Shock Wave" (originally published as "Crescendo")

"'Tis the Season To Be Jelly" (originally published as "Tis the Season To Be Jelly")

"Interest"

"A Drink of Water"

"Therese" (originally published as "Needle in the Heart")

"Prey"

"Button, Button"

"From Dennis Etchison" (by Dennis Etchison)

"By Appointment Only"

"The Finishing Touches"

"'Til Death Do Us Part" (originally published as "Till Death Do Us Part")

"The Near Departed"

"Buried Talents"

"Duel"

"From Richard Christian Matheson" (by Richard Christian Matheson)

Bibliography

*Through Channels* (Footsteps Press, 1989)

Short story. Chapbook. First edition thus. Published in two states: a 500-copy numbered edition signed by Matheson, and a 52-copy lettered edition signed by Matheson and (in red ink) by Vincent Price.

"In Appreciation" (by Vincent Price)

"Through Channels"

Afterword (by Roger Corman)

*The Shrinking Man* (Easton Press, 1990)

Novel. First edition thus. Hardcover, issued without dustjacket. Part of The Easton Press's *The Masterpieces of Science Fiction* series. A leather-bound copy, with gold embossing, gilt edges, and raised spine.

Introduction (by Harlan Ellison)

*The Shrinking Man*

*Somewhere in Time/What Dreams May Come: Two Novels of Love and Fantasy* (Dream/Press, 1991)

Novels. First edition thus, published in three hardcover states: a special commemorative edition with dustjacket (printed for the *Somewhere in Time* Weekend held October 25–27, 1991, at Grand Hotel on Mackinac Island, Michigan, where *Somewhere in Time* was filmed), a 350-copy numbered edition with dustjacket in slipcase, and a trade hardcover edition with dustjacket. The special commemorative edition and the numbered edition are signed by Matheson. The special commemorative edition preceded the numbered edition by several weeks, and is considered the true first edition of this title. Its dustjacket has blank inside flaps, unlike that of the numbered edition, which includes text and a photo of Matheson. The trade edition had multiple printings, the first of which is distinguishable from later printings only by the placement of the text on the inside of the dustjacket, which is ⅛ inch from the bottom border in the first printing and ⅜ inch from the bottom border for the later printings.

"To the Reader"
*Somewhere in Time* (originally published as *Bid Time Return*)
*What Dreams May Come*

*Journal of the Gun Years* (M. Evans & Company, 1991)
    Novel. Hardcover, with dustjacket. True first edition. Winner of the Golden Spur Award from the Western Writers of America for best western novel of 1991.

*Journal of the Gun Years* (Berkley, 1992)
    Novel. First paperback edition.

*The Gun Fight* (M. Evans & Company, 1993)
    Novel. Hardcover, with dustjacket. True first edition.

*7 Steps to Midnight* (Forge, 1993)
    Novel. Hardcover, with dustjacket. True first edition.

*The Gun Fight* (Berkley, 1993)
    Novel. First paperback edition.

*By the Gun* (M. Evans & Company, 1993)
    Short story collection. Hardcover, with dustjacket. True first edi-

tion. Anthology of four previously published and two previously unpublished western short stories.

"Gunsight" (originally published as "They Don't Make 'em Tougher")
"Go West, Young Man" (originally published as "The Conqueror")
"Boy in the Rocks" (originally published as "Son of a Gunman," and also as "Get Off the Circle 7")
"Too Proud to Lose"
"Little Jack Cornered"
"Of Death and Thirty Minutes"

*The Path: Metaphysics for the '90s* (Capra Press, 1993)
Nonfiction. Trade paperback original and true first edition.

*By the Gun* (Berkley, 1994)
Short story collection. First paperback edition. Anthology of six previously published western short stories.

"Gunsight" (originally published as "They Don't Make 'em Tougher")
"Go West, Young Man" (originally published as "The Conqueror")
"Boy in the Rocks" (originally published as "Son of a Gunman," and also as "Get Off the Circle 7")
"Too Proud to Lose"
"Little Jack Cornered"
"Of Death and Thirty Minutes"

*Shadow on the Sun* (M. Evans & Company, 1994)
Novel. Hardcover, with dustjacket. True first edition.

*Shadow on the Sun* (Berkley, 1994)
Novel. First paperback edition.

*The Twilight Zone: The Original Stories* (Edited by Martin H. Greenberg, Richard Matheson, & Charles G. Waugh; MJF Books, c. 1994)
Short story collection. First hardcover edition, with dustjacket. Anthology of thirty previously published stories, including eight by Matheson, that Rod Serling purchased for the television series *The Twilight Zone*. Although the copyright page of this edition lists a publication date of 1985, it was actually published in the mid-1990s after the paperback.

The dustjacket lacks a price, a common practice for books produced for bookstore "bargain" tables.

Preface (by Carol Serling)

Introduction

"Disappearing Act"

"Third From the Sun"

"Little Girl Lost"

"Mute"

"Death Ship"

"Steel"

"Nightmare at 20,000 Feet"

"Long Distance Call" (originally published as "Sorry, Right Number")

*Earthbound* (Tor, 1994)

Novel. Hardcover, with dustjacket. First American edition of Matheson's approved text.

*7 Steps to Midnight* (Tor, 1995)

Novel. First paperback edition.

*Now You See It . . .* (Tor, 1995)

Novel. Hardcover, with dustjacket. True first edition.

*The Incredible Shrinking Man* (Tor, 1995)

Fiction collection. Paperback. First edition thus. This edition contains the novel and nine previously published short stories.

*The Shrinking Man*

"Nightmare at 20,000 Feet"

"The Test"

"The Holiday Man"

"Mantage"

"The Distributor"

"By Appointment Only"

"Button, Button"

"Duel"

"Shoofly" (originally published as "Shoo Fly")

*Earthbound* (Tor, 1995)

Novel. First paperback edition of Matheson's approved text.

*I Am Legend* (Tor, 1995)

Fiction collection. Paperback. First edition thus. This edition contains the novel and ten previously published short stories.

*I Am Legend*

"Buried Talents"

"The Near Departed"

"Prey"

"Witch War"

"Dance of the Dead"

"Dress of White Silk"

"Mad House"

"The Funeral"

"From Shadowed Places"

"Person to Person"

*I Am Legend* (Gauntlet Press, 1995)

Novel. First edition thus. Published as a 500-copy hardcover numbered edition in slipcase, issued without dustjacket, and signed by Matheson, Dan Simmons, George Clayton Johnson, and Dennis Etchison.

"Horror Legend" (by George Clayton Johnson)

Introduction (by Dan Simmons)

Introduction (by Matthew R. Bradley)

*I Am Legend*

Afterword (by Dennis Etchison)

*Robert Bloch: Appreciations of the Master* (Robert Bloch, edited by Richard Matheson & Ricia Mainhardt; Tor, 1995)

Short stories and appreciations. Hardcover, with dustjacket. True first edition. Edited collection of short stories by Robert Bloch, with additional contributions from thirty other authors, filmmakers, and actors.

"Richard Matheson Introduces 'Enoch' "

"Richard Matheson and Ricia Mainhardt Introduce 'The Pied Piper

Fights the Gestapo' " (by Richard Matheson & Ricia Main-hardt)

*The Memoirs of Wild Bill Hickok* ( Jove, 1996)
Novel. Paperback original and true first edition. To date, this is Matheson's only published novel that is not available in a hardcover edition.

*Hell House* (Gauntlet Press, 1996)
Novel. First edition thus. Published in two hardcover states, both issued without dustjacket: a 600-copy numbered edition in slipcase, and a 26-copy lettered edition in traycase, both signed by Matheson.
Introduction (by Dean R. Koontz)
Introduction (by Matthew R. Bradley)
*Hell House*
Afterword (by Richard Christian Matheson)

*Now You See It . . .* (Tor, 1996)
Novel. First paperback edition.

*Noir: Three Novels of Suspense* (G&G Books, 1997)
Novels. First edition thus. First hardcover appearance and first un-abridged reprinting of these three early and hard-to-find Matheson novels. Published in two states, both issued without dustjacket: a 500-copy numbered edition in slipcase, and a 52-copy lettered edition in traycase, both signed by Matheson.
Introduction (by Matthew R. Bradley)
*Someone Is Bleeding*
*Fury on Sunday*
*Ride the Nightmare*

*Robert Bloch: Appreciations of the Master* (Robert Bloch, edited by Richard Matheson & Ricia Mainhardt; Tor, 1997)
Short stories and appreciations. First paperback edition. Edited collection of short stories by Robert Bloch, with additional contributions from thirty authors, filmmakers, and actors.
"Richard Matheson Introduces 'Enoch' "

"Richard Matheson and Ricia Mainhardt Introduce 'The Pied Piper Fights the Gestapo' " (by Richard Matheson & Ricia Mainhardt)

*What Dreams May Come* (Gauntlet Press, 1998)

Novel. First edition thus. Published in two hardcover states, both issued without dustjacket: a 500-copy numbered edition in optional slipcase, and a 52-copy lettered edition in traycase, both signed by Matheson, Douglas E. Winter, and Stephen Simon. The lettered edition includes an afterword by Richard Christian Matheson, who also signed that edition.

Preface

Introduction (by Matthew R. Bradley)

*What Dreams May Come*

Afterword (by Stephen Simon)

"Dreams of Love and Death" (by Douglas E. Winter)

Afterword (by Richard Christian Matheson; lettered edition only)

*Richard Matheson's* The Twilight Zone *Scripts* (Richard Matheson, edited by Stanley Wiater; Cemetery Dance, 1998)

Teleplays. True first edition. Published in two hardcover states, both issued without dustjacket: a 500-copy numbered edition in slipcase, and a 52-copy lettered edition in leather traycase, both signed by Matheson and Stanley Wiater. The lettered edition contains additional artwork.

"Submitted for Your Approval"

Letter from Rod Serling (by Rod Serling)

Prologue (by Stanley Wiater)

"The Last Flight"

"A World of Difference"

"A World of His Own"

"Nick of Time"

"The Invaders"

"Once Upon a Time"

"Little Girl Lost"

"Young Man's Fancy"

"Mute"

"Death Ship"
"Steel"
"Nightmare at 20,000 Feet"
"Night Call"
"Spur of the Moment"
Epilogue (by Stanley Wiater)
Appendix: Suggested Further Reading and Viewing

*Somewhere in Time* (Tor, 1999)
 Novel. Trade paperback. First edition thus.
 *Somewhere in Time* (originally published as *Bid Time Return*)
 "Reading Group Guide to *Somewhere in Time* by Richard Matheson"
  (by Matthew R. Bradley)

*Somewhere in Time* (Gauntlet Press, 1999)
 Novel. First edition thus. Published in two hardcover states, both issued without dustjacket: a 500-copy numbered edition in optional slipcase, and a 52-copy lettered edition in traycase, both signed by Matheson and Bill Shepard. The lettered edition includes additional photographs and a CD of Matheson reading from the book.
 Introduction
 *Somewhere in Time* (originally published as *Bid Time Return*)
 Afterword (by Bill Shepard)
 Stills

*The Path: A New Look at Reality* (Tor, 1999)
 Nonfiction. This is essentially the first hardcover edition of *The Path: Metaphysics for the '90s*, with a modified title. The text is unchanged from the paperback edition, except for a slightly updated foreword.

*The Twilight Zone: The Invaders: The Television Script* (Harvest Moon Publishing, 2000)
 Teleplay. Trade paperback. First separate edition.

*The Twilight Zone: A World of Difference: The Television Script* (Harvest Moon Publishing, 2000)
 Teleplay. Trade paperback. First separate edition.

*The Twilight Zone: Night Call: The Television Script* (Harvest Moon Publishing, 2000)
Teleplay. Trade paperback. First separate edition.

*The Twilight Zone: The Last Flight: The Television Script* (Harvest Moon Publishing, 2000)
Teleplay. Trade paperback. First separate edition.

*Passion Play* (Cemetery Dance, 2000)
Novel. True first edition. Published in two hardcover states: a 1000-copy numbered edition with dustjacket in slipcase, and a 52-copy lettered edition with dustjacket in traycase, both signed by Matheson. The lettered edition contains additional artwork.

*The Twilight Zone: Death Ship: The Television Script* (Harvest Moon Publishing, 2000)
Teleplay. Trade paperback. First separate edition.

*The Twilight Zone: Mute: The Television Script* (Harvest Moon Publishing, 2000)
Teleplay. Trade paperback. First separate edition.

*The Twilight Zone: Nightmare at 20,000 Feet: The Television Script* (Harvest Moon Publishing, 2000)
Teleplay. Trade paperback. First separate edition.

*Mediums Rare* (Cemetery Dance, 2000)
Nonfiction. True first edition. Published in two hardcover states: a 750-copy numbered edition with dustjacket in slipcase, and a 52-copy lettered edition with dustjacket in traycase, both signed by Matheson.

*And in Sorrow* (Gauntlet Press, 2000)
Short story. Chapbook. True first edition. Published in a limited edition of 200 copies. A small number of copies were numbered or lettered, with some signed by Matheson, for use by the publisher as premiums.

*Hunger and Thirst* (Gauntlet Press, 2000)
Novel. True first edition. Published in two hardcover states: a 750-copy numbered edition with dustjacket, and a 52-copy lettered edition

with dustjacket in traycase, both signed by Matheson. A CD of Matheson reading from the book is included with the lettered edition.

Introduction.

*Hunger and Thirst*

Afterword

*Somewhere in Time: The Screenplay* (Harvest Moon Publishing, 2000)
Screenplay. Trade paperback. True first edition.

*The Legend of Hell House: The Screenplay* (Harvest Moon Publishing, 2000)
Screenplay. Trade paperback. First separate edition.

*The Twilight Zone: A World of His Own: The Television Script* (Harvest Moon Publishing, 2000)
Teleplay. Trade paperback. First separate edition.

*The Twilight Zone: Little Girl Lost: The Television Script* (Harvest Moon Publishing, 2000)
Teleplay. Trade paperback. First separate edition.

*The Twilight Zone: Nick of Time: The Television Script* (Harvest Moon Publishing, 2000)
Teleplay. Trade paperback. First separate edition.

*The Twilight Zone: Once Upon a Time: The Television Script* (Harvest Moon Publishing, 2000)
Teleplay. Trade paperback. First separate edition.

*The Twilight Zone: Spur of the Moment: The Television Script* (Harvest Moon Publishing, 2000)
Teleplay. Trade paperback. First separate edition.

*The Twilight Zone: Steel: The Television Script* (Harvest Moon Publishing, 2000)
Teleplay. Trade paperback. First separate edition.

*The Twilight Zone: Young Man's Fancy: The Television Script* (Harvest Moon Publishing, 2000)
Teleplay. Trade paperback. First separate edition.

*Camp Pleasant* (Cemetery Dance, 2001)

Novel. True first edition. Published in two hardcover states: a 1000-copy numbered edition with dustjacket in slipcase, and a 52-copy lettered edition with dustjacket in traycase, both signed by Matheson. The lettered edition contains additional artwork.

*Richard Matheson's* The Twilight Zone *Scripts, Vol. 1* (Richard Matheson, edited by Stanley Wiater; Edge Books, 2001)

Teleplays. First paperback edition.
"Submitted for Your Approval"
Letter from Rod Serling (by Rod Serling)
Prologue (by Stanley Wiater)
"The Last Flight"
"A World of Difference"
"A World of His Own"
"Nick of Time"
"The Invaders"
"Once Upon a Time"
"Little Girl Lost"
"Young Man's Fancy"
Appendix: Suggested Further Reading and Viewing

*The Prisoner* (Gauntlet Press, 2001)

Short story. Chapbook. True first edition. Published in a limited edition of 350 numbered copies. A small number of copies were signed by Matheson for use by the publisher as premiums.

*The Shrinking Man* (Gauntlet Press, 2001)

Novel. First edition thus. Published in two hardcover states, both issued without dustjacket: a 500-copy numbered edition in optional slipcase, and a 52-copy lettered edition in traycase, both signed by Matheson and David Morrell. The lettered edition includes additional photographs and a CD of Matheson reading from the book.

Introduction
*The Shrinking Man*

Afterword (by David Morrell)

Pages from *The Incredible Shrinking Man* script

Stills from *The Incredible Shrinking Man* film

*Purge Among Peanuts* (Gauntlet Press, 2001)

Short story. Chapbook. True first edition. Published in a limited edition of 500 numbered copies. A small number of copies were signed by Matheson for use by the publisher as premiums.

*Abu and the 7 Marvels* (Edge Books, 2001)

Children's novel. True first edition. Published in three limited-edition hardcover states, all issued without dustjacket, and a trade hardcover edition, with dustjacket. The limited editions include a 350-copy numbered edition in optional slipcase, a 52-copy lettered edition in leather traycase, and a 52-copy artist's presentation edition in leather traycase, all signed by Matheson and artist William Stout. The lettered edition includes additional sketches by Stout. The artist's presentation edition includes a bonus color illustration inset into the traycase cover and an illustrated certificate of authenticity mounted on the inside of the traycase, both signed by Stout; and an 8 × 10 portfolio of all the color illustrations from the book. Nominated for the Bram Stoker Award for best work for young readers in 2002.

*Abu and the 7 Marvels*

William Stout Concept Sketches (artwork by William Stout; lettered and artist's presentation editions only)

Additional Artwork (by Stout; artist's presentation edition only)

*A Primer of Reality* (Edited by Richard Matheson; Edge Books, 2002)

Nonfiction. True first edition. Published in three states, all issued without dustjacket: a trade paperback edition, a 100-copy hardcover numbered edition in optional slipcase, and a 26-copy hardcover lettered edition in leather traycase. The numbered and lettered editions are both signed by Matheson. The lettered edition includes the CD *Reality* of Matheson discussing his metaphysical views. A transcript of the CD reading is available online at users.adelphia.net/~sitman/Reality.pdf

*Richard Matheson's* The Twilight Zone *Scripts, Vol. 2* (Richard Matheson, edited by Stanley Wiater; Edge Books, 2002)

Teleplays. First paperback edition.

"Submitted for Your Approval"

Letter from Rod Serling (by Rod Serling)

Prologue (by Stanley Wiater)

"Mute"

"Death Ship"

"Steel"

"Nightmare at 20,000 Feet"

"Night Call"

"Spur of the Moment"

Epilogue (by Stanley Wiater)

Appendix: Suggested Further Reading and Viewing

*Nightmare at 20,000 Feet: Horror Stories by Richard Matheson* (Tor, 2002)

Short story collection. True first edition. Published simultaneously in a trade hardcover edition, with dustjacket, and a trade paperback edition. Anthology of thirteen previously published short stories.

Introduction (by Stephen King)

"Nightmare at 20,000 Feet"

"Dress of White Silk"

"Blood Son" (originally published as " 'Drink My Red Blood . . .' " and also as "Drink My Blood")

"Through Channels"

"Witch War"

"Mad House"

"Disappearing Act"

"Legion of Plotters"

"Long Distance Call" (originally published as "Sorry, Right Number")

"Slaughter House"

"Wet Straw"

"Dance of the Dead"

"The Children of Noah"

*A Stir of Echoes* (Gauntlet Press, 2002)

Novel. First edition thus. Published in two hardcover states, both issued without dustjacket: a 500-copy numbered edition in optional slipcase, and a 52-copy lettered edition in traycase, both signed by Matheson. The lettered edition includes a CD of Matheson reading from the book.

Introduction
*A Stir of Echoes*
*A Stir of Echoes* (screenplay)
Afterword (by David Koepp)

*He Wanted to Live* (Gauntlet Press, 2002)

Short story. Chapbook. True first edition. Published in a limited edition of 552 copies. A small number of copies were numbered or lettered, with some signed by Matheson, for use by the publisher as premiums.

*Hunted Past Reason* (Tor, 2002)

Novel. Hardcover, with dustjacket. True first edition.

*14 Steps to Reality: Metaphysics for the Young* (Gauntlet Press, 2002)

Nonfiction. Chapbook. True first edition. Published in a limited edition of 552 copies. A small number of copies were numbered or lettered, with some signed by Matheson, for use by the publisher as premiums.

*Pride* (Richard Matheson & Richard Christian Matheson; Gauntlet Press, 2002)

Short stories and teleplay. True first edition. Published in two states, both issued without dustjacket: a 1000-copy softcover limited edition in optional (and poorly fitting) slipcase, and a 52-copy hardcover lettered edition in leather traycase, both signed by Matheson and Richard Christian Matheson. The lettered edition includes an additional photograph of the authors, a CD of both authors reading from the book, and a copy of a page from either Matheson's or Richard Christian Matheson's handwritten draft of the story, signed by the respective author.

Introduction
Handwritten Draft
Typed Draft

Handwritten Draft (by Richard Christian Matheson)
1st Typed Draft (by Richard Christian Matheson)
Final Typed Draft (by Richard Christian Matheson)
Teleplay Collaboration (by Richard Matheson & Richard Christian Matheson)
Afterword (by Richard Christian Matheson)
Photo of the Authors (lettered edition only)

*Off Beat: Uncollected Stories* (Richard Matheson, edited by William F. Nolan; Subterranean Press, 2002)

Short story collection. True first edition. Published in two hardcover states: a 750-copy numbered edition with dustjacket, and a 52-copy lettered edition with dustjacket in leather traycase, both signed by Matheson. Both editions include seven previously published stories and five previously unpublished stories. The lettered edition includes an additional previously published story.

Introduction (by William F. Nolan)
"Relies"
"Blunder Buss"
"And Now I'm Waiting"
"All and Only Silence" (also published as "The Last Blah in the ETC")
"Phone Call from Across the Street"
"Maybe You Remember Him"
"Mirror, Mirror . . ."
"Two O'Clock Session"
"And in Sorrow"
"The Prisoner"
"Always Before Your Voice"
"That Was Yesterday"
Afterword
A Checklist of First Editions (by William F. Nolan)
"Life Size" (lettered edition only)

*Professor Fritz and the Runaway House* (Gauntlet Press, 2002)

Short children's story. Chapbook. True first edition. Published in a limited edition of 404 copies. A small number of copies were numbered or lettered, with some signed by Matheson, for use by the publisher as premiums.

*Duel: Terror Stories by Richard Matheson* (Tor, 2003)

Short story collection. True first edition. Published simultaneously in a trade hardcover edition, with dustjacket, and a trade paperback edition. Anthology of seventeen previously published short stories.

"An Appreciation" (by Ray Bradbury)

"Duel"

"When the Waker Sleeps" (originally published as "The Waker Dreams")

"Born of Man and Woman"

"Return"

"Brother to the Machine"

"F—" (originally published as "The Foodlegger")

"Lover When You're Near Me"

"Shipshape Home"

"SRL Ad"

"Death Ship"

"The Last Day"

"Little Girl Lost"

"Trespass" (originally published as "Mother by Protest")

"Being"

"The Test"

"One for the Books"

"Steel"

*Come Fygures, Come Shadowes* (Gauntlet Press, 2003)

Novel. True first edition. Published in two hardcover states: a 500-copy numbered edition with dustjacket in optional slipcase, and a 52-copy lettered edition with dustjacket in traycase, both signed by Matheson. The lettered edition includes a CD of Matheson reading from the book. The first three chapters of this book were originally published in Matheson's short story collection, *Shock Waves*.

*Come Fygures, Come Shadowes*

Afterword
Handwritten Afterword (lettered edition only)

*Man with a Club* (Gauntlet Press, 2003)
Short story. Chapbook. True first edition. Published in a limited edition of 552 copies. A small number of copies were numbered or lettered, with some signed by Matheson, for use by the publisher as premiums.

*Hunted Past Reason* (Forge, 2003)
Novel. First paperback edition.

*Richard Matheson: Collected Stories* (Edited by Stanley Wiater; Edge Books, 2003)
Short story collection. First edition thus. This is an expanded trade paperback edition of the 1989 Dream/Press limited edition, and includes a new introduction by Matheson and his commentary on the "behind-the-scenes" details of each story.
Editor's Preface (by Stanley Wiater)
Introduction
Gauntlet Press Introduction 2003
"Born of Man and Woman"
"Third From the Sun"
"When the Waker Sleeps" (originally published as "The Waker Dreams")
"From Ray Bradbury" (by Ray Bradbury)
"Blood Son" (originally published as " 'Drink My Red Blood . . .' " and also as "Drink My Blood")
"Clothes Make the Man"
"Dress of White Silk"
"Return"
"The Thing"
"Through Channels"
"Witch War"
"From Robert Bloch" (by Robert Bloch)
"Advance Notice" (originally published as "Letter to the Editor")
"Brother to the Machine"

"F—" (originally published as "The Foodlegger")
"Lover When You're Near Me"
"Mad House"
"Shipshape Home"
"SRL Ad"
"To Fit the Crime"
"Death Ship"
"From William F. Nolan" (by William F. Nolan)
"Disappearing Act"
"The Disinheritors"
"Dying Room Only"
"Full Circle"
"The Last Day"
"Lazarus II"
"Legion of Plotters"
"Little Girl Lost"
"Long Distance Call" (originally published as "Sorry, Right Number")

*Richard Matheson's Kolchak Scripts* (Richard Matheson, edited by Mark Dawidziak; Gauntlet Press, 2003)

Teleplays. True first edition. Published in two hardcover states: a 500-copy numbered edition with dustjacket in optional slipcase, and a 52-copy lettered edition with dustjacket in traycase, both signed by Matheson. The lettered edition is additionally signed by William F. Nolan, Dan Curtis, Mark Dawidziak, and (on a separate loose tipsheet) Jeff Rice. Chris Carter of *The X-Files* fame was to have signed as well but did not do so, and his signature space is blank. The lettered edition also includes a copy of a script page for *The Night Killers* signed by Matheson and William F. Nolan.

Introduction to *The Night Stalker* (by Mark Dawidziak)
Cast and Credits for *The Night Stalker*
*The Night Stalker*
Introduction to *The Night Strangler* (by Mark Dawidziak)
Cast and Credits for *The Night Strangler*

*The Night Strangler*
Introduction to *The Night Killers* (by Mark Dawidziak)
*The Night Killers* (by Richard Matheson & William F. Nolan)
Appendix A: The Rest of the Kolchak Story
Appendix A: Photos
Appendix B: Richard Matheson and the TV Movie
Appendix C: Richard Matheson and the Vampire Story
Afterword (by Chris Carter)
Photo Gallery (lettered edition only)

*Darker Places* (Gauntlet Press, 2004)
Short stories and screenplay. True first edition. Published in two hardcover states: a 500-copy numbered edition with dustjacket in optional slipcase, and a 52-copy lettered edition with dustjacket in traycase, both signed by Matheson. The lettered edition includes a copy of a page from one of the following: the handwritten introduction to *Creature*, one of two pages of the handwritten introduction to the book, or one of two handwritten corrected pages from "The Hill," signed by Matheson.
Introduction
"Revolution"
"The Puppy"
"Little Girl Knocking at My Door"
"Cassidy's Shoes"
"The Hill"
"Intergalactic Report"
Introduction to *Creature*
*Creature*: A Screenplay

*The Last Blah in the ETC* (Gauntlet Press, 2004)
Short story. Chapbook. First separate edition; originally published as "All and Only Silence." Published in a limited edition of 552 copies. A small number of copies were numbered or lettered, with some signed by Matheson, for use by the publisher as premiums.

*Counterfeit Bills* (Gauntlet Press, 2004)
Short story. Chapbook. True first edition. Published in a limited edi-

tion of 552 copies. A small number of copies were numbered or lettered, with some signed by Matheson, for use by the publisher as premiums.

*Duel & The Distributor* (Richard Matheson, edited by Matthew R. Bradley; Gauntlet Press, 2004)

Short stories and scripts. True first edition. Published in two hardcover states: a 500-copy numbered edition with dustjacket in optional slipcase, and a 52-copy lettered edition with dustjacket in either a smoke-colored plexiglass traycase or leather traycase, both signed by Matheson. The lettered edition is also signed by actor Dennis Weaver, and includes an original page (not a copy) from Matheson's typewritten script for *The Distributor*, with his handwritten corrections.

> *Playboy* cover 1971
> "Duel": The Foreword (by Matthew R. Bradley)
> "Duel"
> *Duel*: The Script
> "The Duelist: An Interview with Dennis Weaver" (by Matthew R.
>     Bradley)
> "Duel": An Afterword
> *Duel*: Photo Gallery
> *Playboy* cover 1958
> "The Distributor"
> *The Distributor*: The Script
> "The Distributor": An Afterword (by Matthew R. Bradley)
> "The Distributor": An Afterword

*Richard Matheson: Collected Stories, Volume 2* (Edited by Stanley Wiater; Edge Books, 2005)

Short story collection. First edition thus. This is an expanded trade paperback edition of the 1989 Dream/Press limited edition, and includes a new introduction by Matheson and his commentary on the "behind-the-scenes" details of each story.

> Editor's Preface (by Stanley Wiater)
> Introduction
> Gauntlet Press Introduction 2003
> "Slaughter House"

"Trespass" (originally published as "Mother by Protest")
"The Wedding"
"Wet Straw"
"Being"
"The Conqueror" (also published as "Go West, Young Man")
"From Jack Finney" (by Jack Finney)
"The Curious Child"
"Dear Diary"
"Descent"
"The Doll That Does Everything"
"The Man Who Made the World"
"The Test"
"The Traveller"
"When Day Is Dun"
"Dance of the Dead"
"The Funeral"
"Miss Stardust"
"One for the Books"
"Pattern for Survival"
"From George Clayton Johnson" (by George Clayton Johnson)
"A Flourish of Strumpets"
"The Splendid Source"
"Steel"
"A Visit to Santa Claus" (originally published as "I'll Make It Look Good")
"The Children of Noah"
"The Holiday Man"
"Lemmings"
"Old Haunts"
"The Distributor"
"The Edge"

*Woman* (Gauntlet Press, 2005)
Novel and play. True first edition. Published in five states: a trade paperback edition, a 175-copy hardcover numbered edition with dust-

jacket in engraved wooden slipcase, a 31-copy hardcover lettered edition with dustjacket in engraved wooden traycase, a 20-copy hardcover artist's presentation edition with dustjacket in engraved wooden slipcase, and a 100-copy paperback book launch edition. The trade paperback has different cover artwork from that of the limited editions. All except the trade paperback are signed by Matheson and contain his original play upon which the novel was based, along with an afterword by Matheson. The lettered edition also includes a metal labrys bookmark engraved with Matheson's signature and a signed copy of a page from his original handwritten draft of the novel. The artist's presentation edition includes two additional color illustrations and a portrait of Matheson, all signed by artist Harry O. Morris. The book launch edition was distributed to guests at the book's release party held June 7, 2005, at the Peninsula Hotel in Beverly Hills, California. A small number of remaining copies were later made available to the general public by the publisher.

*Woman*: The Novel

*Woman*: The Play (limited editions only)

*Woman*: The Afterword (limited editions only)

Additional Artwork (by Harry O. Morris; artist's presentation edition only)

*Noir: Three Novels of Suspense* (Forge, 2005)

Novels. Published simultaneously in trade hardcover, with dustjacket, and trade paperback editions. The latter is the first paperback edition of this collection.

Introduction (by Matthew R. Bradley)

*Someone Is Bleeding*

*Fury on Sunday*

*Ride the Nightmare*

*1984½* (Gauntlet Press, 2005)

Short story. Chapbook. True first edition. Published in a limited edition of 552 copies. A small number of copies were numbered or lettered, with some signed by Matheson, for use by the publisher as premiums.

*Richard Matheson: Collected Stories, Volume 3* (edited by Stanley Wiater; Edge Books, 2005)

Short story collection. First edition thus. This is an expanded trade paperback edition of the 1989 Dream/Press limited edition, and includes a new introduction by Matheson and his commentary on the "behind-the-scenes" details of each story.

Editor's Preface (by Stanley Wiater)

Introduction

Gauntlet Press Introduction 2003

"Big Surprise" (originally published as "What Was in the Box?")

"The Creeping Terror" (originally published as "A Touch of Grapefruit")

"Deadline" (originally published as "Dead Line")

"Mantage"

"No Such Thing as a Vampire"

"From Harlan Ellison" (by Harlan Ellison)

"Crickets"

"Day of Reckoning" (originally published as "The Faces," and also as "Graveyard Shift")

"First Anniversary"

"From Shadowed Places"

"Nightmare at 20,000 Feet"

"Finger Prints"

"The Likeness of Julie"

"Mute"

"Deus Ex Machina"

"Girl of My Dreams"

"The Jazz Machine"

"From Stephen King" (by Stephen King)

"Shock Wave" (originally published as "Crescendo")

"Tis the Season to Be Jelly" (also published as " 'Tis the Season to Be Jelly")

"Interest"

"A Drink of Water"

"Therese" (originally published as "Needle in the Heart")

"Prey"

"Button, Button"

"From Dennis Etchison" (by Dennis Etchison)

"By Appointment Only"
"The Finishing Touches"
"Till Death Do Us Part" (also published as " 'Til Death Do Us
   Part")
"The Near Departed"
"Buried Talents"
"Duel"
"From Richard Christian Matheson" (by Richard Christian Mathe-
   son)

*Unrealized Dreams* (Gauntlet Press, 2005)
   Screenplays. True first edition. Published in two hardcover states:
a 500-copy numbered edition with dustjacket in optional slipcase, and
a 52-copy lettered edition with dustjacket in traycase, both signed by
Matheson and Dennis Etchison. The lettered edition includes a copy of
a script page from *Appointment in Zahrain* signed by Matheson.
   Introduction (by Dennis Etchison)
   *The Fantastic Little Girl*: An Introduction
   *The Fantastic Little Girl*: First Draft Screenplay
   *Appointment in Zahrain*: An Introduction
   *Appointment in Zahrain*: First Draft Screenplay
   *Sweethearts and Horrors*: An Introduction
   *Sweethearts and Horrors*: The Screenplay

*The Link: A Novel Excerpt* (Gauntlet Press, 2006)
   Novel excerpt. Chapbook. True first edition. Published in a limited
edition of 500 copies. A small number of copies were numbered or lettered,
with some signed by Matheson, for use by the publisher as premiums.
   Introduction
   *The Link: A Novel Excerpt*

*The Link* (Gauntlet Press, 2006)
   Narrative outline. True first edition. Published in two hardcover
states: a 500-copy numbered edition with dustjacket in optional slipcase,
and a 52-copy lettered edition with dustjacket in leather traycase, both
signed by Matheson. The lettered edition includes part of Matheson's
original screenplay and a signed copy of a page from the screenplay.
   *The Link*: An Introduction

*The Link*

*The Link*: The Beginnings of a Screenplay (lettered edition only)

*Bloodlines: Richard Matheson's* Dracula, I Am Legend, *and Other Vampire Stories* (Richard Matheson, edited by Mark Dawidziak; Gauntlet Press, 2006)

Short stories, novel, and scripts. True first edition. Published in two hardcover states: a 500-copy numbered edition in optional leather or wooden slipcase, and a 52-copy lettered edition in wooden traycase, both signed by Matheson and Mark Dawidziak. The lettered edition includes color endpapers and a copy of a script page from *Dracula* signed by Matheson, and is additionally signed by all contributors of appreciations for the book.

"Preface: Tracing the Bloodlines" (by Mark Dawidziak)

"Appreciation One: Under the Influence" (by John Carpenter)

"Introduction One: Richard the Writer, Vlad the Impaler and *Dracula* the Script" (by Mark Dawidziak)

"Appreciation Two: 'X' Marked the Spot" (by Frank Spotnitz)

*Dracula*: Richard Matheson's Script Treatment

Cast and Credits for *Bram Stoker's Dracula* (1974)

*Bram Stoker's Dracula*: The Script

Gallery A: Pictures from *Dracula & The Night Stalker*

"Appreciation Three: Discovering Matheson" (by Mick Garris)

"Introduction Two: The Unfilmed Legend" (by Mark Dawidziak)

The Motion Picture Association Letter: *The Night Creatures* (1957)

*The Night Creatures* Script: From Richard Matheson's Novel *I Am Legend*

"Appreciation Four: The Son Also Apprises" (by Richard Christian Matheson)

Richard Matheson's *I Am Legend*: The Novel (1954)

"Appreciation Five: Matheson and Me" (by Steve Niles)

Cast and Credits for *The Last Man on Earth* (1964)

Cast and Credits for *The Omega Man* (1971)

Gallery B: Pictures from *I Am Legend, The Last Man on Earth & The Omega Man*

"Appreciation Six: Confessions of an Addict" (by Rockne S. O'Bannon)

"Introduction Three: The Short Stories" (by Mark Dawidziak)

"Blood Son" (1951; originally published as "'Drink My Red Blood . . .'" and also as "Drink My Blood")

"The Funeral" (1955)

"No Such Thing as a Vampire" (1959)

Cast and Credits for *The Funeral* (1972)

Cast and Credits for *No Such Thing as a Vampire* (1977)

Gallery C: Pictures from "The Funeral" & "No Such Thing as a Vampire"

"Appreciation Seven: Looks Like the Beginning of a Beautiful Friendship" (by Ray Bradbury)

"Appendix A: Thoughts from the Archive" (by John Scoleri)

"Appendix B: The Unwritten Vampire Story" (by Mark Dawidziak)

*The Funeral* (Gauntlet Press, 2006)

Teleplay. Chapbook. True first edition. Published in a limited edition of 552 copies. A small number of copies were numbered or lettered, with some signed by Matheson, for use by the publisher as premiums.

Introduction (by Mark Dawidziak)

Cast and Credits for "The Funeral"

"The Funeral" (teleplay)

*Visions of Death: Richard Matheson's Edgar Allan Poe Scripts, Volume One* (Richard Matheson, edited by Lawrence French; Gauntlet Press, 2007)

Screenplays. True first edition. Published in two hardcover states: a 500-copy numbered edition with dustjacket in optional slipcase, and a 52-copy lettered edition with dustjacket in traycase, both signed by Matheson. The lettered edition is additionally signed by Roger Corman and Joe Dante, and includes illustrated endpapers.

Introduction (by Roger Corman)

Editor's Introduction (by Lawrence French)

"The House is the Monster: The Making of *House of Usher*" (by Lawrence French)

*The Fall of the House of Usher*

Cast and Credits for *House of Usher*

"The House of the Dead: The Making of *The Pit and the Pendulum*"
(by Lawrence French)
*The Pit and the Pendulum*
Cast and Credits for *The Pit and the Pendulum*
"Richard Matheson on Adapting Edgar Allan Poe for the Screen"
(interview by Lawrence French)
Afterword (by Joe Dante)
American International Pictures *House of Usher* Production Notes
American International Pictures *The Pit and the Pendulum* Production Story
Bibliography

*The Richard Matheson Companion* (Edited by Stanley Wiater, Matthew R. Bradley, and Paul Stuve; Gauntlet Press, 2008).

Nonfiction and novel. First edition. Published in two hardcover states: a 500-copy numbered edition with dustjacket in optional slipcase, and a 52-copy lettered edition with dustjacket in traycase. All numbered copies are signed by co-editors Stanley Wiater and Matthew R. Bradley. Matheson signed 350 of the 500 numbered copies, including those numbered 1–150, but the numbers of the other 200 signed copies are distributed somewhat randomly throughout the remainder of the edition. The entire lettered edition is signed by Matheson and co-editors Wiater and Bradley, as well as by 13 of the volume's 27 contributors, and includes illustrated endpapers designed by Harry O. Morris. Authoritative compendium concerning Matheson and his work containing essays, tributes, and remembrances by various writers, publishers, editors, filmmakers, family members, and fans, as well as a detailed and exhaustive section of bibliographies, filmographies, and assorted other lists. Also includes the only published appearance to date of Matheson's first novel, *The Years Stood Still*, written when he was just 14 years old. The contents of the revised and updated trade edition, retitled *The Twilight and Other Zones: The Dark Worlds of Richard Matheson*, are the same except for the following, which are exclusive to the limited edition.

"A Variation on Vampire Lore That Won't Die" (by Lewis Beale)
Introduction to *The Years Stood Still* (by Richard Christian Matheson)
*The Years Stood Still* (by Richard Matheson)

*Button, Button: Uncanny Stories* (Tor, 2008)

Short story collection. Trade paperback. True first edition. Anthology of twelve previously published short stories.

Introduction

"Button, Button"

"Girl of My Dreams"

"Dying Room Only"

"A Flourish of Strumpets"

"No Such Thing as a Vampire"

"Pattern for Survival"

"Mute"

"The Creeping Terror" (originally published as "A Touch of Grapefruit")

"Shock Wave" (originally published as "Crescendo")

"Clothes Make the Man"

"The Jazz Machine"

"'Tis the Season to Be Jelly" (originally published as "Tis the Season to Be Jelly")

## Book Club/Library Editions and Abridgments

These are book club and library editions of Matheson's work, as well as excerpts and abridged versions of his novels.

"The Frigid Flame" (*Justice*, October 1955)

Short fiction. Although the magazine claims that this is a "complete" reprinting of *Someone Is Bleeding*, it is in fact an abridgment. The original magazine is hard to find, but the piece was reprinted in *American Pulp* (edited by Ed Gorman, Bill Pronzini, and Martin H. Greenberg; Carroll & Graf Publishers, Inc., 1997).

"The Untouchable Divorcee" (*Stag*, May 1956)

Short fiction. An abridgment of *Someone Is Bleeding*, published in this monthly men's magazine.

*Singing in the Shrouds; A Stir of Echoes; The Malignant Heart* (Detective Book Club, 1958)

Novels. Book club edition. Hardcover, with dustjacket. Collects three detective/suspense novels, including Matheson's *A Stir of Echoes.*

"December 14, 1944" (*Charge into Hell*, Popular Library, 1966).

Short fiction. An excerpt from *The Beardless Warriors*, published in this paperback anthology of short stories and abridged versions of war-related fiction.

"Come Fygures, Come Shadowes" (*Shock Waves*, Richard Matheson; Dell Publishing Co, Inc., 1970).

Novel excerpt. The opening section of Matheson's unfinished novel of the same name, subsequently published in a lengthier (but still incomplete) form by Gauntlet Press in 2003.

*I Am Legend* (Nelson Doubleday, Inc., c. 1975)

Novel. Book club edition. Hardcover, with dustjacket. Dustjacket artwork is original to this edition. The actual publication date is unknown, but is thought to be some time in the 1970s. The only date on the copyright page is the date of the original paperback publication.

*The Shrinking Man* (Nelson Doubleday, Inc., c. 1985)

Novel. Book club edition. Hardcover, with dustjacket. Dustjacket artwork is original to this edition. The actual publication date is unknown, but is thought to be some time in the 1980s. The only date on the copyright page is the date of the original paperback publication.

*I Am Legend* (Buccaneer Books, 1991)

Novel. Hardcover, issued without dustjacket. Library edition.

*Journal of the Gun Years* (Thorndike Press, 1992)

Novel. Hardcover. Large print library edition for visually impaired readers.

*The Gun Fight* (Thorndike Press, 1993)

Novel. Hardcover. Large print library edition for visually impaired readers.

*The Shrinking Man* (Buccaneer Books, 1993)

Novel. Hardcover, issued without dustjacket. Library edition.

*Bid Time Return* (Buccaneer Books, 1995)
  Novel. Hardcover, issued without dustjacket. Library edition.

*The Paranoid Fifties: Three Classic Science Fiction Novels* (Quality Paperback Book Club, 1995)
  Novels. Book club edition. Softcover. Collects John Wyndham's *The Day of the Triffids*, Matheson's *I Am Legend*, and Philip K. Dick's *Time Out of Joint*.

*What Dreams May Come* (Transformational Book Circle, 2006)
  Novel. Hardcover, with dustjacket. Published as part of a monthly book service of "transformational" and "life-changing" works. Includes a brief summary and discussion guide, plus a CD of Stephen Simon, the producer of *What Dreams May Come*, discussing the making of the film and how it differs from the novel.

*I Am Legend/Hell House* (Quality Paperback Book Club, 2006)
  Fiction collection. Book club edition. Softcover. Collects two previously published novels and ten previously published short stories.
  *I Am Legend*
  "Buried Talents"
  "The Near Departed"
  "Prey"
  "Witch War"
  "Dance of the Dead"
  "Dress of White Silk"
  "Mad House"
  "The Funeral"
  "From Shadowed Places"
  "Person to Person"
  *Hell House*

## Short Fiction: First Appearances

These are the first appearances of each of Matheson's published short stories, along with information on alternate titles.

"Born of Man and Woman" (*The Magazine of Fantasy and Science Fiction*, Summer 1950)

"Third From the Sun" (*Galaxy*, October 1950)

"The Waker Dreams" (*Galaxy*, December 1950; also published as "When the Waker Sleeps")

"Clothes Make the Man" (*Worlds Beyond*, February 1951)

"Through Channels" (*The Magazine of Fantasy and Science Fiction*, April 1951)

" 'Drink My Red Blood . . .' " (*Imagination*, April 1951; also published as "Blood Son" and "Drink My Blood")

"The Thing" (*Marvel Science Stories*, May 1951)

"Witch War" (*Startling Stories*, July 1951)

"Dress of White Silk" (*The Magazine of Fantasy and Science Fiction*, October 1951)

"They Don't Make 'em Tougher" (*Dime Western*, October 1951; also published as "Gunsight")

"Return" (*Thrilling Wonder Stories*, October 1951)

"Mountains of the Mind" (*Marvel Science Fiction*, November 1951)

"Letter to the Editor" (*Imagination*, January 1952; also published as "Advance Notice")

"SRL Ad" (*The Magazine of Fantasy and Science Fiction*, April 1952)

"The Foodlegger" (*Thrilling Wonder Stories*, April 1952; also published as "F—")

"Lover When You're Near Me" (*Galaxy*, May 1952)

"Shipshape Home" (*Galaxy*, July 1952)

"Brother to the Machine" (*IF Worlds of Science Fiction*, November 1952)

"To Fit the Crime" (*Fantastic*, November–December 1952)

"Wet Straw" (*Weird Tales*, January 1953)

"The Disinheritors" (*Fantastic Story Magazine*, January 1953)

"Mad House" (*Fantastic*, January–February 1953)

"Disappearing Act" (*The Magazine of Fantasy and Science Fiction*, March 1953)

"Death Ship" (*Fantastic Story Magazine*, March 1953)

"The Last Day" (*Amazing Stories*, April–May 1953)

"The Wedding" (*Beyond Fantasy Fiction*, July 1953)

"Legion of Plotters" (*Detective Story Magazine*, July 1953; unconfirmed against actual magazine)

"Slaughter House" (*Weird Tales*, July 1953)

"Lazarus II" (*Fantastic Story Magazine*, July 1953)

"Full Circle" (*Fantastic Universe*, August–September 1953)

"Mother by Protest" (*Fantastic*, September–October 1953; also published as "Trespass")

"Dying Room Only" (*Fifteen Detective Stories*, October 1953)

"Little Girl Lost" (*Amazing Stories*, October–November 1953)

"Sorry, Right Number" (*Beyond Fantasy Fiction*, November 1953; also published as "Long Distance Call")

"The Man Who Made the World" (*Imagination*, February 1954)

"The Conqueror" (*Bluebook*, May, 1954; also published as "Go West, Young Man"; the original magazine is hard to find, due to the first appearance of Ian Fleming's *Live and Let Die*)

"When Day Is Dun" (*Fantastic Universe*, May 1954)

"Descent" (*IF Worlds of Science Fiction*, May 1954)

"The Curious Child" (*Fantastic*, June 1954)

"Being" (*IF Worlds of Science Fiction*, August 1954)

"The Test" (*The Magazine of Fantasy and Science Fiction*, November 1954)

"The Doll That Does Everything" (*Fantastic Universe*, December 1954)

"Dance of the Dead" (*Star Science Fiction Stories No. 3*, edited by Frederik Pohl; Ballantine Books, 1954)

"The Traveller" (*Born of Man and Woman*, Richard Matheson; Chamberlain Press, 1954)

"Dear Diary" (*Born of Man and Woman*)

"Too Proud to Lose" (*Fifteen Western Tales*, February 1955; unconfirmed against actual magazine)

"Miss Stardust" (*Starling Stories*, Spring 1955)

"The Funeral" (*The Magazine of Fantasy and Science Fiction*, April 1955)

"Pattern for Survival" (*The Magazine of Fantasy and Science Fiction*, May 1955)

"One for the Books" (*Galaxy*, September 1955)

"Son of a Gunman" (*Western Magazine*, December 1955; also published as "Boy in the Rocks" and "Get Off the Circle 7")

"Steel" (*The Magazine of Fantasy and Science Fiction*, May 1956)

"The Splendid Source" (*Playboy*, May 1956)

"A Flourish of Strumpets" (*Playboy*, November 1956)

"I'll Make It Look Good" (writing as Logan Swanson; *Alfred Hitchcock's Mystery Magazine*, March 1957; also published as "A Visit to Santa Claus")

"The Children of Noah" (*Alfred Hitchcock's Mystery Magazine*, March 1957)

"The Holiday Man" (*The Magazine of Fantasy and Science Fiction*, July 1957)

"Old Haunts" (*The Magazine of Fantasy and Science Fiction*, October 1957)

"Lemmings" (*The Magazine of Fantasy and Science Fiction*, January 1958)

"The Distributor" (*Playboy*, March 1958)

"The Edge" (*The Magazine of Fantasy and Science Fiction*, August 1958)

"Now Die in It" (*Mystery Tales*, December 1958; later revised and expanded into the novel *Ride the Nightmare*)

"What Was in the Box?" (*Ellery Queen's Mystery Magazine*, April 1959; also published as "Big Surprise")

"No Such Thing as a Vampire" (*Playboy*, October 1959)

"Dead Line" (*Rogue*, December 1959; also published as "Deadline")

"A Touch of Grapefruit" (*Star Science Fiction Stories No. 5*, edited by Frederik Pohl; Ballantine Books, 1959; also published as "The Creeping Terror")

"Mantage" (*Science Fiction Showcase*, edited by Mary Kornbluth; Doubleday & Company, Inc., 1959)

"Crickets" (*Shock*, May 1960)

"First Anniversary" (*Playboy*, July 1960)

"From Shadowed Places" (*The Magazine of Fantasy and Science Fiction*, October 1960)

"The Faces" (*Ed McBain's Mystery Book No. 1*, 1960; also published as "Day of Reckoning" and "Graveyard Shift")

"The Likeness of Julie" (writing as Logan Swanson; *Alone by Night*, edited by Michael Congdon & Don Congdon; Ballantine Books, 1961)

"Nightmare at 20,000 Feet" (*Alone by Night*)

"Mute" (*The Fiend in You*, edited by Charles Beaumont; Ballantine Books, 1962)

"Finger Prints" (*The Fiend in You*)

"The Jazz Machine" (*The Magazine of Fantasy and Science Fiction*, February 1963)

"Tis the Season to Be Jelly" (*The Magazine of Fantasy and Science Fiction*, June 1963; also published as " 'Tis the Season to Be Jelly")

"Girl of My Dreams" (*The Magazine of Fantasy and Science Fiction*, October 1963)

"Crescendo" (*Gamma*, Vol. 1[1], 1963; also published as "Shock Wave")

"Deus Ex Machina" (*Gamma*, Vol. 1[2], 1963)

"Interest" (*Gamma*, September 1965)

"A Drink of Water" (*Signature*, April 1967; unconfirmed against actual magazine)

"Prey" (*Playboy*, April 1969)

"Needle in the Heart" (*Ellery Queen's Mystery Magazine*, October 1969; also published as "Therese")

"By Appointment Only" (*Playboy*, April 1970)

"Button, Button" (*Playboy*, June 1970)

"Till Death Do Us Part" (*Ellery Queen's Mystery Magazine*, September 1970; also published as " 'Til Death Do Us Part")

"The Finishing Touches" (*Shock Waves*, Richard Matheson; Dell Publishing Co., Inc., 1970)

"Duel" (*Playboy*, April 1971)

"Leo Rising" (*Ellery Queen's Mystery Magazine*, May 1972)

"Where There's a Will" (Richard Matheson & Richard Christian Matheson; *Dark Forces*, edited by Kirby McCauley; Viking Press, 1980)

"And Now I'm Waiting" (*Rod Serling's The Twilight Zone Magazine*, April 1983)

"Blunder Buss" (*Rod Serling's The Twilight Zone Magazine*, April 1984)

"Getting Together" (*Rod Serling's The Twilight Zone Magazine*, June 1986)

"Buried Talents" (*Masques II*, edited by J. N. Williamson; Maclay & Associates, Inc., 1987)

"The Near Departed" (*Masques II*)

"Shoo Fly" (*OMNI*, November 1988; also published as "Shoofly")

"Person to Person" (*Rod Serling's The Twilight Zone Magazine*, April 1989)

"CU: Mannix" (*Ellery Queen's Mystery Magazine*, April 1991)

"Two O'Clock Session" (*The Bradbury Chronicles: Stories in Honor of Ray Bradbury*, edited by William F. Nolan & Martin H. Greenberg; Roc/New American Library, 1991)

"Little Jack Cornered" (*By the Gun*, Richard Matheson; M. Evans & Company, 1993)

"Of Death and Thirty Minutes" (*By the Gun*)

"Relics" (*Cemetery Dance* #31, 1999)

"Always Before Your Voice" (*California Sorcery: A Group Celebration*, edited by William F. Nolan & William Schafer; Cemetery Dance, 1999)

"And in Sorrow" (Chapbook; Gauntlet Press, 2000)

"The Prisoner" (Chapbook; Gauntlet Press, 2001)

"Purge Among Peanuts" (Chapbook; Gauntlet Press, 2001)

"Life Size" (*Gauntlet Press Sampler*, Chapbook; Gauntlet Press, 2001)

"He Wanted to Live" (Chapbook; Gauntlet Press, 2002)

"Pride: Handwritten Draft" (*Pride*, Richard Matheson & Richard Christian Matheson; Gauntlet Press, 2002)

"Pride: Typed Draft" (*Pride*)

"That Was Yesterday" (*Off Beat: Uncollected Stories*, Richard Matheson, edited by William F. Nolan; Subterranean Press, 2002)

"All and Only Silence" (*Off Beat: Uncollected Stories*; also published as "The Last Blah in the ETC")

"Phone Call from Across the Street" (*Off Beat: Uncollected Stories*)

"Maybe You Remember Him" (*Off Beat: Uncollected Stories*)

"Mirror, Mirror . . ." (*Off Beat: Uncollected Stories*)

"Professor Fritz and the Runaway House" (Chapbook; Gauntlet Press, 2002)

"Man With a Club" (Chapbook; Gauntlet Press, 2003)

"Portrait" (*Framed: A Gallery of Dark Delicacies*, edited by Del & Sue Howison [writing as Gomez & Morticia Howison]; Dark Delicacies, 2003)

"Revolution" (*Darker Places*, Richard Matheson; Gauntlet Press, 2004)

"The Puppy" (*Darker Places*)

"Little Girl Knocking at My Door" (*Darker Places*)

"Cassidy's Shoes" (*Darker Places*)

"The Hill" (*Darker Places*)

"Intergalactic Report" (*Darker Places*)

"Counterfeit Bills" (Chapbook; Gauntlet Press, 2004)

"1984½" (Chapbook; Gauntlet Press, 2005)

"Haircut" (*Masques V*, edited by J. N. Williamson & Gary Braunbeck; Gauntlet Press, 2006)


## Selected Anthology Appearances

Matheson's work has appeared in countless anthologies since 1951, and a complete list is beyond the scope of this book. What follows is a chronological selection of Matheson's anthology appearances over the past 55 years (most of which we have not been able to examine personally).

*Best Science-Fiction Stories* (Edited by Everett F. Bleiler & T. E. Dikty; Fredrick Fell, 1951)
    "Born of Man and Woman"

*The Best from Fantasy and Science Fiction* (Edited by Anthony Boucher & J. Francis McComas; Little, Brown & Co., 1952)
    "Dress of White Silk"

*The Best Science-Fiction Stories* (Edited by Everett F. Bleiler & T. E. Dikty; Fredrick Fell, 1952)
    "Witch War"

*Galaxy Reader of Science Fiction* (Edited by H. L. Gold; Crown, 1952)
  "Third From the Sun"
  "The Waker Dreams" (also published as "When the Waker Sleeps")

*Omnibus of Science Fiction* (Edited by Groff Conklin; Crown Publishers, 1952)
  "Shipshape Home"

*The Best Science-Fiction Stories: 1953* (Edited by Everett F. Bleiler & T. E. Dikty; Fredrick Fell, 1953)
  "Lover, When You're Near Me"

*Science-Fiction Carnival* (Edited by Fredric Brown & Mack Reynolds; Shasta, 1953)
  "SRL Ad"

*The Best Science-Fiction Stories: 1954* (Edited by Everett F. Bleiler & T. E. Dikty; Fredrick Fell, 1954)
  "The Last Day"

*Star Science Fiction Stories No. 3* (Edited by Frederik Pohl; Ballantine, 1954)
  "Dance of the Dead"

*Science Fiction Terror Tales* (Edited by Groff Conklin; Gnome Press, 1955)
  "Through Channels"

*Terror in the Modern Vein* (Edited by Donald A. Wollheim; Hanover House, 1955)
  "Shipshape Home"

*The Best from Fantasy and Science Fiction, Fifth Series* (Edited by Anthony Boucher; Ace, 1956)
  "Pattern for Survival"

*Science Fiction Showcase* (Edited by Mary Kornbluth; Doubleday & Company, Inc., 1959)
  "Mantage"

*Star Science Fiction Stories No. 5* (Edited by Frederik Pohl; Ballantine Books, 1959)

"A Touch of Grapefruit" (also published as "The Creeping Terror")

*The World That Couldn't Be* (Edited by H.L. Gold; Doubleday, 1959)
"One for the Books"

*Zacherley's Midnight Snacks* (Edited by John Zacherley; Ballantine, 1960)
"Sorry, Right Number" (also published as "Long Distance Call")

*Alone by Night* (Edited by Michael Congdon & Don Congdon; Ballantine Books, 1961)
"Nightmare at 20,000 Feet"
"The Likeness of Julie" (writing as Logan Swanson)

*In the Dead of Night* (Edited by Michael Sissons; Gibbs & Phillips, 1961)
"Crickets"

*75 Masterpieces: Stories from the World's Literature* (Edited by Roger B. Goodman; Bantam, 1961)
"Born of Man and Woman"

*Alfred Hitchcock Presents: A Hangman's Dozen* (Edited by Alfred Hitchcock; Random House, 1962)
"The Children of Noah"

*Asleep in Armageddon* (Edited by Michael Sissons; Panther, 1962)
"Being"

*The Fiend in You* (Edited by Charles Beaumont; Ballantine Books, 1962)
"Mute"
"Finger Prints"

*Alfred Hitchcock Presents: Stories My Mother Never Told Me* (Edited by Alfred Hitchcock; Random House, 1963)
"The Children of Noah"

*And Graves Give Up Their Dead* (Edited by Frederick Pickersgill; Corgi, 1964)
"Girl of My Dreams"

*No Such Thing as a Vampire* (Edited by Frederick Pickersgill; Corgi, 1964)
   "No Such Thing as a Vampire"

*Alfred Hitchcock Presents: Stories Not for the Nervous* (Edited by Alfred Hitchcock; Random House, 1965)
   "Lemmings"

*If This Goes On* (Edited by Charles Nuetzel; Book Company of America, 1965)
   "The Test"

*Invasion of the Robots* (Edited by Roger Elwood; Paperback Library, 1965)
   "Brother to the Machine"

*The Pseudo-People* (Edited by William F. Nolan; Sherbourne, 1965)
   "Steel"

*Beyond Belief* (Edited by Richard J. Hurley; Scholastic, 1966)
   "Third From the Sun"

*Untravelled Worlds* (Edited by Alan F. Barter & Raymond Wilson; Macmillan & Co., 1966)
   "One for the Books"

*A Feast of Blood* (Edited by Charles M. Collins; Avon, 1967)
   " 'Drink My Red Blood . . .' " (also published as "Blood Son" and "Drink My Blood")

*The Playboy Book of Crime and Suspense* (Edited by The Editors of Playboy; Playboy Press, 1967)
   "The Distributor"

*The Midnight People* (Edited by Peter Haining; Leslie Frewin, 1968)
   "Drink My Blood" (originally published as " 'Drink My Red Blood . . .' " and also as "Blood Son")

*The Others* (Edited by Terry Carr; Fawcett Gold Medal, 1969)
   "Shipshape Home"

*The Witchcraft Reader* (Edited by Peter Haining; Dobson, 1969)
  "From Shadowed Places"

*The Hollywood Nightmare* (Edited by Peter Haining; MacDonald & Company, 1970)
  "Mantage"

*Twenty Years of Fantasy and Science Fiction* (Edited by Edward L. Ferman & Robert P. Mills; Berkley, 1970)
  "The Holiday Man"

*Last Train to Limbo* (Edited by the Editors of Playboy; Playboy Press, 1971)
  "The Splendid Source"

*Transit of Earth* (Edited by the Editors of Playboy; Playboy Press, 1971)
  "Button, Button"

*The Year's Best Horror Stories* (Edited by Richard Davis; Sphere, 1971)
  "Prey"

*The Devil's Generation* (Edited by Vic Ghidalia; Lancer, 1973)
  "Mother by Protest" (also published as "Trespass")

*Fantasy: The Literature of the Marvelous* (Edited by Leo P. Kelley; McGraw-Hill, 1973)
  "The Test"

*More Little Monsters* (Edited by Roger Elwood & Vic Ghidalia; Manor Books, 1973)
  "The Doll That Does Everything"

*The Devil's Children* (Edited by Michel Parry; Orbit/Futura, 1974)
  "From Shadowed Places"

*More of Christopher Lee's New Chamber of Horrors* (Edited by Raymond T. McNally; New York Graphic Society, 1974)
  " 'Drink My Red Blood . . .' " (also published as "Blood Son" and "Drink My Blood")

*Alfred Hitchcock Presents: Stories To Be Read with the Door Locked* (Edited by Alfred Hitchcock; Random House, 1975)
"The Distributor"

*Fiends and Creatures* (Edited by Marvin Kaye; Popular Library, 1975)
"Crescendo" (also published as "Shock Wave")

*The Black Magic Omnibus* (Edited by Peter Haining; Taplinger, 1976)
"By Appointment Only"

*Dying of Fright* (Edited by Les Daniels; Charles Scribner's Sons, 1976)
"Born of Man and Woman"

*From the Archives of Evil* (Edited by Christopher Lee & Michel Parry; Warner, 1976)
"Blood Son" (originally published as " 'Drink My Red Blood . . .' " and also published as "Drink My Blood")

*The History of the Science Fiction Magazine Vol. 3 1946–1955* (Edited by Michael Ashley; Contemporary Books, Inc., 1976)
"The Last Day"

*Tales of Mystery and the Unknown* (Edited by Robert Potter; Globe, 1976)
"The Holiday Man"

*Alfred Hitchcock Presents: The Master's Choice* (Edited by Alfred Hitchcock; Random House, 1979)
"Mother by Protest"

*Tales Out of Time* (Edited by Barbara Ireson; Faber & Faber, 1979)
"Deadline" (originally published as "Dead Line")

*Dark Forces* (Edited by Kirby McCauley; Viking, 1980)
"Where There's a Will" (by Richard Matheson and Richard Christian Matheson)

*Science Fiction A to Z* (Edited by Isaac Asimov, Martin H. Greenberg, & Charles G. Waugh; Houghton Mifflin, 1982)
"A Touch of Grapefruit" (also published as "The Creeping Terror")

*65 Great Spine Chillers* (Edited by Mary Danby; Sundial Books, 1982)
  "Deadline" (originally published as "Dead Line")

*The Gruesome Book* (Edited by Ramsey Campbell; Piccolo/Pan, 1983)
  "Long Distance Call" (originally published as "Sorry, Right Number")

*A Treasury of American Horror Stories* (Edited by Frank D. McSherry, Jr., Charles G. Waugh, & Martin H. Greenberg; Bonanza Books, 1985)
  "Being"

*The Twilight Zone: The Original Stories* (Edited by Martin H. Greenberg, Richard Matheson, & Charles G. Waugh; Avon Books, 1985)
  Detailed contents can be found in the "Books: First and Limited Editions" section.

*Masters of Darkness* (Edited by Dennis Etchison; Tor, 1986)
  "Dance of the Dead"

*Masques II* (Edited by J. N. Williamson; Maclay & Associates, Inc., 1987)
  "Buried Talents"
  "The Near Departed"

*Scars and Other Distinguishing Marks* (Richard Christian Matheson; Scream/Press, 1987)
  "Where There's a Will" (by Richard Matheson and Richard Christian Matheson)

*Hot Blood: Tales of Provocative Horror* (Edited by Jeff Gelb & Lonn Friend; Pocket Books, 1989)
  "The Likeness of Julie"

*The Year's Best Fantasy and Horror: Second Annual Collection* (Edited by Ellen Datlow & Terri Windling; St. Martin's Press, 1989)
  "Shoo Fly" (also published as "Shoofly")

*Urban Horrors* (Edited by William F. Nolan & Martin H. Greenberg; Dark Harvest, 1990)
  "Prey"

*The Bradbury Chronicles: Stories in Honor of Ray Bradbury* (Edited by William F. Nolan & Martin H. Greenberg; Roc/New American Library, 1991)
  "Two O'Clock Session"

*Vampires: The Greatest Stories* (Edited by Martin Harry Greenberg; MJF, 1991)
  "No Such Thing as a Vampire"

*Masterpieces of Terror and the Unknown* (Edited by Marvin Kaye; Bantam Doubleday Dell, 1992)
  "Dress of White Silk"

*Playboy Stories: The Best of Forty Years of Short Fiction* (Edited by Alice K. Turner; Penguin/Dutton, 1994)
  "A Flourish of Strumpets"

*Visions of Fear* (Edited by David G. Hartwell; Tor, 1994)
  "Duel"

*The Vampire Omnibus* (Edited by Peter Haining; Artus Books, 1995)
  "First Anniversary"

*A Century of Horror 1970–1979: The Greatest Stories of the Decade* (Edited by David Drake; MJF, 1996)
  "Duel"

*California Sorcery: A Group Celebration* (Edited by William F. Nolan & William Schafer; Cemetery Dance, 1999)
  "Always Before Your Voice"

*My Favorite Horror Story* (Edited by Mike Baker & Martin H. Greenberg; DAW, 2000)
  "The Distributor"

*The American Fantasy Tradition* (Edited by Brian M. Thomsen; Tor, 2002)
  "Prey"

*Framed: A Gallery of Dark Delicacies* (Edited by Del & Sue Howison [writing as Gomez & Morticia Howison]; Dark Delicacies, 2003)
  "Portrait"

*Masques V* (Edited by J. N. Williamson & Gary Braunbeck; Gauntlet Press, 2006)
    "Haircut"

## Introductions, Afterwords, and Other Nonfiction

These are all of Matheson's nonfiction writings, including introductions and afterwords to his own work and that of others. Additional details are included for the various books cited except for Matheson's own books, which are fully described in the "Books: First and Limited Editions" section.

*Writer's Digest* (April, 1956; unconfirmed against actual magazine)
    First appearance of this nonfiction piece, which was later reprinted in *He Is Legend.*
    "SF Unlimited"

*Henry Kuttner: A Memorial Symposium* (Edited by Karen Anderson; Sevagram Enterprises, 1958)
    Nonfiction. Mimeographed pages bound in a three-pronged report cover. Contains tributes, a bibliography, and notes on story bylines.
    " 'Hank Helped Me' "

*SOLACON Final Report* (SOLACON, September 1958)
    Pamphlet. Last of five daily "journals" given out at the 16th World Science Fiction Convention. The original is hard to find, but Matheson's piece was reprinted in *Worldcon Guest of Honor Speeches* (Edited by Mike Resnick and Joe Siclari; Illinois Science Fiction in Chicago Press, 2006).
    "The Coming Together" (Matheson's guest-of-honor address)

*The Magic Man* (Charles Beaumont; Fawcett Gold Medal, 1965)
    Short story collection. Paperback original and true first edition.
    Afterword

"Speech for World Fantasy Convention" (Richard Matheson, 1977)
    Delivered at the third World Fantasy Convention, held at the Los Angeles Biltmore in 1977. Matheson was the guest of honor.

*Rod Serling's Other Worlds* (Edited by Jack C. Haldeman II; Bantam, 1978)

Short stories. Paperback original and true first edition. This is an edited anthology of short fiction, with brief biographical notes on each author.

Introduction

*The Eureka Years: Boucher and McComas's* The Magazine of Fantasy and Science Fiction *1949–1954* (Edited by Annette Peltz McComas; Bantam, 1982)

Short stories and correspondence. Paperback original and true first edition. Collects stories from the first five years of *The Magazine of Fantasy and Science Fiction*, and includes, for each author, relevant correspondence with the magazine's editors.

"Matheson-Editors Correspondence" (Richard Matheson, Anthony Boucher, & J. Francis McComas)

*Rod Serling's The Twilight Zone Magazine* (June 1984)

"Commentary on 'Nightmare at 20,000 Feet'"

*He Is Legend* (Edited by Mark Rathbun & Graeme Flanagan; Mark Rathbun, 1984)

Nonfiction. Chapbook. Contains tributes to Matheson by various writers, a reprint of his nonfiction piece "SF Unlimited," and a bibliography of his film and print work. A loose page containing an introduction by Ray Bradbury is included.

"SF Unlimited"

*Charles Beaumont: Selected Stories* (Edited by Roger Anker; Dark Harvest, 1988)

Short story collection. Published in two states: a trade hardcover edition with dustjacket, and a deluxe numbered edition with dustjacket in slipcase. The deluxe numbered edition is signed by sixteen of the twenty contributors, including Matheson.

"Introduction to 'Last Rites'"

*Holiday* (Richard Christian Matheson; Footsteps Press, 1988)

Short story. Chapbook. Published in two states: a 400-copy numbered edition and a 52-copy lettered edition, both signed by Richard Christian Matheson. The lettered edition is additionally signed by Richard Matheson.

Preface

*Richard Matheson: Collected Stories* (Dream/Press, 1989)

Short story collection. Details in the "Books: First and Limited Editions" section.

"To the Reader"

*INSITE Newsletter* (July 1990)

Newsletter. Stapled pages. Quarterly newsletter of the International Network of *Somewhere in Time* Enthusiasts (INSITE).

"From the desk of . . . Richard Matheson"

*INSITE Newsletter* (October 1990)

Newsletter. Stapled pages. Quarterly newsletter of the International Network of *Somewhere in Time* Enthusiasts (INSITE).

"Richard Matheson on *Somewhere in Time*"

*Somewhere in Time/What Dreams May Come: Two Novels of Love and Fantasy* (Richard Matheson; Dream/Press, 1991)

Novels. Details in the "Books: First and Limited Editions" section.

"To the Reader"

*INSITE Newsletter* (October 1992)

Newsletter. Stapled pages. Quarterly newsletter of the International Network of *Somewhere in Time* Enthusiasts (INSITE).

"A Message from Richard Matheson"

*Mystery Scene* #32 (December-January 1992)

"Crossover Books: *Journal of the Gun Years*"

*The Howling Man* (Charles Beaumont, edited by Roger Anker; Tor, 1992)

Short stories. Trade paperback. First paperback edition, and first edition with this title; the hardcover was called *Charles Beaumont: Selected Stories*.

"Introduction to 'Last Rites' "

*INSITE Newsletter* (July 1993)

Newsletter. Stapled pages. Quarterly newsletter of the International Network of *Somewhere in Time* Enthusiasts (INSITE).

"From Richard Matheson to the Readers of *INSITE*" (also published as "FROM: Richard Matheson TO: *The Overlook Connection* Readers")

*The Path: Metaphysics for the '90s* (Richard Matheson; Capra Press, 1993)

Nonfiction. Details in the "Books: First and Limited Editions" section.

*The Overlook Connection* (Edited by Dave Hinchberger & Laurie Hinchberger; Overlook Connection Press, 1994)

"FROM: Richard Matheson TO: *The Overlook Connection* Readers" (originally published as "From Richard Matheson to the Readers of *INSITE*")

*Psycho: The 35th Anniversary Edition* (Robert Bloch; Gauntlet Press, 1994)

Novel. Published in a 500-copy numbered edition with dustjacket in slipcase, signed by the author and Richard Matheson.

"An Open Letter to Robert Bloch"

*Aardwolf* (February 1995)

"Robert Bloch: A Retrospective" (by Clifford Lawrence; contains a brief reminiscence of Bloch by Matheson)

*What Dreams May Come* (Richard Matheson; Gauntlet Press, 1998)

Novel. Details in the "Books: First and Limited Editions" section. Preface

*Somewhere in Time* (Richard Matheson; Gauntlet Press, 1999)

Novel. Details in the "Books: First and Limited Editions" section. Introduction

*The Path: A New Look at Reality* (Richard Matheson; Tor, 1999)

Nonfiction. Details in the "Books: First and Limited Editions" section.

*Hunger and Thirst* (Richard Matheson; Gauntlet Press, 2000)

Novel. Details in the "Books: First and Limited Editions" section.

Introduction

Afterword

*Dystopia* (Richard Christian Matheson; Gauntlet Press, 2000)

Short story collection. True first edition. Published in three hardcover states: a 500-copy numbered edition with dustjacket, a 250-copy deluxe numbered edition with dustjacket in slipcase, and a 26-copy lettered edition with dustjacket in traycase. All editions are signed by Richard Christian Matheson, Richard Matheson, and Peter Straub. The deluxe numbered edition is additionally signed by illustrator Harry O. Morris and twenty-six of twenty-eight contributors, excluding Ray Bradbury and Stephen King. The lettered edition is signed by all. The deluxe numbered and lettered editions also include a videotape of a short film written and directed by Richard Christian Matheson called *Arousal*, and a CD of him reading several of his short stories and performing several songs with his rock band of the time, The Existers.

Introduction

*Helltracks* (William F. Nolan; Cemetery Dance, 2000)

Novel. True first edition. Published in two hardcover states: a 500-copy numbered edition with dustjacket, and a 26-copy lettered edition with dustjacket in traycase, both signed by William F. Nolan. The lettered edition is additionally signed by Matheson.

"William F. Nolan: A Reminiscence"

*Taps and Sighs* (Edited by Peter Crowther; Subterranean Press, 2000)

Short story collection. True first edition. Published in three hardcover states: a trade edition with dustjacket, a 500-copy numbered edition with dustjacket, and a 52-copy lettered edition with dustjacket in traycase. The numbered and lettered editions are signed by the editor and all story contributors. The lettered edition is additionally signed by Douglas E. Winter, J. K. Potter, and Matheson.

Afterword

*Touch of the Creature* (Charles Beaumont; Subterranean Press, 2000)

Short story collection. True first edition. Published in two hardcover states: a 1000-copy numbered edition with dustjacket signed by Beaumont's son Christopher, and a 13-copy lettered edition, without dustjacket, in cloth traycase signed by Christopher Beaumont and Matheson. The lettered edition is bound in leather and includes additional stories and an original piece of artwork (not a copy) by Charles Beaumont matted to the inside traycase cover.

Introduction

*The Shrinking Man* (Richard Matheson; Gauntlet Press, 2001)

Novel. Details in the "Books: First and Limited Editions" section.

Introduction

*Dark Dreamers: Facing the Masters of Fear* (Photography by Beth Gwinn, commentary by Stanley Wiater; Cemetery Dance, 2001)

Nonfiction. True first edition. A collection of photographs and insightful commentary by (or about) each subject. Published in three hardcover states: a 1250-copy limited trade edition with dustjacket, a 250-copy numbered edition with dustjacket in slipcase, and a 52-copy lettered edition with dustjacket in traycase. The numbered and lettered editions are both signed by the authors, and the lettered edition is also signed by Clive Barker.

"Richard Matheson & R.C. Matheson" (Photograph by Beth Gwinn, commentary by Richard Matheson & Richard Christian Matheson)

*INSITE Newsletter* (Vol. 12[4], Fourth Quarter 2001)

Newsletter. Stapled pages. Quarterly newsletter of the International Network of *Somewhere in Time* Enthusiasts (INSITE).

"Richard Matheson's Other Cameo Role" (Matheson's humorous account of his screen appearance in *Captains and the Kings*)

*A Primer of Reality* (Edited by Richard Matheson; Edge Books, 2002)

Nonfiction. Details in the "Books: First and Limited Editions" section.

Introduction

*A Stir of Echoes* (Richard Matheson; Gauntlet Press, 2002)
  Novel. Details in the "Books: First and Limited Editions" section.
  Introduction

*The Force Is With You: Mystical Movie Messages That Inspire Our Lives* (Stephen Simon; Hampton Roads Publishing Company, 2002)
  Film producer Simon (*Somewhere in Time, What Dreams May Come*) provides his perspectives on the spiritually uplifting and inspiring messages contained in over seventy films representative of "spiritual cinema."
  Afterword

*14 Steps to Reality: Metaphysics for the Young* (Richard Matheson; Gauntlet Press, 2002)
  Nonfiction. Details in the "Books: First and Limited Editions" section.

*Pride* (Richard Matheson & Richard Christian Matheson; Gauntlet Press, 2002)
  Short stories and teleplay. Details in the "Books: First and Limited Editions" section.
  Introduction

*Off Beat: Uncollected Stories* (Richard Matheson, edited by William F. Nolan; Subterranean Press, 2002)
  Short story collection. Details in the "Books: First and Limited Editions" section.
  Afterword

*Come Fygures, Come Shadowes* (Richard Matheson; Gauntlet Press, 2003)
  Novel. Details in the "Books: First and Limited Editions" section.
  Afterword
  Handwritten Afterword (lettered edition only)

*Filet of Sohl: The Classic Scripts and Stories of Jerry Sohl* (Jerry Sohl, edited by Christopher Conlon; BearManor Media, 2003)

Short stories and teleplays. Paperback original and true first edition.

"A Tribute to Jerry Sohl"

*Richard Matheson: Collected Stories, Volume 1* (Edited by Stanley Wiater; Edge Books, 2003)

Short story collection. Details in the "Books: First and Limited Editions" section.

Introduction

Gauntlet Press Introduction 2003

*Vincent Price: The Art of Fear* (Denis Meikle; Reynolds & Hearn Ltd., 2003)

Nonfiction. Extensive chronicle of Vincent Price's career, including scores of photographs and a filmography. Roger Corman provides an afterword.

Foreword

*Darker Places* (Richard Matheson; Gauntlet Press, 2004)

Short stories and screenplay. Details in the "Books: First and Limited Editions" section.

Introduction

Introduction to *Creature*

*Duel & The Distributor* (Richard Matheson, edited by Matthew R. Bradley; Gauntlet Press, 2004)

Short stories and scripts. Details in the "Books: First and Limited Editions" section.

"Duel": An Afterword

"The Distributor": An Afterword

*As Timeless as Infinity: The Complete Twilight Zone Scripts of Rod Serling, Volume One* (Rod Serling, edited by Tony Albarella; Gauntlet Press, 2004)

Teleplays. True first edition. Published in two hardcover states: a 750-copy numbered edition with dustjacket in optional slipcase, and a 52-copy lettered edition with dustjacket in traycase, both signed by Carol Serling. The lettered edition is additionally signed by Rockne S.

O'Bannon and Matheson, and contains an alternate version of the tele-play for "Where Is Everybody?"

"Appreciation: Richard Matheson"

*INSITE Newsletter* (Vol. 15[3], Third Quarter 2004)

Newsletter. Stapled pages. Quarterly newsletter of the International Network of *Somewhere in Time* Enthusiasts (INSITE).

"A Tribute to Christopher Reeve" (by Jo Addie; Matheson provided one of several "Celebrity Messages" that were read at a *Somewhere in Time* weekend memorial for Reeve)

*The Twilight Zone Scripts of Charles Beaumont, Vol. 1* (Charles Beaumont, edited by Roger Anker; Gauntlet Press, 2004)

Teleplays. True first edition. Published in two hardcover states: a 500-copy numbered edition with dustjacket in optional slipcase, and a 52-copy lettered edition with dustjacket in traycase, both signed by Beaumont's son Christopher. The lettered edition is also signed by Roger Anker, Earl Hamner, Jr., and Matheson, and includes an early draft of one of the scripts.

Foreword

*Richard Matheson: Collected Stories, Volume 2* (Edited by Stanley Wiater; Edge Books, 2005)

Short story collection. Details in the "Books: First and Limited Editions" section.

Introduction

Gauntlet Press Introduction 2003

*Woman* (Richard Matheson; Gauntlet Press, 2005)

Novel and play. Details in the "Books: First and Limited Editions."

*Woman*: The Afterword (limited editions only)

*Richard Matheson: Collected Stories, Volume 3* (Edited by Stanley Wiater; Edge Books, 2005)

Short story collection. Details in the "Books: First and Limited Editions" section.

Introduction

Gauntlet Press Introduction 2003

*Unrealized Dreams* (Richard Matheson; Gauntlet Press, 2005)
Screenplays. Details in the "Books: First and Limited Editions" section.
*The Fantastic Little Girl*: An Introduction
*Appointment in Zahrain*: An Introduction
*Sweethearts and Horrors*: An Introduction

*Dark Delicacies* (Edited by Del Howison & Jeff Gelb; Carroll & Graf Publishers Inc., 2005)
Short story collection. Hardcover, with dustjacket. First edition.
"Foreword, Backward, Upside Downward"

*The Link: A Novel Excerpt* (Richard Matheson; Gauntlet Press, 2006)
Novel excerpt. Details in "Books: First and Limited Editions."
Introduction

*The Link* (Richard Matheson; Gauntlet Press, 2006)
Narrative outline. Details in the "Books: First and Limited Editions" section.
*The Link*: An Introduction

*Match to Flame: The Fictional Paths to* Fahrenheit 451 (Ray Bradbury, edited by Donn Albright; Gauntlet Press, 2006)
Novel and short stories. True first edition. Published in two hardcover states: a 750-copy numbered edition with dustjacket in optional wooden slipcase, and a 52-copy lettered edition with dustjacket in traycase, both signed by Bradbury. The lettered edition is additionally signed by Matheson, and also includes copies of various letters and two previously unpublished stories.
Introduction

*Created By* (Richard Christian Matheson; Gauntlet Press, 2007)
Novel. First edition thus. Published in two hardcover states: a 500-copy numbered edition with dustjacket in optional slipcase, and a 52-copy lettered edition with dustjacket in traycase, both signed by the author. The lettered edition is also signed by Richard Matheson, Stephen J. Cannell, and David J. Schow.
Introduction

*It Came from the Kitchen* (Geoff Isaac & Gordon Reid; BearManor Media, 2007)

Cookbook. Paperback original and true first edition. A collection of recipes from science-fiction, fantasy, and horror celebrities with two from Matheson. Brief genre filmographies are included, and many contributors provide anecdotes about their work. Matheson briefly discusses "F—."

"Madres" (a vodka drink)

"Leak [sic] and Stilton Tarts"

*Button, Button: Uncanny Stories* (Richard Matheson; Tor, 2008)

Short story collection. Details in the "Books: First and Limited Editions" section.

Introduction

## Book Dedications

These are the dedications from all of Matheson's books, preserving as closely as possible their original formatting and appearance. Dedications for reprintings of the same title frequently contain some slight variations in formatting from the original printing, but the content of the dedication is typically unchanged (except as noted below), and thus dedications for reprintings are excluded from this list. Clarifying notes are included for dedicatees who may be unfamiliar to the reader.

*Someone Is Bleeding* (Lion Books, Inc., 1953)

to

Bill Gault

a guy you can call your friend

without crossing your fingers

[Matheson met Gault (1910–1985) when he moved to California, and stayed with him briefly until finding his own apartment. Gault was a prolific mystery writer, with several novels to his credit. He also wrote a number of juvenile sports novels.]

*Fury on Sunday* (Lion Books, Inc., 1953)

for

Francis,

cousin and friend

*Born of Man and Woman* (Chamberlain Press, 1954)

to

*Professor William Peden*

of

*The University of Missouri*

with my thanks for
help and encouragement
on the first steps

[Peden (1913–1999) was one of Matheson's professors at the University of Missouri. An author, literary critic, and journal editor, he is credited by many with helping establish the short story as a respected literary form. Matheson took two advanced writing classes from Peden, and maintained correspondence with him for more than thirty years after his graduation.]

*I Am Legend* (Fawcett Gold Medal, 1954)

To

HENRY KUTTNER

with my grateful thanks
for his help and encouragement
on this book.

[Kuttner (1914–1958) was a prolific science-fiction and fantasy author who worked in close collaboration with his wife, C.L. Moore. Much of their work was published under pseudonyms. He was highly regarded by other writers for his support and guidance. Ray Bradbury dedicated *Dark Carnival* to him.]

*The Shrinking Man* (Fawcett Gold Medal, 1956)

To

Harry Altshuler

for faith, hope and clarity.

*I also wish to thank Dr. Sylvia Traube*

*for her generous assistance.*

[Altshuler (1913–1990) was a literary agent who represented Robert Bloch, among others. He was Matheson's first agent. Sylvia Traube was a physician who helped Matheson with technical aspects of his story.]

*A Stir of Echoes* (J.B. Lippincott Company, 1958)

For Chuck and Helen

with affection

[Writer Charles Beaumont (1929–1967) and his wife, Helen (1928–1971). Beaumont was a prolific author, a regular contributor to *Playboy* magazine in its early days, and the screenwriter of more episodes of *The Twilight Zone* than anyone besides Rod Serling himself. He and Matheson were close friends who were very supportive of each other's writing, and collaborated on a number of film and television scripts. An early case of Alzheimer's led to Beaumont's death in 1967. His wife Helen died of cancer in 1971 at the age of 43.]

*The Beardless Warriors* (Little, Brown and Company, 1960)

> *With love, for my sons*
> RICHARD AND CHRISTIAN
> *May the reading of this story*
> *be the closest they ever come to war*

*Shock!* (Dell Publishing Co., Inc., 1961)

> To Philip and Marilyn Woodson
> with great affection

[Ruth Matheson's brother and his former wife.]

*Hell House* (Viking Press, 1971)

> *With love, for my daughters*
>
> **BETTINA and ALISON**
>
> *who have haunted my life so sweetly*

*Bid Time Return* (Viking Press, 1975)

> *With grateful love*
> for my mother
>
> *Recollection of our past together*
> *is the happiest of time travel.*

*What Dreams May Come* (G.P. Putnam's Sons, 1978)

> with grateful love, to my wife
> for adding the sweet measure of her soul to my
> existence

*A Stir of Echoes* (Berkley Books, 1979)

> For CHUCK and HELEN BEAUMONT
> In loving remembrance

[The dedication for this 1979 reprinting of *A Stir of Echoes* differs somewhat from the 1958 first edition.]


*Richard Matheson: Collected Stories* (Dream/Press, 1989)

> with deep gratitude
> I dedicate this collection
>
> *to Don Congdon*
>
> my guiding spirit
> for thirty-three years

[Congdon is Matheson's longtime agent. Upon signing with him in 1956, Matheson wrote to former professor William Peden, "several big editors . . . said that they thought Congdon the best agent operating today *in the whole world!*" Congdon's clients over the years have included Ray Bradbury, Henry Kuttner, John Collier, and Herman Wouk.]


*Journal of the Gun Years* (M. Evans & Company, 1991)

For
William Campbell Gault, William R. Cox,
Henry Kuttner, Les Savage, Jr.,
Joe Brennan, Hal Braham, Malden Grange Bishop,
Chick Coombs, Dean Owens, Bill Fay,
Willard Temple, Frank Bonham,
Todhunter Ballard, Wilbur S. Peacock, and
all my other friends in the Fictioneers.
Happy memories.

[The Fictioneers was a group of Los Angeles–area professional writers, mostly of mysteries and westerns, who met monthly to "talk shop" over dinner and drinks.]

*The Gun Fight* (M. Evans & Company, 1993)

With much gratitude

I dedicate this book to

GARY GOLDSTEIN

for giving me a new literary world to explore.

[Goldstein is an editor who worked with Matheson on his western novels and stories.]

*By the Gun* (M. Evans & Company, 1993)

To our gang
Nick and Judy Perito
Walt and Dody Steiner
Brian and Bunny Herdeg

For the many years of love and laughter

[These are longtime friends of the Mathesons. Nick Perito was musical director for vocalist Perry Como, who recorded two songs that Matheson cowrote with Perito.]

*The Path: Metaphysics for the '90s* (Capra Press, 1993)

*With love*

*To my wife Ruth Ann,*
*To my children Bettina, Richard, Ali and Chris,*
*To my daughters-in-law Marie and Trish,*
*my sons-in-law Bob and Jon,*

*And my grandchildren Robert, Lise,*
*Valerie, Emily, William, Mariel and Kate*

*For all that they have meant to me*
*And all that they truly are.*

*7 Steps to Midnight* (Forge, 1993)

### THIS BOOK IS DEDICATED TO MY LOS ANGELES WRITER FRIENDS

Charles Beaumont, Robert Bloch, Ray
Bradbury, Harlan Ellison, Dennis Etchison,
Brian Garfield, Bill Idelson,
George Clayton Johnson, William F. Nolan,
Ray Russell, Jerry Sohl, John Tomerlin

### THANKS FOR THE MEMORIES

*Earthbound* (Tor, 1994)

*For Ruth Ann*

*Thou art my own, my darling and my wife*
*And when we pass into another life*
*Still thou art mine*

*—A.J. Munby,*
Marriage

*Shadow on the Sun* (M. Evans & Company, 1994)

I dedicate this book
to my dear friend Chad Oliver

*See ya later, pal*

[Oliver (1928—1993) was a writer and close friend of Matheson's. They met in the 1950s when Oliver moved to Los Angeles to attend UCLA.]

*Now You See It . . .* (Tor, 1995)

> To my dear friend Robert Bloch,
> who created magic in all our lives

[Bloch (1917–1994) is the celebrated author of *Psycho* and many other classic works of horror. He contributed a foreword to Matheson's first short story collection, and is the subject of an anthology co-edited by Matheson in 1995; see following entry.]

*Robert Bloch: Appreciations of the Master* (Tor, 1995)

> To the Master, Robert Bloch.
> Thank you for the love, laughs, and scares.

*The Memoirs of Wild Bill Hickok* (Jove, 1996)

I dedicate this book
with much gratitude
to all those who helped me
in my writing career:

William Peden, Anthony Boucher, J. Francis
McComas, H. L. Gold, Harry Altshuler,
Ray Bradbury, Robert Bloch, Howard Browne,
Al Manuel, Albert Zugsmith, Alan Williams,
Malcolm Stuart, Rick Ray, Sam Adams,
Lee Rosenberg, Rod Serling, Buck Houghton,
Jules Schermer, Jim Nicholson, Sam Arkoff,
Roger Corman, Anthony Hinds, Dan Curtis,
Larry Turman, Steven Spielberg, Allen Epstein,
Jim Green, Stan Shpetner, Stephen Deutsch,
Jeannot Szwarc, David Kirschner, Jeff Conner,
David Greenblatt, Gary Goldstein, Bob Gleason,
Greg Cox

and, especially, Don Congdon

[This list includes magazine editors/publishers, fellow writers, film and television producers/directors, book editors/publishers, and agents.]

*Richard Matheson's* The Twilight Zone *Scripts* (Cemetery Dance, 1998)

To Rod Serling
for creating *The Twilight Zone*
and making my years of writing for the show
so pleasant and fulfilling.

To Carol Serling
for being the lovely person she is
and giving me her blessing for this collection of my scripts.

To Buck Houghton
with many thanks for his help and kindness during those enjoyable years.

To Marc Zicree
for his most excellent book about *The Twilight Zone* experience.

To Herb Hirschman and Bert Granet
for enhancing my last two years on the show.

To all the talented and creative people
who worked on *The Twilight Zone*
and left me with a wonderful legacy of lasting shows.

And, finally, to my dear and talented friend
throughout those halcyon days:
Charles Beaumont.

[Houghton, Hirschman, and Granet were producers of *The Twilight Zone*. Zicree is the author of *The Twilight Zone Companion*.]

*Mediums Rare* (Cemetery Dance, 2000)

*To my good friend*
*Stephen Simon*

> *with gratitude and affection*
> *and great admiration for the*
> *spiritual path he has chosen to take*

[Simon (formerly Stephen Deutsch) is the producer of the films *Somewhere in Time* and *What Dreams May Come*.]

*Passion Play* (Cemetery Dance, 2000)

> To Barry Hoffman, Richard Chizmar and Ed Gorman.

> With many thanks for bringing my literary dead back to life.

[Hoffman and Chizmar are publishers and owners of Gauntlet Press and Cemetery Dance Publications, respectively. They have published special editions of Matheson's work over the years. Gorman is an author, and has included Matheson's work in his edited volumes.]

*Hunger and Thirst* (Gauntlet Press, 2000)

> With deep love for my wife Ruth Ann
> and children Tina, Richard, Ali and Chris
> —whose lives were yet to bless mine
> when I wrote this book.

*Abu and the 7 Marvels* (Edge Books, 2001)

> This book, with much love,
> is dedicated to
> William, Kate and Mariel

[Matheson's grandchildren.]

*Camp Pleasant* (Cemetery Dance, 2001)

> *To my father,*
> *Scarcely known*
> *but always remembered*

*Hunted Past Reason* (Tor, 2002)

With deep gratitude to Don Congdon,

My literary bulwark for forty-five years

*Nightmare at 20,000 Feet: Horror Stories by Richard Matheson* (Tor, 2002)

*To Stephen King,*
*with much admiration*
*for taking the ball*
*and running with it*
*all the way*

[King is the most widely read horror writer in the history of the genre. He credits Matheson with being his primary influence as a writer, and in turn dedicated his 2006 novel *Cell* to Matheson and filmmaker George Romero.]

*Richard Matheson: Collected Stories, Volume 1* (Edge Books, 2003)

*This collection of my stories is dedicated to my wife*
*of 51 years, Ruth Ann, my older daughter Tina Louise,*
*my older son Richard Christian, my younger daughter*
*Ali Marie and my younger son Christian Logan. I am*
*very proud of them all and will always love them deeply.*

*—RM*

*Duel: Terror Stories by Richard Matheson* (Tor, 2003)

To Ray Bradbury,
a mentor, guide, and inspiration to me
for more than fifty years.

[Bradbury is one of the world's most prolific and respected fantasy authors. He has written tributes to Matheson on several occasions.]

*Darker Places* (Gauntlet Press, 2004)

> *To Barry Hoffman—with many thanks for resuscitating*
> *so much of my early work.*

> *—RM*

[In addition to publishing twenty special editions of Matheson's work since 1995, Hoffman is also the author of several horror novels and short stories.]

*Duel & The Distributor* (Gauntlet Press, 2004)

> *To Mark Dawidziak and Matthew Bradley*
> *with many thanks for their dedication to my work.*

[Dawidziak and Bradley have written about and interviewed Matheson frequently over the years, and have edited special collections of his work. Bradley is co-editor of *The Twilight and Other Zones.*]

*Woman* (Gauntlet Press, 2005)

> To the women and soon-to-be women in my life.

> My loving mother.

> My Aunts Evelyn and Lise and their daughters Vivian, Helen and Ethel.

> My Sister Gladys and her daughters Doris, Karen and Janet.

> My Sister-in-law Mary and her daughters Pat, Barbara, Maureen, Christine, Kathy and Geraldine.

> My Sisters-in-law Pat and Andrea.

> My Cousin Lily.

> My Daughter Tina and her daughters Lise, Valerie and Emily.

> My Daughter Ali and her daughter Mariel.

My Daughter-in-law Trish and her daughter Kate.

Sweet Diana.

And last but obviously not least, my wife Ruth Ann. The love of my life.

[Diana Mullen is Richard Christian Matheson's fiancée.]

*Richard Matheson: Collected Stories, Volume 2 and 3 (Edge Books, 2005)*

> *With many thanks to Stanley Wiater for his help and dedication on the three volumes of my collected stories.*
>
> *—RM*

[Wiater is a leading expert on horror filmmakers and writers, and is the author of several award-winning collections of interviews. He has interviewed Matheson repeatedly over the years, and is editor or co-editor of several volumes of Matheson's work, as well as *The Twilight and Other Zones*.]

*Unrealized Dreams (Gauntlet Press, 2005)*

> *To Tina, Ali, and Diana who are most definitely realized dreams in my life*
>
> *—Richard Matheson*

*The Link (Gauntlet Press, 2006)*

> To Barry Hoffman—
> With deep gratitude for his faith
> and dedication to this
> admittedly demanding venture.

*Bloodlines (Gauntlet Press, 2006)*

> To my family with love, and Mark Dawidziak
> and Matthew Bradley with gratitude.

[Dawidziak, who edited the book, has a separate dedication, "To Dan and Darren, both legends." Dan Curtis and Darren McGavin, the producer and star, respectively, of Matheson's two Kolchak TV movies, both died in 2006.]

*The Richard Matheson Companion* (Gauntlet Press, 2008)

To my wife, Ruth Ann, for fifty-six years of loving support.

And my children, Tina Louise, Richard Christian, Ali Marie, and Chris Logan, for enriching my life.

—R.M.

*Button, Button: Uncanny Stories* (Tor, 2008)

With love to my son Richard, for protecting
my life in every way.

## Graphic Novel and Comic Book Adaptations

Many of Matheson's works have been adapted into comic books, graphic novels, and, in one case, a "photonovel."

*Master of the World* (Dell Four Color, 1961)
Comic book adaptation of the film scripted by Matheson.

*Edgar Allan Poe's Tales of Terror* (Dell Movie Classics, 1963)
Comic book adaptation of the Roger Corman film, scripted by Matheson.

*Edgar Allan Poe's The Raven* (Dell Movie Classics, 1963)
Comic book adaptation of the Roger Corman film, scripted by Matheson.

*The Incredible Shrinking Woman* (Judy Sibert; Love, 1981)
Photonovel. Paperback. First edition. A photonovel adaptation of the

screenplay by Jane Wagner, which in turn was "suggested by" Matheson's novel. Contains photos from the film, with dialogue contained in conversation "bubbles," as is commonly depicted in comic books.

*Richard Matheson's I Am Legend, Book 1* (Adapted by Steve Niles, illustrated by Elman Brown; Eclipse Books, 1991)
    Graphic novel. Paperback. First edition.

*Richard Matheson's I Am Legend, Book 2* (Adapted by Steve Niles, illustrated by Elman Brown; Eclipse Books, 1991)
    Graphic novel. Paperback. First edition.

*Richard Matheson's I Am Legend, Book 3* (Adapted by Steve Niles, illustrated by Elman Brown; Eclipse Books, 1991)
    Graphic novel. Paperback. First edition.

*Richard Matheson's I Am Legend, Book 4* (Adapted by Steve Niles, illustrated by Elman Brown; Eclipse Books, 1992)
    Graphic novel. Paperback. First edition.

*Kolchak: The Night Stalker* #1 (Story by Jeff Rice, art by Gordon Purcell & Terry Pallot, et al.; Moonstone, 2002)
    Comic book adaptation of Jeff Rice's novel and the TV movie scripted by Matheson; later collected in the trade paperback *Kolchak: The Night Stalker, Volume One* (Moonstone, 2004).

*Richard Matheson's I Am Legend* (Adapted by Steve Niles, illustrated by Elman Brown; IDW Publishing, 2003)
    Graphic novel. First hardcover edition. Combines the contents of the four previously published paperbacks. Also available in paperback.

*Richard Matheson's Hell House, Book 1* (Adapted by Ian Edginton, illustrated by Simon Fraser; IDW Publishing, 2004)
    Graphic novel. Paperback. First edition.

*Richard Matheson's Hell House, Book 2* (Adapted by Ian Edginton, illustrated by Simon Fraser; IDW Publishing, 2005)
    Graphic novel. Paperback. First edition.

*Richard Matheson's Hell House, Book 3* (Adapted by Ian Edginton, illustrated by Simon Fraser; IDW Publishing, 2005)
Graphic novel. Paperback. First edition.

*Richard Matheson's Hell House, Book 4* (Adapted by Ian Edginton, illustrated by Simon Fraser; IDW Publishing, 2005)
Graphic novel. Paperback. First edition.

*Doomed* #1 (Chris Ryall; IDW Publishing, 2005)
Comic book. First edition. Released with two different covers. Includes "Richard Matheson's 'Blood Son' " adapted by Chris Ryall and Ashley Wood.

*Doomed* #2 (Chris Ryall & Dan Taylor; IDW Publishing, 2006)
Comic book. First edition. Released with two different covers. Includes "Richard Matheson's 'Crickets' " adapted by Scott Tipton and illustrated by Mike Hoffman.

*Doomed* #3 (Ted Adams & Chris Ryall; IDW Publishing, 2006)
Comic book. First edition. Released with two different covers. Includes "Richard Matheson's 'Children of Noah' " adapted by Scott Tipton and Nat Jones.

*Doomed* #4 (Ted Adams & Chris Ryall; IDW Publishing, 2006)
Comic book. First edition. Released with two different covers. Includes "Richard Matheson's 'Legion of Plotters' " adapted by Ted Adams and Ashley Wood.

*Totally Doomed* (Ted Adams, Chris Ryall, & Dan Taylor; IDW Publishing, 2007)
Comic book. First edition. Combines the complete contents of the four previously published issues of *Doomed*, including adaptations of Matheson's "Blood Son," "Crickets," "The Children of Noah," and "Legion of Plotters."

*Doomed Presents: Ashley Wood* (Justin Eisinger; IDW Publishing, 2007)
Comic book. First edition. Collects the Ashley Wood adaptations

previously published in *Doomed*, including those of Matheson's "Blood Son" and "Legion of Plotters."

*I Am Legend: Awakening* (DC/Vertigo, 2007)

Graphic novel. Paperback. First edition. Not an adaptation per se but tales by various contributors depicting the effects of the vampire virus from the novel. Book I features: Steve Niles, who wrote the *I Am Legend* graphic novel; Dawn Thomas; Mark Protosevich, one of the screenwriters of *I Am Legend*; Richard Christian Matheson, adapting his story "Vampire"; and artists Bill Sienkiewicz, Jason Chan, and David Levy. This limited edition debuted at Comic-Con International in San Diego, and is also available online at iamlegend.warnerbros.com/comicBook/comicBook.html. A planned Book II was to feature Orson Scott Card, but has not been published and does not appear on the Vertigo website.

*Richard Matheson's Hell House* (Adapted by Ian Edginton, Illustrated by Simon Fraser; IDW Publishing, 2008)

Graphic novel. Paperback. First edition thus. Combines the contents of the four previously published paperbacks.

## Selected Interviews, Profiles, and Other Articles and Books

These are some of the many forewords/afterwords, interviews, profiles, tributes, reviews, and other articles about Matheson and/or his work. Additional details are included for the various books cited, except for Matheson's own books, which are fully described in the "Books: First and Limited Editions" section.

*Born of Man and Woman* (Richard Matheson; Chamberlain Press, 1954)

Short story collection. Details in the "Books: First and Limited Editions" section.

"Introduction: The Art of Richard Matheson" (by Robert Bloch)

*Focus on the Science Fiction Film* (Edited by William Johnson; Prentice-Hall, Inc., 1972)

Nonfiction. A history of science-fiction cinema. Contains references to Matheson's work and a brief interview.

*The Shrinking Man* (Richard Matheson; David Bruce & Watson, 1973)
  Novel. Details in the "Books: First and Limited Editions" section.
  Introduction (by Kingsley Amis)

*Cinefantastique* (Vol. 3[2], 1974)
  "Matheson: A Name to Conjure With" (by Mick Martin; interview
with Matheson)
  "*The Legend of Hell House*" (by Mick Martin; review of the film)
  "*Dracula*" (by Harry Ringel)
  Matheson Filmography

*The Horror People* (John Brosnan; St. Martin's Press, Inc., 1976)
  Nonfiction. Hardcover with dustjacket. First edition. Profiles of and
interviews with important figures in the horror film industry.
  "Writing Horror: Richard Matheson and Robert Bloch" (chapter on
Matheson and Bloch; also contains numerous Matheson comments scat-
tered throughout other chapters)

*Starlog* #11 (January 1978)
  "*The Incredible Shrinking Man*" (by Ed Naha; feature article on the
film)

*Fangoria* #2 (October 1979)
  "Richard Matheson: Master of Fantasy, Part One—The Films of
Richard Matheson" (by Paul Sammon; interview and profile covering
Matheson's early work and films through 1960)

*Fangoria* #3 (December 1979)
  "Richard Matheson: Master of Fantasy, Part Two—The Television
Films of Richard Matheson" (by Paul Sammon; interview and profile
focusing on Matheson's television work, with a filmography of both film
and television work through 1980)

*The Shrinking Man* (Richard Matheson; Gregg Press, 1979)
  Novel. Details in the "Books: First and Limited Editions" section.
  Introduction (by Joseph Milicia)
  Introduction (by Kingsley Amis)

*Rod Serling's The Twilight Zone Magazine* (September 1981)

"Richard Matheson on 'The Honorable Tradition of Writing' " (by James H. Burns; part one of a two-part interview covering Matheson's early career)

"Matheson in the Movies" (by Robert Martin)

*Rod Serling's The Twilight Zone Magazine* (October 1981)

"Richard Matheson: Spinning Fantasy from Daily Life" (by James H. Burns; part two of a two-part interview covering Matheson's later career and forthcoming projects)

*Rod Serling's The Twilight Zone Magazine* (June 1982)

"The Story Behind Richard Matheson's 'The Doll' " (by Marc Scott Zicree; article about Matheson's teleplay, written for the original *Twilight Zone* but not produced until 1986 on *Amazing Stories*)

*The Twilight Zone Companion* (Marc Scott Zicree; Bantam, 1982)

Nonfiction. Trade paperback and true first edition. There is also a hardcover book club edition, as well as an expanded paperback second edition. Matheson is profiled and quoted extensively throughout the book.

*Rod Serling's The Twilight Zone Magazine* (October 1983)

"*TZ* Interview: Richard Matheson" (by Randy Lofficier & Jean-Marc Lofficier; short interview about *Twilight Zone—The Movie*)

*Fangoria* #31 (December 1983)

"Richard Matheson on *Twilight Zone* and *Jaws 3-D*" (by Lawrence French; interview with Matheson)

*He Is Legend* (Mark Rathbun & Graeme Flanagan; Mark Rathbun, 1984)

Nonfiction. Chapbook. Contains tributes to Matheson by various writers, a reprint of his nonfication piece "SF Unlimited," and a bibliography of his film and print work. A loose page containing an introduction by Ray Bradbury is included.

Introduction (by Ray Bradbury)

"The Curious Child: Preface" (by Mark Rathbun)

"Bon Homme Richard" (by Robert Bloch)
"Writing the Nightmare" (by Mark Rathbun)
Comment (by Jack Finney)
"Blood Son: Comments by Richard Christian Matheson" (by Richard Christian Matheson)
Bibliography
Comment (by William F. Nolan)
Filmography
"One for the Books: The Genesis of 'Duel' " (by Jerry Sohl)

*Masques* (Edited by J. N. Williamson; Maclay & Associates, Inc., 1984)
Short story collection. Hardcover, with dustjacket. First edition.
"Master of Imagination: An Interview with Richard Matheson" (by J. N. Williamson)

*Starlog* #100 (November 1985)
"The 100 Most Important People in Science Fiction" (brief profile)
"Profile: Richard Matheson" (by Randy Lofficier & Jean-Marc Lofficier)

*Faces of Fear: Encounters with the Creators of Modern Horror* (Douglas E. Winter; Berkley, 1985)
Interviews. Paperback original and true first edition.
"Richard Matheson" (interview with Matheson)

*Rod Serling's The Twilight Zone Magazine* (June 1986)
"A Richard Matheson Update" (by Michael Blaine; interview with Matheson about his songwriting and musical compositions, the unproduced *Arrow M.E.E.*, his collaborations with and influence on his children, and the *Somewhere in Time* musical)

*Horror: 100 Best Books* (Edited by Stephen Jones; Carroll & Graf Publishers Inc., 1988)
A selection of classic and contemporary horror fiction, with tributes and annotations by top contemporary writers of the genre.
"Richard Matheson: *I Am Legend*" (by Richard Christian Matheson; brief, rather poetic essay on Matheson's novel)

*Starlog* #136 (November 1988)

"Jerry Sohl: The Broken Promise of the Green Hand" (by Edward Gross; interview discussing the corporation formed by Matheson, Sohl, George Clayton Johnson, and Theodore Sturgeon)

*Richard Matheson: Collected Stories* (Dream/Press, 1989)

Short story collection. Details in the "Books: First and Limited Editions" section.

"From Ray Bradbury" (by Ray Bradbury)

"From Robert Bloch" (by Robert Bloch)

"From William F. Nolan" (by William F. Nolan)

"From Jack Finney" (by Jack Finney)

"From George Clayton Johnson" (by George Clayton Johnson)

"From Harlan Ellison" (by Harlan Ellison)

"From Stephen King" (by Stephen King)

"From Dennis Etchison" (by Dennis Etchison)

"From Richard Christian Matheson" (by Richard Christian Matheson)

Bibliography

*Fangoria* #89 (December 1989)

"Richard Matheson and the House of Poe, Part One" (by Tom Weaver & Michael Brunas; interview with Matheson)

*Through Channels* (Chapbook; Footsteps Press, 1989)

Short story. Details in the "Books: First and Limited Editions" section.

"In Appreciation" (by Vincent Price)

Afterword (by Roger Corman)

*Starlog* #150 (January 1990)

"Master of Shrinking Men" (by Tom Weaver; interview with Matheson)

*Fangoria* #90 (February 1990)

"Quoth Matheson, 'Nevermore!' Part Two" (by Tom Weaver & Michael Brunas; interview with Matheson)

*Starlog* #151 (February 1990)

"Master of the Last Men on Earth" (by Tom Weaver; interview with Matheson)

*Dark Dreamers: Conversations with the Masters of Horror* (Stanley Wiater; Underwood-Miller, Publishers, 1990)

Interviews. True first edition. Published in a 405-copy numbered hardcover edition in traycase, issued without dustjacket. The book was to have been signed by all twenty-six contributors, but the accidental destruction of some signature pages resulted in only 297 copies having all signatures. The remaining 108 copies have only one of two signature pages.

"Richard Matheson" (interview with Matheson)

*Dark Dreamers: Conversations with the Masters of Horror* (Stanley Wiater; Avon Books, 1990)

Interviews. First paperback edition.

"Richard Matheson" (interview with Matheson)

*The Shrinking Man* (Richard Matheson; Easton Press, 1990)

Novel. Details in the "Books: First and Limited Editions" section.

Introduction (by Harlan Ellison)

*Paperback, Pulp and Comic Collector Magazine* #4 (1991)

"Richard Matheson: Master of Fantasy and Horror" (by Maurice Flanagan; Matheson profile and film/book bibliography)

*Night Stalking: A 20th Anniversary Kolchak Companion* (Mark Dawidziak; Image Publishing, 1991)

Nonfiction. Trade paperback. True first edition. Detailed reference work on the *Night Stalker* films and television series, including comments by Matheson.

*The Shape Under the Sheet: The Complete Stephen King Encyclopedia* (Stephen J. Spignesi; Overlook Connection Press, 1991)

Nonfiction. True first edition. Published in a limited edition of 350 copies in slipcase, issued without dustjacket, and signed by twenty-seven contributors. Later editions include trade hardcover and trade paperback editions using the truncated title *The Complete Stephen King Encyclopedia*. Exhaustive reference work on King, including previously unpublished photos, interviews with friends, contemporaries, and family members, and a detailed guide to his fiction and film adaptations.

"He Is Legend: An Interview with Richard Matheson"

*Cemetery Dance* #12 (Spring 1992)

"Conversation with Richard Matheson & Richard Christian Matheson" (by Stanley Wiater; interview with the Mathesons, focusing on their personal and professional relationship)

*INSITE Newsletter* (April 1992)

Newsletter. Stapled pages. Quarterly newsletter of the International Network of *Somewhere in Time* Enthusiasts (INSITE).

"The Films of Richard Matheson" (brief profile)

*Midnight Graffiti* (Fall 1992)

"An Interview with Richard Matheson, Part I" (by Paul Sammon; this extremely lengthy interview was conducted in 1978 and previously published in somewhat different form in *Fangoria*)

*Serling: The Rise and Twilight of Television's Last Angry Man* (Gordon F. Sander; Dutton, 1992)

Nonfiction. Hardcover, with dustjacket. First edition. Biography of the groundbreaking writer and creator of *The Twilight Zone* and *Night Gallery*. Contains comments from Matheson and references to his work.

*INSITE Newsletter* (January 1993)

Newsletter. Stapled pages. Quarterly newsletter of the International Network of *Somewhere in Time* Enthusiasts (INSITE).

"The Amused Man" (photo of Matheson from his onscreen appearance in *Somewhere in Time*)

*World Horror Convention III Program* (March 1993)

"1993 Grand Master Richard Matheson" (profile)

*Mystery Scene* #40 (1993)

"Richard Matheson" (by Stefan Dziemianowicz; interview with Matheson)

*Filmfax* #42 (December–January 1994)

"And in the Beginning Was the Word . . . An Interview with Screenwriter Richard Matheson" (by Matthew R. Bradley; lengthy interview focusing on his feature films and TV movies)

*Starlog* #200 (March 1994)

"The 200 Most Important People in Science Fiction & Fantasy" (brief profile)

*The Overlook Connection* (April 1994)

"*The Path: Metaphysics for the '90s*—An Interview with Richard Matheson" (by Marcy Madden; concerns Matheson's book and metaphysical views; previously published in *The Light Connection*)

*Starlog* #203 (June 1994)

"Twilight Testaments: Where the Scripts Are" (by Tom Weaver; interview about newly discovered Rod Serling writings and the associated TV production *Twilight Zone: Rod Serling's Lost Classics*)

*The* Somewhere in Time *Story: Behind the Scenes of the Making of the Cult Romantic Fantasy Motion Picture* (Bill Shepard; INSITE Publications, 1994)

Nonfiction. Paperback and true first edition. A comprehensive history of the making of the film, including rare photographs, preproduction drawings, costume sketches, correspondence, and other documents. Written by the founder of the film's fan club.

*Midnight Graffiti* (Winter 1995)

"An Interview with Richard Matheson, Part II" (by Paul Sammon; this extremely lengthy interview was conducted in 1978 and previously published in somewhat different form in *Fangoria*)

*I Am Legend* (Richard Matheson; Gauntlet Press, 1995)

Novel. Details in the "Books: First and Limited Editions" section.

"Horror Legend" (by George Clayton Johnson)
Introduction (by Dan Simmons)
Introduction (by Matthew R. Bradley)
Afterword (by Dennis Etchison)

*Into the Twilight Zone: The Rod Serling Programme Guide* (Jean-Marc Lofficier & Randy Lofficier; Virgin Books, 1995)
Nonfiction. Paperback and true first edition. In addition to discussing Matheson's work on the various incarnations of *The Twilight Zone*, this contains a "Spotlight" that combines two interviews with Matheson by the authors that originally appeared in the French cinema magazine *L'Ecran Fantastique* (#11, second series, 4th quarter 1979) and in *Rod Serling's The Twilight Zone Magazine* (October 1983).

*Book and Magazine Collector* (February 1996)
"Richard Matheson" (by Richard Dalby; lengthy profile of Matheson and his works, including a bibliography and price guide of UK/US editions)

*SFX* (March 1996)
"The *SFX* Interview: Richard Matheson" (by Christopher Koetting)

*Hell House* (Richard Matheson; Gauntlet Press, 1996)
Novel. Details in the "Books: First and Limited Editions" section.
Introduction (by Dean R. Koontz)
Introduction (by Matthew R. Bradley)
Afterword (by Richard Christian Matheson)

*Cinematic Hauntings* (Edited by Gary J. Svehla & Susan Svehla; Midnight Marquee, 1996)
"*The Legend of Hell House*" (by Robert Alan Crick; lengthy article on the film and Matheson's screenplay adaptation)

*Outré* (Vol. 1[5], 1996)
"The Matheson Years: A Profile in Friendship" (by William F. Nolan; article and interview)
"*I Am Legend*: The Undying Legacy of a Horror Classic" (by Mat-

thew R. Bradley; article and interview adapted from Bradley's introduction to the 1995 Gauntlet Press edition)

*Noir: Three Novels of Suspense* (Richard Matheson; G&G Books, 1997)
  Novels. Details in the "Books: First and Limited Editions" section.
  Introduction (by Matthew R. Bradley)

*Cemetery Dance* #27 (Fall 1997)
  "A Conversation with Richard Matheson" (by Stanley Wiater)

*Backstory 3: Interviews with Screenwriters of the 1960s* (Edited by Pat Mc-Gilligan; University of California Press, 1997)
  Nonfiction. Hardcover, issued without dustjacket.
  "Richard Matheson: Storyteller" (by Pat McGilligan; considered by
    Matheson to be one of the best of his published interviews)

*Keep Watching the Skies!* (Bill Warren; McFarland & Company, Inc., 1997)
  Extensive reference work on science-fiction movies of the 1950s and early 1960s, including photographs, illustrations, and a bibliography. Previously published in two volumes. Lengthy sections are devoted to Matheson's *The Incredible Shrinking Man* and *Master of the World*.

*The Night Stalker Companion: A 25th Anniversary Tribute* (Mark Dawidziak; Pomegranate Press, 1997)
  Nonfiction. Trade paperback. First edition thus. A revised and expanded version of *Night Stalking: A 20th Anniversary Kolchak Companion*.

*What Dreams May Come* (Richard Matheson; Gauntlet Press, 1998)
  Novel. Details in the "Books: First and Limited Editions" section.
  Introduction (by Matthew R. Bradley)
  Afterword (by Stephen Simon)
  "Dreams of Love and Death" (by Douglas E. Winter)
  Afterword (by Richard Christian Matheson; lettered edition only)

*Studies in Weird Fiction* #23 (Summer 1998)
  "Madness or Monster: Textual Ambiguity in Richard Matheson's

'Nightmare at 20,000 Feet' " (by David A. Oakes; essay on Matheson's classic short story)

*Creative Screenwriting* (September–October 1998)
   "The Macabre Cinema of Richard Matheson" (by Christian K. Berger & Robert Arnett; biographical essay and interview with Matheson)

*Entertainment Weekly* (October 1998)
   "Grand Illusionist" (by Tom Russo; brief profile)

*Richard Matheson's* The Twilight Zone *Scripts* (Richard Matheson, edited by Stanley Wiater; Cemetery Dance, 1998)
   Teleplays. Details in the "Books: First and Limited Editions" section.
      "Submitted for Your Approval" (praise for *The Twilight Zone* and Richard Matheson)
      Letter from Rod Serling (by Rod Serling)
      Prologue (by Stanley Wiater)
      Epilogue (by Stanley Wiater)

*Starlog* #256 (November 1998)
   "He Is Legend" (by Marc Shapiro; brief overview with comments from Matheson, focusing on the film version of *What Dreams May Come*)

*Somewhere in Time* (Richard Matheson; Tor, 1999)
   Novel. Details in the "Books: First and Limited Editions" section.
   "Reading Group Guide to *Somewhere in Time* by Richard Matheson" (by Matthew R. Bradley)

*Written By: The Magazine of the Writers Guild of America, West* (March 1999)
   "A Writer's Oeuvre: The House of Matheson" (by Bill Krohn; lengthy profile)

*Somewhere in Time* (Richard Matheson; Gauntlet Press, 1999)
   Novel. Details in the "Books: First and Limited Editions" section.
   Afterword (by Bill Shepard)

*Cinefantastique* (Vol. 31[8], October 1999)

"Stir of Echoes" (by Peter Sobczynski; article about the film version of *A Stir of Echoes*)

*California Sorcery: A Group Celebration* (Edited by William F. Nolan & William Schafer; Cemetery Dance, 1999)

Short story collection. True first edition. Published in two hardcover states: a 1500-copy numbered edition with dustjacket, and a 26-copy lettered edition with dustjacket in traycase, both signed by editors William F. Nolan and William Schafer. The lettered edition is additionally signed by contributors Christopher Conlon, Richard Matheson, Harlan Ellison, John Tomerlin, Jerry Sohl, Charles E. Fritch, George Clayton Johnson, and Ray Bradbury, and includes a double-matted, framed full-color print by artist Erik Wilson.

> Introduction (by Christopher Conlon)
>
> "Remembering 'The Group' " (by William F. Nolan; reminiscence of the renowned group of California writers, including Matheson)

*Rod Serling's Night Gallery: An After Hours Tour* (Scott Skelton & Jim Benson; Syracuse University Press, 1999)

Nonfiction. Published simultaneously in hardcover, issued without dustjacket, and trade paperback editions. Comprehensive reference work on Serling's classic television series, including a detailed synopsis, commentary, and Serling's introduction to each segment. Matheson contributed two segments to the series: "Big Surprise" and "The Funeral." He was interviewed for and is quoted in the book.

*Vampires and Slayers* (Vol. 1[1], undated, c. 1999)

> "Directing 'Legend': An Interview with Rob Bowman" (by Edward Gross; covers Bowman's attempts to direct a third *I Am Legend* film)
>
> "He Is Legend: Richard Matheson on His Vampire Creations" (by Mark Dawidziak; interview with Matheson, and a review of *The Last Man on Earth* and *The Omega Man*)
>
> "Heston: Omega Man" (by Don Shay; interview with Charlton Heston on the making of *The Omega Man*)

*Filmfax* #75–76 (October–January 2000)

> "Enter *The Twilight Zone* with Richard Matheson" (by Matthew R. Bradley; lengthy interview on Matheson's work in episodic television)

*TV Guide* (November 4, 2000)

"The Stalk Market" (by Ted Johnson & Tim Williams; article on the influence of *The Night Stalker* on *The X-Files, Buffy the Vampire Slayer,* etc., with quotes from Matheson as well as Jeff Rice, Dan Curtis, and Chris Carter)

*Starburst* #268 (December 2000)

"Richard Matheson" (by James E. Brooks; article focusing primarily on the film versions of *Somewhere in Time* and *What Dreams May Come* with comments from Matheson)

*Cemetery Dance* #33 (2000)

"California Sorcery Signing" (by Lawrence Dopp; article on the book signing for *California Sorcery* at Dark Delicacies bookstore in Burbank, CA, with photos of Matheson, Ray Bradbury, Harlan Ellison, George Clayton Johnson, William F. Nolan, John Tomerlin, and Jerry Sohl)

*My Favorite Horror Story* (Edited by Mike Baker & Martin H. Greenberg; DAW, 2000)

A selection of classic horror stories, chosen and introduced by top contemporary writers of the genre.

Introduction to "The Distributor" (by F. Paul Wilson)

*Science and Destabilization in the Modern American Gothic: Lovecraft, Matheson, and King* (David A. Oakes; Greenwood Press, 2000)

Nonfiction. Hardcover, issued without dustjacket. A scholarly work on the use of science and technology in the works of writers of modern Gothic fiction.

*Richard Matheson's* The Twilight Zone *Scripts, Vol. 1* (Richard Matheson, edited by Stanley Wiater; Edge Books, 2001)

Teleplays. Details in "Books: First and Limited Editions."

"Submitted for Your Approval" (praise for *The Twilight Zone* and Richard Matheson)

Letter from Rod Serling (by Rod Serling)

Prologue (by Stanley Wiater)

*The Shrinking Man* (Richard Matheson; Gauntlet Press, 2001)
>Novel. Details in the "Books: First and Limited Editions" section.
>Afterword (by David Morrell)

*Firsts: The Book Collector's Magazine* (October 2001)
>"Collecting Richard Matheson" (by William F. Nolan; detailed overview of Matheson's work, and Nolan's personal recollections)
>"Richard Matheson: A Checklist of First Editions" (by William F. Nolan; covers Matheson's books through 2002)

*Video Store Magazine* (December 9–15, 2001)
>"Writer Gets Spotlight in MGM Series" (by Enrique Rivero; brief piece on the "Richard Matheson—Storyteller" series of DVD extras for several of his films)

*INSITE Newsletter* (Vol. 12[3], 2001)
>Newsletter. Stapled pages. Quarterly newsletter of the International Network of *Somewhere in Time* Enthusiasts (INSITE).
>"Richard Matheson: He Is Legend" (by Bill Shepard)
>"Richard Matheson Tribute: The 'Twilight' of his Career" (by Ed Stout; overview and episode guide to Matheson's *Twilight Zone* work)

*Filmfax* #93–94 (October–January 2002)
>"Alpha Male Omega Man!: Behind-the-scenes on the Making of *The Omega Man*" (by Robert Coyle & Mark Phillips; detailed account with extensive quotes from Charlton Heston, Walter Seltzer, and Joyce Carrington)

*Science Fiction Weekly* (www.scifi.com, c. March 2002)
>"Richard Matheson and William Stout Collaborate on a Children's Fantasy" (by Lisa DuMond; interview with Matheson and Stout about *Abu and the 7 Marvels*)

*Richard Matheson's* The Twilight Zone *Scripts, Vol. 2* (Richard Matheson, edited by Stanley Wiater; Edge Books, 2002)
>Teleplays. Details in "Books: First and Limited Editions."
>"Submitted for Your Approval" (praise for *The Twilight Zone* and Richard Matheson)

Letter from Rod Serling (by Rod Serling)
Prologue (by Stanley Wiater)
Epilogue (by Stanley Wiater)

*Nightmare at 20,000 Feet: Horror Stories by Richard Matheson* (Richard Matheson; Tor, 2002)
Short story collection. Details in the "Books: First and Limited Editions" section.
Introduction (by Stephen King)

*Publishers Weekly* (June 17, 2002)
"The Matheson Zone" (by Stefan Dziemianowicz; one of Matheson's favorite profiles, it provides an overview of his work and a discussion of recent publications)

*A Stir of Echoes* (Richard Matheson; Gauntlet Press, 2002)
Novel. Details in the "Books: First and Limited Editions" section.
Afterword (by David Koepp)

*The New York Review of Science Fiction* #169 (September 2002)
"The 'Richard Matheson—Storyteller' Series" (by Matthew R. Bradley; review of the series of interviews with Matheson on current and upcoming DVD releases of his films)

*Pride* (Richard Matheson & Richard Christian Matheson; Gauntlet Press, 2002)
Short stories and teleplay. Details in the "Books: First and Limited Editions" section.
Afterword (by Richard Christian Matheson)

*Off Beat: Uncollected Stories* (Richard Matheson, edited by William F. Nolan; Subterranean Press, 2002)
Short story collection. Details in the "Books: First and Limited Editions" section.
Introduction (by William F. Nolan)
"A Checklist of First Editions" (by William F. Nolan; covers Matheson's books through 2002)

*The Devils of His Own Creation: The Life and Work of Richard Matheson* (Terry Brejla; Writer's Club Press, 2002)

Biography. Trade paperback. True first edition. Matheson initially cooperated with but ultimately disowned this self-published and error-filled project, some of which "borrows" from various sources, notably *The* Somewhere in Time *Story*.

*Duel: Terror Stories by Richard Matheson* (Richard Matheson; Tor, 2003)

Short story collection. Details in the "Books: First and Limited Editions" section.

"An Appreciation" (by Ray Bradbury)

*CFQ* (Vol. 35[1], February–March 2003)

"It Is Legend" (by Jeff Bond; detailed article on the making of *The Omega Man*)

"Taking Their Shots" (by Stanley Manders; sidebar discussing attempts to film a third version of *I Am Legend*)

*Rue Morgue* #32 (March–April 2003)

"Classic Cut Presents *I Am Legend* " (by Chris Alexander; brief article on the novel and screen adaptations)

*Rue Morgue* #35 (September–October 2003)

"Richard Matheson: He Is Legend" (by Chris Alexander; overview of Matheson's work, including a timeline, an interview, and a review of the DVD release of *The Omega Man*)

*Richard Matheson: Collected Stories, Volume 1* (Edited by Stanley Wiater; Edge Books, 2003)

Short story collection. Details in the "Books: First and Limited Editions" section.

Editor's Preface (by Stanley Wiater)

"From Ray Bradbury" (by Ray Bradbury)

"From Robert Bloch" (by Robert Bloch)

"From William F. Nolan" (by William F. Nolan)

*Richard Matheson's Kolchak Scripts* (Richard Matheson, edited by Mark Dawidziak; Gauntlet Press, 2003)

Teleplays. Details in "Books: First and Limited Editions."

Introduction to *The Night Stalker* (by Mark Dawidziak)
Introduction to *The Night Strangler* (by Mark Dawidziak)
Introduction to *The Night Killers* (by Mark Dawidziak)
Appendix A: The Rest of the Kolchak Story
Appendix A: Photos
Appendix B: Richard Matheson and the TV Movie
Appendix C: Richard Matheson and the Vampire Story
Afterword (by Chris Carter)

*INSITE Newsletter* (Vol. 14[2], Second Quarter 2003)
Newsletter. Stapled pages. Quarterly newsletter of the International Network of *Somewhere in Time* Enthusiasts (INSITE).
"Richard Matheson Reflects on *Somewhere in Time*" (by Jim Lundstrom; brief article and interview with Matheson on the novel and film)

*Zoetrope: All-Story* (Spring 2004)
"An Introduction to Richard Matheson's 'Duel' " (by Steven Spielberg; brief article about the making of *Duel*)

*More Giants of the Genre* (Michael McCarty; Wildside Press, 2004)
Nonfiction. Trade paperback and true first edition. Collection of interviews with important figures in the horror, science-fiction, and fantasy fields.
"I Am Legend: Interview with Richard Matheson"

*Filmfax* #103 (July–August 2004)
"About Richard Matheson: The Art of Heart and Brain" (by Ed Gorman; contains Gorman's personal recollections of Matheson, career highlights, and an interview)

*Duel & The Distributor* (Richard Matheson, edited by Matthew R. Bradley; Gauntlet Press, 2004)
Short stories and scripts. Details in the "Books: First and Limited Editions" section.
"Duel": The Foreword (by Matthew R. Bradley)
"The Duelist: An Interview with Dennis Weaver" (by Matthew R. Bradley; covers the making of *Duel*)
"The Distributor": An Afterword (by Matthew R. Bradley)

*Cemetery Dance* #49 (2004)
"A Conversation with Richard Matheson" (by William P. Simmons)

*Richard Matheson: Collected Stories, Volume 2* (Edited by Stanley Wiater; Edge Books, 2005)
Short story collection. Details in the "Books: First and Limited Editions" section.
Editor's Preface (by Stanley Wiater)
"From Jack Finney" (by Jack Finney)
"From George Clayton Johnson" (by George Clayton Johnson)

*H.P. Lovecraft's Magazine of Horror* (Spring 2005)
"A Talk with Richard Matheson" (by Michael McCarty; reprinted from McCarty's *More Giants of the Genre*)
"Matheson's Movies: A Critical Overview" (by Michael McCarty; overview of Matheson's work)

*SFX* (June 2005)
"Richard Matheson" (by Danny Graydon; brief overview and interview)

"Speech by Richard Christian Matheson" (June 2005)
Delivered in honor of his father at the book release party for Matheson's *Woman*.

*Noir: Three Novels of Suspense* (Richard Matheson; Forge, 2005)
Novels. Details in the "Books: First and Limited Editions" section.
Introduction (by Matthew R. Bradley)

*Richard Matheson: Collected Stories, Volume 3* (Edited by Stanley Wiater; Edge Books, 2005)
Short story collection. Details in the "Books: First and Limited Editions" section.
Editor's Preface (by Stanley Wiater)
"From Harlan Ellison" (by Harlan Ellison)
"From Stephen King" (by Stephen King)
"From Dennis Etchison" (by Dennis Etchison)
"From Richard Christian Matheson" (by Richard Christian Matheson)

*Unrealized Dreams* (Richard Matheson; Gauntlet Press, 2005)
   Screenplays. Details in "Books: First and Limited Editions."
   Introduction (by Dennis Etchison)

*Mystery Scene* #95 (Summer 2006)
   "Living Legend: A Talk with Richard Matheson" (by Dick Lochte)

*Bloodlines: Richard Matheson's* Dracula, I Am Legend, *and Other Vampire Stories* (Richard Matheson, edited by Mark Dawidziak; Gauntlet Press, 2006)
   Short stories, novel, and scripts. Details in the "Books: First and Limited Editions" section.
   "Preface: Tracing the Bloodlines" (by Mark Dawidziak)
   "Appreciation One: Under the Influence" (by John Carpenter)
   "Introduction One: Richard the Writer, Vlad the Impaler and *Dracula* the Script" (by Mark Dawidziak)
   "Appreciation Two: 'X' Marked the Spot" (by Frank Spotnitz)
   "Appreciation Three: Discovering Matheson" (by Mick Garris)
   "Introduction Two: The Unfilmed Legend" (by Mark Dawidziak)
   "Appreciation Four: The Son Also Apprises" (by Richard Christian Matheson)
   "Appreciation Five: Matheson and Me" (by Steve Niles)
   "Appreciation Six: Confessions of an Addict" (by Rockne S. O'Bannon)
   "Introduction Three: The Short Stories" (by Mark Dawidziak)
   "Appreciation Seven: Looks Like the Beginning of a Beautiful Friendship" (by Ray Bradbury)
   "Appendix A: Thoughts from the Archive" (by John Scoleri)
   "Appendix B: The Unwritten Vampire Story" (by Mark Dawidziak)

*The Funeral* (Richard Matheson; Gauntlet Press, 2006)
   Teleplay. Details in "Books: First and Limited Editions."
   Introduction (by Mark Dawidziak)

*Doomed* #4 (2006)
   "Buried Treasure: A Richard Matheson Time Capsule" (by Paul Stuve; brief essay on the discovery of rare correspondence between Matheson and his college writing professor, William Peden)

*Visions of Death: Richard Matheson's Edgar Allan Poe Scripts, Volume One*
(Richard Matheson, edited by Lawrence French; Gauntlet Press, 2007)
> Screenplays. Details in the "Books: First and Limited Editions."
> Introduction (by Roger Corman)
> Editor's Introduction (by Lawrence French)
> "The House is the Monster: The Making of *House of Usher*" (by
> Lawrence French)
> "The House of the Dead: The Making of *The Pit and the Pendulum*"
> (by Lawrence French)
> "Richard Matheson on Adapting Edgar Allan Poe for the Screen"
> (interview by Lawrence French)
> Afterword (by Joe Dante)
> American International Pictures *House of Usher* Production Notes
> American International Pictures *The Pit and the Pendulum* Produc-
> tion Story

*Matheson Uncollected: Volume One* (Richard Matheson; Gauntlet Press,
2008)
> Teleplays, novel, and short stories. Details in the "Books: First and
Limited Editions" section.
> Introduction (by George Clayton Johnson)
> "Split Personality: The Evolution of Richard Matheson's 'The En-
> emy Within'" (by Tony Albarella)
> "Richard Matheson's Lost Colony" (by Tony Albarella)

## Selected Websites

The phrase "Richard Matheson" will turn up tens of thousands of hits
on any of the commonly used Internet search engines. While not claim-
ing to have reviewed all of those sites, we have selected a few of our
favorites.

*The Encyclopedia of Fantastic Film and Television*:
www.eofftv.com/names/m/mat/matheson_richard_main.htm
> Contains a biography and filmography of Matheson.

*Fantastic Fiction*:
www.fantasticfiction.co.uk/m/richard-matheson

Bibliographies for thousands of authors. The Matheson entry includes an extensive collection of book cover images.

*Horror-Wood Webzine*:
www.horror-wood.com/matheson.htm
A "webzine for classic and cult horror and monster film fans." Matheson's entry has a profile and an interview with him, and a large collection of book cover art, film posters, and photos from his films.

*I Am Legend*:
iamlegend.warnerbros.com/_main_site/
The official website of the Warner Brothers film starring Will Smith, it includes various photos, screen savers, and other images for downloading, as well as movie previews, an online comic inspired by the novel, an online multiplayer video game, and other features.

*The* I Am Legend *Archive*:
www.iamlegendarchive.com
An impressive website maintained by *I Am Legend* überfan John Scoleri, containing a vast collection of cover images and descriptions of domestic and foreign editions of the novel (some available for trade), information about film adaptations, and interviews with an assortment of people associated with the various print and film incarnations.

*Internet Movie Database*:
www.imdb.com/name/nm0558577
Self-proclaimed as "Earth's biggest movie database." The Matheson entry contains detailed information on his film and television work, although some errors are included.

*The Internet Speculative Fiction Database*:
www.isfdb.org/cgi-bin/ch.cgi? Richard_Matheson
A wiki site devoted to cataloging works of science fiction, fantasy, and horror. Includes detailed bibliographic information on published books, magazines, and anthologies, as well as forthcoming works.

*LOCUS Online—News, Reviews, Resources, and Perspectives of Science Fiction, Fantasy, and Horror*:
www.locusmag.com/index/b331.html#A4644

News of the science-fiction publishing world, including reviews of new books, schedules of upcoming book signings, and an extensive searchable online index of science-fiction writings. Includes a detailed listing of Matheson's publications, including first and later editions of his books, and an extensive listing of magazine and anthology appearances of his short fiction.

*Richard Matheson—Writer of Science Fiction, Terror and Fantasy*:
users.adelphia.net/~sitman/index.html

Contains information about Matheson's print and film work, with many images of book covers and movie posters.

*The Savitar*:
virtuallymissouri.umsystem.edu/t/text/gifcvtdir/sav1947/sav1947p0218
.jpg
virtuallymissouri.umsystem.edu/t/text/gifcvtdir/sav1948/sav1948p0066
.jpg
virtuallymissouri.umsystem.edu/t/text/gifcvtdir/sav1948/sav1948p0135
.jpg

The above links are to college photos of Matheson from the 1947 and 1948 editions of *The Savitar*, the University of Missouri's yearbook.

*Sci-Fi Station*:
www.scifistation.com/matheson/matheson_index.html

Interesting website for collectors of science-fiction memorabilia. Also contains a profile and interview with Matheson, and includes many film photos, movie posters, book cover art, and other images.

*Scifipedia*:
scifipedia.scifi.com/index.php/Richard_Matheson

Extensive online encyclopedia focusing on science-fiction, fantasy, and horror writings and films. Includes a profile of Matheson by Greg Cox, as well as articles by Matthew R. Bradley about *I Am Legend*, *The Incredible Shrinking Man*, and *Master of the World*. A wiki site, with content that can be created and edited by users.

## Films Written by Matheson or Based on His Work

(Key: D = director; P = producer; SP = screenplay; S = story;
b/o = based on; M = music; MU = makeup; SMU = special makeup;
SE = special effects; SVE = special visual effects; SMUE = special
makeup effects; LP = leading players)

Excepting the foreign-language films *Soy Leyenda* and *O Impossível Acontece*, which were sadly unavailable for review, these have all been checked against the actual onscreen credits (although, as noted in the TV movie list that follows, film credits can be inaccurate as well). Many amateur and self-produced films continue to surface on the Internet, in particular on YouTube™, where multiple adaptations of Matheson's "The Near Departed" and a host of short films inspired by *I Am Legend* could be found at the time of this writing. Coverage of these ever-expanding titles is beyond the scope of this list.

*The Incredible Shrinking Man* (Universal-International, 1957) D: Jack Arnold; P: Albert Zugsmith; SP: Matheson/Richard Alan Simmons [uncredited], b/o Matheson's *The Shrinking Man*; M [uncredited]: Irving Gertz/Henry Mancini/Hans J. Salter/Herman Stein; Music Supervision: Joseph Gershenson; Trumpet Soloist: Ray Anthony; MU: Bud Westmore; Special Photography: Clifford Stine; Optical Effects: Roswell A. Hoffman/Everett H. Broussard. Black and white, 81 minutes. LP: Grant Williams, Randy Stuart, April Kent, Paul Langton, Raymond Bailey, William Schallert.

*The Beat Generation* (a.k.a. *This Rebel Age*; MGM, 1959) D: Charles Haas; P: Albert Zugsmith; SP: Matheson/Lewis Meltzer; M: Albert Glasser; MU: William Tuttle. Black and white, 95 minutes. LP: Steve Cochran, Mamie Van Doren, Ray Danton, Fay Spain, Louis Armstrong and His All-Stars, Maggie Hayes, Jackie Coogan, Jim Mitchum, Ray Anthony, Irish McCalla.

*House of Usher* (a.k.a. *The Fall of the House of Usher*; American International, 1960) D/P: Roger Corman; SP: Matheson, b/o Edgar Allan Poe's

"The Fall of the House of Usher"; M: Les Baxter; MU: Fred Phillips; SE: Pat Dinga/Ray Mercer. Color, 79 minutes. LP: Vincent Price, Mark Damon, Myrna Fahey, Harry Ellerbe.

*Master of the World* (American International, 1961) D: William Witney; P: James H. Nicholson; SP: Matheson, b/o Jules Verne's *Robur le Conquérant* (*Robur, the Conqueror* a.k.a. *The Clipper of the Clouds*) and *Maître du Mond* (*Master of the World*); M: Les Baxter; Title Song Lyrics: Lenny Addelson, sung by Darryl Stevens; MU: Fred B. Phillips; SE: Tim Baar [a.k.a. Barr]/Wah Chang/Gene Warren; Photographic Effects: Butler-Glouner, Inc./Ray Mercer, A.S.C.; Special Props and Effects: Pat Dinga. Color, 104 minutes. LP: Vincent Price, Charles Bronson, Henry Hull, Mary Webster, David Frankham, Richard Harrison.

*Pit and the Pendulum* (American International, 1961) D/P: Roger Corman; SP: Matheson, b/o Edgar Allan Poe's "The Pit and the Pendulum"; M: Les Baxter; MU: Ted Coodley; SE: Butler-Glouner, Inc./Ray Mercer/Pat Dinga. Color, 81 minutes. LP: Vincent Price, John Kerr, Barbara Steele, Luana Anders, Antony Carbone, Patrick Westwood.

*Night of the Eagle* (a.k.a. *Burn, Witch, Burn*; Independent Artists/Anglo Amalgamated/American International [GB], 1962) D: Sidney Hayers; P: Albert Fennell; SP: Matheson/Charles Beaumont/George Baxt [uncredited in U.S.], b/o Fritz Leiber's *Conjure Wife*; M: William Alwyn; MU: Basil Newall. Black and white, 87 minutes. LP: Janet Blair, Peter Wyngarde, Margaret Johnston, Anthony Nicholls, Colin Gordon, Kathleen Byron, Reginald Beckwith, Jessica Dunning.

*Tales of Terror* (American International, 1962) D/P: Roger Corman: SP: Matheson; M: Les Baxter; MU: Lou La Cava; SE: Butler-Glouner, Inc./ Ray Mercer Co./Pat Dinga. Color, 89 minutes. "Morella"—b/o Edgar Allan Poe's story; LP: Vincent Price, Maggie Pierce, Leona Gage. "The Black Cat"—b/o Poe's story and "The Cask of Amontillado"; LP: Price, Peter Lorre, Joyce Jameson. "The Case of M. Valdemar"—b/o Poe's "The Facts in the Case of M. Valdemar"; LP: Price, Basil Rathbone, Debra Paget, David Frankham.

*The Raven* (American International, 1963) D/P: Roger Corman; SP: Matheson, b/o Edgar Allan Poe's poem; M: Les Baxter; MU: Ted Coodley; SE: Butler-Glouner, Inc./Pat Dinga. Color, 86 minutes. LP: Vincent Price, Peter Lorre, Boris Karloff, Hazel Court, Olive Sturgess, Jack Nicholson.

*The Comedy of Terrors* (a.k.a. *Graveside Story*; American International, 1963) D: Jacques Tourneur; P: James H. Nicholson/Samuel Z. Arkoff; SP: Matheson; M: Les Baxter; MU: Carlie Taylor; SE: Pat Dinga/Butler-Glouner. Color, 83 minutes. LP: Vincent Price, Peter Lorre, Boris Karloff, Joyce Jameson, Joe E. Brown, Beverly Hills, Basil Rathbone.

*The Last Man on Earth* (*L'Ultimo Uomo della Terra*; Associated Producers/La Regina [U.S./Italy], 1964) D: Sidney Salkow [U.S. version]/ Ubaldo B. Ragona [Italian version]; P: Robert L. Lippert; SP: Logan Swanson [Matheson]/William F. Leicester, b/o Matheson's *I Am Legend*; M: Paul Sawtell/Bert Shefter; MU: Piero Mecacci. Black and white, 87 minutes. LP: Vincent Price, Franca Bettoia, Emma Danieli, Giacomo Rossi-Stuart, Umberto Rau, Christi Courtland.

*Fanatic* (a.k.a. *Die! Die! My Darling!*; Hammer [GB], 1965) D: Silvio Narizzano; P: Anthony Hinds; SP: Matheson, b/o Anne Blaisdell's *Nightmare*; M: Wilfred Josephs; MU: Roy Ashton/Richard Mills. Color, 96 minutes [several sources list U.S. running time as 105 minutes, but home video prints bearing U.S. title run 96 minutes]. LP: Tallulah Bankhead, Stefanie Powers, Peter Vaughan, Maurice Kaufmann, Yootha Joyce, Donald Sutherland.

*I Am Legend* (*Soy Leyenda*; Escuela Oficial de Cinematografia [Spain], 1967) D: Mario Gómez Martín; SP: Martín/Alfonso Núñez Flores, b/o Matheson's novel. Black and white, 15 minutes. LP: Ana Castor, Moisés Menéndez, Ricardo Palacios, Elisa Ramírez, José María Resel.

*The Young Warriors* (a.k.a. *Eagle Warriors*; Universal, 1968) D: John Peyser; P: Gordon Kay; SP: Matheson, b/o his *The Beardless Warriors*; M: Milton Rosen; MU: Bud Westmore. Color, 93 minutes. LP: James

Drury, Steve Carlson, Jonathan Daly, Robert Pine, Jeff Scott, Michael Stanwood, Hank Jones.

*The Devil Rides Out* (a.k.a. *The Devil's Bride*; Seven Arts-Hammer [GB], 1968) D: Terence Fisher; P: Anthony Nelson Keys; SP: Matheson, b/o Dennis Wheatley's novel; M: James Bernard; MU: Eddie Knight; Masks: Roy Ashton [uncredited]; SE: Michael Stainer-Hutchins. Color, 95 minutes. LP: Christopher Lee, Charles Gray, Niké Arrighi, Leon Greene, Patrick Mower, Gwen Ffrangcon-Davies, Sarah Lawson, Paul Eddington.

*"It's Alive!"* (Azalea, 1969 [released directly to television]) D/P/SP/Editor: Larry Buchanan, b/o Matheson's "Being" [uncredited]; SE: Jack Bennett. Color, 80 minutes. LP: Tommy Kirk, Shirley Bonne, Billy Thurman, Annabelle Macadams, Corveth Ousterhouse.

*O Impossível Acontece* (a.k.a. *Believe It or Not*; Minuano/Rio de Janeiro [Brazil], 1969) Black and white, 80 minutes. "O Acidente"—D/P/SP: C. Adolpho Chadler [a.k.a. Cícero Adolpho Vitório da Costa], b/o Matheson's "Disappearing Act" [uncredited]; LP: Chadler, Sanin Cherques, Billy Davis, Dora Palermo, Francisco Santos, Valentina. "Eu, Ela e o Outro"—D/P: Daniel Filho; SP: Filho/Gilvan Pereira; LP: Filho, Rubens de Falco, Glória Menezes. "O Reimplante"—D/SP: Anselmo Duarte; P: Filho; LP: Wilza Carla, Tião Macalé.

*De Sade* (a.k.a. *The Marquis de Sade, Das Ausschweifende Leben des Marquis de Sade, Die Liebesabenteuer des Marquis S*; American International/CCC Film/Trans Continental [U.S./West Germany], 1969) D: Cy Endfield/Roger Corman [uncredited]; P: Samuel Z. Arkoff/James H. Nicholson; SP: Matheson, based on the life and writings of the Marquis de Sade; M: Billy Strange; MU: Freddy Arnold. Color, 104 minutes. LP: Keir Dullea, Senta Berger, Lilli Palmer, Anna Massey, Sonja Ziemann, Christiane Krueger, John Huston.

*Cold Sweat* (a.k.a. *De la Part des Copains, L'Uomo dalle Due Ombre* [*The Man with Two Shadows*]; Films Corona/Comacico/Fair Film [France/Italy], 1970) D: Terence Young; P: Robert Dorfmann; SP: Shimon Wincelberg/Albert Simonin [uncredited]/Jo Eisinger/Dorothea Bennett, b/o Matheson's *Ride the Nightmare*; M: Michel Magne; MU: Marie-Madeleine Paris/Anatole Paris. Color, 94 minutes. LP: Charles Bronson, Liv Ullmann, James Mason, Jill Ireland, Jean Topart, Luigi Pistilli, Yannick de Lulle, Michel Constantin.

*The Omega Man* (Warner Brothers, 1971) D: Boris Sagal; P: Walter Seltzer; SP: John William Corrington/Joyce H. Corrington, b/o Matheson's *I Am Legend*; M: Ron Grainer; MU: Gordon Bau. Color, 98 minutes. LP: Charlton Heston, Anthony Zerbe, Rosalind Cash, Paul Koslo, Eric Laneuville, Lincoln Kilpatrick.

*The Legend of Hell House* (Academy Pictures/20th Century-Fox (GB), 1973) D: John Hough; P: Albert Fennell/Norman T. Herman; SP: Matheson, b/o his *Hell House*; M: Brian Hodgson/Delia Derbyshire; MU: Linda Devetta; SE: Roy Whybrow. Color, 94 minutes. LP: Pamela Franklin, Roddy McDowall, Clive Revill, Gayle Hunnicutt, Roland Culver.

*Icy Breasts* (*Les Seins de Glace*; Lira/Belstar/Capitolina [France/Italy], 1974) D/SP: Georges Lautner, b/o Matheson's *Someone Is Bleeding*: P: Ralph Baum; M: Philippe Sarde. Color, 101 minutes. LP: Alain Delon, Mireille Darc, Claude Brasseur, André Falcon, Nicoletta Machiavelli, Fiore Altoviti.

*Somewhere in Time* (Rastar/Universal, 1980) D: Jeannot Szwarc; P: Stephen Deutsch [a.k.a. Simon]; SP: Matheson, b/o his *Bid Time Return*; M: John Barry; MU: Jack Wilson/Paul Sanchez; SE: Jack Faggard. Color, 103 minutes. LP: Christopher Reeve, Jane Seymour, Christopher Plummer, Teresa Wright, Bill Erwin, George Voskovec, Susan French.

*The Incredible Shrinking Woman* (Universal, 1981) D: Joel Schumacher; P: Hank Moonjean; SP: Jane Wagner, suggested by Matheson's *The Shrinking Man*; M: Suzanne Ciani; MU: Ve Neill; SE: Bruce Logan/Roy Arbogast/Guy Faria/David Kelsey. Color, 88 minutes. LP: Lily Tomlin, Charles Grodin, Ned Beatty, Henry Gibson, Elizabeth Wilson, Mark Blankfield, Maria Smith, Pamela Bellwood, John Glover.

*Twilight Zone—The Movie* (Warner Brothers, 1983) P: Steven Spielberg/John Landis; Inspired by *The Twilight Zone*, created by Rod Serling; M: Jerry Goldsmith; Project Consultant: Carol Serling; Narrator: Burgess Meredith. Color, 101 minutes. Prologue—D/SP: Landis; LP: Dan Aykroyd, Albert Brooks. "Time Out"—D/SP: Landis; MU: Robert Westmoreland/Melanie E. Levitt; SMU: Craig Reardon; SE: Paul Stewart; LP: Vic Morrow, Doug McGrath, Charles Hallahan. "Kick the Can"—D: Spielberg; SP: George Clayton Johnson/Matheson/Josh Rogan [Melissa Mathison]; S: Johnson; MU: John Elliott; LP: Scatman Crothers, Bill Quinn, Martin Garner, Selma Diamond, Helen Shaw, Murray Matheson. "It's a Good Life"—D: Joe Dante; SP: Matheson, b/o Jerome Bixby's story; MU: Elliott; SMU/Monster Effects: Rob Bottin; LP: Kathleen Quinlan, Jeremy Licht, Kevin McCarthy, Patricia Barry, William Schallert. "Nightmare at 20,000 Feet"—D: George Miller; SP: Matheson, b/o his story; MU: Elliott; SMU: Reardon/Michael Mc-Cracken; Visual Effects: Peter Kuran (V.C.E.)/Jim Danforth (Effects Associates)/David Allan; Monster Conceptual Design: Ed Verreaux; LP: John Lithgow, Abbe Lane, Donna Dixon, John Dennis Johnston.

*Jaws III* (a.k.a. *Jaws 3-D*; Universal, 1983) D: Joe Alves; P: Rupert Hitzig; SP: Matheson/Carl Gottlieb, suggested by Peter Benchley's *Jaws*; S: Guerdon Trueblood; M: Alan Parker; Shark Theme: John Williams; MU: Kathryn Bihr; SE: Praxis Film Works, Inc./Robert Blalack [photographic and optical effects]/Private Stock Effects, Inc. [miniatures and electronic composites]. Color, 99 minutes. LP: Dennis Quaid, Bess Armstrong, Simon MacCorkindale, Louis Gossett, Jr., John Putch, Lea Thompson.

*Loose Cannons* (TriStar, 1990) D: Bob Clark; P: Aaron Spelling/Alan Greisman; SP: Richard Christian Matheson/Matheson/Clark; M: Paul Zaza; MU: Michael R. Thomas; SE Supervisor: Roy Arbogast. Color, 94 minutes. LP: Gene Hackman, Dan Aykroyd, Dom DeLuise, Ronny Cox, Nancy Travis, Robert Prosky.

*What Dreams May Come* (PolyGram, 1998) D: Vincent Ward; P: Stephen Simon [a.k.a. Deutsch]/Barnet Bain; SP: Ron Bass, b/o Matheson's novel; M: Michael Kamen; SMUE: Todd Masters; SVE: Mass Illusions/POP Film & Animation/Digital Domain. Color, 114 minutes. LP: Robin Williams, Cuba Gooding, Jr., Annabella Sciorra, Max Von Sydow, Jessica Brooks Grant, Josh Paddock, Rosalind Chao.

*Stir of Echoes* (Artisan, 1999) D/SP: David Koepp, b/o Matheson's *A Stir of Echoes*; P: Gavin Polone/Judy Hofflund; M: James Newton Howard; SMUE: Tony Gardner/Jim Beinke; SE: Banned from the Ranch Entertainment. Color, 99 minutes. LP: Kevin Bacon, Kathryn Erbe, Illeana Douglas, Zachary David Cope, Kevin Dunn, Conor O'Farrell.

*Blood Son* (Buffalonickel Films, 2006) D/SP: Michael McGruther, b/o Matheson's story (a.k.a. " 'Drink My Red Blood . . .' " and "Drink My Blood"); P: Tom MacDonald/Michele Santos; M: Matt Heider; MU: Ingrid Okala. Color, 15 minutes. LP: Lucas Wotkowski, Robert Hancock, Julie M. Finch, Mandi Bedbury, Joseph Michael Somma.

*My Ambition* (k2 Productions, 2006) D/SP: Keith Dinielli, b/o Matheson's "Blood Son" (a.k.a. " 'Drink My Red Blood . . .' " and "Drink My Blood"); P: Robert Myrtle; MU/SEMU: Karen Stein. Color, 8 minutes. LP: Johnny Simmons, Brooke Morgan, Bernard Zilinskas, Jonas Barnes.

*I Am Legend* (Warner Brothers, 2007) D: Francis Lawrence; P: Akiva Goldsman/James Lassiter/David Heyman/Neal H. Moritz; SP: Mark Protosevich/Goldsman, b/o John William & Joyce H. Corrington's screenplay [*The Omega Man*] and Matheson's novel; M: James Newton Howard; VE Supervisor: Janek Sirrs; Creatures Designed by Patrick Tatopoulos; VE: Sony Pictures Imageworks/CIS-Hollywood. Color, 100 minutes, original release; 104 minutes, alternate theatrical and DVD version. LP: Will Smith, Alice Braga, Charlie Tahan, Salli Richardson, Willow Smith.

## TV Movies and Miniseries Written by Matheson or Based on His Work

(Key: D = director; P = producer; TP = teleplay; S = story; b/o = based on; M = music; MU = makeup; SE = special effects; SEMU = special effects makeup; LP = leading players)

Sharp-eyed viewers may notice some discrepancies between these credits and those of the many TV movies Matheson wrote for producer Dan

Curtis. Unfortunately, Curtis appears to have taken a rather cavalier attitude toward credits; several misspelled names are corrected herein.

*Duel* (ABC-TV, 11/13/71) D: Steven Spielberg; P: George Eckstein; TP: Matheson, b/o his story; M: Billy Goldenberg. Color, 74 minutes, original broadcast version; 90 minutes, syndicated/home video/theatrical release version. LP: Dennis Weaver, Jacqueline Scott, Eddie Firestone, Lou Frizzell, Gene Dynarski, Lucille Benson.

*The Night Stalker* (ABC-TV, 1/11/72) D: John Llewellyn Moxey; P: Dan Curtis; TP: Matheson, b/o Jeff Rice's unpublished novel *The Kolchak Papers*; M: Robert Cobert; MU: Jerry Cash. Color, 74 minutes. LP: Darren McGavin, Carol Lynley, Simon Oakland, Ralph Meeker, Claude Akins, Charles McGraw, Kent Smith, Elisha Cook, Jr., Stanley Adams, Larry Linville, Jordan Rhodes, Barry Atwater.

*The Night Strangler* (ABC-TV, 1/16/73) D/P: Dan Curtis; TP: Matheson, b/o some characters created by Jeff Rice; M: Robert Cobert; MU: William J. Tuttle; SE: Ira Anderson. Color, 74 minutes, original broadcast version; 90 minutes, syndicated/home video/overseas theatrical release version. LP: Darren McGavin, Jo Ann Pflug, Simon Oakland, Richard Anderson, Scott Brady, Wally Cox, Margaret Hamilton, John Carradine.

*Dying Room Only* (ABC-TV, 9/18/73) D: Philip Leacock; P: Allen S. Epstein; TP: Matheson, b/o his story; M: Charles Fox; MU: Mel Berns, Jr. Color, 74 minutes. LP: Cloris Leachman, Ross Martin, Ned Beatty, Dana Elcar, Louise Latham, Dabney Coleman.

*Scream of the Wolf* (ABC-TV, 1/16/74) P/D: Dan Curtis; TP: Matheson, b/o David Case's "The Hunter"; M: Robert Cobert; MU: Mike Westmore; SE: Roger George. Color, 74 minutes. LP: Peter Graves, Clint Walker, Jo Ann Pflug, Philip Carey, Don Megowan.

*Dracula* (a.k.a. *Bram Stoker's Dracula*; CBS-TV, 2/8/74 [postponed from 10/12/73]) D/P: Dan Curtis; TP: Matheson, b/o Bram Stoker's novel; M: Robert Cobert; MU: Paul Rabiger; SE: Kit West. Color, 98 minutes.

LP: Jack Palance, Simon Ward, Nigel Davenport, Pamela Brown, Fiona Lewis, Penelope Horner, Murray Brown.

*The Morning After* (ABC-TV, 2/13/74) D: Richard T. Heffron; P: Stan Margulies; TP: Matheson, b/o Jack B. Weiner's novel; M: Mike Post/ Pete Carpenter; MU: Bob Westmoreland. Color, 73 minutes. LP: Dick Van Dyke, Lynn Carlin, Don Porter, Linda Lavin, Jewel Blanch, Sam Gilman, Joshua Bryant, Richard Derr.

*The Stranger Within* (ABC-TV, 10/1/74) D: Lee Philips; P: Neil T. Maffeo; TP: Matheson, b/o his "Trespass" (a.k.a. "Mother by Protest"); M: Charles Fox; MU: Karl Herlinger. Color, 78 minutes. LP: Barbara Eden, George Grizzard, Joyce Van Patten, David Doyle, Nehemiah Persoff.

*All Together Now* (ABC-TV, 2/5/75) D: Randal Kleiser; P: Ron Bernstein; TP: Jeff Andrus/Rubin Carson; S: Carson; M: John Rubinstein; Songs: Tim McIntire/Rubinstein. Color, 90 minutes less commercials. LP: Rubinstein, Glynnis O'Connor, Brad Savage, Helen Hunt, Dori Brenner, Bill Macy, Jane Withers. [Matheson made uncredited revisions to this script—which fictionalized the struggle of Charles Beaumont's eldest child, Chris, to obtain guardianship of his three siblings—but how much, if any, of his material was used is unknown.]

*Trilogy of Terror* (ABC-TV, 3/4/75) D/P: Dan Curtis; M: Robert Cobert; MU: Mike Westmore; SE: Richard Albaine; Puppet Master: Erik M. Von Buelow. Color, 72 minutes. "Julie"—TP: William F. Nolan, b/o Matheson's "The Likeness of Julie"; LP: Karen Black, Robert Burton, James Storm. "Millicent and Therese"—TP: Nolan, b/o Matheson's "Therese" (a.k.a. "Needle in the Heart"); LP: Black, George Gaynes, John Karlen. "Amelia"—TP: Matheson, b/o his "Prey"; LP: Black.

*The Strange Possession of Mrs. Oliver* (NBC-TV, 2/28/77) D: Gordon Hessler; P: Stan Shpetner; TP: Matheson; M: Morton Stevens; MU: Stephen B. Gautier. Color, 78 minutes. LP: Karen Black, George Hamilton, Robert F. Lyons, Lucille Benson, Jean Allison.

*Dead of Night* (NBC-TV, 3/29/77) D: Dan Curtis; P: Robert Singer; M: Robert Cobert; MU: Frank Westmore; SE: Cliff Wenger. Color, 73 minutes. "Second Chance"—TP: Matheson, b/o Jack Finney's story; LP: Ed Begley, Jr., Ann Doran, Christine Hart, Orin Cannon. "No Such Thing as a Vampire"—TP: Matheson, b/o his story; LP: Patrick Macnee, Anjanette Comer, Elisha Cook, Jr., Horst Buchholz. "Bobby"—TP: Matheson; LP: Joan Hackett, Lee H. Montgomery, Larry Green.

*The Martian Chronicles* (NBC-TV, 1/27–29/80) D: Michael Anderson; P: Andrew Donally/Milton Subotsky; TP: Matheson, b/o Ray Bradbury's book and the story "The Fire Balloons" from Bradbury's *The Illustrated Man*; M: Stanley Myers; MU: George Frost/Mark Reedall/Colin Arthur; SE: John Stears. Color, 289 minutes. LP: Rock Hudson, Gayle Hunnicutt, Bernie Casey, Christopher Connelly, Nicholas Hammond, Roddy McDowall, Darren McGavin, Bernadette Peters, Maria Schell, Joyce Van Patten, Fritz Weaver.

*The Dreamer of Oz* (a.k.a. *The Dreamer of Oz: The L. Frank Baum Story*; NBC-TV, 12/10 /90) D: Jack Bender; P: Ervin Zavada; TP: Matheson; S: David Kirschner/Matheson, suggested in part by a book by Michael Patrick Hearn; M: Lee Holdridge; MU/Oz characters: Craig Reardon; SE: Stargate Films. Color, 93 minutes. LP: John Ritter, Annette O'Toole, Rue McClanahan, Charles Haid, David Schramm.

*Twilight Zone: Rod Serling's Lost Classics* (CBS-TV, 5/19/94) D: Robert Markowitz; P: S. Bryan Hickox; M: Patrick Williams; SEMU: Alterian Studios/Jim Beinke. Color, 92 minutes. Host: James Earl Jones. "The Theatre"—TP: Matheson; S: Rod Serling; LP: Amy Irving, Gary Cole. "Where the Dead Are"—TP: Serling; LP: Patrick Bergin, Jack Palance, Jenna Stern, Julia Campbell.

*Trilogy of Terror II* (USA Network, 10/30/96) D: Dan Curtis; P: Julian Marks; M: Bob Cobert; Creature Effects: Eric Allard; Prosthetics: Rick Stratton; MU: Marie Nardella; SE: Frank C. Carere. Color, 91 minutes. "The Graveyard Rats"—TP: William F. Nolan/Curtis, b/o Henry Kuttner's story; LP: Lysette Anthony, Geraint Wyn Davies, Matt Clark, Geoffrey Lewis. "Bobby"—TP: Matheson; LP: Lysette Anthony, Blake Heron, Joe Geib. "He Who Kills"—TP: Nolan/Curtis, b/o the Zuni doll from Matheson's "Prey"; LP: Lysette Anthony, Richard Fitzpatrick, Thomas Mitchell, Alex Carter.

*Stir of Echoes: The Homecoming* (Sci-Fi Channel, 8/11/07) D/TP: Ernie Barbarash, b/o characters created by Matheson [uncredited]; P: Philip Stilman/Claire Welland; M: Norman Orenstein; MU: Sarah Fairbairn; SEMU and Prosthetics: DeWilde FX Studio; SE: Invisible Pictures. Color, 89 minutes. LP: Rob Lowe, Marnie McPhail, Vik Sahay, Katya Gardner, Ben Lewis, Tatiana Maslany, Shawn Roberts, Zachary Bennett.

## Television Episodes Written by Matheson or Based on His Work

(Key: D = director; TP = teleplay; S = story; b/o = based on)

Every effort has been made to confirm these credits and original airdates against the actual episodes or, where unavailable, multiple sources. Matheson reportedly wrote teleplays for *Richard Diamond, Private Detective* and *Philip Marlowe*, alone or in collaboration with Charles Beaumont, for which no information could be found.

"Young Couples Only" (*Studio 57*; DuMont, 9/3/55) D: Richard Irving; TP: Lawrence Kimble, b/o Matheson's "Shipshape Home"

"Thy Will Be Done" (unaired pilot for *Now Is Tomorrow*; Roncom Telefilms, c. 1958) D: Irvin Kershner; TP: Matheson

"Iron Mike Benedict" (*The D.A.'s Man*; NBC, 2/14/59) D: unknown; TP: Charles Beaumont/Matheson

"Act of Faith" (*Buckskin*; NBC, 3/23/59) D: Earl Bellamy [unconfirmed]; TP: Charles Beaumont/Matheson

"The Marble Face" (*Markham*; CBS, 4/59 [exact airdate unknown]) D: Bretaigne Windust; TP: John Kneubuhl; S: Charles Beaumont/Matheson [apparently drafted as "Spirit Unwilling"]

"The Healing Woman" (*Wanted: Dead or Alive*; CBS, 9/12/59) D: Donald McDougall; TP: Charles Beaumont; S: Beaumont/Matheson

"And When the Sky Was Opened" (*The Twilight Zone*; CBS, 12/11/59) D: Douglas Heyes; TP: Rod Serling, b/o Matheson's "Disappearing Act"

"Third from the Sun" (*The Twilight Zone*; CBS, 1/8/60) D: Richard L. Bare; TP: Rod Serling, b/o Matheson's story

"The Last Flight" (*The Twilight Zone*; CBS, 2/5/60) D: William Claxton; TP: Matheson

"The Lady on the Wall" (*Have Gun—Will Travel*; CBS, 2/20/60) D: Ida Lupino; TP: Charles Beaumont/Matheson

"Target of Hate" (*Bourbon Street Beat*; ABC, 3/7/60) D: Leslie H. Martinson; TP: Matheson/William L. Stuart; S: Matheson

"A World of Difference" (*The Twilight Zone*; CBS, 3/11/60) D: Ted Post; TP: Matheson

"Home Is the Brave" (*Cheyenne*; ABC, 3/14/60) D: Emory Horger; TP: Matheson; S: George Waggner

"Thirty Minutes" (*Lawman*; ABC, 3/20/60) D: Robert T. Sparr; TP: Matheson, b/o his "Of Death and Thirty Minutes" [uncredited]

"A World of His Own" (*The Twilight Zone*; CBS, 7/1/60) D: Ralph Nelson; TP: Matheson, b/o his "And Now I'm Waiting" [uncredited]

"Yawkey" (*Lawman*; ABC, 10/23/60) D: Stuart Heisler; TP: Matheson

"Nick of Time" (*The Twilight Zone*; CBS, 11/18/60) D: Richard L. Bare; TP: Matheson

"Samson the Great" (*Lawman*; ABC, 11/20/60) D: Stuart Heisler; TP: Matheson

"Cornered" (*Lawman*; ABC, 12/11/60) D: Marc Lawrence; TP: Matheson, b/o his "Little Jack Cornered" [uncredited]

"The Invaders" (*The Twilight Zone*; CBS, 1/27/61) D: Douglas Heyes; TP: Matheson

"Homecoming" (*Lawman*; ABC, 2/5/61) D: Robert B. Sinclair; TP: Matheson

"The Return of Andrew Bentley" (*Thriller*; NBC, 12/11/61) D: John Newland; TP: Matheson, b/o August Derleth and Mark Schorer's story

"Once Upon a Time" (*The Twilight Zone*; CBS, 12/15/61) D: Norman Z. McLeod/Les Goodwins [uncredited]; TP: Matheson

"Little Girl Lost" (*The Twilight Zone*; CBS, 3/16/62) D: Paul Stewart; TP: Matheson, b/o his story

"Young Man's Fancy" (*The Twilight Zone*; CBS, 5/11/62) D: John Brahm; TP: Matheson

"The Actor" (*Lawman*; ABC, 5/27/62) D: Richard C. Sarafian; TP: Matheson

"Forgotten Front" (*Combat!*; ABC, 10/2/62) D: Robert Altman; TP: Logan Swanson [Matheson], b/o Jerome Coopersmith's story

"Ride the Nightmare" (*The Alfred Hitchcock Hour*; CBS, 11/29/62) D: Bernard Girard; TP: Matheson, b/o his novel

"The Thirty-first of February" (*The Alfred Hitchcock Hour*; CBS, 1/4/63) D: Alf Kjellin; TP: Logan Swanson [Matheson], b/o Julian Symons's novel

"Mute" (*The Twilight Zone*; CBS, 1/31/63) D: Stuart Rosenberg; TP: Matheson, b/o his story

"Death Ship" (*The Twilight Zone*; CBS, 2/7/63) D: Don Medford; TP: Matheson, b/o his story

"Steel" (*The Twilight Zone*; CBS, 10/4/63) D: Don Weis; TP: Matheson, b/o his story

"Nightmare at 20,000 Feet" (*The Twilight Zone*; CBS, 10/11/63) D: Richard Donner; TP: Matheson, b/o his story

"Night Call" (*The Twilight Zone*; CBS, 2/7/64) D: Jacques Tourneur; TP: Matheson, b/o his "Long Distance Call" (a.k.a. "Sorry, Right Number")

"Spur of the Moment" (*The Twilight Zone*; CBS, 2/21/64) D: Elliot Silverstein; TP: Matheson

"Time of Flight" (*Bob Hope Presents the Chrysler Theatre*; NBC, 9/21/66) D: Joseph Sargent; TP: Matheson

"The Enemy Within" (*Star Trek*; NBC, 10/6/66) D: Leo Penn; TP: Matheson

"The Atlantis Affair" (*The Girl from U.N.C.L.E.*; NBC, 11/15/66) D: E. Darrell Hallenbeck; TP: Matheson

"No Such Thing as a Vampire" (*Late Night Horror*; BBC, 4/19/68) D: Paddy Russell; TP: Hugh Leonard, b/o Matheson's story

"Girl of My Dreams" (*Journey to the Unknown*; ABC, 12/26/68) D: Peter Sasdy; TP: Robert Bloch/Michael J. Bird, b/o Matheson's story

"Big Surprise" (*Night Gallery*; NBC, 11/10/71) D: Jeannot Szwarc; TP: Matheson, b/o his story (a.k.a. "What Was in the Box?")

"The Funeral" (*Night Gallery*; NBC, 1/5/72) D: John Meredyth Lucas; TP: Matheson, b/o his story

"The New House" (*Ghost Story*; NBC, 3/17/72) D: John Llewellyn Moxey; TP: Matheson, b/o Elizabeth Walter's story

"L'Esame" ["The Test"] (*I Racconti di Fantascienza di Blasetti*; 1/31/79) D/TP: Alessandro Blasetti, b/o Matheson's story [unconfirmed]

"Button, Button" (*The Twilight Zone*; CBS, 3/7/86) D: Peter Medak; TP: Logan Swanson [Matheson], b/o Matheson's story

"The Doll" (*Amazing Stories*; NBC, 5/4/86) D: Phil Joanou; TP: Matheson

"One for the Books" (*Amazing Stories*; NBC, 5/11/86) D: Lesli Linka Glatter; TP: Matheson, b/o his story

"Miss Stardust" (*Amazing Stories*; NBC, 4/10/87) D: Tobe Hooper; TP: Thomas Szollosi/Richard Christian Matheson, b/o Matheson's story

"First Anniversary" (*The Outer Limits*; Showtime, 2/16/96) D: Brad Turner; TP: Jon Cooksey/Ali Marie Matheson, b/o Matheson's story

"Dance of the Dead" (*Masters of Horror*; Showtime, 11/11/05) D: Tobe Hooper; TP: Richard Christian Matheson, b/o Matheson's story

## Unproduced Scripts, Outlines, and Treatments

Although Matheson himself has not kept complete records of his screenwriting work, exhaustive efforts have been made to ensure that this list is as inclusive as possible. In the mid-1960s, Matheson, George Clayton Johnson, Jerry Sohl, and Theodore Sturgeon formed a corporation called The Green Hand, pitching various series to the networks without success. Sohl told *Starlog*'s Edward Gross that these included *Hunter*, *E.T.* (no connection with Steven Spielberg's film of the same name), *Gestalt Team*, the anthology *A Touch of Strange*, and a series about an android, but how much Matheson actually wrote for any of these proposals is unknown. We are deeply indebted to collectors Don Cannon and Brian Kirby, who own copies of many of Matheson's scripts, outlines, and treatments, both produced and unproduced, and have generously shared information regarding them. Due to the difficulty of dating some of these projects, they are listed alphabetically, rather than chronologically.

*Adam and Eve* (c. 1959): written for producer Albert Zugsmith; filmed in 1961 as *The Private Lives of Adam and Eve* from a script by Robert Hill.

*Ali Baba and the Seven Marvels of the World* (1961): a treatment for an animated feature written with William F. Nolan for American International Pictures (AIP).

*Appointment in Zahrain* (c. 1960): adapted from the novel by Michael Barrett (filmed in 1961 as *Escape from Zahrain* from a script by Robin Estridge) for Clark Gable and director Edward Dmytryk.

*Arrow M.E.E. [Mystery Evaluation and Explanation]* (c. 1986): a pilot based on the nonfiction book *The Evidence Never Lies* by Alfred Lewis for ABC/Lorimar and producers David Goldsmith and Linda Yellen.

*Baseball Movie* (title unknown; c. 1960s): a screenplay about a baseball team going out West, written with William R. Cox.

*Being* (a.k.a. *G.O.O. [Galactic Octopoidal Ooze]*; 1960s): adapted by Matheson from his story (filmed [uncredited] in 1969 as "*It's Alive!*" from a script by Larry Buchanan) for AIP.

*Bid Time Return* (1970s): a teleplay adapted by Matheson from his novel (filmed in 1980 as *Somewhere in Time* from a separate Matheson script) for producer Stan Shpetner.

*Call for Small* (1950s): a television series idea about a tiny adventurer, based on *The Shrinking Man*, for producer Albert Zugsmith.

"The Children of Noah" (c. 1973?): adapted by Matheson from his story, presumably as an episode of the abortive *Dead of Night* anthology series, for producer-director Dan Curtis.

*Creature* (c. 1991): adapted from the novel by John Saul for Universal, and rewritten by director Frank LaLoggia, whose version also remains unproduced.

*Cybernia* (c. 1960s/1970s): adapted from the novel by Lou Cameron for producer John Cutts.

*The D.A.'s Man* (c. 1959): according to William F. Nolan, archivist extraordinaire, Matheson and Charles Beaumont wrote a second script (title unknown) for this series, but whether it was produced is unconfirmed.

*The Deadly Powder of Thomas Roch* (1950s): a teleplay adapted from Jules Verne's *Facing the Flag* for producer Albert Zugsmith; Matheson included Verne's character of Captain Nemo, who does not appear in the novel.

*The Disappearance* (1990s): a six-hour miniseries adapted from the novel by Philip Wylie for actor-producer Peter Strauss.

*The Distributor* (c. 1965): adapted by Matheson from his story.

*Double, Double* (1962): written with William F. Nolan (according to whom "the plot was based on some real-life experiences of mine in which I had used the name 'Frank Anmar' ") as a vehicle for Tony Randall.

*The Dreamers* (c. 1958): adapted from the novel by Roger Manvell for Hill-Hecht-Lancaster Productions.

*Earthbound* (a.k.a. *The Cold and Alien Kiss of Death*; c. 1970?): written for producer Stan Shpetner; adapted by Matheson into his novel.

*Fade-Out* (1980s): adapted from the novel by Patrick Tilley for producer Tony Bill and director Ulu Grosbard.

*The Fantastic Little Girl* (a.k.a. *The Fantastic Shrinking Girl*; 1956): a se-quel to *The Incredible Shrinking Man*, written for Universal-International and producer Albert Zugsmith (who received original story credit on Matheson's first-draft screenplay).

*Fear* (c. 1992): adapted from the novel by L. Ron Hubbard for NBC.

*Forbidden Land*: listed among Matheson's unfilmed screenplays in the sixth edition of Susan Avallone's *Film Writers Guide* (Lone Eagle Publishing Co., 1996)—which, among other errors, attributes a number of Richard Christian Matheson's scripts to his father—but when asked, the elder Matheson could remember nothing about the project.

*The French Villa* (a.k.a. *Nicole*): an original screenplay written for producer Stan Shpetner.

*Fury on Sunday* (c. 1989): adapted by Matheson from his novel for producer Allen Epstein and director James Sadwith.

*Galaxy* (1980s): a pilot for an abortive anthology series written with Richard Maibaum, and adapted in part from Matheson's "The Holiday Man" and "Lover When You're Near Me," for executive producer David Gerber.

*Gresham's People* (a.k.a. *The "R" Project*; 1960s): According to Rod Serling's biographer, Gordon F. Sander, this script, "a *Frankenstein*-like story about a military man who invents a race of robots in an attempt to end war, was eventually assigned to Richard Matheson, to Serling's dismay."

*Gulliver's Travels* (1957): a treatment adapted with producer Albert Zugsmith from the novel by Jonathan Swift for Universal-International; this was intended as a vehicle for David Niven and Cantinflas, following their success in *Around the World in 80 Days*.

*The Gun Fight* (1960s): adapted with William R. Cox from Matheson's then-unpublished novel.

*Implosion* (1960s): adapted from the novel by D.F. Jones for AIP.

*Journal of the Gun Years* (1990s): a four-hour miniseries adapted by Matheson from his novel, for TNT and producer-director Dan Curtis.

"The Joust" (c. 1959): an episode of *Have Gun—Will Travel* written with Charles Beaumont.

*Kingdom of Nemo*: a pilot written with Charles Beaumont.

"The Last Hour of John Butler Hickock" (1962): an episode of *Cheyenne* that did not reach the script stage.

*The Last Revolution* (1968): rewritten by Matheson from an earlier script by Rod Serling, based on the novel by Lord Dunsany, for producer George Pal.

*The Link* (1970s): a miniseries outline and partial teleplay about psychic events, written for ABC and producer Stephen Deutsch (a.k.a. Simon), and adapted by Matheson into his unfinished novel.

*The Lost World* (c. 1992): adapted from the novel by Sir Arthur Conan Doyle for director John Landis, who later served as executive producer of the eponymous syndicated series, in which Matheson was not involved.

"The Love Letter" (1973): adapted from the story by Jack Finney (filmed in 1998 from a script by James Henerson) as an episode of the abortive *Dead of Night* anthology series for producer-director Dan Curtis.

*Midvale* (1995): a speculative script about life after death, written with Richard Christian Matheson and sold to producer-director Ivan Reitman.

*The Nature of Evil* (1998): a script about supernatural horror on a college campus, written with Richard Christian Matheson for producer-director Ivan Reitman.

*Needle in a Timestack* (1990s/2000s): based on the story by Robert Silverberg.

*Night Gallery* (c. 1971): Matheson adapted several unused stories by other writers for this anthology series.

*The Night Killers* (1973): written with William F. Nolan for producer-director Dan Curtis.

*One Cut to Paradise* (c. 1993): rewritten by Matheson from an original screenplay by Crash Leyland (filmed in 1995 as *The Final Cut* from a script by Raul Inglis) for director John Landis.

*Ossian's Ride*: an outline adapted from the novel by Fred Hoyle for producer Sydell Albert and director Daniel Petrie.

*Out There* (c. 1960): Matheson wrote one or more scripts for this abortive anthology series created by Charles Beaumont.

*Power and Light* (c. 1990): a screenplay about Nikola Tesla written for Lucasfilm and director Walter Murch.

*Pride* (2002): a teleplay adapted by Matheson and Richard Christian Matheson from their respective of the eponymous story.

*Private Parts in Public Places* (1960s): adapted from the novel by Robin Cook (originally published in England as *Public Parts and Private Places*) for AIP.

*Progeny of the Adder*: an outline adapted from the novel by Leslie H. Whitten.

*PSI* (1972): a one-hour pilot about the work of the UCLA parapsychology lab, written with Richard Christian Matheson for Lorimar Television and ABC.

*The Raft* (1974): a teleplay adapted from the nonfiction book by Robert Trumbull for Paramount Television and producer Emmet Lavery, Jr.

*The Rogue*: a script that Matheson may have adapted from Jay Williams's *The Good Yeoman* for producer John Cutts.

*The Search for King Tut's Tomb* (exact title unknown; 1978): a six-hour miniseries, possibly adapted from *Tutankhamun: The Untold Story* by Thomas Hoving, the director of New York City's Metropolitan Museum of Art at the time of the wildly popular Tut exhibit in the 1970s.

*7 Steps to Midnight*: adapted by Matheson from his novel.

*Shadow on the Sun*: adapted by Matheson into his novel.

*Shadowed Places*: a four-hour miniseries.

*Shifter* (c. 1991): a speculative script about a sociopathic shape-shifter, written with Richard Christian Matheson and sold to producer-director Richard Donner.

*Shipshape Home* (c. 1957): adapted by Matheson from his story (previously filmed in 1955 as "Young Couples Only," an episode of *Studio 57*, from a script by Lawrence Kimble).

*Skedaddle* (c. 1978): a comedy western written for producer Stan Shpetner and director Hal Needham.

*Slaughter House* (1975): a teleplay adapted by William F. Nolan from Matheson's story.

*A Stir of Echoes* (1959): adapted by Matheson from his novel (filmed in 1999 as *Stir of Echoes* from a script by David Koepp) for Universal and producer William Sackheim.

*Sweethearts and Horrors* (c. 1964): written as a follow-up to *The Comedy of Terrors* for AIP.

*Through the Golden Horn* (c. 1990): a musical teleplay written for producer David Kirschner.

*To Live* (c. 2003): adapted by Matheson from his novel *Hunted Past Reason* (and restoring his preferred title).

*Twilight Zone—The Movie* (1983): a Halloween segment (title unknown) written for producer-director Steven Spielberg that was eventually replaced with a remake of "Kick the Can."

*Under the Bounding Main* (1962): a treatment adapted with William F. Nolan from Jack Finney's *Assault on a Queen* (filmed in 1966 from a script by Rod Serling) for Columbia.

*Voyage to Lilliput* (1956): a "step outline" adapted from Jonathan Swift's *Gulliver's Travels* for Universal-International and producer Albert Zugsmith.

"The Wedding" (1980s): adapted by Matheson from his story for the anthology series *Amazing Stories*.

*What Dreams May Come* (c. 1980s): adapted by Matheson from his novel (filmed in 1998 from a script by Ron Bass) for director Wolfgang Petersen.

*When the Sleeper Wakes* (1960s): adapted from the novel by H.G. Wells for AIP.

*Wild Bill*: adapted by Matheson into his novel *The Memoirs of Wild Bill Hickok*.


## Published Scripts

These are the first appearances of all of Matheson's published scripts. Additional details for the Matheson books cited can be found in the "Books: First and Limited Editions" section, which also includes information on subsequent printings.

"The Doll" (*Rod Serling's The Twilight Zone Magazine*, June 1982)

"A World of His Own" (*Rod Serling's The Twilight Zone Magazine*, April 1983)

"Nightmare at 20,000 Feet" (*Rod Serling's The Twilight Zone Magazine*, June 1984)

*Screamplays* (Edited by Richard Chizmar; Del Rey Books, 1997)
Screenplays. Trade paperback and true first edition. Includes Matheson's screenplay for *The Legend of Hell House.*

*Richard Matheson's* The Twilight Zone *Scripts* (Richard Matheson, edited by Stanley Wiater; Cemetery Dance, 1998)
Includes the first appearances of the following teleplays:
"The Last Flight"
"A World of Difference"
"Nick of Time"
"The Invaders"
"Once Upon a Time"
"Little Girl Lost"
"Young Man's Fancy"
"Mute"
"Death Ship"
"Steel"
"Night Call"
"Spur of the Moment"

*Somewhere in Time: The Screenplay* (Richard Matheson; Harvest Moon Publishing, 2000)

*A Stir of Echoes* (Richard Matheson; Gauntlet Press, 2002)
Includes Matheson's screenplay adaptation of his novel.

*Pride* (Richard Matheson & Richard Christian Matheson; Gauntlet Press, 2002)
Includes the teleplay collaboration *Pride* by Matheson and his son.

*Richard Matheson's Kolchak Scripts* (Richard Matheson, edited by Mark Dawidziak; Gauntlet Press, 2003)
Includes the following teleplays:
*The Night Stalker*
*The Night Strangler*
*The Night Killers* (with William F. Nolan)

*Darker Places* (Richard Matheson; Gauntlet Press, 2004)
Includes Matheson's screenplay *Creature.*

*As Timeless as Infinity: The Complete Twilight Zone Scripts of Rod Serling, Volume One* (Rod Serling, edited by Tony Albarella; Gauntlet Press, 2004)
Includes the teleplay "Third From the Sun," adapted by Rod Serling from Matheson's story.

*Duel & The Distributor* (Richard Matheson, edited by Matthew R. Bradley; Gauntlet Press, 2004)
Includes the following scripts:
*Duel*
*The Distributor*

*Unrealized Dreams* (Richard Matheson; Gauntlet Press, 2005)
Includes the following screenplays:
*The Fantastic Little Girl*
*Appointment in Zahrain*
*Sweethearts and Horrors*

*The Link* (Richard Matheson; Gauntlet Press, 2006)
Includes Matheson's narrative outline; the lettered edition includes an excerpt from Matheson's partial teleplay.

*Bloodlines: Richard Matheson's* Dracula, I Am Legend, *and Other Vampire Stories* (Richard Matheson, edited by Mark Dawidziak; Gauntlet Press, 2006)
Includes the following:
*Dracula*: Richard Matheson's Script Treatment
*Bram Stoker's Dracula*: The Script
*The Night Creatures* Script: From Richard Matheson's Novel *I Am Legend*

*The Funeral* (Chapbook; Gauntlet Press, 2006)
Includes Matheson's teleplay "The Funeral."

*Visions of Death: Richard Matheson's Edgar Allan Poe Scripts, Volume One*
(Richard Matheson, edited by Lawrence French; Gauntlet Press, 2007)
  Includes the following scripts:
  *The Fall of the House of Usher*
  *The Pit and the Pendulum*


## Stage Plays and Musicals

Matheson has a great love of the theater, and has been involved in a local community theater group, The Hidden Hills Players, for many years. He has also written several stage plays and musicals, as well as having written songs for college productions.

*When Nights Were Bold* (Melvin Goodman, 1947)
  A musical comedy produced for "The J-Show" at the University of Missouri while Matheson was a student. Matheson wrote the musical numbers and is listed in the program as the director, but reports: "Why I even attempted that is beyond me. I got another guy to do it as soon as I could. They probably had the program made up already by the time I begged him to take over." His bio in the program reads: "Richard B. Matheson (Director)—Song writing's just Dick's hobby, but he wrote seven of this show's tunes and has written more than fifty others. Writing is another sideline, and he's been doing plenty for Radio Workshop. But he wants to be a public relations man and enters Journalism School soon to find out how. He's been active in Workshop." Other material suggests that he wrote eight, not seven, of the show's songs. The show had three performances on the University of Missouri campus May 23–24, 1947.

*The Eyes Have It* (Norman Kennelly & Richard Matheson, 1948)
  A musical comedy produced for "The J-Show" at the University of Missouri while Matheson was a student. Matheson cowrote the script and wrote the musical numbers. The show had two performances on the University of Missouri campus May 14–15, 1948.

*A Stir of Echoes* (Richard Matheson, 1958)

Unproduced play based on Matheson's novel of the same name. Regarding the play, Matheson commented in a letter to his former professor William Peden in 1959 that "I did it too fast and it got nowhere."

*Do Not Go Gentle* (Richard Matheson & Charles Beaumont, c. 1960)

In the early 1960s, Matheson and Beaumont collaborated on this play about an alcoholic poet, based loosely on Dylan Thomas. They completed the first act, but the play was never finished.

*Magician's Choice* (Richard Matheson, c. 1970)

A mystery/suspense play written by Matheson in the 1970s and later revised into his novel *Now You See It*. . . . A Broadway production got as far as rehearsals before being cancelled; it was to have been directed by Robert Altman and starred Jack Palance, Susannah York, and Paul Dooley. It was later reconsidered for a 2002 or 2003 bow on the London stage, but again failed to come to fruition.

*Woman* (Richard Matheson, 2005)

Unproduced play that was the basis for Matheson's novel of the same name. Published, with the novel, in a limited edition by Gauntlet Press in 2005.

*Somewhere in Time* (Richard Matheson)

This stage musical based on Matheson's novel and screenplay has been in the works for twenty years. Matheson has done an outline and a script, and another script by Ken Davenport apparently also exists. Songs have been written, with music by Billy Goldenberg and lyrics by Harry Shannon, but it is not clear at present if those songs will be used for the production currently being planned.

*Wild Bill and His Lady* (Richard Matheson)

Unproduced play based on Matheson's novel *The Memoirs of Wild Bill Hickok*. Matheson has turned it into a one-man play and reports having "an excellent director" attached. The project is apparently nearing production.

## Adaptations of Matheson Scripts

These are novelizations and related adaptations of Matheson screenplays and teleplays.

*The Beat Generation* (Albert Zugsmith; Bantam, 1959)
　　Novelization based on Matheson and Lewis Meltzer's screenplay. Paperback original and true first edition.

*The Pit and the Pendulum* (Lee Sheridan; Lancer Books, 1961)
　　Novelization based on Matheson's screenplay *Pit and the Pendulum*. Paperback original and true first edition.

*Poe's Tales of Terror* (Eunice Sudak; Lancer Books, 1962)
　　Novelization based on Matheson's screenplay *Tales of Terror*. Paperback original and true first edition.

*The Raven* (Eunice Sudak; Lancer Books, 1963)
　　Novelization based on Matheson's screenplay. Paperback original and true first edition.

*Comedy of Terrors* (Elsie Lee; Lancer Books, 1964)
　　Novelization based on Matheson's screenplay *The Comedy of Terrors*. Paperback original and true first edition.

*De Sade* (Henry Clement; Signet Books, 1969)
　　Novelization based on Matheson's screenplay. Paperback original and true first edition.

*Star Trek 8* (James Blish; Bantam, 1972)
　　Short story adaptations of six *Star Trek* episodes, including Matheson's teleplay "The Enemy Within." Paperback original and true first edition.

*The Night Stalker* (Jeff Rice; Pocket Books, 1973)
　　Novel. Unlike the other items on this list, Rice's novel—originally entitled *The Kolchak Papers*—was written (although not published) prior to Matheson's teleplay, and served as its source material. It is therefore

not an adaptation of Matheson's work, but is sought after by Matheson collectors due to its relationship to the Kolchak series, and is listed here for that reason. Paperback original and true first edition.

*The Night Strangler* (Jeff Rice; Pocket Books, 1974)
    Novelization based on Matheson's original teleplay. Paperback original and true first edition.

*Twilight Zone—The Movie* (Robert Bloch; Warner Books, 1983)
    Novelization based on Matheson, John Landis, George Clayton Johnson, and Josh Rogan's screenplay. Paperback original and true first edition.

*De Sade: "Kiss the Whip"* (Robert Bloch, Jeremy Reed, Jean-Paul Denard, et al.; Creation Books, 2005)
    Contains several pieces on Sade, including a reprint of Henry Clement's novelization of Matheson's screenplay.

## Film, Television, and Documentary Appearances

These are Matheson's onscreen appearances. Despite his longtime involvement with community theater, these appearances are few, and confined mostly to interview segments.

*Jefferson and Hamilton* (date unknown): In this educational film from Bernie Willits, Matheson noted that he played a "diabolical master of ceremonies who brings Alexander Hamilton and Thomas Jefferson back from the grave to debate."

*Captains and the Kings* (1976): Matheson played President Garfield in this NBC miniseries, which also featured future *Somewhere in Time* star Jane Seymour. Adapted by Stephen and Elinor Karpf from the novel by Taylor Caldwell, it was scripted and codirected by Matheson's *Twilight Zone* colleague, Douglas Heyes.

*Somewhere in Time* (1980): Matheson cameoed as the "Astonished Man."

"Rod Serling: Submitted for Your Approval" (1995): Matheson was interviewed in this episode of the PBS series *American Masters*.

Somewhere in Time *15th Anniversary Celebration with Jane Seymour* (1996): The fourth in a series of videos released by the International Network of *Somewhere in Time* Enthusiasts, this documents the event held in May 1995 at Universal City, California. It includes a panel discussion with Matheson and producer Stephen Deutsch, and is available from INSITE (www.somewhereintime.tv).

*100 Years of Horror* (1996): According to the IMDb, Matheson was interviewed in several episodes of writer-director Ted Newsom's video documentary series: "Giants and Dinosaurs," "The Evil Unseeable," "The Aristocrats of Evil," and "Sorcerers."

"Vincent Price" (1998): Matheson was interviewed in this episode of the Sci-Fi Channel series *Masters of Fantasy*.

*Back to* Somewhere in Time (2000): Matheson was interviewed in this documentary written, directed, and produced by Laurent Bouzereau for the Universal DVD of *Somewhere in Time*.

*Dark Dreamers* (2000): Matheson appeared in an episode of Stanley Wiater's Canadian-produced interview series (as yet unaired in the U.S., but telecast elsewhere, and now available on DVD domestically).

*Richard Matheson—Storyteller* (2001): These interview segments, filmed back to back, appear as extras on MGM's DVD releases of Matheson's *De Sade, The Raven, The Comedy of Terrors,* and *The Last Man on Earth*; others created for *Master of the World* and *Burn, Witch, Burn* are as yet unreleased. Another segment, in which Matheson discusses the origin of "Duel," appears as an "Easter egg," or hidden feature, on MGM's DVD release of *Jeepers Creepers* (2001), whose writer-director, Victor Salva, was influenced by the 1971 film version.

*Richard Matheson: The Writing of* Duel (2004): Written, directed, and produced by Laurent Bouzereau, this documentary appeared as an extra on the Universal DVD of *Duel*.

*Shadows in the Dark: The Val Lewton Legacy* (2005): Matheson was interviewed for this documentary, included in the Warner Brothers "Val Lewton Horror Collection" DVD set.

*The Twilight Zone—The Definitive Edition: Season 5* (2005): Video interview clips with Matheson are included as bonus features on "Steel," "Nightmare at 20,000 Feet," "Night Call," and "Spur of the Moment," and he is seen but not heard in highlights from the Museum of Radio and Television's *Twilight Zone* seminar. The set also contains "Rod Serling: Submitted for Your Approval."

*Richard Matheson: Terror Scribe* (2006): This interview featurette appears as an extra on the Dark Sky Films DVD of *Trilogy of Terror.*

*Masters of Horror: Dance of the Dead* (2006): Matheson can be seen but not heard during an on-set visit in several of the featurettes on this Anchor Bay DVD.

## Musical Compositions

Matheson has a great love of music and composition, and at one time considered a career as a composer. He wrote a number of reviews of local concerts for the school newspaper while he was a student at the University of Missouri. Most of his musical work is unpublished, but a number of his songs were performed in musical theater productions while he was in college. Additionally, vocalist Perry Como has recorded two Matheson songs, one of which, a Christmas song, has also been recorded by several other performers, including Bob Hope.

Selections from *When Nights Were Bold*
    Play. Melvin Goodman. Songs by Richard B. Matheson. Performed at the University of Missouri, May 1947.
    "My Heart Is Taken"
    "A Princess Has a Full Time Job"
    "Marriage"
    "In King Arthur"
    "I'd Rather Be in Love"
    "Laughing Is Easy"
    "Up Til Now"
    "From Fairy Tales"

Selections from *The Eyes Have It*
> Play. Norman Kennelly & Richard B. Matheson. Songs by Richard
B. Matheson. Performed at the University of Missouri, May 1948.
> "In the Night"
> "Words"
> "Because of You"
> "My Heart Tells Me Different"
> "Abnormal You"
> "Here in the Darkness"
> "I Can't"
> "Sadie"
> "Won't You Come a Little Closer"
> "Whether It's December . . ."
> "You've Never Kissed Me!"
> "I Didn't Know What I Was Talking About"
> "Senorita, Where I Come From . . ."
> "Sadie (English Version)"
> "Sadie (Russian Version)"
> "There Doesn't Seem to Be!"
> "It's a Wonderful Life!"

"I Wish It Could Be Christmas Forever"
> Song. Lyrics by Richard B. Matheson, music by Nick Perito.
> *I Wish It Could Be Christmas Forever* (LP. Perry Como. RCA, 1982)
> *A Shiny New Christmas* (CD. Ed Vodicka. Best Recordings, 1990)
> *Christmas Classics* (CD. Various contributors. RCA, 1993)
> *Perry Como's Christmas Concert* (CD. Perry Como. RCA, 1994)
> *Hopes for the Holidays* (CD. Bob Hope. Varese Sarabande, 1996)
> *A Perry Como Christmas* (CD. Perry Como. RCA, 2001)
> *The Perry Como Christmas Album* (CD. Perry Como. RCA, 2001)
> *Noël Pianissimo* (CD. Duo Campion-Vachon. Analekta, 2004)

"Do You Remember Me"
> Song. Lyrics by Richard B. Matheson, music by Nick Perito.
> *Today* (CD. Perry Como. RCA, 1987)

## Audio Recordings

These are readings by Matheson of selections from his books, as well as related items.

*INSITE Presents The Original Audio Notes for* Somewhere in Time (IN-SITE Publications, 1993)

Cassette tapes in plastic storage case. First edition. Four tapes, approximately four hours. In November of 1971, Matheson drove from his home in L.A. to San Diego and the Hotel Del Coronado to do research for his novel *Bid Time Return.* During the trip, while speaking in character, Matheson dictated story notes, details, and his protagonist's thoughts into a handheld voice recorder. These audio notes are in unedited form, including automobile and other background noise, occasional pauses, and the start/stop sounds of the recorder. Published in two states: a standard edition of unknown size, and a 50-copy numbered edition, signed by Matheson.

*Burn, Witch, Burn* (Image Entertainment, 1995)

Laserdisc. Matheson provides a separate audio commentary track, reminiscing on the making of the film (a.k.a. *Night of the Eagle*) and other aspects of his career.

*Somewhere in Time: CD Reading* (Gauntlet Press, 1999)

Compact disc. First edition. Selected passages read by Matheson.

*Hunger and Thirst: CD Reading* (Gauntlet Press, 2000)

Compact disc. First edition. Chapter One read by Matheson.

*The Shrinking Man: CD Reading* (Gauntlet Press, 2001)

Compact disc. First edition. Chapter Two read by Matheson.

*A Stir of Echoes: CD Reading* (Gauntlet Press, 2002)

Compact disc. First edition. Selected passages read by Matheson.

*Pride: CD Reading* (Richard Matheson & Richard Christian Matheson; Gauntlet Press, 2002)

Compact disc. First edition. Selected passages read by Matheson and Richard Christian Matheson.

*Reality: CD Reading* (Gauntlet Press, 2002)

Compact disc. First edition. Matheson reads from a paper about his metaphysical views. A transcript of the reading is available online at: users.adelphia.net/~sitman/Reality.pdf

*Come Fygures, Come Shadowes: CD Reading* (Gauntlet Press, 2003)

Compact disc. First edition. Selected passages read by Matheson.

*The Twilight Zone—The Definitive Edition: Season 1* (2004)

An audio interview with Matheson by Marc Scott Zicree is included as a bonus feature on "A World of His Own."

## Audio Adaptations of Matheson's Work

These are audio adaptations of Matheson's novels and short stories.

*Somewhere in Time* (Books on Tape, Inc., 1989)

Audio book. Available on seven cassette tapes. An unabridged reading by Christopher Hurt of Matheson's novel.

*Murder in Hollywood: Stories from Ellery Queen's Mystery Magazine* (Audio Renaissance, 1992)

Audio book. Approximately three hours. Contains six short stories from *EQMM*, read by Morgan Fairchild and Roddy McDowall. McDowall reads Matheson's short story "CU: Mannix."

*I Am Legend/The Shrinking Man* (Books on Tape, Inc., 1992)

Audio book. Available on nine cassette tapes. Approximately twelve hours. Unabridged readings by Walter Lawrence of Matheson's novels.

*Journal of the Gun Years* (Books on Tape, Inc., 1992)

Audio book. Available on eight cassette tapes. Approximately eight hours. Unabridged reading by Larry McKeever of Matheson's novel.

*Great Mystery Series: Twelve of the Best Mystery Short Stories from Ellery Queen's Mystery Magazine* (Media Books Audio Publishing, 2000)

Audio book. Approximately six hours. Abridged. Contains a dozen short stories from *EQMM*, read by Morgan Fairchild and Roddy McDowall. McDowall reads Matheson's short story "CU: Mannix."

*The Incredible Shrinking Man* (Blackstone Audiobooks, 2006)

Audio book. Available on six cassette tapes, seven CDs, or one MP3-CD. Approximately eight hours. An unabridged reading by Yuri Rasovsky of Matheson's novel.

*I Am Legend* (Blackstone Audiobooks, 2007)

Audio book. Available on four cassette tapes, five CDs, or one MP3-CD. Approximately five and a half hours. An unabridged reading by Robertson Dean of Matheson's novel.

*I Am Legend and Other Stories* (Blackstone Audiobooks, 2007)

Audio book. Available on eight cassette tapes, ten CDs, or one MP3-CD. Approximately eleven hours. Includes the unabridged reading by Robertson Dean of *I Am Legend*, as well as readings by Yuri Rasovsky of Matheson's "Buried Talents," "The Near Departed," "Prey," "Witch War," "Dance of the Dead," "Dress of White Silk," "Mad House," "The Funeral," "From Shadowed Places," and "Person to Person."

## Movie and Television Soundtracks

These are some of the many soundtracks and compilations that include music from films and television programs written by Matheson or based on his work. All were released on CD, unless otherwise noted. Entries labeled as "Soundtracks" can be expected to contain extensive music from the designated film/TV program. Other entries typically include only a single track from the designated film/TV program, usually the main theme music, unless otherwise noted. Music from television series will generally not be from the specific Matheson-scripted episode(s), although there are some exceptions to this for *The Twilight Zone*, as indicated.

*De Sade* (score composed by Billy Strange)

*De Sade*—Original Motion Picture Soundtrack (LP only)

*Dead of Night* (score composed by Robert Cobert)

The Night Stalker *and Other Classic Thrillers*

*The Devil Rides Out* (score composed by James Bernard)
    *A History of Horror from* Nosferatu *to* The Sixth Sense
    *The Best of Hammer Horror*
    *The Devil Rides Out*—Original Motion Picture Soundtrack
    The Devil Rides Out: *Horror, Adventure and Romance—Music from*
        *Hammer Films*
    *The Hammer Film Music Collection, Volume One*

*Dracula* (score composed by Robert Cobert)
    *The Night Stalker* and Other Classic Thrillers
    Vampire Circus *Featuring* The Return of Dracula: *The Essential*
        *Vampire Theme Collection*

    *The Dreamer of Oz* (score composed by Lee Holdridge)
    *The Dreamer of Oz*—Original Television Soundtrack

*Duel* (score composed by Billy Goldenberg)
    *Music from the Films of Steven Spielberg*

*The Girl from U.N.C.L.E.* (theme composed by Jerry Goldsmith)
    *Television's Greatest Hits Vol. V—In Living Color*

*Have Gun—Will Travel* (theme composed by Bernard Herrmann)
    *Bernard Herrmann: The CBS Years Volume 1—The Westerns*
    *Have Gun—Will Travel* (LP only)
    Rio Bravo: *Western and Other Movie & TV Themes*
    *Themes from the Hip* (LP only)

*I Am Legend* (score composed by James Newton Howard)
    *I Am Legend*—Original Motion Picture Soundtrack

*The Incredible Shrinking Man* (score composed by Hans J. Salter, Irving
Gertz, Herman Stein, Foster Carling, & Earl E. Lawrence)
    *Sci-Fi's Greatest Hits Vol. 2: The Dark Side*
    *Themes from Classic Science Fiction, Fantasy and Horror Films* (LP and CD)

*Jaws 3-D* (score composed by Alan Parker)
    *Jaws 3-D*—Music from the Original Motion Picture Soundtrack
    (LP only)

*Lawman* (theme composed by Jerry Livingstone and Mack David)
 *Themes from the Hip* (LP only)

*The Martian Chronicles* (score composed by Stanley Myers; additional music by Richard Harvey & Laurence Holloway)
 *Ray Bradbury's "The Martian Chronicles"*—Original Television Score

*Master of the World* (score composed by Les Baxter)
 *Les Baxter's Original Soundtrack Music from Jules Verne's* Master of the World (LP only)

*Night Gallery* (main theme composed by Gil Mellé)
 *Sci-Fi's Greatest Hits Vol. 2: The Dark Side*
 *Television's Greatest Hits Vol. V—In Living Color*

*The Night Stalker* (score composed by Robert Cobert)
 The Night Stalker *and Other Classic Thrillers*

*The Night Strangler* (score composed by Robert Cobert)
 The Night Stalker *and Other Classic Thrillers*

*The Omega Man* (score composed by Ron Grainer)
 *The Omega Man*—Original Motion Picture Soundtrack

*The Outer Limits* (1995–1998; main theme composed by Mark Mancina & John Van Tongeren)
 *The Outer Limits*—Original Television Score

*Les Seins de Glace* (*Icy Breasts*; score composed by Philippe Sarde)
 *Du Rififi Au Ciné, Vol. 2*
 *Les Meilleurs Bandes Originales Des Films D'Alain Delon* (LP only)
 *Les Seins de Glace/Vincent, François, Paul et les Autres*

*Somewhere in Time* (score composed by John Barry)
 *In Session: A Film Music Collaboration*
 *John Barry*—Moviola
 *John Barry*—Somewhere in Time
 *John Barry The Collection: 40 Years of Film Music*
 *Somewhere in Time*—Original Motion Picture Soundtrack (LP and CD)
 *The Classic John Barry*

*Stir of Echoes* (score composed by James Newton Howard)
  *Stir of Echoes*—Original Motion Picture Soundtrack

*Trilogy of Terror* (score composed by Robert Cobert)
  The Night Stalker *and Other Classic Thrillers*

*The Twilight Zone* (theme composed by Marius Constant)
  *Bernard Herrmann*: The Twilight Zone (includes the full score from the episode "Little Girl Lost")
  *Chiller*
  *John Williams and the Boston Pops Orchestra: Space and Time*
  *John Williams and the Boston Pops: Out of This World*
  *Rod Serling's* The Twilight Zone: *The Original Television Scores I* (includes music by Jerry Goldsmith from the episode "The Invaders"; LP and CD)
  *Rod Serling's* The Twilight Zone: *The Original Television Scores III* (includes music by Leonard Rosenman from the episode "And When the Sky Was Opened," and by Nathan Van Cleave from the episode "A World of Difference"; LP and CD)
  *Sci-Fi's Greatest Hits Vol. 2: The Dark Side*
  *The Best of Rod Serling's* The Twilight Zone (includes music by Jerry Goldsmith from the episode "The Invaders")
  *The Best of Rod Serling's* The Twilight Zone *Volume II* (includes music by Leonard Rosenman from the episode "And When the Sky Was Opened")
  *The Cult Files Re-Opened—Volume Two of the Ultimate Collection of Cult TV and Film Themes*

*Twilight Zone—The Movie* (score composed by Jerry Goldsmith)
  *Great Movie Scores from the Films of Steven Spielberg*
  *Jerry Goldsmith—Frontiers*
  *Jerry Goldsmith 40 Years of Film Music*
  *The Film Music of Jerry Goldsmith*
  The Omen: *The Essential Jerry Goldsmith Film Music Collection*
  *The Spielberg Collection*
  *Twilight Zone—The Movie*—Original Motion Picture Soundtrack (LP and CD)
  *Warner Bros. 75 Years Entertaining the World: Film Music*

*Wanted: Dead or Alive* (theme composed by Rudy Schrager)
   *Themes from the Hip* (LP only)

*What Dreams May Come* (score composed by Michael Kamen)
   *What Dreams May Come*—Original Motion Picture Soundtrack

## Collectibles

These are various collectibles related to Matheson and his work.

*World Horror Convention II* (Edited by Maurine Dorris; World Horror Society, 1992)
   Program from the second annual convention of the World Horror Society, held in Nashville, Tennessee, on March 5–8, 1992. Matheson was a guest of honor (as was artist Harry O. Morris, who often illustrates Matheson's books). The program reprints Matheson's short story "Prey."

*World Horror Convention III* (Edited by Suzan Gervais, Stanley Wiater, and Jill Bauman; World Horror Society, 1993)
   Program from the third annual convention of the World Horror Society, held in Stamford, Connecticut, on May 4–7, 1993. The program contains a profile and brief bio of Matheson, who was named grand master by the Society.

*Twilight Zone* Series 1: Premiere Edition (Rittenhouse Archives, 1999)
   Trading cards. Set of 72 "base cards" with additional autograph cards and other special cards, for a total of 113 cards in this series. The set includes six base cards plus an autograph card of Rod Taylor from "And When the Sky Was Opened," and six base cards plus an autograph card of William Shatner from "Nightmare at 20,000 Feet." There are also additional "Twilight Star" cards of Taylor and Shatner.

Gauntlet Press Gift Card (Gauntlet Press, 2000)
   Signed print/gift card. Published in a numbered edition of 25 copies, signed by Matheson. Consists of a print of the *Hunger and Thirst* cover art by Harry O. Morris on 8 × 11 card stock. The bottom 3½ inches is perforated and functions as a gift certificate for the publisher's titles.

*Somewhere in Time* Collectibles (INSITE Publications, 2000)

The International Network of *Somewhere in Time* Enthusiasts (IN-SITE) has produced a line of collectibles inspired by the film, including such items as t-shirts, mugs, mousepads, stationery, and keychains, as well as CDs, videos, books, jewelry and other items. Available from the INSITE website: www.somewhereintime.tv

*Twilight Zone* Series 2: The Next Dimension (Rittenhouse Archives, 2000)

Trading cards. Set of 72 "base cards" with additional autograph cards and other special cards, for a total of 112 cards in this series. The set includes six base cards plus an autograph card of William Shatner from "Nick of Time," and six base cards from "A World of His Own." There is also an additional "Twilight Star" card of Shatner.

Dr. Erasmus Craven from *The Raven* (Neca Toys, 2002)

Figure. Fully articulated (even the fingers are posable) 12-inch-tall figure of the Vincent Price character from *The Raven*. Includes a velour robe, silk shirt, pants, belt, and hat. A raven rounds out the ensemble. Limited to an edition of 5000.

Gremlin from "Nightmare at 20,000 Feet" (Sculpted by Mat Falls; Sideshow Collectibles, 2002)

Figure. Highly articulated 12-inch-tall figure of the famed creature from the classic episode of *The Twilight Zone*. Includes a damaged airplane wing panel and a stand.

*Twilight Zone* Series 3: Shadows and Substance (Rittenhouse Archives, 2002)

Trading cards. Set of 72 "base cards" with additional autograph cards and other special cards, for a total of 115 cards in this series. The set includes autograph cards of Patricia Breslin from "Nick of Time," Gloria Pall from "And When the Sky Was Opened," and Asa Maynor from "Nightmare at 20,000 Feet." There is also a card with a sketch by Pablo Raimondi of the fortune-telling machine from "Nick of Time."

The Invader from "The Invaders" (Sculpted by Mat Falls; Sideshow Collectibles, 2003)

Figure. Rotocast 12-inch-tall vinyl figure, which rotates at its head and its antenna. Comes with wand.

*Trilogy of Terror* Zuni Fetish Warrior (Majestic Studios, 2004)
Figure. A 13-inch-tall plastic figure, with cloth skirt, spear, warrior feathers, and charmed waist chain. Comes with a display stand.

Metal Labrys Bookmark (Gauntlet Press, 2005)
Metal labrys bookmark engraved with Matheson's signature. Included with the purchase of the lettered edition of *Woman*, but also available separately.

*Twilight Zone* Series 4: Science and Superstition (Rittenhouse Archives, 2005)
Trading cards. Set of 72 "base cards" with additional autograph cards and other special cards, for a total of 149 cards in this series. The set includes six base cards from "Night Call," plus "Twilight Star" and "Hall of Fame" cards of Gladys Cooper, and a card with a sketch by Pablo Raimondi of the gremlin from "Nightmare at 20,000 Feet."

*I Am Legend* Playaway (Playaway, 2007)
A small MP3 player wrapped in a customized label and pre-loaded with the audiobook read by Robertson Dean (see "Audio Adaptations").

## Awards and Honors

These are awards and honors accorded to Matheson, his work, and adaptations of his work.

Hugo Award (1958)
Outstanding Movie, *The Incredible Shrinking Man* (Winner)

*Playboy* Writing Award (1958)
Best Short Story, "The Distributor" (Winner)

Writers Guild Award (1961)
Best Writing, Television Episodic Drama, Half-Hour, *Lawman* episode "Yawkey" (Winner)

Hugo Award (1963)
    Dramatic Presentation, *Burn, Witch, Burn* (Nominee)

Emmy Award (1972)
    Cinematography, *Duel* (Nominee)
    Film Sound Editing, *Duel* (Winner)

Golden Globe Award (1972)
    Best Television Movie, *Duel* (Nominee)

Writers Guild Award (1972)
    Best Writing, Television Anthology, Adapted, *Duel* (Nominee)

Edgar Allan Poe Award (1973)
    Best TV Feature or Miniseries, *The Night Stalker* (Winner)

Writers Guild Award (1973)
    Best Writing, Television Anthology, Adapted, *The Night Stalker* (Winner)

British Fantasy Award (1974)
    Best Film, *The Legend of Hell House* (Winner)

Emmy Award (1974)
    Best Lead Actor in a Drama, *The Morning After* (Dick Van Dyke, Nominee)

Writers Guild Award (1975)
    Best Writing, Television Anthology, Adapted, *The Morning After* (Nominee)

World Fantasy Award (1976)
    Best Novel, *Bid Time Return* (Winner)

Academy Award (1980)
    Costume Design, *Somewhere in Time* (Nominee).

Golden Globe Award (1980)
    Best Original Score, *Somewhere in Time* (Nominee)

Hugo Award (1981)
Dramatic Presentation, *The Martian Chronicles* (Nominee)

Writers Guild Award (1981)
Best Writing, Television Longform, Multi-part, *The Martian Chronicles Part II* (Nominee)

George Pal Lecture on Fantasy in Film (1983)
Established in 1980 by the Academy of Motion Picture Arts and Sciences in honor of the science-fiction and fantasy film producer, director, and special effects wizard. Matheson delivered the 1983 lecture, which included film clips from his own and others' films. Jack Arnold (director of *The Incredible Shrinking Man*) was a special guest at the lecture.

World Fantasy Award (1984)
Life Achievement (Winner)

Emmy Award (1986)
Best Guest Performer in a Drama Series, *Amazing Stories* episode "The Doll" (John Lithgow, Winner)

Bram Stoker Award (1989)
Fiction Collection, *Richard Matheson: Collected Stories* (Winner)

Bram Stoker Award (1990)
Lifetime Achievement (Winner)

World Fantasy Award (1990)
Best Collection, *Richard Matheson: Collected Stories* (Winner)

Christopher Award (1991)
Cable and Television Programming, *The Dreamer of Oz* (Winner)

Golden Spur Award (1991)
Western Novel, *Journal of the Gun Years* (Winner)

World Horror Literary Society (1992)
Guest of Honor, World Horror Convention II

World Horror Literary Society (1993)
Grand Master (Winner)

Academy Award (1998)
> Art Direction, *What Dreams May Come* (Nominee)
> Visual Effects, *What Dreams May Come* (Winner)

International Horror Guild Award (1999)
> Best Film, *Stir of Echoes* (Winner)
> Living Legend Award (Winner)

1951 Retro Hugo Award (2001)
> Short Story, "Born of Man and Woman" (Nominee)

Bram Stoker Award (2002)
> Work for Young Readers, *Abu and the 7 Marvels* (Nominee)

Ben Franklin Award (2003)
> Juvenile—Young Adult Fiction, *Abu and the 7 Marvels* (Winner)

Legend Award (2005)
> Named for Matheson (who was the first recipient), the Legend Award is given to authors who are both exceptional writers and outstanding human beings. Future recipients will be decided by a distinguished panel that includes members of the Matheson family.

Trenton Film Festival (2006)
> Best Direction for Narrative Short, *Blood Son* (Winner)

Eisner Award (2006)
> Best Short Story, "Richard Matheson's 'Blood Son' " from *Doomed* #1 (Nominee)

Image Awards (2008)
> Best Movie, *I Am Legend* (Nominee)
> Best Male Performance, *I Am Legend* (Will Smith, Nominee)

MTV Movie Awards (2008)
> Best Movie, *I Am Legend* (Nominee)
> Best Male Performance, *I Am Legend* (Will Smith, Winner)

Saturn Awards (2008)
> Best Movie, *I Am Legend* (Nominee)
> Best Male Performance, *I Am Legend* (Will Smith, Nominee)

## Forthcoming Publications

Matheson titles continue to be published regularly, and each year sees another two to three titles become available. Here are some projects planned for the next few years. Publication dates are provided when known, but should be considered tentative.

*Matheson Uncollected* (Richard Matheson; Gauntlet Press, 2008 & 2009)
    Teleplay, novels, and short stories. To be published in two volumes. Collects Matheson's teleplay for the *Star Trek* episode "The Enemy Within," three previously unpublished novels that Matheson abandoned before completing them, and seventeen short stories that have never before been collected. Lettered and numbered editions are planned.

*Visions Deferred* (Edited by Mark Dawidziak; Edge Books, 2009)
    Screenplays. Collects three unproduced Matheson scrips: *The Night Creatures* (based on his novel *I Am Legend*), *Sweethearts and Horrors* (a follow-up to *The Comedy of Terrors*), and *The Distributor* (based on his short story). All appeared previously in limited-edition collections from Gauntlet Press (see "Published Scripts"). A trade paperback edition is planned.

*He Is Legend* (Edited by Christopher Conlon; Gauntlet Press, 2009)
    Short stories, screenplay. Tribute anthology to contain original stories by contemporary authors written in the style of Richard Matheson, and inspired by his work. It will also include the screenplay for the cult classic *Burn, Witch, Burn* (a.k.a. *Night of the Eagle*), written by Matheson and Charles Beaumont. Lettered and numbered editions are planned.

*The Beardless Warriors* (Richard Matheson; Gauntlet Press, 2009)
    Limited edition of Matheson's classic World War II novel. Lettered and numbered editions are planned.

*Earthbound* (Richard Matheson; Gauntlet Press, 2010)
    Limited edition of Matheson's horror novel. Lettered and numbered editions are planned.

*Omnibus Westerns Collection* (Richard Matheson; Gauntlet Press, 2011)

Title unconfirmed. Planned collection of Matheson's western novels. Lettered and numbered editions are planned.

*The Fort College Stories* (Richard Matheson; Borderlands Press)

Title undecided. Short story collection. Contains Matheson's previously published short stories set in fictional Fort College. This was originally to have been part of the publisher's limited edition "Little Book" series, with the title *A Little Silver Book of Sterling Stories*. That title has since been reassigned to a different author in the series, and the Matheson project is presently on hold, per the publisher. Its publication may be in some form other than a "Little Book."

## Unrealized Editions and Errata

The careful Matheson collector will occasionally stumble upon bibliographies and other sources that list impossible-to-find titles—impossible because they do not actually exist. The following either were announced but never published, or have been otherwise erroneously attributed to Matheson. In addition, the literary and screen credits of Richard Matheson, Richard Christian Matheson, and Christian (Chris) Matheson are often hopelessly confused.

"The Solid Gold Patrol" (1958)

The IMDb currently credits Matheson as the cowriter with Irving Wallace of this episode of *Have Gun—Will Travel*, but both tv.com and the exhaustive *Have Gun—Will Travel Companion* by Martin Grams, Jr., and Les Rayburn list only Wallace as the screenwriter.

"No Such Thing as a Vampire" (1968)

Several sources assert that Matheson adapted his story of the same name for this episode of the BBC-TV series *Late Night Horror.* Matheson had no involvement with the series; the teleplay was adapted from his story by Hugh Leonard.

*The House That Dripped Blood* (1970)

"Sweets to the Sweet," one segment of this horror anthology film, is sometimes attributed to Matheson. It was written by Robert Bloch, based on his own short story. Matheson had nothing to do with it.

## The Godfather Part II (1974)

The IMDb, Wikipedia, and other websites have recently asserted that Matheson played a senator in Francis Ford Coppola's film. This is untrue, although Matheson's frequent collaborator, Roger Corman (of whom Coppola is one of many famous protégés), did.

## Young Warriors (1983)

This 1983 film written by Russell W. Colgin and Lawrence D. Foldes is sometimes attributed to Matheson, undoubtedly confusing it with Matheson's 1968 film *The Young Warriors*.

## Someone Is Bleeding (Richard Matheson, Evening Star Press)
## Fury on Sunday (Richard Matheson, Evening Star Press)

These books were scheduled to be published in August and September of 1985, respectively, each in two states: a 750-copy unnumbered edition, and a 250-copy numbered edition in slipcase, both to have been issued without dustjacket, and both 6 × 9 inches in dimension, with a Smyth-sewn binding. The numbered editions were to be signed by Matheson. Artist Brent Anderson was retained to do the dustjacket designs, but Matheson later requested that both covers be changed to a uniform design stamped in gold and silver. Neither book was published.

## Darker (Richard Matheson, Scream/Press)

This planned Scream/Press title would have been the first unabridged reprinting of Matheson's early novels *Someone Is Bleeding, Fury on Sunday*, and *Ride the Nightmare*. Publication was planned for the early 1990s in two states: a trade edition, and a numbered edition of 300 copies to have been signed by Matheson. It was never published, although cover artwork by Josh Gosfield was produced, and Scream/Press catalogs indicate that it progressed to the point of being typeset. A small number of galleys is known to exist, consisting of 275 uncorrected laser-printed pages with a plastic cover in Velobind binding. This same trio of novels was eventually published in a limited edition as *Noir: Three Novels of Suspense* by G&G Books in 1997.

*Born of Man and Woman* (Richard Matheson, Buccaneer Books)
*The Beardless Warriors* (Richard Matheson, Buccaneer Books)
*Hell House* (Richard Matheson, Buccaneer Books)

Buccaneer Books has reprinted three of Matheson's books, but these are not among them. They are sometimes incorrectly listed as Buccaneer titles.

*Ghost Trilogy* (Richard Matheson, Scream/Press)

This planned Scream/Press omnibus title was to have included three of Matheson's ghost-themed novels: *A Stir of Echoes*, *Hell House*, and *Earthbound*. It remained unpublished when Scream/Press went out of business in the mid-1990s.

*Born of Man and Woman* (Richard Matheson; Chapbook, Cemetery Dance Publications)

In 2000, Cemetery Dance announced the upcoming publication of a special 50th anniversary chapbook of Matheson's classic story. Apparently the interior pages were printed, but not the cover, and the pages were never assembled. This project has been cancelled.

*Lost Angels* (David J. Schow; Babbage Press, 2000)

The introduction to this novel is sometimes erroneously attributed to Matheson; it was written by his son, Richard Christian Matheson.

*Things Beyond Midnight* (William F. Nolan; Babbage Press, 2000)

The introduction to this short story anthology is sometimes erroneously attributed to Matheson; it was written by his son, Richard Christian Matheson.

*Shadow on the Sun* (Richard Matheson, Cemetery Dance)

A planned limited edition of Matheson's novel, to have been published in two states: a 1000-copy numbered edition and a 52-copy lettered edition in traycase, both to have been signed by Matheson. The title was dropped from the publisher's website in 2006, and the project appears to have been abandoned.

# About the Contributors

GREG COX is a consulting editor at Tor/Forge Books, where he has worked with Matheson for some eighteen years. He is also the *New York Times* best-selling author of numerous books and short stories based on such popular movie, TV, and comic-book series as *Alias, Batman, Buffy the Vampire Slayer, Daredevil, Fantastic Four, Farscape, Ghost Rider, Infinite Crisis, Iron Man, Roswell, Star Trek, Underworld, Xena,* and *X-Men*. He lives in Oxford, Pennsylvania.

HARLAN ELLISON has written more than forty books, dozens of scripts for movies and such television shows as *Star Trek* and *The Outer Limits*, and more than 1,000 essays, reviews, articles, short stories (including the classic "A Boy and His Dog"), and newspaper columns. He has also won more awards for imaginative literature than any other living author; been nominated for Emmys, Grammys, and Humanitas Prizes; and received the coveted Milford Award for lifetime excellence as an editor.

DENNIS ETCHISON's short stories have appeared in numerous magazines and anthologies since 1961, and in his collections *The Dark Country, Red Dreams, The Blood Kiss,* and *The Death Artist*. He is also an editor (*Cutting Edge, MetaHorror, Masters of Darkness, The Museum of Horrors*), novelist (*Darkside, California Gothic, Double Edge*), past president of the Horror Writers of America, and the winner of five British Fantasy and World Fantasy Awards. He recently wrote 135 episodes for the *Twilight Zone* radio series.

GARY GOLDSTEIN is a senior editor at Kensington Publishing, and previously worked for Bantam, Doubleday, Penguin USA, and Simon & Schuster. He lives on Long Island, New York, with his wife and their two cats.

ED GORMAN is the author of more than twenty novels, five story collections, and three screenplays. Previously he spent twenty years in advertising, mostly writing and directing TV commercials in the Midwest. Primarily a crime novelist, he has also written a number of westerns and horror novels, and several of his books and stories have been optioned for TV and movies. He lives in Cedar Rapids with his wife, novelist Carole Gorman, and their three cats.

BARRY HOFFMAN is the publisher and owner of Gauntlet Press. In addition to publishing more than twenty special editions of Matheson's work since 1995, he is also the author of the "Eyes" series (*Hungry Eyes, Eyes of Prey, Judas Eyes, Blindsided*, and the forthcoming *Blind Vengeance*), one stand-alone novel (*Born Bad*), and two collections (*Guardian of Lost Souls* and *Love Hurts*). Other forthcoming works include an untitled sixth "Eyes" novel and *Curse of the Shamra*, the first of a young adult dark fantasy trilogy.

GEORGE CLAYTON JOHNSON is best known for his contributions to *The Twilight Zone* (published as *Twilight Zone Scripts & Stories*) and as the author, with William F. Nolan, of the classic SF novel *Logan's Run*. His retrospective collection *All of Us Are Dying and Other Stories* includes scripts and treatments, some unproduced, and nonfiction. He wrote episodes of *Honey West, Kentucky Jones, Kung Fu, The Law and Mr. Jones, Mr. Novak*, and *Route 66*, and shared story credit on *Ocean's Eleven* (1960).

JACK KETCHUM, an award-winning writer of psychological horror, is considered by Stephen King to be "probably the scariest writer in the country." His work includes such novels as *Off Season, Red, Joy Ride, She Wakes*, and *The Girl Next Door*, plus the short story collection *Peaceable Kingdoms*. His novel *The Lost* was recently made into a feature film.

DEAN KOONTZ is the author of ten #1 *New York Times* hardcover bestsellers: *One Door Away From Heaven, From the Corner of His Eye,*

*Midnight, Cold Fire, The Bad Place, Hideaway, Dragon Tears, Intensity, Sole Survivor* and *The Husband*. His books are published in thirty-eight languages, selling more than seventeen million copies per year, and have been major bestsellers in countries as diverse as Japan and Sweden. He and his wife, Gerda, live in southern California with their dog, Trixie.

JOE R. LANSDALE has written more than twenty books and won a host of awards. These include five Bram Stoker Horror Awards, a British Fantasy Award, the American Mystery Award, the Horror Critics Award, the "Shot in the Dark" International Crime Writer's Award, the *Booklist* Editor's Award, the Critic's Choice Award, and a *New York Times* "Notable Book" Award. Lansdale lives in Nacogdoches, Texas, with his wife, Karen, a writer and editor.

BRIAN LUMLEY is undoubtedly best known for his international book phenomenon known as the Necroscope®, in which Harry Koegh—who has the ability to speak to the dead—fights a never-ending battle with the forces of evil and the undead. He has written several other series of best-selling horror novels and several short story collections, and co-edited with Stanley Wiater the definitive *The Brian Lumley Companion*.

ALI MATHESON is a successful television writer and producer whose credits include the series *The Collector* and *So Weird*, which she cocreated and executive produced. She has also written for *Moonlighting* and *Rugrats*, as well as the Disney Channel original movie *Halloweentown* and its sequel. She cowrote the *Outer Limits* adaptation of her father's story "First Anniversary," and wrote the original script "Lane Change" for Steven Spielberg's anthology series *Amazing Stories*. She is the younger daughter of Richard and Ruth Ann Matheson.

BETTINA MATHESON is a successful career woman in the field of social work. She is the eldest child of Richard and Ruth Ann Matheson, and an incident from her childhood inspired his classic short story and the *Twilight Zone* teleplay "Little Girl Lost."

CHRIS MATHESON is a successful screenwriter whose credits include *Bill & Ted's Excellent Adventure, Bill & Ted's Bogus Journey, Mom and Dad Save the World, A Goofy Movie, Mr. Wrong*, and *Stepsister from the Planet*

*Weird*. The youngest child of Richard and Ruth Ann Matheson, he has also written and directed *The Wise Ones* and *Evil Alien Conquerors*.

RICHARD CHRISTIAN MATHESON is a successful novelist (*Created By*), short story writer (*Scars and Other Distinguishing Marks*, *Dystopia*), and television and motion picture screenwriter and producer. The older son of Richard and Ruth Ann Matheson, he has adapted his father's work on *Amazing Stories* and *Masters of Horror*, and collaborated with him on several scripts and stories. Among his many screenwriting and producing credits are such films as *Three O'Clock High* and *Full Eclipse* in addition to the adaptations of Dean Koontz's *Sole Survivor* as a miniseries and Stephen King's "Battleground" as an episode of *Nightmares and Dreamscapes*. He is also a professional drummer.

RUTH ANN MATHESON, Ph.D., is a successful psychologist, and has been married to Richard Matheson since 1952. He has named characters after her in many of his scripts and stories, and fictionalized their meeting on a California beach in his first novel, *Someone Is Bleeding*. Matheson also dedicated his novel *What Dreams May Come* to Ruth "for adding the sweet measure of her soul to my existence." They live in Calabasas, California, and have four children and several grandchildren.

DAVID MORRELL is an award-winning author universally recognized as the creator of the wildly successful character John Rambo, who first appeared in Morrell's debut novel, *First Blood*. Although much of his short fiction delves into the darkest aspects of horror, he is known to the mainstream for his best-selling novels of espionage and high adventure.

HARRY O. MORRIS lives with his wife, Christine, and three cats in Albuquerque in what is locally known as "The Witch House." He published the fanzine *Nyctalops* from 1970 to 1990, and has done illustration work since 1985. Morris is inspired by the contradictory philosophies of surrealist leader Andre Breton and Howard Pyle, "The Father of American Illustration."

WILLIAM F. NOLAN designed greeting cards for Hallmark and attended the Kansas City Art Institute before giving up art to concentrate on writing. His output includes scores of books, hundreds of articles, and more than 150 short stories, in genres from SF and mystery-suspense to westerns. His best-known novels are *Logan's Run* (written with George Clayton Johnson) and two sequels, and he has also written a number of movie and television scripts, many of them produced by Dan Curtis.

STEPHEN SIMON's more than twenty credits as a Hollywood producer and executive include the Matheson adaptations *Somewhere in Time* and *What Dreams May Come*. He is the author of *The Force Is With You: Mystical Movie Messages That Inspire Our Lives* and the cofounder of the DVD subscription service, The Spiritual Cinema Circle (www. spiritualcinemacircle.com). Simon made his directorial debut with *Indigo*, and recently produced and directed the adaptation of Neale Donald Walsch's *Conversations with God*.

F. PAUL WILSON has been writing fiction and practicing medicine since he was a first-year medical student. His novels include such horror thrillers as the *New York Times* bestsellers *The Keep* and *The Tomb*. *Soft & Others* is a collection of short fiction from his first twenty years as a writer, and he edited the Horror Writers of America anthology *Freak Show*. Married to his high school sweetheart, he lives on the Jersey Shore with their two daughters and three cats.

GAHAN WILSON is known primarily for his hundreds of wonderfully weird and strange cartoons, most of which first appeared in either *The New Yorker* or *Playboy*, and have since been gathered into such wonderfully weird and strange collections as *Is Nothing Sacred*, *Gahan Wilson's America*, *And Then We'll Get Him!* and *The Best of Gahan Wilson*. Wilson is also an accomplished novelist, short story writer, anthologist, computer game creator, and screenwriter.

# About the Editors

STANLEY WIATER is a widely acclaimed observer of the dark side of popular culture. He has interviewed more major horror and suspense authors, filmmakers, actors, and artists than any other journalist. He is the creator and host of *Dark Dreamers*, a television series profiling those personalities. Wiater has been recognized as "the world's leading expert on horror filmmakers and authors" (*Radio-TV Interview Report*) and "the top horror journalist in North America for the past twenty-five years" (*Rue Morgue*).

His first collection of exclusive interviews, *Dark Dreamers: Conversations with the Masters of Horror* (1990) won the Bram Stoker Award from the Horror Writers Association in 1991. A companion volume, *Dark Visions: Conversations with the Masters of the Horror Film* (1992) was a Bram Stoker Award finalist. *Dark Thoughts: On Writing—Advice and Commentary from Fifty Masters of Fear and Suspense* (1997) won the Bram Stoker Award in 1998. A unique collection of photographs (by Beth Gwinn) and commentary entitled *Dark Dreamers: Facing the Masters of Fear* (2001) won the Bram Stoker Award the following year. His work has also been nominated for the Hugo, Eisner, Harvey, Readercon, and International Horror Guild Awards.

Wiater's first published story "The Toucher" was the sole winner of a competition judged by Stephen King in 1980. Other stories have since appeared in such award-winning series as Peter Crowther's *Narrow Houses*, Thomas F. Monteleone's *Borderlands*, and J.N. Williamson's

*Masques.* He has edited two anthologies of original dark fiction, *Night Visions* 7 (1989) and *After the Darkness* (1993).

Wiater is the coauthor of *The Collected Stephen King Universe* (2006) and *Comic Book Rebels: Conversations with the Creators of the New Comics* (1997). He is also the co-editor of *The Brian Lumley Companion* (2002) and has edited *Richard Matheson's* The Twilight Zone *Scripts* (2001) and the three-volume *Richard Matheson: Collected Stories* (2005–2006). Wiater's books—and more than 750 interviews, articles, comic book scripts, reviews, stories, and DVD liner notes—have been translated into ten languages. In 1993 and 2005 he was master of ceremonies at the World Horror Convention. His official website is www.stanleywiater.com, while further information about the television series may be found at www.darkdreamers.com.

Wiater lives in Massachusetts with his wife and daughter.

MATTHEW R. BRADLEY is a recognized authority on Richard Matheson, having written introductions, articles, interviews, reviews, press releases, website content, and a reading group guide devoted to him and his work. He has extensively interviewed Matheson's fellow members of the Southern California School of Writers (a.k.a. "The Group"), such as Robert Bloch, Ray Bradbury, George Clayton Johnson, William F. Nolan, and Jerry Sohl, and intends to publish a collection of his Group interviews.

This is the second book Bradley has edited about Matheson and his work, following Gauntlet's *Duel & The Distributor* (2004), and he is currently completing a comprehensive study of his film and television oeuvre entitled *Richard Matheson on Screen*, which is forthcoming from McFarland. He has also written introductions to Matheson's *Noir: Three Novels of Suspense* (G&G Books, 1997; Tor/Forge, 2005), and to the Gauntlet limited editions of his *I Am Legend* (1995), *Hell House* (1996), and *What Dreams May Come* (1998), as well as of William Peter Blatty's *The Exorcist* (1997).

Bradley's articles, reviews, and interviews with a wide variety of filmmakers, authors, and other literary figures have appeared for more than a decade in the pages of *Filmfax, Outré, Mystery Scene, VideoScope,* and *The New York Review of Science Fiction*. He has contributed interviews to two separate editions of *Invasion of the Body Snatchers: A Tribute* (Berkley Boulevard, 1999; Stark House Press, 2006), and written dozens of film-related articles and profiles for the Scifipedia site that was launched by scifi.com in 2006.

A lifelong resident of Connecticut, Bradley has a B.A. in English literature from Trinity College in Hartford, and worked for twenty years in New York City in the book-publishing and home-video industries. Currently the copy specialist for MBI, Inc., in Norwalk, he still lives in the area with his wife, Loreen, and their daughter, Alexandra.

PAUL STUVE is a clinical psychologist when he's not reading, collecting or, most recently, writing about Richard Matheson. Over the years, he has assembled an outstanding collection of books, magazines, and other items relating to Matheson, some of which he graciously allowed Gauntlet Press to reproduce in Matheson's *Duel & The Distributor*. He lives in Columbia, Missouri.

# Index